Joseph S. Nye, Jr. | David A. Welch

UNDERSTANDING GLOBAL CONFLICT AND COOPERATION

AN INTRODUCTION TO THEORY AND HISTORY

Ninth Edition

PEARSON

Original Edition entitled *Understanding Global Conflict: Pearson New International Edition: An Introduction to Theory and History , Ninth Edition,* by Nye Joseph S, Welch David A published by Pearson Education, Inc, publishing as Pearson International, Copyright © 2013 by Pearson Education, Inc.

Indian edition published by Pearson India Education Services Pvt. Ltd. Copyright @ 2015

ISBN: 978-93-325-4313-3

First Impression, 2015

Published by Pearson India Education Services Pvt.Ltd,CIN:U72200TN2005PTC057128.
Formerly known as TutorVista Global Pvt Ltd, licensees of Pearson Education in South Asia

Head Office:15th Floor, Tower-B, World Trade Tower, Plot No. 1, Block-C, Sector 16,
Noida 201 301, Uttar Pradesh, India.

Registered Office: 4th floor, Software Block, Elnet Software City, TS 140 Block 2 & 9,
Rajiv Gandhi Salai, Taramani, Chennai - 600 113, Tamil Nadu, Fax: 080-30461003,
Phone: 080-30461060, www.pearson.co.in email id: companysecretary.india@pearson.com

Digitally printed in India by CMS IT Services Private Limited, New Delhi in the year of 2017.

Table of Contents

GLOSSARY

Actor Any person or body whose decisions and actions have repercussions for international politics. States, non-governmental organizations, multinational corporations, and even occasionally individuals qualify as international actors.

Alliances Formal or informal arrangements made between sovereign states, usually to ensure mutual security.

Anarchy The absence of hierarchy. The Westphalian system of sovereign states is anarchic because there is no authority above states. When used in the study of international politics, anarchy is generally not used as a synonym for chaos, since anarchic systems can be very orderly.

Appeasement Generally, the act or policy of accommodating the demands of an assertive power in an attempt to prevent conflict; more specifically, when referring to British policy between the two world wars, the policy of satisfying Germany's legitimate grievances.

Arab Spring The wave of protests and uprisings against authoritarian regimes in North Africa and the Middle East that began in Tunisia in December 2010.

Asymmetry Situations in which states or other actors with unbalanced power capabilities are in opposition to one another. The U.S. war against al Qaeda is widely regarded as an asymmetrical conflict.

Balance of power A term commonly used to describe (1) the distribution of power in the international system at any given time, (2) a policy of allying with one state or group of states so as to prevent another state from gaining a preponderance of power, (3) a realist theory about how states behave under anarchy, or (4) the multipolar system of Europe in the nineteenth century.

Bipolarity The structure of an international system in which two states or alliances of states dominate world politics. The Cold War division between the United States and the Soviet Union is often referred to as a bipolar system.

Bretton Woods New Hampshire resort where a 1944 conference established the International Monetary Fund (IMF) and World Bank.

Cold War The standoff between the United States and the Soviet Union that lasted from roughly the end of World War II until the fall of the Berlin Wall in 1989. Though proxy wars were fought on behalf of both sides around the globe, U.S. and Soviet troops did not engage in direct combat, making this a "cold" war rather than a "hot" shooting war.

Collective security A means of maintaining peace in which a group of states agree on an institutional framework and legal mechanism to prevent or respond to aggression. Two examples of collective security actions under the auspices of the United Nations were the Korean War (1950–1953) and the Persian Gulf War (1991).

Congress of Vienna An 1815 agreement that marked the end of the Napoleonic Wars and established the general framework for the European international system in the nineteenth century.

Constructivism An analytical approach to international relations that emphasizes the importance of ideas, norms, cultures, and social structures in shaping actors' identities, interests, and actions. John Ruggie, Alexander Wendt, and Peter Katzenstein are considered constructivists.

Containment A foreign policy designed to prevent a potential aggressor from expanding its influence geographically.

Containment was the cornerstone of American foreign policy toward Soviet communism during the Cold War.

Cosmopolitanism The view that individuals, not sovereign states, are the relevant moral units in world affairs, and that moral principles such as human rights are universal rather than culture-specific. Charles Beitz is a prominent cosmopolitan theorist.

Counterfactuals Thought experiments that imagine situations with a carefully selected change of facts. These are often phrased as "what if" questions and are employed in the analysis of scenarios in international relations to explore causal relationships.

Crisis stability A measure of the pressure leaders feel to escalate to war during an international crisis.

Cuban missile crisis A standoff in October 1962 between the United States and the Soviet Union over the deployment of Soviet nuclear missiles in Cuba. The crisis was resolved when the Soviets removed their missiles, partly in exchange for a secret agreement that the United States would remove similar missiles based in Turkey.

Dependency theory A theory of development inspired by Marxism, popular in the 1960s and 1970s, that predicted wealthy countries at the "center" of the international system would hold back "peripheral" developing countries.

Deterrence A strategy of dissuading a potential aggressor through threat or fear.

Economic interdependence Situations characterized by reciprocal economic effects among countries or actors in different countries. See *Interdependence*.

Fourteen Points Woodrow Wilson's blueprint for a settlement at the end of World War I. Among its most important features was a call for an international institution that would safeguard collective security. See *League of Nations*.

Game Theory The analysis of how rational actors will behave in contexts of strategic interaction.

GATT (General Agreement on Tariffs and Trade) An international agreement on tariffs and trade that began in 1947 and was replaced in 1994 by the WTO (World Trade Organization).

Geopolitics A theory of international politics that considers the location, proximity, and power of a state a key cause of its behavior.

Globalization At its broadest, the term is used to describe worldwide networks of interdependence. It has a number of dimensions, including economic, cultural, military, and political globalization. It is not a new phenomenon—it dates back at least to the Silk Road—but due to the information revolution, its contemporary form is "thicker and quicker" than previous ones.

Global Public Goods Extension of the public goods concept in economics, which refers to goods that are nonrival and nonexcludable. Examples include knowledge and a stable climate.

Hard power The ability to obtain desired outcomes through coercion or payment.

Hegemony The ability to exercise control within a system of states. The United States is often said to exercise military hegemony today.

IGO (intergovernmental organization) An organization whose members are sovereign states. The United Nations, IMF, and World Bank are examples of IGOs. Commonly referred to as *international institutions*.

IMF (International Monetary Fund) An international institution set up after World War II to lend money, primarily to developing countries, to help stabilize currencies or cover balance-of-payments problems. See *Bretton Woods*.

INGO (international nongovernmental organizations) A subset of NGOs with an international focus. See *NGO*.

Interdependence Situations characterized by reciprocal effects among countries or other actors.

International Court of Justice (ICJ) An international tribunal for settling disputes between *states* and for providing legal opinions on questions submitted to it by the UN General Assembly and other authorized bodies. The Statute of the International Court of Justice is an integral part of the UN Charter (Chapter XIV). Based in the Hague, the ICJ is the successor to the League of Nations' Permanent Court of International Justice.

International Criminal Court (ICC) A permanent tribunal of last resort for trying *individuals* charged with genocide, crimes against humanity, or war crimes. Established by the Rome Statute (1999) and in operation since July 1, 2002.

International Criminal Tribunal for the Former Yugoslavia (ICTY) An ad hoc tribunal established by the UN Security Council to prosecute those charged with committing genocide, crimes against humanity, or war crimes during the violent breakup of Yugoslavia (1991–1995).

International Criminal Tribunal for Rwanda (ICTR) An ad hoc tribunal established by the UN Security Council to prosecute those charged with committing genocide, crimes against humanity, or war crimes in Rwanda (1994).

International institutions See *IGO*.

International law The collective body of treaties and accepted customary practices that regulate the conduct of states. International law can also apply to individuals who act in an international context.

International society A way of conceptualizing the international system that stresses the importance of international law, norms, and rules (including rules of protocol and etiquette), as well as the rights and obligations of states. Constructivists and British scholars of the "English School" of International Relations theory (some of whom are classical realists) generally prefer to speak of international society rather than the international system. Neorealists prefer the opposite.

International system See *System*.

Intervention External actions that influence the domestic affairs of a sovereign state. Most often this term is used to refer to forcible interference by one or more states in another state's domestic affairs.

Jus ad bellum That part of just war doctrine that specifies the conditions under which states may morally resort to war. Traditionally, these include just cause, right intention, legitimate authority, last resort, and reasonable chance of success. From the Latin "justice to war."

Jus in bello That part of just war doctrine that specifies the ways in which wars may morally be fought. Traditionally, these include observing the laws of war, maintaining proportionality between the amount of force used and the objective sought, and observing the principle of noncombatant immunity. From the Latin "justice in war."

Just war doctrine An intellectual tradition with origins in ancient Rome and the early Christian church that provides moral guidelines for the resort to force and the use of force in war. St. Augustine and St. Thomas Aquinas are important historical figures in this tradition; Michael Walzer is a well-known modern just war theorist. Sometimes called "just war theory." See *jus ad bellum* and *jus in bello*.

League of Nations An international organization dedicated to collective security founded at the end of World War I. Woodrow Wilson, the League's chief advocate, called for its creation in his Fourteen Points at the end of the war. The League failed owing to its inability to prevent the aggressions that led to World War II.

Liberalism An analytical approach to international relations in which states function as part of a global society that sets the context for their interactions and that stresses the domestic sources of foreign policy. Classical liberalism has intellectual roots in the writings of Immanuel Kant, Jeremy Bentham, and John Stuart Mill. Richard Rosecrance is considered a liberal.

Marxism An analytical approach to international relations, inspired by the writings of Karl Marx and Friedrich Engels, that sees economic classes as the primary actors, and that explains patterns and events in world affairs in terms of the interactions between classes. Immanuel Wallerstein is a prominent Marxist international relations theorist.

Milieu goals Intangible goals such as democracy or human rights, in contrast to tangible possession goals such as territory.

Multipolarity The structure of an international system in which three or more states or alliances dominate world politics. Many scholars describe nineteenth-century Europe as multipolar.

NAFTA (North American Free Trade Agreement) A 1994 agreement among the United States, Canada, and Mexico that created a free-trade zone in North America.

Nation A group of people who have some combination of common language, culture, religion, history, mythology, identity, or sense of destiny, as well as strong ties to a particular territory, and, usually, aspirations for political autonomy. All nations are peoples (see *People*). Confusingly, the word "nation" is often used to mean "state" (see *State*).

Nation-state An ethnically homogenous state; that is, a state whose citizens are all, or virtually all, members of a single nation. Used both descriptively (e.g., with respect to Korea, Japan, and other ethnically homogenous states) and prescriptively (i.e., as a philosophical ideal—impossible to realize in practice—that all nations should have states of their own).

National interest A state's perceptions of its goals in the international system. Realists, liberals, and constructivists all have different accounts of how states formulate their national interests.

Nationalism A celebration or assertion of national identity that commonly finds political expression in the claim of a right of self-determination or self-government. See *Nation, Self-determination,* and *Self-government.*

Neoliberalism An analytical approach to international relations in which the actions of states are constrained by economic interdependence and international institutions. Robert Keohane is considered a neoliberal. See *Interdependence* and *International institutions.*

Neorealism An analytical approach to international relations, inspired by the objectivity and rigor of natural science, that sees the actions of states as constrained primarily by the distribution of power in the international system. Kenneth Waltz and John Mearsheimer are well-known neorealists.

NGO (nongovernmental organization) In the broadest definition, any organization that represents interests other than those of a state or multinational corporation. Most references concern transnational or international groups (sometimes referred to as INGOs). Examples of well-known NGOs include the Catholic Church, Greenpeace, and the International Red Cross.

Nuclear deterrence A strategy used by both the United States and Soviet Union during the Cold War to dissuade each other from provocative acts by threat of annihilation. See *Deterrence.*

OPEC (Organization of Petroleum Exporting Countries) An organization of the world's largest oil-producing states that tries to coordinate policy on oil production and pricing among its members.

Peacebuilding A term coined by UN Secretary-General Boutros Boutros-Ghali in 1992 describing a range of activities by foreign military and civilian personnel intended to stabilize war-torn societies, build durable governance structures, and lay the groundwork for long-term peace, security, and development.

Peace enforcement The deployment of well-armed foreign troops to compel one or more warring parties to comply with UN resolutions calling for a cessation of hostilities.

Peacekeeping The deployment of neutral, lightly armed foreign troops or police to prevent conflict or maintain peace in a state or between states. Many peacekeeping operations are conducted under UN auspices, but peacekeeping can also be conducted by a regional organization or a group of countries acting outside the United Nations.

Peace of Westphalia The 1648 treaties that formally concluded the Thirty Years' War and established state sovereignty as the chief organizing principle in the international system.

People A group united by common culture, tradition, or sense of kinship (though not necessarily by blood, race, or political ties), typically sharing a language and system of beliefs. A people with a sense of territorial homeland and a shared political identity are a *nation*.

Peloponnesian War More accurately, the Second Peloponnesian War, documented by Thucydides; a conflict between Athens and Sparta lasting from 431 to 404 BCE that resulted in the defeat of Athens and the end of the Golden Age of Athenian democracy. See *Thucydides*.

Power Generally, the ability to achieve one's purposes or goals; more specifically, the ability to affect others to get the outcomes one wants. In a more restricted definition, Robert Dahl defines power as "the ability to get others to do what they otherwise would not do."

Prisoner's Dilemma A classic strategic interaction in which two independent decision makers, each attempting to pursue his or her rational self-interest, will choose not to cooperate with each other (i.e., to defect) and will thereby end up worse off than if they had both chosen to cooperate. Since the best possible outcome in Prisoner's Dilemma is to defect while the other cooperates, the noncooperative outcome is a function of their inability to trust. See *Game theory*.

Realism An analytical approach to international relations in which the primary actors are states and the central problems are war and the use of force. Thucydides, Otto von Bismarck, E. H. Carr, Hans Morgenthau, and Henry Kissinger are all considered realists.

Self-determination The right of a people to decide their own political fate.

Self-government The right of a people to rule themselves.

Sensitivity The degree and rapidity of the effects of interdependence. Describes how quickly a change in one part of a system leads to a change in another part.

Skeptics Those who believe that moral categories have no place in discussions of international relations because of the lack of an international community that can sanction rights and duties.

Soft power The ability to obtain desired outcomes through attraction or persuasion rather than coercion or payment.

Sovereignty An absolute right to rule.

Stability See *Crisis stability* and *System stability*.

State A sovereign, territorial political unit.

State moralism The view that international morality depends on a society of sovereign states playing by certain rules, even if those rules are not always obeyed; that moral obligations within state borders are much greater than across them.

Structure The configuration of units within a *system*. Structures characterize how units relate. Realists consider the distribution of power the most important structural feature of the international system; constructivists emphasize its social dimensions (e.g., norms, rules, and identity relationships).

Symmetry Situations in which states or agents with relatively balanced power capabilities are in opposition to one another. The latter half of the Cold War is widely regarded as a symmetrical conflict because of the rough nuclear balance between the United States and the Soviet Union.

System A set of interrelated units that interact in a regular way. The international system is a particular system whose units are international *actors*, of which sovereign states are currently the most significant, and whose processes of interaction include such things as diplomacy, negotiation, trade, and war.

System stability Generally, a measure of the ability of a system to absorb shocks without breaking down or becoming disorderly; with respect specifically to the international system, a measure of its war-proneness.

Thirty Years' War A series of European wars fueled by international, religious, and dynastic conflicts that took place from 1618 to 1648. See *Peace of Westphalia.*

Thucydides An Athenian commander whose book *History of the Peloponnesian War,* a chronicle of the war between Athens and Sparta, is one of the earliest known works of history and international relations. Thucydides is widely considered the father of realism.

Transgovernmental relations Relations between sub-units of national governments.

Transnational actor Any nonstate actor that acts across international borders. See *Actor*.

Treaty of Rome The 1957 treaty that laid the groundwork for European integration, which led first to the creation of a European Common Market and eventually to the European Union and the common euro currency.

Treaty of Utrecht The 1713 treaty that ended the Wars of Spanish Succession and established the legitimacy of both British and French holdings in North America.

Treaty of Westphalia See *Peace of Westphalia.*

Unipolarity The structure of an international system in which one state exercises preponderant power. Some analysts refer to the current military power structure as a unipolar system dominated by the United States.

Virtual history A particular style of counterfactual analysis that infers what would have happened had something been different (the counterfactual) from what actually did happen beforehand.

Vulnerability The relative cost of changing the structure of a system of interdependence. Can also be thought of as the cost of escaping or changing the rules of the game.

Westphalia See *Peace of Westphalia.*

World Bank An institution set up after World War II to provide loans, technical assistance, and policy advice to developing countries. See *Bretton Woods.*

WTO (World Trade Organization) An international organization created in 1994 to regulate trade and tariffs among its member states. See *GATT.*

Are There Enduring Logics of Conflict and Cooperation in World Politics?

Marble relief commemorating Athenians who died in the Peloponnesian War

The world is shrinking. The *Mayflower* took three months to cross the Atlantic. In 1924, Charles Lindbergh's flight took 33 hours. Fifty years later, the Concorde did it in three hours. Ballistic missiles can do it in 30 minutes. At the beginning of the twenty-first century, a transatlantic flight cost one-third of what it did in 1950, and a call from New York to London cost only a small percentage of what it did at midcentury. Global Internet communications are nearly instantaneous, and transmission costs are negligible. An environmentalist in Asia or a human rights activist in Africa today has a power of communication once enjoyed only by large organizations such as governments or transnational corporations. On a more somber note, nuclear weapons have added a new dimension to war that one writer calls "double death," meaning that not only could individuals die, but under some circumstances the whole human species could be threatened. And as the September 11 terrorist attacks on New York and Washington in 2001 ("9/11") illustrated, technology is putting into the hands of nonstate actors destructive powers that once were reserved solely for governments. As the effects of distance shrink, conditions in remote, poor countries such as Afghanistan suddenly become highly relevant to people around the globe.

Marble memorial commemorating Americans who died in the Vietnam War

Yet some other things about international politics have remained the same over the ages. Thucydides' account of Sparta and Athens fighting the Peloponnesian War 2,500 years ago bears an eerie resemblance to the Arab-Israeli conflict after 1947. Pliny the Elder complained about imbalances in Rome's (mutually beneficial) trade with India nearly 2,000 years ago in almost exactly the same language with which members of Congress today complain about imbalances in the United States' (mutually beneficial) trade with China. There are basic logics to conflict and cooperation that have remained surprisingly constant over the millennia, even if the forms they take and the issues that give rise to them change (the ancient world never had to worry about nuclear weapons, HIV/AIDS, or climate change). The world is a strange cocktail of continuity and change.

The task for students of world politics is to build on the past but not be trapped by it—to understand the continuities as well as the changes. We must learn the traditional theories and then adapt them to current circumstances.

> "I found in my experience in government that I could ignore neither the age-old nor the brand-new dimensions of world politics."
>
> —Joseph S. Nye, Jr.

World politics would be transformed if separate states were abolished, but world government is not around the corner. And while nonstate actors such as transnational corporations, nongovernmental organizations, and terrorist groups present new challenges to governments, they do not replace states. The peoples who live in the nearly 200 states on this globe want their independence, separate cultures, and different languages. In fact, rather than vanishing, nationalism and the demand for separate states have increased. Rather than fewer states, this century will probably see more. World government would not automatically solve the problem of war. Most wars today are civil or ethnic wars. In the two decades after the fall of the Berlin Wall in November 1989, 220 armed conflicts occurred in 75 different locations around the world. Nine were interstate wars, and 24 were intrastate wars with foreign intervention.[1] In fact, the bloodiest wars of the nineteenth century were not among the quarreling states of Europe but rather the Taiping Rebellion in China and the American Civil War. We will continue to live in a world of rival communities and separate states for quite some time, and it is important to understand what that means for our prospects.

WHAT IS INTERNATIONAL POLITICS?

The world has not always been divided into a system of separate states. Over the centuries there have been three basic forms of world politics. In a *world imperial system*, one government controls most of the world with which it has contact. The greatest example in the Western world was the Roman Empire. Spain in the sixteenth century and France in the late seventeenth century tried to gain similar supremacy, but they failed. In the nineteenth century, the British Empire spanned the globe, but even the British had to share the world with other strong states. Ancient world empires—the Roman, Sumerian, Persian, and Chinese—were actually regional empires. They thought they ruled the world, but they were protected from conflict with other empires by lack of communication. Their fights with barbarians on the peripheries of their empires were not the same as wars among roughly equal states.

A second basic form of international politics is a *feudal system,* in which human loyalties and political obligations are not fixed primarily by territorial boundaries. Feudalism was common in Europe after the collapse of the Roman Empire. An individual had obligations to a local lord, but might also owe duties to some distant noble or bishop, as well as to the pope in Rome. Political obligations were determined to a large extent by what happened to one's superiors. If a ruler married, an area and its people might find their obligations rearranged as part of a wedding dowry. Townspeople born French might suddenly find themselves Flemish or even English. Cities and leagues of cities sometimes had a special semi-independent status. The crazy quilt of wars that accompanied the feudal situation did not much resemble modern territorial wars. These wars could occur within as well as across territories and were shaped by crosscutting, nonterritorial loyalties and conflicts.

A third form of world politics is an *anarchic system of states,* composed of states that are relatively cohesive but with no higher government above them. Examples include the city-states of ancient Greece or Machiavelli's fifteenth-century Italy. Another example of an anarchic state system is the dynastic territorial state whose coherence comes from control by a ruling family. Examples can be found in India or China in the fifth century BCE. Large territorial dynasties reemerged in Europe in about 1500, and other forms of polities such as city-states or loose leagues of territories began to vanish. In 1648, the *Peace of Westphalia* ended Europe's Thirty Years' War, sometimes called the last of the great wars of religion and the first of the wars of modern states. In retrospect, we can see that the Peace of Westphalia enshrined the territorial sovereign state as the dominant political unit.

Today when we speak of the international system, we usually mean this territorial system of sovereign states (or simply the "Westphalian system" for short), and we define *international politics* as politics in the absence of a common sovereign—politics among entities with no ruler above them. International politics is a self-help system. The English philosopher Thomas Hobbes (1588–1679) called such an anarchic system a "state of nature." For some, the words *state of nature* may conjure up images of a herd of cows grazing peacefully on a farm, but that is not what Hobbes meant. Think of a Texas town without a sheriff in the days of the Old West, or Lebanon after its government broke down in the 1970s, or Somalia in the 1990s. Hobbes did not think of a state of nature as benign; he saw it as a war of all against all, because there was no higher ruler to enforce order. As Hobbes famously declared, life in such a world would be nasty, brutish, and short.

Because there is no higher authority above states, there are important legal, political, and social differences between domestic and international politics. Domestic law is relatively clear and consistent. Police and courts enforce it. By contrast, international law is patchy, incomplete, and rests on sometimes vague foundations. There is no common enforcement mechanism. The world lacks a global police force, and while there are international courts, they can do little when sovereign states choose to ignore them.

Force plays a different role in domestic and international politics as well. In a well-ordered domestic political system, the government has a monopoly on the legitimate use of force. In international politics, no one has such a monopoly. Because international politics is the realm of self-help, and some states are stronger than others, there is always a danger that they may resort to force. When force cannot be ruled out, mistrust and suspicion are common.

Domestic and international politics also differ in their underlying sense of community. In a well-ordered domestic society, a widespread sense of community gives rise to common loyalties, standards of justice, and views of legitimate authority. On a global scale, people have competing loyalties. Any sense of global community is weak. People often disagree about what is just and legitimate. The result is a great gap between two basic political values: order and justice. In such a world, most people place national concerns before international justice. Law and ethics play a role in international politics, but in the absence of a sense of community norms, they are weaker forces than in domestic politics.

Some people speculate that of the three basic systems—world imperial, feudal, and Westphalian—the twenty-first century may see the gradual evolution of a new feudalism, or less plausibly, an American world empire.

Differing Views of Anarchic Politics

International politics is anarchic in the sense that there is no government above sovereign states. But political philosophy offers different views of how harsh a state of nature need be. Hobbes, who wrote in a seventeenth-century England wracked by civil war, emphasized insecurity, force, and survival. He described humanity as being in a constant state of war. A half century later, John Locke (1632–1704), writing in a more stable England, argued that although a state of nature lacked a common sovereign, people could develop ties and make contracts, and therefore anarchy was not necessarily an obstacle to peace. Those two views of a state of nature are the philosophical precursors of two current views of international politics, one more pessimistic and one more optimistic: *realism* and *liberalism*.

Realism has been the dominant tradition in thinking about international politics for centuries. For the realist, the central problem of international politics is war and the use of force, and the central actors are states. Among modern Americans, realism is exemplified by the writings and policies of President Richard Nixon and his secretary of state, Henry Kissinger. The realist starts from the assumption of the anarchic system of states. Kissinger and Nixon, for example, sought to maximize the power of the United States and to minimize the ability of other states to jeopardize U.S. security. According to the realist, the beginning and the end of international politics is the individual state in interaction with other states.

The other tradition, *liberalism*, can be traced back in Western political philosophy to Baron de Montesquieu and Immanuel Kant in eighteenth-century France and Germany respectively, and such nineteenth-century British philosophers as Jeremy Bentham and John Stuart Mill. A modern American example can be found in the writings and policies of the political scientist and president, Woodrow Wilson.

Liberals see a global society that functions alongside states and sets an important part of the context for state action. Trade crosses borders, people have contacts with each other (such as students studying in foreign countries), and international institutions such as the United Nations mitigate some of the harsher aspects of anarchy. Liberals complain that realists portray states as billiard balls careening off one another in an attempt to balance power. They claim that this explanation is not adequate, as people do have contacts across borders and because there is an international society. Realists, claim liberals, overstate the difference between domestic and international politics. Because the realist picture of anarchy as a Hobbesian "state of war" focuses only on extreme situations, in the liberals' view it misses the growth of economic interdependence and the evolution of a transnational global society.

Realists respond by quoting Hobbes: "Just as stormy weather does not mean perpetual rain, so a state of war does not mean constant war."[2] Just as Londoners carry umbrellas on sunny April days, the prospect of war in an anarchic system makes states keep armies even in times of peace. Realists point to previous liberal predictions that went awry. For example, in 1910, the president of Stanford University said future war was no longer possible because it was too costly. Liberal writers proclaimed war obsolete; civilization had grown out of it, they argued. Economic interdependence, ties between labor unions and intellectuals, and the flow of capital all made war impossible. Of course, these predictions failed catastrophically when World War I broke out in 1914, and the realists felt vindicated.

1910: THE "UNSEEN VAMPIRE" OF WAR

If there were no other reason for making an end of war, the financial ruin it involves must sooner or later bring the civilized nations of the world to their senses. As President David Starr Jordan of Leland Stanford University said at Tufts College, "Future war is impossible because the nations cannot afford it." In Europe, he says, the war debt is $26 billion, "all owed to the unseen vampire, and which the nations will never pay and which taxes poor people $95 million a year." The burdens of militarism in time of peace are exhausting the strength of the leading nations, already overloaded with debts. The certain result of a great war would be overwhelming bankruptcy.

—*The New York World*[3]

Neither history nor the argument between the realists and liberals stopped in 1914. The 1970s saw a resurgence of liberal claims that rising economic and social interdependence was changing the nature of international politics. In the 1980s, Richard Rosecrance wrote that states can increase their power in two ways, either aggressively by territorial conquest or peacefully through trade. He used the experience of Japan as an example: In the 1930s, Japan tried territorial conquest and suffered the disaster of World War II. But after the war, Japan used trade and investment to become the second largest economy in the world (measured by official exchange rates) and a significant power in East Asia. Japan succeeded while spending far less on its military, proportionately to the size of either its population or its economy, than other major powers. Thus Rosecrance and modern liberals argue that the nature of international politics is changing.

Some new liberals look even further to the future and believe that dramatic growth in ecological interdependence will so blur the differences between domestic and international politics that humanity will evolve toward a world without borders. For example, everyone will be affected without regard to boundaries if greenhouse gas emissions warm the planet. Problems such as HIV/AIDS and drugs cross borders with such ease that we may be on our way to a different world. Professor Richard Falk of Princeton argues that transnational problems and values will alter the state-centric orientation of the international system that has dominated for the last 400 years. Transnational forces are undoing the Peace of Westphalia, and humanity is evolving toward a new form of international politics.

In 1990, realists replied, "Tell that to Saddam Hussein!" Iraq showed that force and war are ever-present dangers when it invaded its small neighbor Kuwait. Liberals responded by arguing that politics in the Middle East is the exception. Over time, they said, the world is moving beyond the anarchy of the sovereign state system. These divergent views on the nature of international politics and how it is changing will not soon be reconciled. Realists stress continuity; liberals stress change. Both claim to be more "realistic." Liberals tend to see realists as cynics whose fascination with the past blinds them to change. Realists, in turn, think liberals are utopian dreamers peddling "globaloney."

Who's right? Both are right and both are wrong. A clear-cut answer might be nice, but it would also be less accurate and less interesting. The mix of continuity and change that characterizes today's world makes it impossible to arrive at one simple, synthetic explanation.

Realism and liberalism are not the only approaches. For much of the past century *Marxism* was a popular alternative for many people. Originally developed by Karl Marx and Friedrich Engels and subsequently enhanced and adapted by other theorists, Marxism focused on the domestic economic structure of capitalist states. Its concentration on economic class, production, and property relations has sometimes been called "economic reductionism" or "historical materialism." Marxists believed that politics is a function of economics and predicted that the greed of capitalists would drive important events in international relations, ultimately proving their own undoing as socialist revolution swept the globe. But Marxists underestimated the forces of nationalism, state power, and geopolitics. Their lack of attention to the importance of diplomacy and the balance of power led to a flawed understanding of international politics and incorrect predictions. Even before the collapse of the Soviet Union in 1991, the failure of Marxist theory to account for peace among major capitalist states and warfare among various communist states undermined its explanatory value. For example, it was difficult for Marxists to explain clashes between China and the Soviet Union in 1969, the Vietnamese invasion of Cambodia in 1978, or the Sino-Vietnamese War of 1979.

In the 1960s and 1970s, *dependency theory*, which builds on Marxism, was popular. It predicted that the wealthy countries in the "center" of the global marketplace would control and hold back poorer countries on the "periphery." According to dependency theorists, the global economic and political division between the First World (rich, liberal, capitalist countries) and the Third World (developing countries), also known as the North-South divide, is the result of both historical imperialism and the nature of capitalist globalization. Dependency theory enjoyed some explanatory successes, such as accounting for the failure of many poor countries to benefit from global economic liberalization to the extent that orthodox liberal economic theory predicted. It also drew attention to the curious and important phenomenon of the "dual economy" in developing countries, in which a small, wealthy, educated, urban economic elite interacted with and profited handsomely from globalization, while the vast majority of impoverished, largely rural farmers, laborers, and miners did not. But while dependency theory helped illuminate some important structural causes of economic inequality, it had difficulty explaining why, in the 1980s and 1990s, "peripheral" countries in East Asia, such as South Korea, Singapore, and Malaysia, grew more rapidly than "central" countries in North America and Europe. South Korea and Singapore are now wealthy "developed" countries in their own right, and Malaysia is a rising middle-income country. These weaknesses of dependency theory were underlined when Fernando Henrique Cardoso, a leading dependency theorist in the 1970s, turned to liberal economic policies after being elected president of Brazil in the 1990s.

In the 1980s, analysts on both sides of the realist-liberal divide attempted to emulate microeconomics by developing formal, deductive theories. *Neorealists* such as Kenneth Waltz and *neoliberals* such as Robert Keohane developed structural models of states as rational actors constrained by the international system. Neorealists and neoliberals increased the simplicity and elegance of theory, but they did so at the cost of discarding much of the rich complexity of classical realism and liberalism. "By the end of the 1980s, the theoretical contest that might have been was reduced to relatively narrow disagreements within one state-centric rationalist model of international relations."[4]

More recently, a diverse group of theorists labeled *constructivists* has argued that realism and liberalism both fail to explain long-term change in world politics adequately. For example, neither realists nor liberals predicted the end of the Cold War, nor could they explain it satisfactorily after the fact. Constructivists emphasize the importance of ideas and culture in shaping both the reality and the discourse of international politics. They stress the ultimate subjectivity of interests and their links to changing identities. There are many types of constructivists, but they all tend to agree that neither realism nor liberalism paints a true picture of the world and that we need not just explanations of how things are, but explanations of how they come to be. Constructivists have focused on important questions about identities, norms, culture, national interests, and international governance.[5] They believe that leaders and other people are motivated not only by material interests, but also by their sense of identity, morality, and what their society or culture considers appropriate. These norms change over time, partly through interaction with others. Constructivists agree that the international system is anarchic, but they argue that there is a spectrum of anarchies ranging from benign, peaceful, even friendly ones to bitterly hostile, competitive ones. The nature of anarchy at any given time depends upon prevailing norms, perceptions, and beliefs. As the prominent constructivist scholar Alexander Wendt puts it, anarchy is what states make of it. That is why Americans worry more about one North Korean nuclear weapon than 500 British nuclear weapons, and why war between France and Germany, which occurred twice in the last century, seems unthinkable today.[6]

Realists and liberals take for granted that states seek to promote their "national interest," but they have little to say about how those interests are shaped or change over time. Constructivists draw on different disciplines to examine the processes by which leaders, peoples, and cultures alter their preferences, shape their identities, and learn new behaviors. For example, both slavery in the nineteenth century and racial apartheid in South Africa in the twentieth century were accepted by most states once upon a time. But both later came to be widely condemned. Constructivists ask: Why the change? What role did ideas play? Will the practice of war go the same way someday? What about the concept of the sovereign state? The world is full of political entities such as tribes, nations, and nongovernmental organizations. Only in recent centuries has the sovereign state been dominant. Constructivists suggest that concepts such as "state" and "sovereignty" that shape our understandings of world politics and that animate our theories are, in fact, socially constructed; they are not given. Nor are they permanent. Even our understanding of "security" evolves. Traditional international relations theories used to understand security strictly in terms of preventing violence or war among states, but in today's world "human security"—a relatively new concept—seems at least as problematic. Moreover, a wider range of phenomena have become "securitized," that is, treated politically as dire threats warranting extraordinary efforts to address them. Scholars and politicians worry today not only about interstate war, but also about poverty, inequality, and economic or ecological catastrophe.

Feminist constructivists add that the language and imageries of war as a central instrument of world politics have been heavily influenced by gender. *Feminism* gained strength as a critical approach in the early 1990s when traditional security concerns lost some of their apparent urgency in the wake of the Cold War. By focusing on social processes, nonelite issues, and transnational structures, and by rejecting the established, limited focus on interstate relations, feminism aims to study world politics more inclusively and reveal "the processes through which identities and interests, not merely of states but of key social constituencies, are shaped at the global level."[7] Feminist scholars highlight disparities between the sexes. For example, out of 193 members of the United Nations, only 23 had female presidents, chancellors, or prime ministers in 2011. Feminist critiques also illuminate problematic aspects of globalization, such as the "export" or trafficking of women and children and the use of rape as an instrument of war.

Constructivism is an approach that rejects neorealism's or neoliberalism's search for scientific laws. Instead, it seeks contingent generalizations and often offers thick description as a form of explanation. Some of the most important debates in world politics today revolve around the meanings of terms such as *sovereignty, humanitarian intervention, human rights*, and *genocide*, and constructivists have much more to say about these issues than do older approaches.[8] Constructivism provides both a useful critique and an important supplement to realism and liberalism. Though sometimes loosely formulated and lacking in predictive power, constructivist approaches remind us of what realism and liberalism often miss. It is important to look beyond the instrumental rationality of pursuing current goals and to ask how changing identities and interests can sometimes lead to subtle shifts in states' policies, and sometimes to profound changes in international affairs. Constructivists help us understand how preferences are formed and judgments are shaped. In that sense, constructivist thought complements rather than opposes the two main approaches.

> "When I was working in Washington and helping formulate American foreign policies as an assistant secretary in the State Department and the Pentagon, I found myself borrowing elements from all three types of thinking: realism, liberalism, and constructivism. I found all of them helpful, though in different ways and in different circumstances."
>
> —Joseph S. Nye, Jr.

Sometimes practical men and women wonder why we should bother with theory at all. The answer is that theory provides a road map that allows us to make sense of unfamiliar terrain. We are lost without it. Even when we think we are just using common sense, there is usually an implicit theory guiding our actions. We simply do not know or have forgotten what it is. If we were more conscious of the theories that guide us, we would be better able to understand their strengths and weaknesses, and when best to apply them. As the British economist John Maynard Keynes once put it, practical men who consider themselves above theory are usually listening to some dead scribbler from the past whose name they have long forgotten.[9]

Building Blocks

Actors, goals, and *instruments* are three concepts that are basic to theorizing about international politics, but each is changing. In the traditional realist view of international politics, the only significant "actors" are the states, and only the big states really matter. But this is changing. The number of states has grown enormously in the last half century: In 1945 there were about 50 states in the world; by the beginning of the twenty-first century, there were nearly four times that many, with more to come. More important than the number of states is the rise of *nonstate actors*. Today large multinational corporations straddle international borders and sometimes command more economic resources than many states do (Table 1). At least 192 corporations have annual sales that are larger than the gross domestic product (GDP) of more than half the states in the world.[10] While multinational corporations lack some types of power such as military force, they are very relevant to a country's economic goals. In terms of the economy, IBM is more important to Belgium than is Burundi, a former Belgian colony.

A picture of the Middle East without warring states and outside powers would be downright silly, but it would also be woefully inadequate if it did not include a variety of nonstate actors. Multinational oil companies such as Shell, British Petroleum, and Exxon Mobil are one type of nonstate actor, but there are others. There are large intergovernmental organizations (IGOs) such as the United Nations, and smaller ones such as the Arab League and the Organization of Petroleum Exporting Countries (OPEC). There are nongovernmental organizations (NGOs), such as the Red Cross and Amnesty International. There are also a variety of transnational ethnic groups, such as the Kurds who live in Turkey, Syria, Iran, and Iraq, and the Armenians, scattered throughout the Middle East and the Caucasus. Terrorist groups, drug cartels, and criminal organizations span national borders and often divide their resources among several states. International religious movements, particularly political Islam in the Middle East and North Africa, add a further dimension to the range of nonstate actors.

The question is not whether state or nonstate groups are more important—usually the states are—but how new, complex coalitions affect the politics of a region in a way that the traditional realist views fail to disclose. States are the major actors in current international politics, but they do not have the stage to themselves.

What about goals? Traditionally the dominant goal of states in an anarchic system is military security. Countries today obviously care about their military security, but they often care as much or more about their economic wealth, about social issues such as stopping drug trafficking or the spread of AIDS, or about ecological changes. Moreover, as we noted above, as threats change, the definition of security changes; military security is not the only goal that states pursue. Looking at the relationship between the United States and

TABLE 1

The World's 100 Largest Economic Units (2010)

RANK	COUNTRY or CORPORATION	PPP GDP (Country) or REVENUE (Corporation), $million
1	United States	$14,657,800
2	People's Republic of China	$10,085,708
3	Japan	$4,309,432
4	India	$4,060,392
5	Germany	$2,940,434
6	Russia	$2,222,957
7	United Kingdom	$2,172,768
8	Brazil	$2,172,058
9	France	$2,145,487
10	Italy	$1,773,547
11	Mexico	$1,629,917
12	South Korea	$1,459,246
13	Spain	$1,368,642
14	Canada	$1,330,272
15	Indonesia	$1,029,884
16	Turkey	$960,511
17	Australia	$882,362
18	Republic of China (Taiwan)	$821,781
19	Iran	$818,653
20	Poland	$721,319
21	Netherlands	$676,700
22	Argentina	$632,223
23	Saudi Arabia	$619,826
24	Thailand	$584,768
25	South Africa	$524,341
26	Egypt	$498,176
27	Pakistan	$464,711
28	Colombia	$429,866
29	Malaysia	$412,302
30	Walmart	$408,214
31	Belgium	$392,862
32	Nigeria	$374,323
33	Sweden	$352,327
34	Philippines	$350,279
35	Venezuela	$346,973
36	Austria	$330,496
37	Switzerland	$325,305
38	Greece	$322,555

(Continued)

RANK	COUNTRY or CORPORATION	PPP GDP (Country) or REVENUE (Corporation), $million
39	Hong Kong	$322,486
40	Ukraine	$302,679
41	Singapore	$291,712
42	Royal Dutch Shell	$285,129
43	Exxon Mobil	$284,650
44	Vietnam	$275,639
45	Peru	$274,276
46	Czech Republic	$260,566
47	Chile	$257,546
48	Bangladesh	$257,545
49	Norway	$255,505
50	Algeria	$252,189
51	Romania	$252,173
52	BP	$246,138
53	Portugal	$245,860
54	Israel	$218,490
55	Toyota	$204,106
56	Denmark	$203,159
57	Japan Post Holdings	$202,196
58	Kazakhstan	$193,261
59	Hungary	$188,403
60	Sinopec	$187,518
61	United Arab Emirates	$186,908
62	Finland	$185,019
63	State Grid	$184,496
64	AXA	$175,257
65	Ireland	$173,614
66	China National Petroleum	$165,496
67	Chevron	$163,527
68	ING Group	$163,204
69	General Electric	$156,779
70	Total	$155,887
71	Morocco	$152,619
72	Bank of America	$150,450
73	Qatar	$149,995
74	Volkswagen	$146,205
75	ConocoPhillips	$139,515
76	Kuwait	$138,099
77	Belarus	$130,780
78	BNP Paribas	$130,708
79	Assicurazioni Generali	$126,012

(*Continued*)

RANK	COUNTRY or CORPORATION	PPP GDP (Country) or REVENUE (Corporation), $million
80	Allianz	$125,999
81	AT&T	$123,018
82	Carrefour	$121,452
83	Slovak Republic	$120,758
84	New Zealand	$119,791
85	Ford Motor	$118,308
86	ENI	$117,235
87	J.P. Morgan Chase & Co.	$115,632
88	Iraq	$115,330
89	Hewlett-Packard	$114,552
90	Angola	$114,343
91	E.ON	$113,849
92	Ecuador	$113,825
93	Berkshire Hathaway	$112,493
94	GDF Suez	$111,069
95	Daimler	$109,700
96	NTT	$109,656
97	Samsung	$108,927
98	Citigroup	$108,785
99	McKesson	$108,702
100	Verizon	$107,808

Source: "The Fortune Global 500," *Fortune;* International Monetary Fund, *World Economic Outlook Database,* April 2011, http://www.imf.org/external/pubs/ft/weo/2010/01/weodata/index.aspx.

Canada, where the prospects of war are essentially zero, a Canadian diplomat once said his fear was not that the United States would march into Canada and sack Toronto as it did in 1813, but that Toronto would be programmed out of relevance by computers in Texas—a rather different dilemma from the traditional one of states in an anarchic system. Economic strength has not replaced military security (as Kuwait discovered when Iraq invaded in August 1990), but the agenda of international politics has become more complex as states pursue a wider range of goals, including human security.

Along with the goals, the *instruments* of international politics are also changing. The realist view is that military force is the only instrument that really matters. Describing the world before 1914, the British historian A. J. P. Taylor defined a great power as one able to prevail in war. States obviously use military force today, but the past half century has seen changes in its role. Many states, particularly large ones, find it more costly to use military force to achieve their goals than was true in earlier times. As Professor Stanley Hoffmann of Harvard University has put it, the link between military strength and positive achievement has been loosened.

What are the reasons? One is that the ultimate means of military force, nuclear weaponry, is hopelessly muscle-bound. Although they once numbered more than 50,000, nuclear weapons have not been used in war since 1945. The disproportion between the vast devastation nuclear weapons can inflict and any reasonable political goal has made leaders understandably loath to employ them. So the ultimate form of military force is for all practical purposes too costly for national leaders to use in war.

Even conventional force has become more costly when used to rule nationalistic populations. In the nineteenth century, European countries conquered other parts of the globe by fielding a handful of soldiers armed with modern weapons and then administered their colonial possessions with relatively modest garrisons. But in an age of socially mobilized populations, it is difficult to rule an occupied country whose people feel strongly about their national identity. Americans found this out in Vietnam in the 1960s and 1970s; the Soviets discovered it in Afghanistan in the 1980s. Vietnam and Afghanistan had not become more powerful than the nuclear superpowers, but trying to rule these nationalistically aware populations was too expensive for either the United States or the Soviet Union. Foreign rule is very costly in an age of nationalism. In the nineteenth century, Britain was able to rule India with a handful of soldiers and civil servants, which would be impossible in today's world.

A third change in the role of force relates to internal constraints. Over time there has been a growing ethic of antimilitarism, particularly in democracies. Such views do not prevent the use of force, but they make it a politically risky choice for leaders, particularly when it is massive or prolonged. It is sometimes said that democracies will not accept casualties, but that is too simple. The United States, for example, expected some 10,000 casualties when it planned to enter the Gulf War in 1990, but it was loath to accept casualties in Somalia or Kosovo, where its national interests were less deeply involved. And if the use of force is seen as unjust or illegitimate in the eyes of other states, this can make it costly for political leaders in democratic polities. Force is not obsolete, and terrorist nonstate actors are less constrained than states by such moral concerns, but force is more costly and more difficult for most states to use than in the past.

Finally, a number of issues simply do not lend themselves to forceful solutions. Take, for example, economic relations between the United States and Japan. In 1853, Commodore Matthew Perry sailed his "black ships" into the harbor at Uraga and threatened bombardment unless Japan opened its ports to trade. This would not be a very useful or politically acceptable way to solve current U.S.-Japan trade disputes. Thus, while force remains a critical instrument in international politics, it is not the only instrument. The use of economic interdependence, communication, international institutions, and transnational actors sometimes plays a larger role than force. Military force is not obsolete as a state instrument—witness the fighting in Afghanistan, where the Taliban government had sheltered the terrorist network that carried out the 9/11 attacks on the United States, or the American and British use of force to overthrow Saddam Hussein in 2003. But it was easier to win the war than to win the peace in Iraq, and military force alone is not sufficient to protect against terrorism. While military force remains the ultimate instrument in international politics, changes in its cost and effectiveness make today's international politics more complex.

The basic game of security goes on. Some political scientists argue that the balance of power is usually determined by a leading, or hegemonic, state—such as Spain in the sixteenth century, France under Louis XIV, Britain in most of the nineteenth century, and the United States in most of the twentieth century. Eventually the top country will be challenged, and this challenge will lead to the kind of vast conflagrations we call hegemonic, or world, wars. After world wars, a new treaty sets the new framework of order: the Treaty of Utrecht in 1713, the Congress of Vienna in 1815, the League of Nations in 1919, and the United Nations in 1945. If nothing basic has changed in international politics since the struggle for supremacy between Athens and Sparta, will a new challenge lead to another world war, or is the cycle of hegemonic war over? Will a rising China challenge the United States? Has nuclear technology made world war too devastating? Has economic interdependence made it too costly? Will nonstate actors such as terrorists force governments to cooperate? Has global society made war socially and morally unthinkable? We have to hope so, because the next hegemonic war could be the last. But first, it is important to understand the case for continuity.

Follow Up

- Kenneth Waltz, *Man, the State, and War: A Theoretical Analysis* (New York: Columbia University Press, 1959), pp. 1–15.
- Richard Ned Lebow, *A Cultural Theory of International Relations* (Cambridge: Cambridge University Press, 2008), pp. 1–28.

THE PELOPONNESIAN WAR

Thucydides (c. 460–400 BCE) is widely considered the father of realism, the perspective most people use when thinking about international politics even when they do not know they are thinking theoretically. Theories are the indispensable tools we use to organize facts. Many of today's leaders and editorial writers use realist theories even if they have not heard of Thucydides. A member of the Athenian elite who lived during Athens' greatest age, Thucydides participated in some of the events described in his *History of the Peloponnesian War*. Robert Gilpin, a notable realist, asserted, "In honesty, one must inquire whether or not twentieth-century students of international relations know anything that Thucydides and his fifth-century [BCE] compatriots did not know about the behavior of states." He then answered his own query: "Ultimately international politics can still be characterized as it was by Thucydides."[11] Gilpin's proposition is debatable, but to debate it, we must know what Thucydides said. And what better introduction to realist theory is there than one of history's great stories? However, like many great stories, it has its limits. One of the things we learn from the Peloponnesian War is to avoid too simplistic a reading of history.

A Short Version of a Long Story

Athens and Sparta (Figure 1) were allies that had cooperated to defeat the Persian Empire in 480 BCE. Sparta was a conservative, land-oriented state that turned inward after the victory over Persia; Athens was a commercial, sea-oriented state that turned outward. In the middle of the century, Athens had 50 years of growth that led to the development of an Athenian empire. Athens formed the Delian League, an alliance of states around the Aegean Sea, for mutual protection against the Persians. Sparta, in turn, organized its neighbors on the Peloponnesian Peninsula into a defensive alliance. States that had joined Athens freely for protection against the Persians soon had to pay taxes to the Athenians. Because of the growing strength of Athens and the resistance of some to its growing empire, a war broke out in 461. By 445, the first Peloponnesian

FIGURE 1
Classical Greece

War ended and was followed by a treaty that promised peace for 30 years. Thus Greece enjoyed a period of stable peace before the second, more significant, Peloponnesian War.

In 434, a civil war broke out in the small, peripheral city-state of Epidamnus. Like a pebble that begins an avalanche, this event triggered a series of reactions that led ultimately to the second Peloponnesian War. Large conflicts are often precipitated by relatively insignificant crises in out-of-the-way places, as we shall see when we discuss World War I.

In Epidamnus, the democrats fought with oligarchs over how the country would be ruled. The democrats appealed to the city-state of Corcyra, which had helped establish Epidamnus, but were turned down. They then turned to another city-state, Corinth, and the Corinthians decided to help. This angered the Corcyraeans, who sent a fleet to recapture Epidamnus, their former colony. In the process, the Corcyraeans defeated the Corinthian fleet. Corinth was outraged and declared war on Corcyra. Corcyra, fearing the attack from Corinth, turned to Athens for help. Both Corcyra and Corinth sent representatives to Athens.

The Athenians, after listening to both sides, were in a dilemma. They did not want to break the truce that had lasted for a decade, but if the Corinthians (who were close to the Peloponnesians) conquered Corcyra and took control of its large navy, the balance of power among the Greek states would tip against Athens. The Athenians felt they could not risk letting the Corcyraean navy fall into the hands of the Corinthians, so they decided to become "a little bit involved." They launched a small endeavor to scare the Corinthians, sending

Bust of Thucydides

ten ships with instructions not to fight unless attacked. But deterrence failed; Corinth attacked, and when the Corcyraeans began to lose the battle, the Athenian ships were drawn into the fray more than they had intended. The Athenian involvement infuriated Corinth, which in turn worried the Athenians. In particular, Athens worried that Corinth would stir up problems in Potidaea, which, although an Athenian ally, had historic ties to Corinth. Sparta promised to help Corinth if Athens attacked Potidaea. When a revolt did occur in Potidaea, Athens sent forces to put it down.

At that point there was a great debate in Sparta. The Athenians appealed to the Spartans to stay neutral. The Corinthians urged the Spartans to go to war and warned them against failing to check the rising power of Athens. Megara, another important city, agreed with Corinth because contrary to the treaty, the Athenians had banned Megara's trade. Sparta was torn, but the Spartans voted in favor of war, according to Thucydides, because they were afraid that if Athenian power was not checked, Athens might control the whole of Greece: In other words, Sparta went to war to maintain the balance of power among the Greek city-states.

Athens rejected Sparta's ultimatum, and war broke out in 431. The Athenian mood was one of imperial greatness, with pride and patriotism about their city and their social system, and optimism that they would prevail in the war. The early phase of the war came to a stalemate. A truce was declared after ten years (421), but the truce was fragile and war broke out again. In 413, Athens undertook a very risky venture. It sent two fleets and infantry to conquer Sicily, the great island off the south of Italy, which had a number of Greek colonies allied to Sparta. The result was a terrible defeat for the Athenians. At the same time, Sparta received additional money from the Persians, who were only too happy to see Athens trounced. After the defeat in Sicily, Athens was internally divided. In 411 the oligarchs overthrew the democrats, and 400 of them attempted to rule Athens. These events were not the end, but Athens never really recovered. An Athenian naval victory in 410 was followed five years later by a Spartan naval victory, and by 404 Athens was compelled to sue for peace. Sparta demanded that Athens pull down the long walls that protected it from attack by land-based powers. Athens' power was broken.

Causes and Theories

This is a dramatic and powerful story. What caused the war? Thucydides is very clear. After recounting the various events in Epidamnus, Corcyra, and so forth, he said that those were not the real causes. What made the war inevitable was the growth of Athenian power and the fear this caused in Sparta.

Did Athens have a choice? With better foresight, could Athens have avoided this disaster? Pericles, the Athenian leader in the early days of the war, had an interesting answer for his fellow citizens. "[Y]our country has a right to your services in sustaining the glories of her position. . . . You should remember also that what you are fighting against is not merely slavery as an exchange for independence, but also loss of empire and danger from the animosities incurred in its exercise. Besides, to recede is no longer possible . . . [f]or what you hold is, to speak somewhat plainly, a tyranny; to take it was perhaps wrong, but to let it go is unsafe."[12] In other words, Pericles told his fellow Athenians that they had no choice. Perhaps they should not be where they were, but once they had an empire, there was not much they could do about it without even larger risks. Thus Pericles favored war. But there were other voices in Athens, such as those of the Athenian delegates to the debate in Sparta in 432 BCE who urged the Spartans to "consider the vast influence of accident in war, before you are engaged in it."[13] That turned out to be good advice; why didn't the Athenians heed their own counsel? Perhaps the Athenians were carried away by emotional patriotism or anger that clouded their reason. But there is a more interesting possibility: Perhaps the Athenians acted rationally but were caught in a security dilemma.

Security dilemmas are related to the essential characteristic of international politics: *anarchy*, the absence of a higher authority. Under anarchy, independent action taken by one state to increase its security may make all states less secure. If one state builds its strength to make sure that another cannot threaten it, the other, seeing the first getting stronger, may build its strength to protect itself against the first. The result is that the independent effort of each to improve its security makes both more insecure. It is an ironic result, yet neither has acted irrationally. Neither has acted from anger or pride, but from fear caused by the threat perceived in the growth of the other. After all, building defenses is a rational response to a perceived threat. States could cooperate to avoid this security dilemma; that is, they could agree that neither should build up its defenses and all would be better off. If it seems obvious that states should cooperate, why don't they?

An answer can be found in the game called the *Prisoner's Dilemma*. (Security dilemmas are a specific type of Prisoner's Dilemma.) The Prisoner's Dilemma scenario goes like this: Imagine that somewhere the police arrest two men who have small amounts of drugs in their possession, which would probably result in one-year jail sentences. The police have good reason to believe these two are really drug dealers, but they do not have enough evidence for a conviction. As dealers, the two could easily get 25-year jail sentences. The police know that the testimony of one against the other would be sufficient to convict the other to a full sentence. The police offer to let each man off if he will testify that the other is a drug dealer. They tell them that if both testify, both will receive ten-year sentences. The police figure this way these dealers will be out of commission for ten years; otherwise they are both in jail for only a year and soon will be out selling drugs again.

The suspects are put in separate cells and are not allowed to communicate with each other. Each prisoner has the same dilemma: If the other stays silent, he can secure his own freedom by squealing on the other, sending him to jail for 25 years, and go free himself; or he can stay silent and spend a year in jail. But if both prisoners squeal, they each get ten years in jail. Each prisoner thinks, "No matter what the other guy does, I'm better off if I squeal. If he stays quiet, I go free if I squeal and spend a year in jail if I don't. If he squeals,

I get ten years if I squeal and 25 years if I don't." If both think this way, both will squeal and spend ten years in jail each. If they could trust each other not to squeal, however, they would both be much better off, spending only one year in jail.

That is the basic structural dilemma of independent rational action in a situation of this kind. If the two could talk to each other, they might agree to make a deal to stay silent and both spend one year in jail. But even if communication were possible, there would be another problem: trust and credibility. Continuing with the metaphor in the Prisoner's Dilemma, each suspect could say to himself, "We are both drug dealers. I have seen the way the other acts. How do I know that after we've made this deal, he won't say, 'Great! I've convinced him to stay quiet. Now I can get my best possible outcome: freedom!'?" Similarly, in international politics the absence of communication and trust encourages states to provide for their own security, even though doing so may reduce all states to mutual insecurity. In other words, one state could say to another, "Don't build up your armaments and I will not build up my armaments, and we will both live happily ever after," but the second state may wonder whether it can afford to trust the first state.

The Athenian position in 432 looks very much like the Prisoner's Dilemma. In the middle of the century, the Athenians and Spartans agreed they were both better off having a truce. Even after the events in Epidamnus and the dispute between Corcyra and Corinth, the Athenians were reluctant to break it. The Corcyraeans ultimately convinced the Athenians with the following argument: "[T]here are but three considerable naval powers in Hellas [Greece], Athens, Corcyra, and Corinth, and . . . if you allow two of these three to become one, and Corinth to secure us for herself, you will have to hold the sea against the united fleets of Corcyra and the Peloponnesus. But if you receive us, you will have our ships to reinforce you in the struggle."[14]

Should Athens have cooperated with the Peloponnesians by turning Corcyra down? If they had, what would have happened if the Peloponnesians had captured the Corcyraean fleet? Then the naval balance would have been two to one against Athens. Should Athens have trusted the Peloponnesians to keep their promises? The Athenians decided to ally with Corcyra, thereby risking the treaty—the equivalent of squealing on the other prisoner. Thucydides explains why: "For it began now to be felt that the coming of the Peloponnesian War was only a question of time, and no one was willing to see a naval power of such magnitude as Corcyra sacrificed to Corinth."[15]

Inevitability and the Shadow of the Future

Ironically, the belief that war was inevitable played a major role in causing it. Athens felt that if the war was going to come, it was better to have two-to-one naval superiority rather than one-to-two naval inferiority. The belief that war was imminent and inevitable was critical to the decision. Why should that be so? Look again at the Prisoner's Dilemma. At first glance, it is best for each prisoner to cheat and let the other fellow be a sucker, but because each knows the situation, they also know that if they can trust each other, both should go for second best and cooperate by keeping silent. Cooperation is difficult to develop when playing the game only once. Playing a game time after time, people can learn to cooperate, but if it is a one-time game, whoever "defects" can get the reward and whoever trusts is a sucker. Political scientist Robert Axelrod played the Prisoner's Dilemma on a computer with different strategies. He found that after many games, on average the best results were obtained with a strategy he called *tit for tat*—"I will cooperate on my first move, and after that I will do to you what you last did to me. If on the first move you defect, I will defect. If you defect again, I should defect again. If you cooperate, I will cooperate. If you cooperate again, I cooperate again." Eventually, players find that the total benefit from the game is higher by learning to cooperate. But Axelrod warns that tit for tat is a good strategy only when you have a chance to continue the game for a long period, when there is a "long shadow of the future." On the last move, it is always rational to defect.

That is why the belief that war is inevitable is so corrosive in international politics. When you believe war is inevitable, you believe that you are very close to the last move, and you worry about whether you can still trust your opponent. If you suspect your opponent will defect, it is better to rely on yourself and take the risk of defecting rather than cooperating. That is what the Athenians did. Faced with the belief that war would occur, they decided they could not afford to trust the Corinthians or the Spartans. It was better to have the Corcyraean navy on their side than against them when it looked like the last move in the game and inevitable war.

Was the Peloponnesian War really inevitable? Thucydides had a pessimistic view of human nature: "I have written my work," he wrote, "not as an essay which is to win the applause of the moment, but as a possession for all time."[16] His history shows human nature caught in the situation of the Prisoner's Dilemma then and for all time. Thucydides, like all historians, had to emphasize certain things and not others. Thucydides concluded that the cause of the war was the growth of the power of Athens and the fear it caused in Sparta. But the Yale classicist Donald Kagan argues that Athenian power was in fact *not* growing: Before the war broke out in 431 BCE the balance of power had begun to stabilize. And though the Spartans worried about the rise of Athenian power, Kagan says, they had an even greater fear of a slave revolt. Both Athens and Sparta were slave states and both feared that going to war might provide an opportunity for the slaves to revolt. The difference was that the slaves, or Helots, in Sparta were 90 percent of the population—far greater than Athens' slave percentage—and the Spartans had recently experienced a Helot revolt in 464 BCE.

Thus the immediate or precipitating causes of the war, according to Kagan, were more important than Thucydides' theory of inevitability admits. Corinth, for example, thought Athens would not fight; it misjudged the Athenian response, partly because it was so angry at Corcyra. Pericles overreacted; he made mistakes in giving an ultimatum to Potidaea and in punishing Megara by cutting off its trade. Those policy mistakes made the Spartans think that war might be worth the risk after all. Kagan argues that Athenian growth caused the first Peloponnesian War but that the Thirty-Year Truce doused that flame. So, to start the second Peloponnesian War, "the spark of the Epidamnian trouble needed to land on one of the rare bits of flammable stuff that had not been thoroughly drenched. Thereafter it needed to be continually and vigorously fanned by the Corinthians, soon assisted by the Megarians, Potidaeans, Aeginetans, and the Spartan War Party. Even then the spark might have been extinguished had not the Athenians provided some additional fuel at the crucial moment."[17] In other words, the war was not caused by impersonal forces but by bad decisions in difficult circumstances.

It is perhaps impudent to question Thucydides, a father figure to historians, but very little is ever truly inevitable in history. Human behavior is voluntary, although there are always external constraints. Karl Marx observed that men make history, but not in conditions of their own choosing. The ancient Greeks made flawed choices because they were caught in the situation well described by Thucydides and by the Prisoner's Dilemma. The security dilemma made war highly probable, but *highly probable* is not the same as *inevitable*. After all, the Joker in *The Dark Knight* constructed a version of the Prisoner's Dilemma for the passengers on the two Gotham City ferries wired with explosives, but they opted to cooperate rather than defect. The 30-year unlimited war that devastated Athens was not inevitable. Human decisions mattered. Accidents and personalities make a difference even if they work within limits set by the larger structure, the situation of insecurity that resembles the Prisoner's Dilemma.

What modern lessons can we learn from this ancient history? We need to be aware of both the continuities and the changes. Some structural features of international politics predispose events in one direction rather than another. That is why it is necessary to understand security dilemmas and the Prisoner's Dilemma. On the other hand, such situations do not prove that war is inevitable. There are degrees of freedom, and human decisions can sometimes prevent the worst outcomes. Cooperation does occur in international affairs, even though the general structure of anarchy often tends to discourage it.

It is also necessary to be wary of patently shallow historical analogies. During the Cold War, it was often popular to say that because the United States was a democracy and a sea-based power while the Soviet Union was a land-based power and had slave labor camps, America was Athens and the Soviet Union was Sparta, locked into replaying a great historical conflict. But such shallow analogies ignored the fact that ancient Athens was a slave-holding state, wracked with internal turmoil, and that democrats were not always in control. Moreover, unlike in the Cold War, Sparta won.

Another lesson is to be aware of the selectivity of historians. No one can tell the whole story of anything. Imagine trying to tell everything that happened in the last hour, much less the entire story of your life or a whole war. Too many things happened. A second-by-second account in which everything was reported would take much longer to tell than it took for the events to happen in the first place. Thus historians always abstract. To write history, even the history of the last hour or the last day, we must simplify. We must select. What we select is obviously affected by the values, inclinations, and theories in our minds, whether explicit or inchoate.

Historians are affected by their contemporary concerns. Thucydides was concerned about how Athenians were learning the lessons of the war, blaming Pericles and the democrats for miscalculating. He therefore stressed those aspects of the situation we have described as the Prisoner's Dilemma. Yet while these aspects of the war were important, they are not the whole story. Thucydides did not write much about Athenian relations with Persia, or about the decree that cut off Megara's trade, or about Athens raising the amount of tribute that others in the Delian League had to pay. We have no reason to suspect that Thucydides' history was deliberately misleading or biased, but it is an example of how each age tends to rewrite history because the questions brought to the vast panoply of facts tend to change over time.

The need to select does not mean that everything is relative or that history is bunk. Such a conclusion is unwarranted. Good historians and social scientists do their best to ask questions honestly, objectively bringing facts to bear on their topic. But they and their students should be aware that what is selected is by necessity only part of the story. Always ask what questions the writer was asking as well as whether he or she carefully and objectively ascertained the facts. Beware of biases. Choice is a very important part of history and of writing history. The cure to misunderstanding history is to read more, not less.

Follow Up

- Robert B. Strassler, ed., *The Landmark Thucydides: A Comprehensive Guide to the Peloponnesian War*, trans. Richard Crawley (New York: Touchstone, 1996).
- Donald Kagan, *The Outbreak of the Peloponnesian War* (Ithaca, NY: Cornell University Press, 1969), pp. 31–56, 345–356.

THE RISE OF CHINA

Ever since Thucydides' explanation of the Peloponnesian War, historians have known that the rise of a new power has been attended by uncertainty and anxieties. Often, though not always, violent conflict has followed. The rise in the economic and military power of China, the world's most populous country, will be a central question for Asia and for American foreign policy at the beginning of a new century. Explaining why democratic Athens decided to break a treaty that led to war, Thucydides pointed to the power of expectations of inevitable conflict. "The general belief was that whatever happened, war with the Peloponnese was bound to come," he wrote. Belief in the inevitability of conflict with China could have similar self-fulfilling effects.

— *The Economist, June 27, 1998*[18]

ETHICAL QUESTIONS AND INTERNATIONAL POLITICS

Given the nature of the security dilemma, some realists believe that moral concerns play no role in international conflicts. However, ethics do play a role in international relations, although not quite the same role as in domestic politics.

Moral arguments have been used since the days of Thucydides. When Corcyra went to Athens to plead for help against Corinth, it used the language of ethics: "First, . . . your assistance will be rendered to a power which, herself inoffensive, is a victim to the injustice of others. Second, you will give unforgettable proof of your goodwill and create in us a lasting sense of gratitude."[19] Substitute *Kosovo* for *Corcyra* and *Serbia* for *Corinth,* and those words could be uttered in modern times.

Moral arguments move and constrain people. In that sense, morality is a powerful reality. However, moral arguments can also be used rhetorically as propaganda to disguise less elevated motives, and those with more power are often able to ignore moral considerations. During the Peloponnesian War, the Athenians sailed to the island of Melos to suppress a revolt. In 416 BCE, the Athenian spokesmen told the Melians that they could fight and die or they could surrender. When the Melians protested that they were fighting for their freedom, the Athenians responded that "the strong do what they can and the weak suffer what they must."[20] In essence, the Athenians stated that in a realist world, morality has little place. Might makes right. When Iraq invades Kuwait, or the United States invades Grenada or Panama, or the Indonesians suppress a revolt in East Timor, they all to some degree employ similar logic. But, in the modern world, it is increasingly less acceptable to articulate one's motives as plainly as Thucydides suggests the Athenians did in Melos. Does this mean that morality has come to occupy a more prominent place in international relations, or simply that states have become more adept at propaganda? Has international politics changed dramatically, with states more attuned to ethical concerns, or is there a clear continuity between the actions of the Athenians 2,500 years ago and the actions of Iraq or Serbia in the late twentieth century?

Moral arguments are not all equal. Some are more compelling than others. We ask whether they are logical and consistent. For instance, when the activist Phyllis Schlafly argued that nuclear weapons are a good thing because God gave them to the free world, we should wonder why God also gave them to Stalin's Soviet Union and Mao's China.

A basic touchstone for many moral arguments is impartiality—the view that all interests are judged by the same criteria. Your interests deserve the same attention as mine. Within this framework of impartiality, however, there are two different traditions in Western political culture about how to judge moral arguments. One descends from Immanuel Kant, the eighteenth-century German philosopher, the other from British utilitarians of the early nineteenth century such as Jeremy Bentham. As an illustration of the two approaches, imagine walking into a poor village and finding that a military officer is about to shoot three people lined up against the wall. You ask, "Why are you shooting these peasants? They look quite harmless." The officer says, "Last night somebody in this village shot one of my men. I know somebody in this village is guilty, so I am going to shoot these three to set an example." You say, "You can't do that! You're going to kill an innocent person. If only one shot was fired, then at least two of these people are innocent, perhaps all three. You just can't do that." The officer takes a rifle from one of his men and hands it to you, saying, "If you shoot one of them for me, I'll let the other two go. You can save two lives if you will shoot one of them. I'm going to teach you that in civil war you can't have these holier-than-thou attitudes."

What are you going to do? You could try to mow down all the troops in a Rambo-like move, but the officer has a soldier aiming his gun at you. So your choice is to kill one innocent person in order to save two or to drop the gun and have clean hands. The Kantian tradition says that all deliberate killing is wrong, so you should refuse to perpetrate the evil deed. The utilitarian tradition suggests that if you can save two lives, you should do it. Now, suppose that you sympathize with the Kantian perspective; imagine now that the numbers were increased. Suppose there were 100 people against the wall. Or imagine you could save a city full of people from a terrorist's bomb by shooting one possibly innocent person. Should you refuse to save a million people in order to keep your hands and conscience clean? At some point, consequences matter. Moral arguments can be judged in three ways: by the motives or intentions involved, by the means used, and by their consequences or net effects. Although these dimensions are not always easily reconciled, good moral argument tries to take all three into account.

Limits on Ethics in International Relations

Ethics plays less of a role in international politics than in domestic politics for four reasons. One is the weak international consensus on values. There are cultural and religious differences over the justice of some acts. Second, states are not like individuals. States are abstractions, and although their leaders are individuals, statesmen are judged differently than when they act as individuals. For instance, when picking a roommate, most people want a person who believes "thou shalt not kill." But the same people might vote against a presidential candidate who says, "Under no circumstances will I ever take an action that will lead to a death." A president is entrusted by citizens to protect their interests, and under some circumstances this may require the use of force. Presidents who saved their own souls but failed to protect their people would not be good trustees.

In private morality, sacrifice may be the highest proof of a moral action, but should leaders sacrifice their whole people? During the Peloponnesian War, the Athenians told the leaders of the island of Melos that if they resisted, Athens would kill all the men and sell the women and children into slavery. Melos resisted and was destroyed. Should they have come to terms? In 1962, should President Kennedy have run a risk of nuclear war to force the Soviets to remove missiles from Cuba when the United States had similar missiles in Turkey? Different people may answer these questions differently. The point is, when individuals act as leaders of states, their actions are judged somewhat differently.

A third reason ethics plays a lesser role in international politics is the complexity of causation. It is hard enough to know the consequences of actions in domestic affairs, but international relations has another layer of complexity: the interaction of states. That extra dimension makes it harder to predict consequences accurately. A famous example is the 1933 debate among students at the Oxford Union, the debating society of Oxford University. Mindful of the 20 million people killed in World War I, the majority of students voted for a resolution that they would never again fight for king and country. But someone else was listening: Adolf Hitler. He concluded that democracies were soft and that he could press them as hard as he wanted because they would not fight back. In the end, he pressed too far and the result was World War II, a consequence not desired or expected by those students who voted never to fight for king and country. Many later did, and many died.

A more trivial example is the "hamburger argument" of the early 1970s, when people were worried about shortages of food in the world. A number of students in American colleges said, "When we go to the dining hall, refuse to eat meat because a pound of beef equals eight pounds of grain, which could be used to feed poor people around the world." Many students stopped eating hamburger and felt good about themselves, but they did not help starving people in Africa or Bangladesh one bit. Why not? The grain freed up by some people not eating hamburgers in America did not reach the starving people in Bangladesh because those starving had no money to buy the grain. The grain was simply a surplus on the American market, which meant American prices went down and farmers produced less. To help peasants in Bangladesh required getting money to them so they could buy some of the excess grain. By launching a campaign against eating hamburger and failing to look at the complexity of the causal chain that would relate their well-intended act to its consequences, the students failed.

Finally, there is the argument that the institutions of international society are particularly weak and that the disjunction between order and justice is greater in international than in domestic politics. Order and justice are both important. In a domestic polity we tend to take order for granted. In fact, sometimes protesters purposefully disrupt order for the sake of promoting their view of justice. But if there is total disorder, it is very hard to have any justice; witness the bombing, kidnapping, and killing by all sides in Lebanon in the 1980s, in Somalia since the end of the Cold War, and in many parts of Afghanistan today. Some degree of order is a prior condition for justice. In international politics, the absence of a common legislature, central executive, or strong judiciary makes it much harder to preserve the order that precedes justice.

Three Views of the Role of Morality

At least three different views of ethics exist in international relations: those of the *skeptics,* the *state moralists,* and the *cosmopolitans.* Although there is no logical connection, people who are realists in their descriptive analysis of world politics often tend to be either skeptics or state moralists in their evaluative approach, whereas those who emphasize a liberal analysis tend toward either the state moralist or cosmopolitan moral viewpoints.

Skeptics The skeptic says that moral categories have no meaning in international relations because no institutions exist to provide order. In addition, there is no sense of community, and therefore there are no moral rights and duties. For the skeptics, the classic statement about ethics in international politics was the Athenians' response to the Melians' plea for mercy: "The strong do what they can and the weak suffer what they must." Might makes right. And that, for the skeptics, is all there is to say.

Philosophers often say that *ought* (moral obligation) implies *can* (the capacity to do something). Morality requires choice. If something is impossible, we cannot have an obligation to do it. If international relations are simply the realm of "kill or be killed," then presumably there is no choice, and that would justify the skeptics' position. But international politics consists of more than mere survival. If choices exist in international relations, pretending choices do not exist is merely a disguised form of choice. To think only in terms of narrow national interests is simply smuggling in values without admitting it. The French diplomat who once said, "What is moral is whatever is good for France," was ducking hard choices about why only French interests should be considered. The leader who says, "I had no choice," often did have a choice, albeit not a pleasant one. If there is some degree of order and of community in international relations—if it is not constantly "kill or be killed"—then there is room for choices. Anarchy means "without government," but it does not necessarily mean chaos or total disorder. There are rudimentary practices and institutions that provide enough order to allow some important choices: balance of power, international law, and international organizations. Each is critical to understanding why the skeptical argument is not sufficient.

Thomas Hobbes argued that to escape from "the state of nature" in which anyone might kill anyone else, individuals give up their freedom to a "leviathan," or government, for protection, because life in the state of nature is nasty, brutish, and short. Why then don't states form a superleviathan? Why isn't there a world government? The reason, Hobbes said, is that insecurity is not so great at the international level as at the individual level. Governments provide some degree of protection against the brutality of the biggest individuals taking whatever they want, and the balance of power among states provides some degree of order. Even though states are in a hostile posture of potential war, "they still uphold the daily industry of their subjects." The international state of nature does not create the day-to-day misery that would accompany a state of nature among individuals. In other words, Hobbes believed that the existence of states in a balance of power alleviates the condition of international anarchy enough to allow some degree of order.

Liberals point further to the existence of international law and customs. Even if rudimentary, such rules put a burden of proof on those who break them. Consider the Persian Gulf crisis in 1990. Saddam Hussein claimed that he annexed Kuwait to recover a province stolen from Iraq in colonial times. But because international law forbids crossing borders for such reasons, an overwhelming majority of states viewed his action as a violation of the UN charter.

The twelve resolutions passed by the UN Security Council showed clearly that Saddam's view of the situation ran against international norms. Law and norms did not stop Saddam from invading Kuwait, but they did make it more difficult for him to recruit support, and they contributed to the creation of the coalition that expelled him from Kuwait.

International institutions, even if rudimentary, also provide a degree of order by facilitating and encouraging communication and some degree of reciprocity in bargaining. Given this situation of nearly constant communication, international politics is not always, as the skeptics claim, "kill or be killed." The energies and attention of leaders are not focused on security and survival all the time. Cooperation (as well as conflict) occurs in large areas of economic, social, and military interaction. And even though cultural differences exist about the notion of justice, moral arguments take place in international politics and principles are enshrined in international law.

Even in the extreme circumstances of war, law and morality may sometimes play a role. *Just war doctrine,* which originated in the early Christian church and became secularized after the seventeenth century, prohibits the killing of innocent civilians. The prohibition on killing innocents starts from the premise "thou shalt not kill." But if that is a basic moral premise, how is any killing ever justified? Absolute pacifists say that no one should kill anyone else for any reason. Usually this is asserted on Kantian grounds, but some pacifists add a consequentialist argument that "violence only begets more violence." Sometimes, however, the failure to respond to violence can also beget more violence. For example, it is unlikely that Osama bin Laden would have left the United States alone if President George W. Bush had turned the other cheek after 9/11. In contrast to pacifism, the just war tradition combines a concern for the intentions, means, and consequences of actions. It argues that if someone is about to kill you and you refuse to act in self-defense, the result is that evil will prevail. By refusing to defend themselves, the good die. If one is in imminent peril of being killed, it can be moral to kill in self-defense. But we must distinguish between those who can be killed and those who cannot be killed. For example, if a soldier rushes at you with a rifle, you can kill him in self-defense, but the minute the soldier drops the rifle, puts up his hands, and says, "I surrender," he is a prisoner of war and you have no right to take his life. In fact, this is enshrined in international law, and also in the U.S. military code. An American soldier who shoots an enemy soldier after he surrenders can be tried for murder in an American court. Some American officers in the Vietnam and Iraq wars were sent to prison for violating such laws. The prohibition against intentionally killing people who pose no harm also helps explain why terrorism is wrong. Some skeptics argue that "one man's terrorist is just another man's freedom fighter." However, under just war doctrine, you can fight for freedom, but you cannot target innocent civilians. Though they are often violated, some norms exist even under the harshest international

JUST WAR DOCTRINE

Classical just war doctrine grew out of the Roman and Christian traditions. Cicero, St. Augustine, and St. Thomas Aquinas were key early thinkers. Today, just war doctrine has broad appeal. There are many possible formulations, but all have two components: principles of *jus ad bellum,* which specify the conditions under which it is morally permissible to use force, and principles of *jus in bello,* which specify how force may be used morally.

The five standard principles of *jus ad bellum* include (1) just cause, (2) right intention, (3) legitimate authority, (4) last resort, and (5) reasonable chance of success. Over the centuries, interpretations of these principles have changed. Just cause used to be restricted almost entirely to self-defense, for example, but today may include counterintervention or preventing humanitarian catastrophe. Kings and emperors used to enjoy unquestioned legitimate authority, but increasingly world opinion requires the approval of an international body such as the United Nations Security Council.

The three main principles of *jus in bello* are (1) observe the laws of war, (2) maintain proportionality, and (3) observe the principle of noncombatant immunity. The laws of war have also evolved over the centuries and represent a much more stringent set of constraints today than in medieval times. Modern military technology makes it more difficult in some respects to maintain proportionality and protect innocent civilians, since the destructive power of modern weaponry is vastly greater than in the age of the sword and spear, but modern precision-guided munitions and advanced battlefield management systems can compensate for this to some extent.

circumstances. The rudimentary sense of justice enshrined in an imperfectly obeyed international law belies the skeptics' argument that no choices exist in a situation of war.

We can therefore reject complete skepticism because some room exists for morality in international politics. Morality is about choice, and meaningful choice varies with the conditions of survival. The greater the threats to survival, the less room for moral choice. At the start of the Peloponnesian War, the Athenians argued, "[P]raise is due to all who, if not so superior to human nature as to refuse dominion, yet respect justice more than their position compels them to do."[21] Unfortunately, the Athenians lost sight of that wisdom later in their war, but it reminds us that situations with absolutely no choice are rare and that national security and degrees of threat are often ambiguous. Skeptics avoid hard moral choices by pretending otherwise. To sum up in an aphorism: Humans may not live wholly by the word, but neither do they live solely by the sword.

Not all realists are skeptics, but those who take morality seriously consider order at least as important. Without order, justice is difficult or impossible. Moral crusades can even cause disorder. If the United States becomes too concerned about spreading democracy or human rights throughout the world, for example, it may create disorder that will actually do more damage than good in the long run. The realist theologian and public affairs commentator

Reinhold Niebuhr considered "moral and political factors" equally important. Writing in the aftermath of World War II, Niebuhr insisted that "[w]e can save mankind from another holocaust only if our nerves are steady and if our moral purpose is matched by strategic shrewdness."[22]

The realists have a valid argument, up to a point. International order is important, but it is a matter of degrees, and there are trade-offs between justice and order. How much order is necessary before we start worrying about justice? For example, after the 1990 Soviet crackdown in the Baltic republics in which a number of people were killed, some Americans urged a break in relations with the Soviet Union. In their view, Americans should express their values of democracy and human rights in foreign policy, even if that meant instability and the end of arms control talks. Others argued that while concerns for peace and for human rights were important, it was more important to control nuclear weapons and negotiate an arms reduction treaty. In the end, the American government went ahead with the arms negotiations, but linked the provision of economic aid to respect for human rights. Over and over in international politics, the question is not absolute order versus justice, but how to trade off choices in particular situations. The realists have a valid point of view, but they overstate it when they argue that it has to be all order before any justice.

State Moralists *State moralists* argue that international politics rests on a society of states with certain rules, although those rules are not always perfectly obeyed. The most important rule is state sovereignty, which prohibits states from intervening across borders into others' jurisdiction. The political scientist Michael Walzer, for example, argues that national boundaries have a moral significance because states represent the pooled rights of individuals who have come together for a common life. Thus, respect for the sovereignty and territorial integrity of states is related to respect for individuals. Others argue more simply that respect for sovereignty is the best way to preserve order. "Good fences make good neighbors," in the words of the poet Robert Frost.

In practice, these rules of state behavior are frequently violated. In the last few decades, Vietnam invaded Cambodia, China invaded Vietnam, Tanzania invaded Uganda, Israel invaded Lebanon, the Soviet Union invaded Afghanistan, the United States invaded Grenada and Panama, Iraq invaded Iran and Kuwait, the United States and Britain invaded Iraq, and NATO bombed Serbia because of its mistreatment of ethnic Albanians in the province of Kosovo—to name just a few examples. Determining when it is appropriate to respect another state's sovereignty is a long-standing challenge. In 1979, Americans condemned the Soviet invasion of Afghanistan in strong moral terms. The Soviets responded by pointing to the Dominican Republic, where in 1965 the United States sent 25,000 troops to prevent the formation of a communist government. The intention behind the American intervention in the Dominican Republic—preventing a hostile regime from coming to power in the Caribbean—was quite similar to the intention of the Soviet Union's intervention in Afghanistan: that is, preventing the formation of a hostile government on its border.

To find differences, we have to look further than intentions. In terms of the means used, very few people were killed by the U.S. intervention in the Dominican Republic, and the Americans soon withdrew. In the Afghan case, many people were killed, and the Soviet forces remained for nearly a decade. In the 1990s, some critics compared the Iraqi invasion of Kuwait with the American invasion of Panama. In December 1989, the United States sent troops to overthrow the Panamanian dictator Manuel Noriega, and in August 1990, Iraq sent troops into Kuwait to overthrow the emir. Both the United States and Iraq violated the rule of nonintervention. But again there were differences in means and consequences. In Panama, the Americans put into office a government that had been duly elected but that Noriega had not permitted to take power. The Americans did not try to annex Panama. In Kuwait, the Iraqi government tried to annex the country and caused much bloodshed in the process. Such considerations do not mean that the Panama case was all right or all wrong, but problems often arise when applying simple rules of nonintervention and sovereignty.

Cosmopolitans *Cosmopolitans* such as the political theorist Charles Beitz see international politics not just as a society of states, but as a society of individuals. When we speak about justice, say the cosmopolitans, we should speak about justice for individuals. They argue that realists focus too much on issues of war and peace. Cosmopolitans contend that if realists focused on issues of distributive justice—that is, who gets what—they would pay more attention to the interdependence of the global economy. Constant economic intervention across borders can sometimes have life-or-death consequences. For example, it is a life-or-death matter if you are a peasant in the Philippines and your child

INTERVENTION

Imagine the following scene in Afghanistan in December 1979:

An Afghan communist leader came to power promoting a platform of greater independence from the Soviet Union. This worried Soviet leaders, because an independent regime on their border might foment trouble throughout Central Asia (including Soviet Central Asia) and would create a dangerous precedent of a small communist neighbor escaping the Soviet Empire. Imagine the Russian general in charge of the Soviet invasion force confronting the renegade Afghan leader, whom he is about to kill, explaining why he is doing these things against the international rules of sovereignty and nonintervention. "As far as right goes, other countries in our sphere of influence think one has as much of it as the other, and that if any maintain their independence it is because they are strong, and that if we do not molest them it is because we are afraid; so that besides extending our empire we should gain in security by your subjection; the fact that you are a border state and weaker than others, rendering it all the more important that you should not succeed in thwarting the masters of Central Asia."

Thus spoke the Athenians to the leaders of Melos (5.97), with but minor substitutions! Intervention is not a new problem.

dies of a curable disease because the local boy who went to medical school is now working in the United States for a much higher salary.

Cosmopolitans argue that national boundaries have no moral standing; they simply defend an inequality that should be abolished if we think in terms of distributive justice. Realists (who include both moral skeptics and some state moralists) reply that the danger in the cosmopolitans' approach is that it may lead to enormous disorder. Taken literally, efforts at radical redistribution of resources are likely to lead to violent conflict, because people do not give up their wealth easily. A more limited cosmopolitan argument rests on the fact that people often have multiple loyalties—to families, friends, neighborhoods, and nations; perhaps to some transnational religious groups; and to the concept of common humanity. Most people are moved by pictures of starving Somali children or Darfur refugees, for some common community exists beyond the national level, albeit a weaker one. We are all humans.

Cosmopolitans remind us of the distributive dimensions to international relations in which morality matters as much in peace as in war. Policies can be designed to assist basic human needs and basic human rights without destroying order. And in cases of gross abuse of human rights, cosmopolitan views have been written into international laws such as the international convention against genocide. As a result, policy makers are more conscious of moral concerns. For example, President Bill Clinton has said that one of his worst mistakes was not to have done more to stop genocide in Rwanda in 1994, and the United States and other countries later supported African peacekeeping troops in efforts to suppress genocidal violence in the Sudanese province of Darfur.

Of the approaches to international morality, the skeptic makes a valid point about order being necessary for justice but misses the trade-offs between order and justice. The state moralist who sees a society of states with rules against intervention illustrates an institutional approach to order but does not provide enough answers regarding when some interventions may be justified. Finally, the cosmopolitan who focuses on a society of individuals has a profound insight about common humanity but runs the risk of fomenting enormous disorder by pursuing massive redistributive policies. Most people develop a hybrid position; labels are less important than the central point that trade-offs exist among these approaches.

Because of the differences between domestic and international politics, morality is harder to apply in international politics. But just because there is a plurality of principles, it does not follow that there are no principles at all. How far should we go in applying morality to international politics? The answer is to be careful, for when moral judgments determine everything, morality can lead to a sense of outrage, and outrage can lead to heightened risk. Prudence can be a virtue, particularly when the alternative is disastrous unintended consequences. After all, there are no moral questions among the dead. But we cannot honestly ignore morality in international politics. Each person must study events and make his or her own decisions about judgments and trade-offs. The enduring logic of international conflict does not remove the responsibility for moral choices, although it does require an understanding of the special setting that makes those choices difficult.

While the specific moral and security dilemmas of the Peloponnesian War are unique, many of the issues recur over history. As we trace the evolution of international relations, we will see again and again the tension between realism and liberalism, between skeptics and cosmopolitans, between an anarchic system of states and international organizations. We will revisit the Prisoner's Dilemma and continue to grapple with the ethical conundrums of war. We will see how different actors on the world stage have approached the crises of their time and how their goals and instruments vary. As mentioned at the outset, certain variables that characterize international politics today simply did not exist in Thucydides' day: no nuclear weapons; no United Nations; no Internet; no transnational corporations; no cartels. The study of international conflict is an inexact science combining history and theory. In weaving our way through theories and examples, we try to keep in mind both what has changed and what has remained constant so we may better understand our past and our present and better navigate the unknown shoals of the future.

Follow Up

- Joel H. Rosenthal, ed., *Ethics & International Affairs: A Reader*, 3rd ed. (Washington, DC: Georgetown University Press, 2009).
- David A. Welch, "Can We Think Systematically About Ethics and Statecraft?" *Ethics & International Affairs*, Vol. 8 (1994), pp. 23–37.

CHRONOLOGY: PELOPONNESIAN WARS

490 BCE	First Persian War
480 BCE	Second Persian War
478 BCE	Spartans abdicate leadership
476 BCE	Formation of Delian League and Athenian empire
464 BCE	Helot revolt in Sparta
461 BCE	Outbreak of first Peloponnesian War
445 BCE	Thirty-Year Truce
445–434 BCE	Ten years of peace
434 BCE	Epidamnus and Corcyra conflicts
433 BCE	Athens intervenes in Potidaea
432 BCE	Spartan Assembly debates war
431 BCE	Outbreak of second Peloponnesian War
430 BCE	Pericles' Funeral Oration
416 BCE	Melian dialogue
413 BCE	Athens' defeat in Sicily
411 BCE	Oligarchs revolt in Athens
404 BCE	Athens defeated, forced to pull down walls

STUDY QUESTIONS

1. What role should ethical considerations play in the conduct of international relations? What role *do* they play? Can we speak meaningfully about moral duties to other countries or their populations? What are America's moral obligations in Iraq? In Afghanistan?
2. How well did the Iraq war satisfy the principles of *jus ad bellum* and *jus in bello?* What about Afghanistan?
3. Is there a difference between moral obligations in the realms of domestic politics and international politics? On the basis of the Melian dialogue, did the Athenians act ethically? Did the Melian elders?
4. What is realism? How does it differ from the liberal view of world politics? What does constructivism add to realism and liberalism?
5. What does Thucydides pinpoint as the main causes of the Peloponnesian War? Which were immediate? Which were underlying?
6. What sort of theory of international relations is implicit in Thucydides' account of the war?
7. Was the Peloponnesian War inevitable? If so, why and when? If not, how and when might it have been prevented?

NOTES

1. Calculated from UCDP/PRIO Armed Conflict Dataset and Codebook, version 4-2009; see also Nils Petter Gleditsch, Peter Wallensteen, Mikael Eriksson, Margareta Sollenberg, and Håvard Strand, "Armed Conflict 1946–2001: A New Dataset," *Journal of Peace Research* 39:5 (September 2002), pp. 615–637.
2. Thomas Hobbes, *Leviathan*, ed. C. B. MacPherson (London: Penguin, 1981), p. 186.
3. *The New York World*, "From Our Dec. 13 Pages, 75 Years Ago," *International Herald Tribune*, December 13, 1985.
4. Miles Kahler, "Inventing International Relations: International Relations Theory After 1945," in Michael W. Doyle and G. John Ikenberry, eds., *New Thinking in International Relations Theory* (Boulder, CO: Westview, 1977), p. 38.
5. Emanuel Adler, "Constructivism in International Relations: Sources, Contributions, Debates and Future Directions," in Walter Carlsnaes, Thomas Risse, and Beth Simmons, eds., *Handbook of International Relations* (Thousand Oaks, CA: Sage, 2003).
6. Ian Hurd, quoting Alexander Wendt, "Constructivism," in Christopher Reus-Smit and Duncan Snidal, eds., *Oxford Handbook of International Relations* (Oxford: Oxford University Press, 2008).
7. Jacqui True, "Feminism," in Scott Burchill and Andrew Linklater, eds., *Theories of International Relations*, 3rd ed. (New York: Palgrave Macmillan, 2005), p. 233.

8. Michael Barnett, "Social Constructivism," in John Baylis and Steve Smith, eds., *The Globalization of World Politics*, 3rd ed. (Oxford: Oxford University Press, 2005), p. 260.
9. John Maynard Keynes, *The General Theory of Employment, Interest and Money* (London: Macmillan, 1936), p. 383.
10. Sales and GDP are different measures, so the comparison is imperfect. Nonetheless, it understates the importance of corporations, since corporate sales are a component of GDP.
11. Robert Gilpin, *War and Change in World Politics* (Cambridge: Cambridge University Press, 1981), pp. 227–228.
12. Thucydides, *History of the Peloponnesian War* 2.63, trans. Richard Crawley; in Robert B. Strassler, ed., *The Landmark Thucydides: A Comprehensive Guide to the Peloponnesian War* (New York: Touchstone, 1996), pp. 125–126.
13. 1.78; ibid., p. 44.
14. 1.36; ibid., p. 24.
15. 1.44; ibid., p. 28.
16. 1.22; ibid., p. 16.
17. Donald Kagan, *The Outbreak of the Peloponnesian War* (Ithaca, NY: Cornell University Press, 1969), p. 354. For an alternative interpretation of the realities of Athenian expansion, see G. E. M. de Ste. Croix, *The Origins of the Peloponnesian War* (Ithaca, NY: Cornell University Press, 1972), pp. 60, 201–203.
18. Joseph S. Nye, Jr., "As China Rises, Must Others Bow?" *The Economist*, June 27, 1998, p. 23.
19. Thucydides, *History of the Peloponnesian War* 1.33, p. 22.
20. 5.89; ibid., p. 352.
21. 1.76; ibid., p. 43.
22. Reinhold Niebuhr, "For Peace, We Must Risk War," *Life*, September 20, 1948, p. 39.

PHOTO CREDITS

Credits are listed in order of appearance:

Alinari/Art Resource, NY.

David Welch.

With permission of the Royal Ontario Museum © ROM.

BOX CREDIT

"1910: The Unseen Vampire of War": Excerpted from "From Our December 13 Pages, 75 Years Ago," *International Herald Tribune*, December 13, 1985. Copyright 1985 *International Herald Tribune* and The New York Times Syndicate. Reprinted by permission.

MAP CREDIT

Map is drawn from Brian Catchpole, *A Map History of the Modern World* (Oxford: Heinemann Publishers, 1982), reprinted with adjustments by permission.

Explaining Conflict and Cooperation: Tools and Techniques of the Trade

German chancellor Prince Otto von Bismarck (1815–1898)

From Chapter 2 of *Understanding Global Conflict and Cooperation*, Ninth Edition. Joseph S. Nye, Jr., David A. Welch.

KEY CONCEPTS

To make sense of something, you need an appropriate conceptual toolkit that includes a useful vocabulary, ways of drawing inferences that help you see how things work, and strategies for solving problems. Understanding global conflict and cooperation is no exception.

Unlike physicians, engineers, or natural scientists, people who study world politics have relatively little in the way of highly specialized vocabulary. We borrow words from other fields, or from common usage. The upside of this is that the barriers to entry are low; almost anyone can have a sensible discussion about world politics. How many people can have a casual dinnertime conversation about plasmapheresis or quantum tunneling? The downside is that there is an unusually high risk of ambiguity and confusion, because the same word can mean quite different things in different contexts, and many words have two or more possible meanings in the same context. Ambiguity is not something that we can purge from the English language, but we can learn to spot potentially confusing usages. Before we delve too deeply into the interplay of theory and history, therefore, it is useful to spend some time exploring key concepts. We will then go on to examine some useful tools and techniques for drawing inferences about world politics.

States, Nations, and Nation-States

Perhaps the single most important concept used in the study of world politics is the *sovereign state*. Unfortunately, it is also one of the most confusing—partly because it is two concepts bundled together, *sovereignty* and *state*. Most people would agree that the state is the most important actor in the international system (we will explore the terms "actor" and "system" more closely in a moment), although realists and liberals would disagree about the relative importance of other actors. Realists would insist that states are the only significant actors, while liberals would argue that states are only the most important among many. But what, exactly, *is* a "state"?

A state is a particular type of political unit that has two crucial characteristics: *territoriality* and *sovereignty*. Territoriality is straightforward: A state governs a specific, identifiable portion of the Earth's surface. Sovereignty is the absolute right to govern it. In most cases, when you encounter the word "state" in a discussion of world politics, the best single synonym would be "country." Britain, France, Argentina, and Japan are all states. Being sovereign means that they have no higher authority to which they must answer. Different countries have different political systems that locate sovereignty in different places. In traditional monarchies, kings or queens are sovereign and enjoy supreme authority over the territories they govern. In democracies, the people hold sovereignty and delegate government to their elected representatives and other state officials. But whatever the ultimate source of sovereignty, all states have governments that pass laws, enforce order, and are supposed to defend the people who live within their borders.

The United States of America is a state in this sense as well. However, it is a federation of lower-level political units that rather inconveniently also happen to be called "states." The same is true for a number of other countries, such as Australia, India, and Mexico. This is one obvious possible source of confusion. Michigan, New South Wales, Uttar Pradesh, and Chihuahua are all states, but they are not countries. They are territorial, but they are not sovereign. While they have delegated areas of jurisdiction, they are answerable to their federal constitutions.

> "When concepts are used in more than one way, confusion is easy. A southern colleague of mine began her university teaching career in the upper Midwest. The first course she taught was a comparative politics course titled 'The State in Western Europe.' In it she explored the wide variety of structures and practices of various European political systems. After a few weeks, one student timidly approached her after class with a puzzled look on his face. 'Professor,' he said, 'I know you're from Georgia and this is Wisconsin; but when you talk about "the state," you do mean Wisconsin, don't you?'"
>
> —Joseph S. Nye, Jr.

A third possible source of confusion is that the word "state" is often used to refer to the *government* of a country—or, more precisely, to the structure and practices of the institutions and offices that make up the government. This usage is common in the comparative politics subfield of political science, where you will often hear Singapore (for example) described as a "strong state" because its central government has a great deal of authority, and the United States as a "weak" state because of its system of checks and balances and a very generous set of constitutionally protected individual rights. Obviously, in terms of material power, the United States is much stronger than Singapore, so one must be very careful to interpret phrases such as "strong state" and "weak state" appropriately. Context is key.

Another word often used as a synonym for state is "nation." This is a particularly unfortunate practice, because the word "nation" is commonly used to denote a group of people who have some combination of common language, culture, religion, history, mythology, identity, or sense of destiny. A decent but imperfect synonym for this kind of "nation" is "ethnic group."[1] Kurds, Tamils, Québécois, and Navajo are all nations in this sense, but none of them is a state. Abraham Lincoln famously said in his Gettysburg Address, "Four score and seven years ago, our forefathers brought forth upon this continent a

ARE EU MEMBERS "SOVEREIGN STATES"?

The European Union (EU) is a fascinating example of supranational integration. Its 27 member states have agreed to set up supranational institutions such as the European Parliament and Council of Ministers (which are responsible for legislation), a European Commission (the EU's executive arm), and the European Court of Justice and Court of First Instance (judicial arms). The EU is a single market and customs union with free movement of goods, services, capital, and people; it attempts to harmonize policies in a wide range of issue areas; and it strives to speak with one voice on the world stage. Sixteen EU members have embraced a common currency, the euro, which is second in importance only to the U.S. dollar in the world economy. At the same time, the members only loosely coordinate their common defense and foreign policies.

Does all of this mean that the members are no longer sovereign states? Technically, no; every member country retains the right to withdraw from the EU at any time it chooses. However, withdrawal would be very costly, and it is difficult to imagine anything other than very extreme circumstances prompting it. Indeed, no state is contemplating withdrawal at the moment, while several states, such as Turkey, are seeking entry.

The EU is the best, but not the only, example of supranational integration. Egypt and Syria formed the United Arab Republic (UAR) in 1958, but it fell apart after only three years. A more interesting and somewhat more successful experiment was the East African Community (EAC) in 1967, binding Kenya, Tanzania, and Uganda. The EAC fared quite well until torn apart by ideological differences and personality clashes among the three countries' leaders. In 2001, the EAC was reborn, and in 2007, Burundi and Rwanda joined as well. Yet the reincarnation of the EAC has a long way to go before it proves as effective as the EU in promoting the common and individual interests of its member states.

new nation, conceived in liberty, and dedicated to the proposition that all men are created equal." It would have been much better if he had said *state* rather than *nation*, because the United States of America is a multinational state.

It was common among eighteenth- and nineteenth-century liberal political philosophers to believe that every nation should have a state of its own, and groups such as the Kurds and Tamils struggled for this for years. A state whose citizens are overwhelmingly members of a single nation is a *nation-state*. There are few true nation-states in the world today. Japan and the two Koreas are notable exceptions; 98.5 percent of the inhabitants of Japan are ethnic Japanese, and an even higher proportion of the inhabitants of North and South Korea are ethnic Koreans. Most countries of the world today are far from being ethnically homogenous.

National groups within states often claim a right to *self-government* or *self-determination*. Self-determination is the ability to decide one's own political fate. This frequently includes a claim to a state of one's own. Québec separatists, for example, claim a right to self-determination for the purpose of carving a new country out of Canada. Sometimes groups claiming a right to self-determination seek to detach the territories in which they live from one country and join it to another, as did ethnic Germans in Austria, Czechoslovakia, and Poland between the two world wars.[2] Groups that claim a right to self-government may be happy to live within the territory of an existing multinational state, but may seek extensive rights and prerogatives to look after their own affairs. Wales, for example, is not a sovereign state—it is part of the United Kingdom—but the Welsh enjoy quite a significant degree of self-government, which is exercised by the aptly named Welsh National Assembly.

The difficulty with the idea of the nation-state as a philosophical ideal is that nations are often intermingled and spread out in diasporas over vast distances. It would be impossible to draw borders in such a way as to give each nation a state of its own. Even if this were possible, a powerful norm against redrawing settled borders has emerged over the course of the last century, in part in reaction to the carnage caused by the partial, inconsistent, and unsuccessful attempt to realize the nation-state ideal in Europe after World War I. In another era, Kurds and Tamils might have been in luck: Their claims to self-determination might have been greeted with sympathy from powerful countries, and possibly even with active political support. Nowadays the international community is reluctant to recognize secession in all but the most severe cases of genocide, oppression, violent state collapse, or rare mutual agreements such as the Czech and Slovak "velvet divorce" in 1993.

For the sake of clarity, it is always important to pay careful attention to what people actually mean when they use terms such as *state, nation*, and *nation-state*. You will find them being used interchangeably a large proportion of the time. It does not help that the world's preeminent organization of sovereign states is called the United "Nations," or that we call what happens between states "inter*national*" politics!

How do states come to be? A group of people cannot simply mark out some turf, run up a flag, and call themselves a state (though one disgruntled Australian farmer and his family tried to do exactly this in 1970).[3] To be a state, one must be recognized *as* a state—by other states. In this sense, being a state is a bit like being a member of a club: Existing members must admit you.

What do other states look at to decide whether to recognize a new sovereign state? There is no generally agreed-upon checklist, but five issues tend to dominate their deliberations: first, whether there is a government with de facto control over a certain territory; second, whether other states claim the territory, and if so, how strong their claim is; third, whether the people seeking to establish a new state are historically oppressed; fourth, whether those people consider their government legitimate; and fifth, but not least important, whether recognizing the new state as sovereign would affect their own claims and interests. Countries such as China that face significant domestic secessionist movements are often reluctant to recognize new states out of fear of setting a precedent that could backfire, even if in other respects the case for statehood is sound. With some critical mass of recognition—being accepted as a member of the United Nations is the gold standard—a new state takes its place among the countries of the world and shoulders the rights, privileges, and obligations of statehood. Its government comes to be accepted internationally—for the most part, at any rate—as the rightful spokesperson for the inhabitants of the territory and the ultimate authority within its borders. The two newest aspirants for sovereign statehood are Kosovo, which declared unilateral independence from Serbia in 2008, and Palestine, which made a push for recognition in 2011. Most observers believe that they will attain UN membership in the fullness of time. Somaliland has had less luck: Despite its unilateral declaration of independence from Somalia in 1991, it remains unrecognized by any UN member state.

The club-membership dimension of statehood is functional, but not perfect; it does generate occasional anomalies. Taiwan, for example, is for all practical purposes an independent country, but only 23 sovereign states recognize it as such. It does not have a seat at the UN. Since the People's Republic of China considers Taiwan a renegade province, Taiwanese officials must conduct most of their international business in a roundabout way. At the same time, there are many countries in the world—Somalia, Zimbabwe, and Afghanistan come to mind—that are recognized globally as sovereign states, but that fail to satisfy the most basic condition of sovereign statehood: namely, having a legitimate government that exercises effective control within its borders.

International Actors, Power, and Authority

Realists and liberals disagree on whether the state is the only significant actor in world politics. An *actor* is any person or body whose decisions and actions have repercussions for international politics. When speaking about actors in general, we don't use proper nouns; when we speak of particular actors, we do. Of course, technically only people make decisions and take actions, so when we talk of "the state" as an actor, we are abstracting for the sake of simplicity. You will commonly hear or read (for example) that Germany attacked Poland in 1939, although it would be more accurate

SYSTEMS AND WAR

After the last war, the international system developed two rigid camps. This bipolarity led to a loss of flexibility and heightened insecurity. One of the new alliances developed around an authoritarian land-based power, the other around a democratic power with an expansive commerce and culture that held naval supremacy. Each side feared that the other would achieve a decisive advantage in the conflict that both expected. Ironically, it was civil conflict in a small, weak state threatening a marginal change in the alliances that heightened the sense of threat in both alliances and actually triggered the war.

Which war does this describe: the Peloponnesian War, World War I, or the Cold War?

to say that Germans attacked Poles. This kind of anthropomorphizing is very standard. It is important to be aware of it, however, because when we anthropomorphize the state—or any other collective actor, such as a multinational corporation or an NGO—it can incline us to assume wrongly that these are *unitary* actors with interests, minds, and wills of their own. Very often, what happens in the world can only be understood if we pay attention to the disagreements, debates, and sometimes even struggles that take place inside states. A major reason why President John F. Kennedy and Soviet Chairman Nikita Khrushchev cut an abrupt deal to end the Cuban missile crisis in 1962 was because both had become frightened of the unanticipated, inadvertent, and sometimes insubordinate actions of their own militaries, which threatened to drag the superpowers into nuclear war. This was a situation in which those who should really only have been *agents* of the state (soldiers, diplomats, and bureaucrats are only ever supposed to act in accordance with superiors' instructions) were behaving inappropriately as *actors*. Of course, not all actors are anthropomorphized collectivities. Individual human beings can be international actors as well. Osama bin Laden was an international actor, as is Bono—not to put them on the same moral plane, of course! Even movie actors can be actors.[4] Mia Farrow, for example, managed to influence China's policy on Darfur.

While liberals are more inclined than realists to believe that multinational corporations, NGOs, churches, diasporas, transnational criminal networks, drug cartels, terrorist groups, charitable foundations, celebrities, and any number of other types of actors can do things that have real consequences in international politics, both agree that states are the most important, for four main reasons. First, all but "failed" states (the Somalias, Zimbabwes, and Afghanistans of the world)[5] have the capacity in principle to control the flow of people, goods, and money across borders. No state controls this perfectly, but most states control it fairly effectively. Second, states normally are the only actors that wield significant armies. Some other actors are capable of organized violence on a small scale, but functioning states have an unusual capacity to wield organized violence on a massive scale. (In failed states or states that are experiencing civil war, substate actors occasionally have this capacity.) Third, only states have the power to tax and spend in significant amounts. The Mafia taxes by running protection rackets, and drug cartels raise significant funds by illegal business, but on a scale dwarfed by most states, and only as long as they manage to avoid or corrupt the law. Fourth, only states promulgate and enforce laws. States are answerable to no higher authority.

These four considerations demonstrate that, compared to other actors, the state typically wields more *power*. Power is another key concept in the study of global conflict and cooperation. However, like love, it is easier to experience than to define or measure.

Power is the ability to achieve one's purposes or goals. More specifically, it is the ability to affect others to get the outcomes one wants. Robert Dahl, a Yale political scientist, defines power as the ability to get others to do what they otherwise would not do. But when we measure power in terms of the changed behavior of others, we have to know their preferences. Otherwise, we may be as mistaken about our power as was the fox who thought he was hurting Br'er Rabbit when he threw him into the briar patch. Knowing in advance how other people or states would behave in the absence of our efforts is often difficult.

The behavioral definition of power can be useful to analysts and historians who devote considerable time to reconstructing the past, but to practical politicians and leaders it may seem too ephemeral. Because the ability to influence others is usually associated with the possession of certain resources, political leaders commonly define power this way. These resources include population, territory, natural resources, economic size, military forces, and political stability, among others. The virtue of this definition is that it makes power appear more concrete, measurable, and predictable than the behavioral definition. Power in this sense means holding the high cards in the international poker game. A basic rule of poker is that if your opponent is showing cards that can beat anything you hold, fold. If you know you will lose a war, don't start it.

Some wars, however, have been started by the eventual losers, which suggests that political leaders sometimes take risks or make mistakes. Japan in 1941 and Iraq in 1990 are examples. Often the opponent's cards are not all showing in the game of international politics. As in poker, bluffing and deception can make a big difference. Even without deception, mistakes can be made about which power resources are most relevant in particular situations. For example, France and Britain had more tanks than did Nazi Germany in 1940, but Hitler's tanks were better engineered, and his generals used them more effectively.

Power conversion is a basic problem that arises when we think of power in terms of resources. Some countries are better than others at converting their resources into effective influence over other countries' behavior, just as some skilled card players win despite being dealt weak hands. Power conversion is the capacity to convert potential power, as measured by resources, to realized power, as measured by the changed behavior of others. To predict outcomes correctly, we need to know about a country's skill at power conversion as well as its possession of power resources.

Another problem is determining which resources provide the best basis for power in any particular context. Tanks are not much good in swamps; uranium was not a power resource in the nineteenth century. In earlier periods, power resources were easier to judge. For example, in the agrarian economies of eighteenth-century Europe, population was a critical power resource because it provided a base for taxes and recruitment of infantry. In terms of population, France dominated Western Europe. Thus at the end of the Napoleonic Wars (1799–1815), Prussia presented its fellow victors at the Congress of Vienna (1815) with a precise plan for its own reconstruction in order to maintain the balance of power. Its plan listed the territories and populations it had lost since 1805 and the territories and populations it would need to regain equivalent numbers. In the prenationalist period, it was not significant that many of the people in those provinces did not speak German or feel themselves to be Prussian. However, within half a century, nationalist sentiments would matter very much.

Another change of context that occurred during the nineteenth century was the growing importance of industry and rail systems that made rapid mobilization possible. In the 1860s, Chancellor Otto von Bismarck's Germany pioneered the use of railways to transport armies in Europe for quick victories. Although Russia had always had greater population resources than the rest of Europe, they were difficult to mobilize. The growth of the rail system in western Russia at the beginning of the twentieth century was one of the reasons the Germans feared rising Russian power in 1914. Further, the spread of rail systems on the continent helped deprive Britain of the luxury of concentrating on naval power. There was no longer time, should it prove necessary, to insert an army to prevent another great power from dominating the continent.

The application of industrial technology to warfare has long had a powerful impact. Advanced science and technology have been particularly critical power resources since the beginning of the nuclear age in 1945. But the power derived from nuclear weapons has proven to be so awesome and destructive that its actual application is muscle-bound. Nuclear war is simply far too costly. Indeed, there are many situations where any use of force may be inappropriate or too costly.

Even if the direct use of force were banned among a group of countries, military force would still play an important background role. For example, the American military role in deterring threats to allies, or of assuring access to a crucial resource such as oil in the Persian Gulf, means that the provision of protective force can be used in bargaining situations. Sometimes the linkage may be direct; more often it is a factor not mentioned openly but present in the back of leaders' minds.

Coercing other states to change is a direct or commanding method of exercising power. Such *hard power* can rest on payments ("carrots") or threats ("sticks"). But there is also a soft or indirect way to exercise power. A country may achieve its preferred outcomes in world politics because other countries want to emulate it or have agreed to a system that produces such effects. In this sense, it can be just as important to set the agenda and attract others in world politics as it is to force others to change in particular situations. This aspect of power—that is, getting others to want what you want—is called attractive or *soft power*. Soft power can rest on such resources as the appeal of one's ideas or on the ability to set the political agenda in a way that shapes the preferences others express. Parents of teenagers know that if they have structured their children's beliefs and preferences, their power will be greater and will last longer than if they had relied only on active control. Similarly, political leaders and constructivist theorists have long understood the power that comes from setting the agenda and determining the framework of a debate. The ability to establish preferences is often associated with intangible power resources such as culture, ideology, and institutions that constructivists emphasize.

Soft power is not automatically more effective or ethical than hard power. Twisting minds is not necessarily better than twisting arms. Moral judgments depend on the purposes for which power is used. The terrorist leader Osama bin Laden, for example, had soft power in the eyes of his followers who carried out the 9/11 attacks. Nor is soft power necessarily more closely associated with liberal than realist theory. Neorealists such as Kenneth Waltz tend to be materialists who pay little attention to the role of ideas. In their efforts to be parsimonious they impoverished realist theory. Classical realists such as Machiavelli and Morgenthau never neglected ideas as a source of power.

Power is the ability to affect others to get the outcomes you want regardless of whether its sources are tangible or not. Soft power is often more difficult for governments to wield and slower to yield results. Sometimes it is completely ineffective. But analysts ignore it at their peril. For example, in 1762, when Frederick the Great of Prussia was about to be defeated by a coalition of France, Austria, and Russia, he was saved because the new Russian tsar, Peter III (1728–1762), idolized the Prussian monarch and pulled his troops out of the anti-Prussian coalition. In 1917, Great Britain had greater soft power than Germany over American opinion, and that affected the United States' entry on Britain's side in World War I. More recently, the election of Barack Obama in 2008 gave an immediate boost to American soft power because his image and his message held great appeal even in parts of the world that had become notably hostile to U.S. policy. But translating these enhanced soft power resources into tangible outcomes has been neither linear nor easy.

Hard and soft power are related, but they are not the same. Material success makes a culture and ideology attractive, and decreases in economic and military success lead to self-doubt and crises of identity. But soft power does not rest solely on hard power. The soft power of the Vatican did not wane as the size of the Papal States diminished in the nineteenth century. Canada, Sweden, and the Netherlands today tend to have more influence than some other states with equivalent economic or military capability. The Soviet Union had considerable soft power in Europe after World War II but squandered it after its invasions of Hungary in 1956 and Czechoslovakia in 1968. Many would argue that the United States enjoyed enormous soft power in the immediate wake of 9/11, but squandered much of it in the aftermath through artless, muscular unilateralism.

What resources are the most important sources of power today? A look at the five centuries since the birth of the sovereign state shows that different power resources played critical roles in different periods. The sources of power are never static, and they continue to change in today's world. Moreover, they vary in different parts of the world. Soft power is becoming more important in relations among the postindustrial societies in an information age in which the democratic peace prevails; hard power is often more important in industrializing and preindustrial parts of the world.

In an age of information-based economies and transnational interdependence, power is becoming less transferable, less tangible, and less coercive. Traditional analysts would predict the outcome of conflict mainly on the basis of whose army wins. Today, in conflicts such as the struggle against transnational terrorism, it is equally important whose story wins. Hard power is necessary against hard-core terrorists, but it is equally important to use soft power to win the hearts and minds of the mainstream population that might otherwise be won over by the terrorists.

> "The capacity to know when to use hard power, when to use soft power, and when to combine the two, I call *smart power*."
>
> —Joseph S. Nye, Jr.

The transformation of power is not the same in all parts of the world. The twenty-first century will certainly see a greater role for informational and institutional power, but as events in the Middle East demonstrate, hard military power remains an important instrument. Economic scale, both in markets and in natural resources, will also remain important. The service sector grows within modern economies, and the distinction between services and manufacturing continues to blur. Information will become more plentiful, and the critical resource will be organizational capacity for rapid and flexible response. Political cohesion will remain important, as well as the nurturing of a universalistic, exportable popular culture.

Note the slightly complicated relationship between *power* and *authority*. Authority can be a power resource when others respect it, but you can have power without having authority. The United States had the power to oust the duly elected Guatemalan president, Jacobo Árbenz Guzmán, in a CIA-engineered coup in 1954, but it did not have the authority to do so. Guatemala was a sovereign state. Power is an empirical notion, whereas authority is a moral, normative, or juridical concept. Authority requires legitimacy. While the international system of sovereign states is anarchic in the legal distribution of authority, it is never truly anarchic in the distribution of power. In *unipolar* systems, one country enjoys a preponderance of power and can effectively set the terms of international cooperation and enforce or elicit compliance. In a *bipolar* system, two countries of similar power enjoy primacy within their particular sphere or among other states aligned with them (lesser powers or client states). In a *multipolar* system, three or more countries wield an unusual degree of power. We usually call the strongest country within a unipolar system a *hegemon* (from the Greek meaning "leader"); we call the strongest countries in a modern bipolar system *superpowers;* and we call the strongest countries within multipolar systems *great powers*.

International System and International Society

We have been using the word "system" frequently to this point. What do we mean by it? According to the dictionary, a *system* is a set of interrelated units. The units or components of systems interact in a regular way that may be more or less complicated. We use the terms *structure* to describe the configuration of the units, and *process* to capture their interactions. The distinction between structure and process at any given time can be illustrated by the metaphor of a poker game. The *structure* of a poker game is in the distribution of power, that is, how many chips the players have and how many high cards they are dealt. The *process* is how the game is played and the types of interactions among the players. (How are the rules created and understood? Are the players good bluffers? Do they obey the rules? If players cheat, are they likely to get caught?) For example, allowing the players in Prisoner's Dilemma games to communicate with one another alters the nature of the game. So, too, when states communicate with one another and reach mutually beneficial agreements or create well-understood norms and institutions, they add to the repertoire of state strategies and can thus alter political outcomes.

The international system is an example of a particular kind of system, namely, a *political* system. In contrast to many domestic political systems, which are easy to identify because of their clear institutional referents (the presidency, Congress, Parliament, and so forth), the current international political system is less centralized and less tangible. Without the United Nations, an international system would still exist. Do not be misled, however, by the institutional concreteness of domestic political systems. They also include intangible aspects such as public attitudes, the role of the press, or some of the unwritten conventions of constitutions. Put another way, systems can be material, ideational, or both. Computers, human bodies, and the ecosphere are all material systems. Computers have power supplies, processors, memory chips, buses, keyboards, storage devices, and screens, all of which interact electromechanically according to the laws of physics. Languages are ideational systems; their components are words, and their processes of interaction are captured by rules of grammar and syntax. The international system is a combination of material things and ideas.

To some extent representing something as a "system" is an exercise in mental housekeeping, because at the end of the day everything is connected to everything else. We can more easily make sense of the world, for example, by distinguishing a computer from the electrical grid required to operate it, and by distinguishing the electrical grid from the hydrological processes that make it possible for dams to generate power on flowing rivers. But in fact these all interact. The international system is a mental construction as well. What happens in it is affected not only by state and nonstate actors, but also by other systems. Greenhouse gas emissions, for example, will result in climate change, altered sea levels, altered rainfall patterns, changes in vegetation, and large-scale migrations. These are likely to trigger intrastate conflicts, as has already happened in Darfur, and may trigger interstate conflicts as well. We might literally say that the solar system affects the international political system via the atmospheric system. But it is unwieldy and counterproductive to attempt to think of everything as part of one enormous system. Treating the international system as something discrete makes it possible to talk more sensibly of what happens in the world than would be possible otherwise, even if, in a technical sense, everything is connected to everything else.

While the ordering principle of the international system is anarchic, the system itself is not chaotic. Most global interactions are orderly in the sense that they follow regular, largely predictable patterns. In most respects, these interactions are rule-governed. International law is a weak cousin of domestic law, but in fact rates of compliance with international law are often not that different from those with domestic law. If anything, egregious violations of international law are comparatively rare, while most countries' domestic legal systems groan under a heavy caseload of both criminal and civil violations. The marks of an orderly social system (such as the international system of sovereign states) are that institutions and practices exist for handling disputes; that most conflicts are resolved peacefully; that there exists an authoritative body of rules (laws, regulations, guidelines, acceptable practices, etc.); that there is a good level of compliance with the rules; and that there are methods of dealing with noncompliance. How can we explain this?

The answer is that relatively few parts of the world can accurately be described as being in a Hobbesian state of nature. The international system is not a pool table on which states-as-billiard-balls careen off one another blindly in an endless series of conflicts. The international system is *social*. Just because there is no world government (i.e., the international system is anarchic in the distribution of authority) does not mean that there is no such thing as an *international society*. There are rules of conduct, an increasingly rich body of international law, well-specified rights and obligations, even rules of international etiquette—diplomatic practices, honors, and so on—in short, all of the features of "polite society." Slights can trigger international conflict, just as they can trigger interpersonal conflict in everyday life. Indeed, Bismarck deliberately engineered the Franco-Prussian War (1870–1871) by violating well-entrenched norms of diplomatic protocol: first by attempting to place a Prussian king on the throne of Spain without consulting France beforehand, and then by leaking confidential French diplomatic communications to the international press (the famous "Ems Telegram").[6] Realists on the one hand, and liberals and constructivists on the other, disagree on the degree to which the international system is genuinely social. Realists think it is social only in a thin, superficial sense, while liberals and constructivists think the social constraints on action are much thicker. But virtually all agree that the social dimensions of international politics promote orderly interaction.

System Stability and Crisis Stability

International systems are stable if they are able to absorb shocks without breaking down. Systems break down when they are no longer able to serve their intended purposes. A major purpose of the international system is to safeguard the sovereignty and security of its members. Minor wars are not necessarily evidence of system breakdown, since sometimes the only way to protect the sovereignty and security of certain states is to wage war against others. For this reason, the renowned Australian scholar Hedley Bull wrote at length about war as an institution—in the sense of a recognized and regulated practice—for maintaining order.[7] But major wars jeopardize the sovereignty and security of most or all states and are evidence of system instability.

What makes a system stable? One important factor is the quality of the social fabric of international society. The stronger the normative and institutional threads binding states, and the denser the connections between them, the greater the stake states have in preventing system breakdown, and the more avenues they have available for resolving disagreements before they can get out of hand. The weaker the social context—the more the system resembles a Hobbesian state of nature, in other words—the more states depend upon self-help.

In a Hobbesian anarchy, according to systems theorists such as Kenneth Waltz, distributions of power are crucial to system stability. Unipolar systems tend to erode as states try to preserve their independence by balancing against the hegemon, or a rising state eventually challenges the leader. In multipolar or dispersed-power systems, states form alliances to balance power, but alliances are flexible. Wars may occur, but they will be relatively limited in scope. In bipolar systems, alliances become more rigid, which in turn contributes to the probability of a large conflict, perhaps even a global war. Some analysts say that "bipolar systems either erode or explode." This happened in the Peloponnesian War when Athens and Sparta tightened their grips on their respective alliances. It was also true before 1914, when the multipolar European balance of power gradually consolidated into two strong alliance systems that lost their flexibility. But predictions about war based on multipolarity versus bipolarity encountered a major anomaly after 1945. During the Cold War the world was bipolar with two big players, the United States and its allies and the Soviet Union and its allies, yet no overall central war occurred for more than four decades before the system eroded with the decline of the Soviet Union. Some people say nuclear weapons made the prospect of global war too awful. Thus the structure of the international system offers a rough explanation for system stability, but does not explain enough all by itself.

Arguably, the Cold War system was stable because it also exhibited *crisis stability*. In a crisis-unstable situation, if two or more countries find themselves in an acute international crisis, they will feel enormous pressure to strike the first blow. To use a simple metaphor, imagine you and an adversary are standing in the open, each armed with a gun. Neither of you is quite sure of the other's intentions. If either of you thinks there is a chance that shots might be fired, then you both have a powerful incentive to shoot first. Whoever shoots first is more likely to survive. A situation such as this is very likely to escalate quickly to violence.

Now imagine that you and your adversary are locked in a room, knee-deep in gasoline, armed only with a match. In this situation, neither of you has a strong incentive to strike the first match. If you did, your adversary would surely be killed or badly injured, but so would you. You both have a powerful incentive to try to find a peaceful way out. Such a situation is highly crisis-stable.

To a very significant degree, crisis stability is a function of technology—or, perhaps more accurately, prevailing beliefs about technology, as reflected in military doctrine. When the prevailing military technology is believed to favor the offense, decision makers feel pressure to strike the first blow. When it is believed to favor the defense, they do not. At the beginning of World War I, European leaders believed that there was a great advantage in taking the offensive, and the July crisis of 1914 escalated very quickly. (In this belief they were tragically mistaken. As the carnage of the following four years would demonstrate, well-entrenched infantry armed with machine guns and backed by mass artillery cut attacking armies to pieces.) During the Cold War, prevailing beliefs about military technology were almost certainly correct: Neither the United States nor the Soviet Union could defend against a nuclear attack, but there was little doubt that they could count upon being able to launch a devastating retaliatory blow. This situation, aptly called "Mutual Assured Destruction" (or MAD), was highly crisis-stable.

The "National Interest"

The final key concept that needs clarification before we proceed further is the *national interest*. Leaders and analysts alike assert that "states act in their national interest." That statement is normally true, but it does not tell us much unless we know how states define their national interests.

Realists say that states have little choice in defining their national interest because of the international system. They must define their interest in terms of power or they will not survive, just as a company in a perfect market that wants to be altruistic rather than maximize profits will not survive. So for the realists, a state's position in the international system determines its national interests and predicts its foreign policies.

Liberals and constructivists argue that national interests are defined by much more than the state's position in the international system, and they have a richer account of how state preferences and national interests are formed. The definition of the national interest depends in large part on the type of domestic society and culture a state has. For example, a domestic society that values economic welfare and places heavy emphasis on trade, or that views wars against other democracies as illegitimate, defines its national interests very differently from a despotic state that is similarly positioned in the international system. Liberals argue that this is particularly true if international institutions and channels of communication enable states to build trust; this helps them escape from the Prisoner's Dilemma.

Because nonpower incentives can help shape how states define their interests, it is important to know how closely a particular situation approximates a Hobbesian state of nature. In a Hobbesian system, you may be killed by your neighbor tomorrow, and limited opportunities exist for democracy or trade preferences to influence foreign policy. Survival comes first. But if institutions and stable expectations of peace moderate the Hobbesian anarchy, then some of these other factors related to domestic society and culture are likely to play a larger role. Realist predictions are more likely to be accurate in the Middle East, for example, and liberal predictions in Western Europe. Knowing the context helps us gauge the likely predictive value of different theories.

It is important to bear in mind that the national interest is almost always contested. People who would agree at an abstract level that power and security are important national interests very often disagree about the concrete policies that would promote them. Sometimes policy preferences are completely opposite and incompatible. During the period between the two World Wars, there was a vibrant debate in the United States between those who believed that the best way to promote American security was to avoid becoming entangled in the thorny power politics of Europe and East Asia, and those who believed that American security depended upon actively working with others to check the rising power and imperial ambitions of Germany and Japan. There is also a historically important debate between those who see morality and the pursuit of the national interest as separate and incompatible, and those who think that a country's conception of what is right and just is a fundamental part of its national interest. What is not open for debate is the fact that anyone seeking to promote a particular foreign policy will inevitable try to wrap it in the mantle of the national interest. The concept, in other words, is not merely a shorthand for vital state goals—it is also a playing field on which policy makers and policy entrepreneurs contend.

Follow Up

- Barry Buzan, "From International System to International Society: Structural Realism and Regime Theory Meet the English School," *International Organization*, Vol. 47, No. 3 (Summer 1993), pp. 327–352.
- Joseph S. Nye, Jr., *The Future of Power* (New York: PublicAffairs, 2011).

LEVELS OF ANALYSIS

A system is greater than the sum of its parts. Systems can create consequences not intended by any of their components. Think of the market system in economics. Every firm in a perfect market tries to maximize its profits, but the market system produces competition that reduces profits to the break-even point, thereby benefiting the consumer. The businessperson does not set out to benefit the consumer, but individual firms' pattern of behavior in a perfect market leads to that effect. In other words, the system produces the consequences, which may be quite different from the intention of the actors in the system.

The international political system can similarly lead to effects the actors did not originally intend. For example, in 1917 when the Bolsheviks came to power in Russia, they regarded the whole system of interstate diplomacy that had preceded World War I as bourgeois nonsense. They intended to sweep away the interstate system and hoped that revolutions would unite all the workers of the world and abolish borders. Transnational proletarian solidarity would replace the interstate system. Indeed, when Leon Trotsky took charge of the Russian Foreign Ministry, he said his intent was to issue some revolutionary proclamations to the peoples of the world and then "close up the joint." But the Bolsheviks found that their actions were soon affected by the nature of the interstate system. In 1922, the new communist state signed the Treaty of Rapallo with Germany. It was an alliance of the outcasts, the countries that were not accepted in the post–World War I diplomatic world. In 1939, Josef Stalin entered a pact with his ideological archenemy, Adolf Hitler, in order to turn Hitler westward. Soviet behavior, despite Trotsky's initial proclamations and illusions, soon became similar to that of other actors in the international system.

The distribution of power among states in an international system helps us make predictions about certain aspects of states' behavior. The tradition of *geopolitics* holds that location and proximity will tell a great deal about how states will behave. Because neighbors have more contact and points of potential friction, it is not surprising that half of the military conflicts between 1816 and 1992 began between neighbors.[8] A state that feels threatened by its neighbor is likely to act in accord with the old adage that "the enemy of my enemy is my friend." This pattern has always been found in anarchic systems. For example, the Indian writer Kautilya pointed out in the third century BCE that the states of the Indian subcontinent tended to ally with distant states to protect themselves against their neighbors, thus producing a checkerboard pattern of alliances. Machiavelli noted the same behavior among the city-states in fifteenth-century Italy. In the early 1960s, as West African states emerged from colonial rule, there was a great deal of talk about African solidarity, but the new states soon began to produce a checkerboard pattern of alliances similar to what Kautilya described in ancient India. Ghana, Guinea, and Mali were ideologically radical, while Senegal, Ivory Coast, and Nigeria were relatively conservative, but they were also balancing against the strength of their neighbors. Another example was the pattern that developed in East Asia after the Vietnam War. If the Soviet Union were colored black, China would be red, Vietnam black, and Cambodia red. A perfect checkerboard pattern developed. Ironically, the United States entered the Vietnam War because policy makers believed in the "domino theory," according to which one state would fall to communism, leading another state to fall, and so forth. With more foresight, the United States should have realized that the game in East Asia was more like checkers than dominoes, and the United States might have stayed out. The checkerboard pattern based on "the enemy of my enemy is my friend" is an old tradition of geopolitics that helps us make useful predictions in an anarchic situation.

How can we make sense of a pattern or tendency such as this? World politics is not something one can manipulate the way a physicist or a chemist can manipulate the conditions of an experiment in the lab. What happens, happens, and we must try to make sense of it without the benefit of controlled experiments. This almost always means that we must be more guarded in our conclusions, because certain valuable strategies for identifying and ruling out spurious explanations are simply not available. Yet we do make judgments about why things happen in world politics, and we never do so without reason. What tips and tricks can we use? How reliable are they?

Systems are not the only way of explaining what happens in international politics. In *Man, the State, and War,* Kenneth Waltz distinguishes three levels of causation for war, which he calls "images": the *individual,* the *state,* and the *international system.* The checkerboard pattern that so frequently develops as a result of "the enemy of my enemy is my friend" could be a function of dynamics at any one (or more) of these levels of analysis. So a good place to start, when attempting to determine why things happen in world politics, is to see whether we get the most explanatory power by looking at the reasons why people (such as leaders) do what they do (the individual level of analysis), by looking at what happens within individual states (the state level), or by looking at the interactions between actors (the system level).

The Individual Level

Explanations at the level of the individual are useful when it genuinely matters who is making decisions. Most analysts believe that the United States would have attacked al Qaeda training camps in Afghanistan after 9/11 and toppled the Taliban regime if it failed to cooperate no matter who was president. If Al Gore rather than George W. Bush had won the 2000 presidential election, we probably still would have seen Operation Enduring Freedom, or something very much like it. But few analysts think that a President Gore would have attacked Iraq in 2003. Neither domestic political nor systemic imperatives made that likely, the way they made Afghanistan likely. The Iraq War was very much a war of choice, and to explain it we have to look at the specific reasons why President Bush and his senior advisors chose it.

There is little doubt that individuals sometimes matter. Pericles made a difference in the Peloponnesian War. In 1991, Saddam Hussein was a critical factor in the Gulf War. Sometimes individuals matter, but not in isolation from other considerations. In the 1962 Cuban missile crisis, Kennedy and Khrushchev faced the possibility of nuclear war and the ultimate decision was in their hands. But why they found themselves in that position cannot be explained at the level of individuals. Something in the structure of the situation brought them to that point. Similarly, knowing something about the personality of Kaiser Wilhelm II or Hitler is necessary to an understanding of the causes of World War I and World War II, but it is not a sufficient explanation. It made a difference that Kaiser Wilhelm fired his chancellor, Otto von Bismarck, in 1890; but that does not mean World War I was brought about primarily by Kaiser Wilhelm.

While one way of using the individual level of analysis is to focus on features specific to individual people (their personalities, their life histories, and so forth), another way is to look for explanations in people's common characteristics—in the "human nature" common to all individuals. For example, we could take a Calvinist view of international politics and assign the ultimate cause of war to the evil that lies within each of us. That would explain war as the result of an imperfection in human nature. But such an explanation overpredicts: It does not tell us why some evil leaders go to war and others do not, or why some good leaders go to war and others do not. Sometimes generalizations about human nature lead to unfalsifiable explanations. Some realists locate the ultimate source of conflict in a relentless drive for power. The Australian historian Geoffrey Blainey, for example, argues: "One generalization about war aims can be offered with confidence. The aims are simply varieties of power. The vanity of nationalism, the will to spread an ideology, the protection of kinsmen in an adjacent land, the desire for more territory or commerce, the avenging of a defeat or insult, the craving for greater national strength or independence, the wish to impress or cement alliances—all these represent power in different wrappings. The conflicting aims of rival nations are always conflicts of power."[9] If every goal counts as a quest for power, then the statement "the quest for power causes wars" is an unfalsifiable tautology. Something that explains everything explains nothing.

More fruitful are explanations that leverage psychological tendencies. Many students of international politics assume that psychological considerations do not matter: Leaders of states either are, or can be assumed to be, "rational" actors. If they are rational, then all we need to know in order to understand or predict the choices they make are the costs and benefits of each. Any rational actor facing a situation reminiscent of the Prisoner's Dilemma, according to this view, can be expected to defect rather than cooperate. But while some people do make decisions on the basis of good-quality cost-benefit analysis, there are many situations in which this is simply not possible, owing to a lack of information. In any case, we know that many people do not, or cannot, make decisions in this way even when it is possible to do so. Using psychological considerations to explain apparent deviations from "rational" actions can be very helpful.

This is precisely how the field of political psychology examines global conflict and cooperation. There are four main approaches. One is *cognitive psychology*. Cognitive psychology examines the processes by which people seek to make sense of raw information about the world. Cognitive psychologists have shown that people do this by looking for commonalities between what they are trying to make sense of and things they already know or believe—between the unfamiliar, in other words, and the familiar. Shocked by the horrors inflicted upon the world by dictators such as Adolf Hitler and Benito Mussolini, for instance, Western leaders after World War II tended to think that any dictator claiming to have suffered some injustice at the hands of other countries was, in fact, an opportunistic aggressor. Sometimes they were right. But sometimes they were wrong. A case in which they were wrong was 1956, when Egyptian president Gamal Abdel Nasser asserted Egypt's right to control the Suez Canal because it cut through Egyptian territory. When Nasser nationalized the canal, French and British leaders leapt to the conclusion that Nasser was "just like Hitler" and had to be resisted. The result was an unnecessary war that greatly complicated Middle Eastern politics, divided NATO allies, distracted the world's attention from the Soviet crackdown in Hungary, and severely damaged Britain's power and prestige.

A second approach is *motivational psychology*. Motivational psychologists explain human behavior in terms of deep-seated psychological fears, desires, and needs. These needs include self-esteem, social approval, and a sense of efficacy. Motivational psychology helps us understand, for example, why almost all German diplomats before World War I gave false or misleading reports on the likely reactions of European countries to Austrian and German military moves. They were simply frightened of the consequences of not telling the notoriously intolerant German foreign ministry what it wanted to hear. The one German diplomat who accurately reported the likely response of Britain to a German violation of Belgian neutrality, Ambassador Prince Karl Lichnowsky in London, was dismissed in Berlin as having "gone native"—a judgmental error that itself can be explained in terms of a well-documented motivational-psychological tendency: namely, the desire to avoid the psychological pain of admitting one's own error. Since Germany's entire strategy for swift victory in 1914 depended upon Britain staying out of the war, Lichnowsky's reports would have been extremely unsettling if they had been accepted.

A third approach, and a more recent one, is to apply insights from *behavioral economics*, and particularly from *prospect theory*. Prospect theory explains deviations from rational action by noting that people make decisions very differently depending upon whether they face prospects of gain or prospects of loss. Most notably, people take much greater risks to avoid losses than they would be willing to take to achieve gains. Identifying how leaders frame their choices can help us understand and even anticipate how willing they will be to take risks. Indeed, since many choice situations can be described equally well in the language of losses or gains (ten lives out of a hundred lost is the same as ninety lives saved), strategically reframing choices can induce people to make different choices. The general tendency people exhibit toward loss-aversion helps us understand, for example, why people escalate commitments to losing courses of action. The more a gambler loses at the slot machines in Las Vegas, the less willing he or she will be to stop playing, because the desire to recoup the loss gets stronger and stronger. Similarly, the more lives the United States lost in the Vietnam War, the less willing it was to throw in the towel. Unlucky gamblers and leaders who fight losing battles often quit only when they exhaust their resources.

Finally, the fourth approach, *psychobiography*, explains leaders' choices in terms of their psychodynamics. This approach locates idiosyncratic personality traits in generally recognized neuroses and psychoses. A fascinating example of this is Alexander and Juliette George's psychobiography of Woodrow Wilson and Colonel House, which seeks to explain America's heavy hand at the Paris peace talks of 1919 and its subsequent failure to join the League of Nations—President Wilson's pet project—in terms of Wilson's need for control, his unwillingness to compromise, and his intolerance of opposition, all of which, the Georges argue, can be traced to traumatic childhood experiences at the hands of an overbearing father.[10] Equally fascinating are the many psychobiographies of Adolf Hitler, which stress the importance of his desire to compensate for self-loathing and sexual frustration.[11] It is now routine for the U.S. intelligence community to compile psychological profiles of foreign leaders, with an eye toward better predicting their behavior. But while psychobiography is always fascinating, it shares many of the weaknesses of the Freudian tradition out of which it springs, the most important of which are unfalsifiability and the difficulty of independent corroboration. When explanations for international political events rest upon the subconscious fears, needs, and desires of world leaders—many of whom are dead or otherwise unavailable for close examination—it is difficult to know how to have high confidence in them.

The State Level

When we seek to explain things at the state level of analysis, we ask whether what happens in world politics is a function of domestic politics, various features of domestic society, or the machinery of government. Domestic considerations clearly sometimes matter. After all, the Peloponnesian War began with a domestic conflict between the oligarchs and the democrats in Epidamnus. The domestic politics of Germany and the Austro-Hungarian Empire played significant roles in the onset of World War I. To understand the end of the Cold War, we must look inside the Soviet Union at the failure of its centrally planned economy. It is easy to find examples in which domestic considerations mattered, but can we generalize about them? After we have said that they are important, is there anything else to say?

Marxism and liberalism both put a great deal of emphasis on the state level of analysis. Both hold that states will act similarly in the international system if they are similar domestically. Marxists argue that the source of war is capitalism. In Lenin's view, monopoly capital requires war: "Inter-imperialist alliances are inevitably nothing more than a truce in the periods between wars."[12] War can be explained by the nature of capitalist society, whose inequitable distribution of wealth leads to underconsumption, stagnation, and lack of domestic investment. As a consequence, capitalism leads to imperialist expansionism abroad, which helps sell surplus production in foreign markets, creates foreign investment opportunities, and promises access to natural resources. Such imperialism also fuels the domestic economy through higher military spending. Thus, Marxism predicts arms races and conflict between capitalist states. The theory did not do a very good job of explaining the onset of World War I. Moreover, it does not fit the experience of the second half of the twentieth century. Communist states, such as the Soviet Union, China, and Vietnam, were involved in military clashes with each other, while the major capitalist states in Europe, North America, and Japan maintained peaceful relations. The arguments that capitalism causes war do not stand up in historical experience.

Classical liberalism, the philosophy that dominated much of British and American thought in the nineteenth century, came to the opposite conclusion: According to liberal thinkers, capitalist states tend to be peaceful because war is bad for business. One strand of classical liberalism was represented by free traders such as Richard Cobden (1804–1865), who led the successful fight to repeal England's Corn Laws, protectionist measures that had regulated Britain's international grain trade for 500 years. Like others of the Manchester School of British economists, he believed that it was better to trade and to prosper than to go to war. If we are interested in getting richer and improving the welfare of citizens, asserted Cobden, then peace is best. In 1840 he expressed the classical view, saying "We can keep the world from actual war, and I trust that the world will do that through trade."[13]

The liberal view was very powerful on the eve of World War I. A number of books, including a classic by Norman Angell, *The Great Illusion* (1910), said that war had become too expensive. To illustrate the optimism of classical liberalism on the eve of World War I, we can look at the philanthropists of that era. Andrew Carnegie, the steel magnate, established the Carnegie Endowment for International Peace in 1910. Carnegie worried about what would happen to the money he had given to this foundation after lasting peace broke out, so he put a provision in his will to cover this possibility. Edward Ginn, a Boston publisher, did not want Carnegie to get all the credit for the forthcoming permanent peace, so he set up the World Peace Foundation devoted to the same cause. Ginn also worried about what to do with the rest of the money after peace was firmly established, so he designated it for low-cost housing for young working women.

This liberal outlook was severely discredited by World War I. Even though bankers and aristocrats had frequent contact across borders, and labor also had transnational contacts, none of this helped stop the European states from going to war with each other. Statistical analysis has found no strong correlation between states' involvement in war and whether they are capitalist or democratic. The classical Marxist and liberal views are opposites in their understandings of the relationship between war and capitalism, but they are similar in locating the causes of war in domestic politics, and especially in the nature of the economic system.

State-level explanations of this kind suffer from some of the same difficulties as human-nature explanations. If certain types of societies cause war, then why do some "bad" societies or "bad" states not go to war? And why do some "good" societies or "good" states go to war? Insert your favorite description for "good" and "bad"—"democratic," "communist," "capitalist," or whatever. For example, after World War I there was a great deal of enthusiasm for the belief that the victory of the democracies would mean less danger of war. But clearly democracies can go to war and often do. After all, Athens was a democracy. Marxist theorists argued that war would be abolished when all states were communist, but obviously there have been military clashes among communist countries—witness China versus the Soviet Union or Vietnam versus Cambodia. Thus the nature of the society, democratic or capitalist or communist, is not a predictor of whether it will go to war.

One proposition is that if *all* countries were democratic, there would be less war. In fact, cases in which liberal democracies have fought against other liberal democracies are difficult to find, although democracies have fought against authoritarian states in many situations. The reasons for this empirical finding and whether it will continue to hold in the future are not clear, but it suggests something interesting to investigate at this second level of analysis.

A relatively recent state-level line of inquiry is the *bureaucratic politics* approach. Bureaucratic politics explanations look not to the domestic political or economic arrangements of states, but to the interplay of governmental agencies and officials. One strand focuses on organizational dynamics, and in particular the routines and standard operating procedures upon which all complex organizations depend in order to function. Arguably, an important reason why World I War broke out was because European armies in general and the German army in particular had crafted rigid military plans that limited leaders' choices in the heat of crisis. This, coupled with the "cult of the offensive," which glorified the cavalry and tactics of maneuver, made the situation in July and August 1914 highly crisis-unstable. A second strand stresses the role of parochial bureaucratic interests. It is possible, for example, to explain some arms races by noting how competition for resources between branches of the military leads to escalating budgets, adversaries feeling less secure, adversaries spending more on defense, and ultimately a classic security dilemma. Perhaps the most famous insight from bureaucratic politics is captured by Miles's Law: "Where you stand depends on where you sit." If Miles's Law were correct, then decision makers engaged in policy debates would seek to promote not national interests, but the interests of the departments, agencies, or branches of government that they represent. Evidence for Miles's Law is mixed. There are cases that fit the pattern. When he was the state of California's director of finance under Governor Ronald Reagan, Caspar Weinberger was known as "Cap the Knife" for the gusto with which he slashed budgets. Later, as President Reagan's secretary of defense, his enthusiastic advocacy for ever higher military spending prompted one Republican senator to call him "a draft dodger in the war on the federal deficit."[14] Yet other studies show at most a weak link between bureaucratic position and policy preferences, or no link at all. In any case, while it is possible to imagine that bureaucratic considerations can help us understand specific policy choices states make, it is harder to imagine how they might be harnessed to explanations of general patterns in world politics.

The System Level

Interesting explanations often involve interplay between two or more levels of analysis. A satisfying explanation of the outbreak of World War I might invoke a combination of three factors: rigid bipolarity (a structural feature of the international system); crisis-unstable military plans and doctrines (a result of military cultures within states, particularly Germany); and serious motivated errors of judgment by key leaders (a psychological consideration). But how do we know which is most important? And where do we start when we want to explain the outbreak of war? Do we start from the outside in? This would mean starting with system-level analysis, looking at the way the overall system constrains state action. Or do we start from the inside out? This would mean starting with the individual or state level.

Because we often need information about more than one level of analysis, a good rule of thumb is to start with the simplest approach. If a simple explanation is adequate, it is preferable to a more complicated one. This is called the *rule of parsimony* or *Occam's razor*, after the philosopher William of Occam (c. 1287–1347), who argued that good explanations shave away unnecessary detail. *Parsimony*—the ability to explain a lot with a little—is only one of the criteria by which we judge the adequacy of theories. We are also interested in the *range* of a theory (how much behavior it covers) and its *explanatory fit* (how many loose ends or anomalies it accounts for). Nonetheless, parsimony suggests a place to start. Because systemic explanations tend to be the simplest, they provide a good starting point. If they prove to be inadequate, then we can look at the units of the system or at individual decision makers, adding complexity until a reasonable fit is obtained.

How simple or complicated should a systemic explanation be? Some neorealists, such as Kenneth Waltz, argue for extreme parsimony and focus only on structure. Liberals and constructivists argue that Waltz's concept of system is so spare that it explains very little.

Economists characterize the structure of markets by the concentration of sellers' power. A monopoly has one big seller, a duopoly two big sellers, and an oligopoly several big sellers. In a perfect market, selling power is widely dispersed. Firms that maximize profits in a perfect market benefit the consumer. But the result would be different for a monopoly or oligopoly. In these systems, large firms can increase profits by restricting production in order to raise prices. Thus when the structure of the system is known, economists are better able to predict behavior and who will benefit. So it is that the structure of the international system can help us understand behavior within it. Note that in a perfect market, we do not need to look inside firms or at the personalities of CEOs in order to understand or predict the behavior of the market as a whole. We can assume that firms are rational, unitary actors, because over time those who do not make business decisions *as if* they were rational, unitary actors (or very close to the ideal) will fail. They will be selected out of the system, to use a Darwinian metaphor. Over the long run, only firms that respond well to the incentives of the marketplace will survive. This is not necessarily true of firms in monopolistic or oligopolistic markets. If we want to understand those markets, sometimes we must understand something about the firms and personalities that dominate them.

Does the international system resemble a perfectly competitive market? Not exactly. There are many states in the world, certainly, but they rarely get "selected out of the system," so it is more difficult to justify the assumption that they can be treated "as if" they were unitary, rational actors. Still, in a Hobbesian world, states would face powerful incentives to be on their guard, make adequate provision for their security, and take advantage of opportunities to increase their wealth and power. States that could not provide for their own security—owing, perhaps, to having much bigger and much more powerful neighbors—would face strong incentives to find allies. They might seek to

DEMOCRACY AND PEACE

A coalition for democracy—it's good for America. Democracies, after all, are more likely to be stable, less likely to wage war. They strengthen civil society. They can provide people with the economic opportunities to build their own homes, not to flee their borders. Our efforts to help build democracies will make us all more secure, more prosperous, and more successful as we try to make this era of terrific change our friend and not our enemy.

—President William J. Clinton, remarks to the 49th Session of the UN General Assembly, September 26, 1994

The survival of liberty in our land increasingly depends on the success of liberty in other lands. The best hope for peace in our world is the expansion of freedom in all the world. America's vital interests and our deepest beliefs are now one. . . . So it is the policy of the United States to seek and support the growth of democratic movements and institutions in every nation and culture, with the ultimate goal of ending tyranny in our world.

—President George W. Bush, second inaugural address, Washington, DC, January 20, 2005

balance the power of the strongest states. This logic has given rise to the most extensive body of systemic theory in the study of international politics—realist balance-of-power theory—about which we will have more to say later in this chapter.

Non-Hobbesian systems behave very differently. The more social the system, the less the logic of self-help applies. Liberalism and constructivism are better suited to the study of highly social systems, because the interactions of the units are more reliably governed by laws, rules, norms, expectations, and taboos. Liberalism and constructivism pay a great deal of attention to the origin and evolution of these social constraints on state action. Since explaining them often requires examining the role of domestic political considerations or of individual norm entrepreneurs, liberal and constructivist theories tend to cross levels of analysis.

Follow Up

- J. David Singer, "The Levels of Analysis Problem in International Relations," in James N. Rosenau, ed., *International Politics and Foreign Policy* (New York: Free Press, 1969), pp. 20–29.
- Jack S. Levy, "Contending Theories of International Conflict: A Levels-of-Analysis Approach," in Chester A. Crocker and Fen Osler Hampson, eds., *Managing Global Chaos: Sources of and Responses to International Conflict* (Washington, DC: United States Institute of Peace, 1996), pp. 3–24.

PARADIGMS AND THEORIES

To study something systematically, you need a way of organizing the tools and techniques that you use. The conceptual toolkit and the "handbook" (as it were) for using the tools is called a "paradigm." As Columbia University sociologist Robert Merton put it, a paradigm is "a systematic statement of the basic assumptions, concepts, and propositions employed by a school of analysis." Paradigms, according to Merton, serve a "notational function," keeping concepts in order; they specify assumptions and the logical connections between them; they promote the cumulation of useful theories that explain things we observe in the world; they help us identify new puzzles; and they promote rigorous analysis instead of mere description.[15] Paradigms can be thought of as the foundations on which we build ever-taller (and narrower) structures of knowledge.

The structures themselves are theories. Theories are provisional statements about how the world works. We derive theories from paradigms.

We use *hypotheses* to test theories. A hypothesis is a statement about what we should expect to observe in the world if our theories were true. If our expectations are dashed, we reject the hypothesis and rework (or discard) the theory. If our expectations are met, we consider the theory confirmed and go on to expand it, refine it, or build other theories compatible with it, gradually building up a body of propositions about the world in which we can have confidence. From time to time we abandon one paradigm in favor of another if it cannot perform as well. The Newtonian paradigm dominated physics for almost 300 years, and it did an excellent job of helping us explain how the physical world worked under most conditions (indeed, it is still useful for many practical applications). But Newtonian physics could not help us explain how things behaved at extremely small time and distance scales, or at speeds approaching the speed of light. A later paradigm—Einstein's relativity—performed much better.

We have already met the four dominant paradigms in the study of world politics: realism, liberalism, Marxism, and constructivism. Each begins with certain unquestioned assumptions called "axioms" (axioms are always necessary; it is impossible to question everything, because one would never actually get around to explaining anything). Each employs a particular set of concepts, though in the case of these four paradigms they often employ many of the same ones. Each generates particular bodies of theory. Table 1 provides a snapshot comparison.

Realism

By now the contours of realism as a paradigm should be familiar. It is worth recalling, though, that despite the apparent simplicity of realism as reflected in Table 1, realism is actually a fairly large tent. Realists of all stripes agree that states are the most important actors in the international system, that anarchy has a powerful effect on state behavior, and that at the end of the day all politics is power politics. But classical realism differs quite significantly from neorealism (sometimes called "structural realism"). As we have seen, classical realists such as Machiavelli and Morgenthau paid attention to ideas as well as material power. They saw foreign policy as something that could spring

TABLE 1

Key Features of Paradigms

		REALISM	LIBERALISM	MARXISM	CONSTRUCTIVISM
Key actors		States	States, nonstate actors	Economic classes	States, nonstate actors
Key Axioms	Dominant human drive(s)	Fear, desire to dominate	Fear, desire to live well	Greed	Need for orderly, meaningful social life
	Actors' primary goals	All states seek power or security	Actors seek welfare and justice in addition to security	The capital-owning class seeks to maximize profit; the working class seeks fair wages and working conditions	Actors' interests are socially constructed through interaction
	Actors' dominant instrument	Military power	Military power, trade, investment, negotiation, persuasion	Wealth (capital-owning class); labor (working class)	Depends upon historical period and social context
	Dominant processes of interaction	Competition	Competition and cooperation	Exploitation	Depends upon historical period and social context
	Dominant structural feature of international system	Hobbesian anarchy	Non-Hobbesian anarchy	Economic inequality	Social constraints (e.g., laws, rules, norms, taboos)
Dominant bodies of theory		Balance-of-power theory; theories of hegemonic transition and hegemonic war	Neoliberal institutionalism; "Democratic Peace."	Dependency theory; theories of revolution	Structuration; theories of norm evolution

from domestic sources as well as from systemic pressures. They even noted the important role considerations of ethics would play in shaping foreign policy, though they tended to bemoan this as insufficiently hard-nosed and practical. Classical realists had more of a humanistic approach to world politics than a scientific one. Many of them were prominent historians or philosophers. In contrast, neorealists seek to emulate the natural sciences and are much more concerned with generating purely systemic theories.

There are other distinctions to make within realism as well. "Defensive realists" tend to stress security as the dominant state goal, whereas "offensive" realists tended to stress power. These are both varieties of what Cambridge University political scientist James Mayall calls "hard realists," in contrast to "soft realists," who would include the maintenance of international order among state goals. Many of the so-called English School writers on international relations, such as Hedley Bull, fall broadly within this category.

So realism is a bit like Baskin-Robbins: There may be 31 flavors, but they are all ice cream. What realists of all kinds share is a commitment to the view that there is an immutable logic to world politics that is perhaps best summed up by the aphorism inspired by an 1848 statement Lord Palmerston made in the British House of Commons: namely, that states have no permanent friends or permanent enemies, merely permanent interests. But there is ample room for debate within realism, and vibrant ongoing research programs that attempt to help us answer questions such as: Do states balance power, or do they balance threat? When do they balance, and when do they bandwagon? What is the fate of American leadership in the world? How will world politics change as countries such as China and India rise?

Liberalism

We have not yet had as much chance to explore liberalism as we have realism, so it would be helpful here to unpack it in somewhat more detail, particularly since it is enjoying a recent resurgence. The two world wars and the failure of collective security in the interwar period had discredited liberal theories. Most writing about international politics in the United States after World War II was strongly realist. However, as transnational economic interdependence increased, the late 1960s and 1970s saw a revival of interest in liberal theories.

There are three strands of liberal thinking: *economic, social*, and *political*. The political strand has two parts, one relating to institutions and the other to democracy.

The economic strand of liberalism focuses heavily on trade. Liberals argue that trade is important, not because it prevents states from going to war, but because it may lead states to define their interests in a way that makes war less important to them. Trade offers states a way to transform their position through economic growth rather than through military conquest. Richard Rosecrance points to the example of Japan.[16] In the 1930s, Japan thought the only way to gain access to markets was to create a "Greater East Asia Co-Prosperity Sphere," which in turn required conquering its neighbors and

The Berlin wall coming down

requiring them to trade preferentially with Japan. Already in 1939, Eugene Staley, a Chicago economist, argued that part of Japan's behavior in the 1930s could be explained by economic protectionism. Staley believed that when economic walls are erected along political boundaries, possession of territory is made to coincide with economic opportunity. A better solution for avoiding war is to pursue economic growth in an open trading system without military conquest. In the postwar period, Japan successfully transformed its position in the world through trade. It is now the world's third largest national economy, measured in purchasing power parity terms—behind only the United States and China.

Realists reply that Japan was able to accomplish this amazing economic growth because somebody else was providing for its security. Specifically, Japan relied on the United States for security against its large nuclear neighbors, the Soviet Union and China. Some realists predicted that, with the Soviet Union gone, the United States would withdraw its security presence in East Asia and raise barriers against Japanese trade. Japan would remilitarize, and eventually there would be conflict between Japan and the United States. But liberals replied that modern Japan is a very different domestic society from the Japan of the 1930s. It is among the least militaristic in the world, partly because the most attractive career opportunities in Japan are in business, not in the military. Liberals argue that the realists do not pay enough attention to domestic politics and the way that Japan has changed as a result of economic opportunities. Trade may not prevent war, but it does change incentives, which in turn may lead to a social structure less inclined to war.

The second form of liberalism is social. It argues that person-to-person contacts reduce conflict by promoting understanding. Such transnational contacts occur at many levels, including through students, businesspeople, and tourists. Such contacts make others seem less foreign and less hateful. That, in turn, leads to a lower likelihood of conflict. The evidence for this view is mixed. After all, bankers, aristocrats, and labor union officials had broad contacts in 1914, but that did not stop them from killing one another once they put on military uniforms. Obviously, the idea that social contact breeds understanding and prevents war is far too simple. Nonetheless, it may make a modest contribution to understanding. Western Europe today is very different from 1914. There are constant contacts across international borders in Europe, and text editors try to treat other nationalities fairly. The images of the other peoples of Europe are very different from the images of 1914. Public opinion polls show that a sense of European identity coexists with a sense of national identity. The Erasmus Program of the European Union encourages students to study in the universities of other European countries. Transnational society affects what people in a democracy want from their foreign policy. It is worth noting how France responded to the reunification of Germany in 1990. A residue of uncertainty and anxiety remained among the foreign policy experts, but public opinion polls showed that most French people welcomed German unification. Such attitudes were a sharp contrast to those when Germany first unified in 1871.

The first version of the third form of liberalism emphasizes the role of institutions; this strand is often labeled "neoliberalism." Why do international institutions matter? According to Princeton political scientist Robert O. Keohane, they provide information and a framework that shapes expectations. They allow people to believe there is not going to be a conflict. They lengthen the shadow of the future and reduce the acuteness of the security dilemma. Institutions mitigate the negative effects of anarchy (uncertainty and an inability to cultivate trust). Hobbes saw international politics as a state of war. He was careful to say that a state of war does not mean constant fighting, but a propensity to war, just as cloudy weather means a likelihood of rain. In the same sense, a state of peace means a propensity toward peace: people can develop peaceful expectations when anarchy is stabilized by international institutions.

Institutions stabilize expectations in four ways. First, they provide a sense of continuity; for example, most Western Europeans expect the European Union to last. It is likely to be there tomorrow. At the end of the Cold War, many Eastern European governments agreed and made plans to join the European Union. That affected their behavior even before they eventually joined in 2004. Second, institutions provide an opportunity for reciprocity. If the French get a little bit more today, the Italians might get a little more tomorrow. There is less need to worry about each transaction because over time it will likely balance out. Third, institutions provide a flow of information. Who is doing what? Are the Italians actually obeying the rules passed by the European Union? Is the flow of trade roughly equal? The institutions of the union provide information on how it is all working out. Finally, institutions provide ways to resolve conflicts. In the European

Union, bargaining goes on within the Council of Ministers and in the European Commission, and there is also a European court of justice. Thus institutions create a climate in which expectations of stable peace develop.

Classical liberals also expect to see islands of peace where institutions and stable expectations have developed. The political scientist Karl Deutsch called such areas "pluralistic security communities" in which war between countries becomes so unthinkable that stable expectations of peace develop. Institutions helped reinforce such expectations. The Scandinavian countries, for example, once fought each other bitterly, and the United States fought Britain and Mexico. Today such actions are unthinkable. The advanced industrial countries seem to have a propensity for peace, and institutions such as the European Union, the North American Free Trade Agreement (NAFTA), and the Organization of American States create a culture in which peace is expected and provide forums for negotiation. Expectations of stability can provide a way to escape the Prisoner's Dilemma.

Some realists expect the security dilemma to reemerge in Europe despite the liberal institutions of the European Union. After the high hopes that greeted European integration in 1992, some opposition arose to further unity, particularly in disputes over the single European currency, the euro, which entered circulation in 2002. Countries such as Great Britain feared that ceding further power to the European Union would jeopardize the autonomy and prosperity of the individual states. Efforts in 2003 and 2004 to develop a new European constitution proved difficult, and in 2005, voters in France and the Netherlands refused to ratify it. At the same time, Britain and others worried that if they opted out of the European Union entirely, countries such as Germany, France, and Italy that opted in would gain a competitive edge. Despite such obstacles to further integration, the former communist countries of central Europe were attracted to joining. While the European Union is far from being a true superstate, its institutions helped transform relations between European states.

Liberals also argue that realists pay insufficient attention to democratic values. Germany today is a different country from the Germany of 1870, 1914, or 1939. It has experienced a half century of democracy, with parties and governments changing peacefully. Public opinion polls show that the German people do not seek an expansive international role. Thus liberals are skeptical of realist predictions that fail to account for the effects of democracy.

Is there a relationship between domestic democracy and a state's propensity to go to war? Current evidence suggests that the answer is yes, but with qualifications, and for reasons that are not yet entirely clear. The Prussian philosopher Immanuel Kant (1724–1804) was among the first to suggest that democracies are less warlike than authoritarian states. Absolute rulers can easily commit their states to war, as did Frederick the Great when he wanted Silesia in 1740 or Saddam Hussein when he invaded Kuwait in 1990. But Kant and other classical liberals pointed out that in a democracy the people can vote against war. Moreover, it is the people, rather than the rulers, who bear the heaviest costs of war. It stood to reason, Kant believed, that the people would be less inclined to war than would their leaders. But the fact that a country is democratic does not mean its people will always vote against war. As we have seen, democracies are likely to be involved in wars as often as other countries, and democratic electorates often vote for war. In ancient Greece, Pericles roused the people of Athens to go to war; in 1898, the American electorate dragged a reluctant President McKinley into the Spanish-American War. In 2003, opinion polls and a congressional vote supported President Bush's calls for war against Iraq, though public opinion later soured as the conflict dragged on.

Michael Doyle, a political scientist at Columbia, has pointed to a more limited proposition that can be derived from Kant and classical liberalism, namely, the idea that liberal democracies do not fight *other liberal democracies.* The fact that two democratic states do not fight each other is a correlation, and some correlations are spurious. Fires and the presence of fire engines are highly correlated, but we do not suspect fire engines of causing fires. One possible source of spurious causation is that democratic countries tend to be rich countries, rich countries tend to be involved with trade, and according to trade liberalism, they are not likely to fight each other. But that dismissal does not fit with the fact that rich countries have often fought each other—witness the two world wars. Liberals suggest that the cause behind the correlation is a question of legitimacy. Maybe people in democracies think it is wrong to fight other democracies because there is something wrong with solving disputes through killing when the other people have the right of consent. In addition, constitutional checks and balances on making war may work better when there is widespread public debate about the legitimacy of a battle. It is harder to rouse democratic peoples when there is no authoritarian demon like Hitler or Saddam Hussein.

Although "democratic peace" theory requires further exploration and elaboration, it is striking how difficult it is to find cases of liberal democracies waging war against other liberal democracies. Whatever the reason—whether liberal democracies share and respect a common set of principles of peaceful dispute resolution, whether they identify with each other, or whether because of something else (perhaps different explanations work best in different cases)—democratic peace theory suggests that if the number of democracies in the world grows, interstate war should decline. The past two decades have been somewhat encouraging. According to Freedom House, the number of "free countries"—truly liberal democracies—has risen since the end of the Cold War from 65 to 87 (i.e., from 40 percent to 45 percent).[17] But caution is in order. The democratic peace theory may be less true in the early stages of transition to democracy, and may not fit states whose democratic transition is unfinished. Some of the new democracies may be plebiscitary democracies without a liberal domestic process of free press, checks on executive power, and regular elections. The warring governments of Croatia, Serbia, and Bosnia were elected, though they were far from liberal democracies. The same was true of Ecuador and Peru, which fought a border skirmish in 1995. The character of a democracy matters a great deal.

Keeping these qualifications in mind, we should be cautious about making foreign policy recommendations on the basis of the democratic peace theory alone. Elections do not guarantee peace. International democracy promotion, as advocated by presidents Clinton and Bush, may help promote peace and security in the long term, but democratic transitions may increase the proclivity for war in the early stages of transition.

Marxism

A third major paradigm of International Relations is Marxism. As we have seen, it was clear enough in its predictions about the world that we are in a fairly good position to assess it. Marxists clearly but inaccurately predicted the death of capitalism as a result of imperialism, major war, socialist revolution, and the rise of communism. Instead we have seen changes in the nature of capitalism, an end to imperialism, the decline of major interstate war, a slowing of the rate of socialist revolution (and even the transformation of some revolutionary socialist states into liberal capitalist ones), and the collapse of communism.

Marxism appears to have suffered from three main weaknesses. First, it attempted to reduce politics to economics. People care about economics, of course, but they care about many other things as well. People's primarily loyalties rarely lie with their economic class. Second, it erred in conceiving of the state as a simple tool of a particular class. While wealthy capitalists are often very influential in the politics of their country, their narrow, self-serving interests rarely drive foreign policy, and never for terribly long. (The best examples, perhaps, would be the ability of certain U.S. multinational corporations to persuade policy makers in Washington to try to overthrow Latin American governments that had nationalized their properties, or seemed likely to do so, during the Cold War. Certainly corporate interests played a role in shaping various unsuccessful attempts to overthrow Cuban president Fidel Castro and successful attempts to overthrow socialist governments in Guatemala in 1954 and Chile in 1973.) Third, Marxism had an overly rigid understanding of the progress of history. Marx and his followers spoke at length about the inevitable collapse of capitalism and the inevitable triumph of communism, but they seem to have underestimated the role of both chance and human choice. Arguably, nothing in life is inevitable, except for death and taxes.

Still, Marxism has contributed something valuable, via dependency theory, to our understanding of patterns of development and underdevelopment, and also to the problem of growing global inequality. Marx did not err when he saw the potential of capitalism to concentrate wealth, and he was certainly correct to draw our attention to the dangers of gross economic inequality—one of the most significant drivers of substate conflict in the world today. Smart people are rarely wrong about everything, just as no one is ever right about everything.

Constructivism

Constructivism is a relatively new paradigm for the study of world politics that draws heavily from the field of sociology. Constructivism makes use of a "thicker" understanding of "structure" than do earlier paradigms. For constructivists, structures include not just the number or configuration of units, but also the "intersubjective meanings"—the shared discourses, ideas, practices, norms, rules, and logics of appropriateness—that help make them who they are and enable them to interact in an intelligible way. Social structures thus understood shape both identities and interests. Someone who grows up in rural Afghanistan will be a dramatically different person, with rather different goals, from someone who grows up in Los Angeles.

At the same time, when people interact in a social context, they alter it, if only marginally. Accordingly, social structures change over time. The concept of agent-structure interaction is a bit like the "karma" score in the popular *Fallout* series of video games: whether your character does nice things or nasty things, thus gaining or losing karma, affects how nonplayer characters interact with you and can even affect the ending of the game.

The crucial insights of constructivism, therefore, are (1) that "agents" and structures interact in a cyclical and reciprocal way; (2) that the identities and interests of agents are not given, but are instead the product of social interaction; and (3) that over time, intersubjective meanings change as a result of social interaction, resulting in changes in rules, norms, legitimate expectations, and even, eventually, in the very character of the international system itself.

Compared to realism, liberalism, and Marxism, constructivism is relatively new—so new that there remain fundamental differences among constructivists as to its status as a paradigm. One view, championed by Ohio State political scientist Alexander Wendt, is that constructivism is a purely formal approach to international politics, not a substantive one. As such, it is not directly comparable to realism, liberalism, or Marxism. Unlike these other paradigms, constructivism makes no strong assumptions about human nature, and cannot therefore generate substantive claims or expectations about how actors behave. In this sense it is a bit like *game theory*, which is a purely formal mathematical technique for representing interactions. Another view, however, is that constructivism merely qualifies the ways in which human nature expresses itself by noting the importance of social and cultural context. On this view, constructivism is a bit like the "nurture" view in the nature vs. nurture debate. Realism, liberalism, and Marxism all tend to cluster closer to the "nature" end of the spectrum (with neorealism arguably furthest along)—but since all four perspectives lie on a single spectrum, they are all essentially comparable.

The differences between these two views of constructivism are important to people whose primary interest is ironing out the wrinkles in International Relations theory, but for someone interested primarily in explaining why things happen in the world—and, if possible, anticipating how things will unfold in the future—they have a common practical implication: namely, that there is no way of avoiding hard work! We cannot simply assume that people will behave in such-and-such a way. We need to know who they are, what they want, and how they see the world in order to understand what they do, and to know these things, we have to understand the social and cultural contexts in which they are embedded. We have to "reconstruct" the world in order to explain it, and this requires a great deal of information—and a correspondingly great deal of time and energy. But constructivist scholars willing to invest the effort have succeeded in explaining things that are difficult to explain from realist, liberal, or Marxist perspectives: for example, the rise of antimilitarism in Japan; the spread of powerful international norms against slavery, territorial revision, and weapons of mass destruction; the rapid evolution of the global human rights regime; the spread of feminism and environmentalism; and the development of pluralistic security communities.[18]

Since realism packs a lot of punch into assumptions, it has a much easier time than constructivism in generating predictions. Realist predictions are not always right—the end of the Cold War did not, in fact, weaken Western solidarity, contrary to the prognostications of many prominent realists—but at least realism gives us ready tools for making predictions. One of the crucial axioms of constructivism is that international politics is "path-dependent": What will happen tomorrow is less a function of immutable mechanisms such as the balance of power than of the historical background against which leaders must choose today. Prediction, on this view, requires being able to tease out plausible future paths and identifying those that are most likely. Not only is this task inherently harder, it means that our confidence in our predictions must rapidly decline the further we project into the future.

Constructivist explanations are not always incompatible with realist, liberal, or Marxist ones. The liberal story about postwar antimilitarism in Japan, for instance—the story that appeals to economic opportunity—is fully compatible with a constructivist story that stresses the reaction of the Japanese people to the shame, betrayal, and suffering they experienced at the hands of earlier militaristic leaders. We do not have to choose between them; both stories can be true in their own way. Moreover, in some circumstances it may be possible to "nest" other paradigms' explanations within a constructivist one. There is reason to believe, for example, that realism works best when explaining periods of history in which key practitioners of diplomacy were themselves believers in realism. U.S. foreign policy was never more "realist" than when Henry Kissinger was secretary of state. Liberalism performs best when explaining periods of history in which key players were devout liberals, such as Woodrow Wilson. From a constructivist perspective, this strong interaction of agents and structures is hardly surprising.

Follow Up

- Annette Freyberg-Inan, Ewan Harrison, and Patrick James, eds., *Rethinking Realism in International Relations: Between Tradition and Innovation* (Baltimore, MD: Johns Hopkins University Press, 2009).
- Andrew Moravcsik, "Taking Preferences Seriously: A Liberal Theory of International Politics," *International Organization*, Vol. 51, No. 4 (Autumn 1997), pp. 513–553.
- Immanuel Wallerstein, *World-Systems Analysis: An Introduction* (Durham, NC: Duke University Press, 2004).
- Stefano Guzzini and Anna Leander, eds., *Constructivism and International Relations: Alexander Wendt and His Critics* (London: Routledge, 2006).

COUNTERFACTUALS AND "VIRTUAL HISTORY"

In 1990, President Václav Havel of Czechoslovakia spoke before the U.S. Congress. Six months earlier he had been a political prisoner. "As a playwright," Havel said, "I'm used to the fantastic. I dream up all sorts of implausible things and put them in my plays. So this jolting experience of going from prison to standing before you today, I can adjust to this. But pity the poor political scientists who are trying to deal with what's probable."[19] Few people, including Soviets and Eastern Europeans, predicted the collapse of the Soviet Empire in Eastern Europe in 1989. Humans sometimes make surprising choices, and human history is full of uncertainties. How can we sort out the importance of different causes at different levels of analysis?

International politics is not like a laboratory science. We cannot do controlled experiments because it is impossible to hold other things constant while looking at one thing that changes. Aristotle said one should be as precise in any science as the subject matter allows: Do not try to be too precise if the precision will be spurious. International politics involves so many variables, so many changes occurring at the same time, that events are often overdetermined. But as analysts, we still want to sort out causes to get some idea of which ones are more important than others. Mental experiments called counterfactuals can be useful tools in helping us determine this.

Counterfactuals are *contrary-to-fact conditionals,* but it is simpler to think of them as thought experiments to explore causal claims. Because there is no actual, physical laboratory for international politics, we imagine situations in which one thing changes while other things are held constant and then construct a picture of how the world would look. In fact, we use counterfactuals every day. Many students might say, "If I had not eaten so much dinner, I could concentrate better on this reading."

Though often without admitting it, historians use a more elaborate version of the same procedure to weigh causes. For example, imagine that the kaiser had not fired Bismarck in 1890. Would that have made World War I less likely? Would Bismarck's policies have continued to lower the sense of threat that other countries felt from Germany and thus curbed the growing rigidity of the two alliance systems? In this instance, the use of a counterfactual examines how important a particular personality was in comparison to structural factors. Here is another counterfactual related to World War I: Suppose Franz Ferdinand's driver in Sarajevo had not mistakenly turned down the wrong street, unexpectedly presenting Gavrilo Princip with a target of opportunity. Would war have still started? This counterfactual illuminates the role of the assassination (as well as the role of accident). How important was the assassination? Given the overall tensions inherent in the alliance structure, might some other spark have ignited the flame had this one not occurred? Did the assassination affect anything other than the timing of the outbreak of war?

Contrary-to-fact conditional statements provide a way to explore whether a cause is significant, but there are also pitfalls in such "iffy history." Poorly handled counterfactuals may mislead by destroying the meaning of history.

The fact is that once something has happened, other things are not equal, because events are path-dependent: Once something happens, the probabilities of possible futures change. Some events become more likely, others less.

We can use four criteria to test whether our counterfactual thought experiments are good or useful: plausibility, proximity, theory, and facts.

Plausibility

A useful counterfactual has to be within the reasonable array of options. This is sometimes called *cotenability*. It must be plausible to imagine two conditions existing at the same time. Suppose someone said that if Napoleon had had stealth bombers, he would have won the Battle of Waterloo (1815). She may say that such a counterfactual is designed to test the importance of military technology, but it makes little sense to imagine twentieth-century technology in a nineteenth-century setting. The two are not cotenable. Although it might be good for laughs, it is not a fruitful use of counterfactual thinking because of the anachronism involved. In real life, there never was a possibility of such a conjunction.

Proximity in Time

Each major event exists in a long chain of causation, and most events have multiple causes. The further back in time we go, the more causes that must be held constant. The closer in time the questioned event is to the subject event (did A cause B?), the more likely the answer is yes. Consider Pascal's (1623–1662) famous counterfactual statement that if Cleopatra's nose had been shorter, she would have been less attractive to Marc Antony, and the history of the Roman Empire would have been different. If the history of the Roman Empire had been different, the history of Western European civilization would have been different. Thus the length of Cleopatra's nose was one of the causes of World War I. In some trivial sense, that may be true, but millions of events and causes channeled down to August 1914. The contribution of Cleopatra's nose to the outbreak of World War I is so small and so remote that the counterfactual is more amusing than interesting when we try to ascertain why the war broke out. Proximity in time means that the closeness of two events in the chain of causation allows us to better control other causes and thereby obtain a truer weighing of factors.

Relation to Theory

Good counterfactual reasoning should rely on an existing body of theory that represents a distillation of what we think we know about things that have happened before. We should ask whether a counterfactual is plausible considering what we know about all the cases that have given rise to these theories. Theories provide coherence and organization to our thoughts about the myriad causes and help us to avoid random guessing. For example, there is no theory behind the counterfactual that if Napoleon had had stealth aircraft he would have won the Battle of Waterloo. The very randomness of the example helps explain why it is amusing, but also limits what we can learn from the mental exercise.

But suppose we were considering the causes of the Cold War and asked, what if the United States had been a socialist country in 1945; would there have been a Cold War? Or suppose the Soviet Union had come out of World War II with a capitalist government; would there have been a Cold War? These counterfactual questions explore the theory that the Cold War was caused primarily by ideology. An alternative hypothesis is that the bipolar international structure caused the Cold War—that some sort of tension was likely even if the United States had been socialist, as balance-of-power theory would predict. Counterfactual inferences can be bolstered by looking at *factual* patterns invoking factual comparisons. After the Cold War, we did not witness a wholesale reconfiguration of alliances designed to balance the now unchallenged supremacy of the United States, suggesting that ideological affinity trumps balance of power considerations at least among liberal states. But during the Cold War, at least in certain parts of the world, we did see communist states balancing against each other, and since the Cold War both Russia and China have been wary of the United States. So we are on fairly firm ground concluding that both ideology and balance of power were relevant, but that they were not equally relevant to all players. In general, counterfactuals related to theory are more interesting and more useful because the mental exercise ties into a broader body of knowledge, and by focusing our attention on theoretically informed counterfactuals, we can often come up with something new and interesting to say about the theories themselves.

Facts

It is not enough to imagine fruitful hypotheses. They must be carefully examined in relation to the known facts. Counterfactuals require accurate facts and careful history. In examining the plausibility of a mental experiment, we must ask whether what is held constant is faithful to what actually happened. We must be wary of piling one counterfactual on top of another in the same thought experiment. Such multiple counterfactuals are confusing because too many things are being changed at once, and we are unable to judge the accuracy of the exercise by a careful examination of its real historical parts.

A particularly good way of disciplining a counterfactual is *virtual history*, a term coined by Harvard historian Niall Ferguson. Done properly, it limits the dangers of implausibility and remoteness in time by answering questions about what *might* have happened strictly in terms of what *did* happen. In the 2008 film *Virtual JFK*, Koji Masutani explores the question of whether President Kennedy would have committed U.S. troops heavily to the Vietnam War, as his successor did, had he lived to win reelection in 1964. He answers the question by looking carefully at what Kennedy did whenever he faced a decision about committing American troops to battle overseas. Six times in his presidency, Kennedy confronted just such a decision; all six times he avoided it. Not only did Kennedy demonstrate a powerful aversion to militarizing disputes, he also displayed deep skepticism about the advice he was receiving from his military and intelligence officials who were urging him to do so. By extrapolating from Kennedy's actual behavior and known disposition, it is possible to discipline the counterfactual in a way that increases our confidence in the judgment that Kennedy would not have committed large numbers of American troops to Vietnam.

Some historians are purists who say counterfactuals that ask what might have been are not real history. Real history is what actually happened. Imagining what might have happened is not important. But such purists miss the point that we try to understand not just *what* happened, but *why* it happened. To do that, we need to know what else *might* have happened, and that brings us back to counterfactuals. So while some historians interpret history as simply the writing down of what happened, many historians believe that good counterfactual analysis is essential to good historical analysis. The purists help warn us against poorly disciplined counterfactuals such as Napoleon's stealth bombers. But, there is a distinction between saying that some counterfactual analysis is trivial and saying that good counterfactual analysis is essential to clear thinking about causation.

Follow Up

- Philip E. Tetlock and Aaron Belkin, eds., *Counterfactual Thought Experiments in World Politics: Logical, Methodological, and Psychological Perspectives* (Princeton, NJ: Princeton University Press, 1996).
- James G. Blight, Janet M. Lang, and David A. Welch, *Virtual JFK: Vietnam If Kennedy Had Lived* (Lanham, MD: Rowman & Littlefield, 2010).

STUDY QUESTIONS

1. What are the relationships among the concepts "state," "nation," and "nation-state"?
2. How might authority be a source of power? Would it be a source of hard power or soft power?
3. What is the relationship between system stability and crisis stability?
4. What are Waltz's three images? Can they be combined? If so, how?
5. Why do liberals think democracy can prevent war? What are the limits to their view?
6. What is the difference between the structure and process of an international system? Is constructivism useful for understanding how processes change?
7. What is counterfactual history? Can you use it to explain the causes of the war in Afghanistan?

NOTES

1. A nation is an "imagined community," in the words of Benedict Anderson, and so it is often difficult to define objectively; to some extent a nation is a self-defined entity. Benedict Anderson, *Imagined Communities: Reflections on the Origin and Spread of Nationalism* (London: Verso, 1991).

2. A claim by one state to the territory of another state on grounds of self-determination of the inhabitants is called *irredentism*, from the Italian *irredenta*, meaning "unredeemed."
3. See http://www.huttriver.net/.
4. Andrew F. Cooper, *Celebrity Diplomacy* (Boulder, CO: Paradigm Publishers, 2008).
5. See http://www.fundforpeace.org/web/index.php?option=com_content&task=view&id=99&Itemid=140.
6. David A. Welch, *Justice and the Genesis of War* (Cambridge: Cambridge University Press, 1993), pp. 76–94.
7. Hedley Bull, *The Anarchical Society: A Study of Order in World Politics* (London: Macmillan, 1977).
8. Paul R. Hensel, "Territory: Theory and Evidence on Geography and Conflict," in John A. Vazquez, ed., *What Do We Know About War?* (New York: Rowman & Littlefield, 2000), p. 62.
9. Geoffrey Blainey, *The Causes of War* (New York: Free Press, 1973), p. 150.
10. Alexander L. George and Juliette L. George, *Woodrow Wilson and Colonel House* (New York: John Day Co., 1956).
11. Perhaps the best is Fritz Redlick, *Hitler: Diagnosis of a Destructive Prophet* (New York: Oxford University Press, 1999).
12. V. I. Lenin, *Imperialism: The Highest Stage of Capitalism* (New York: International Publishers, 1977), p. 119.
13. Richard Cobden, quoted in Kenneth N. Waltz, *Man, the State, and War: A Theoretical Analysis* (New York: Columbia University Press, 1959), p. 104.
14. Barry M. Blechman, *The Politics of National Security: Congress and U.S. Defense Policy* (New York: Oxford University Press, 1990), pp. 36–37.
15. Robert K. Merton, *Social Theory and Social Structure*, rev. and enl. ed. (New York: Free Press, 1965), pp. 12–16.
16. Richard Rosecrance, *The Rise of the Trading State: Commerce and Conquest in the Modern World* (New York: Basic, 1986), p. ix.
17. *Freedom in the World 2011: The Authoritarian Challenge to Democracy* (Freedom House, January 2011), p. 25.
18. Peter J. Katzenstein, *Rethinking Japanese Security: Internal and External Dimensions* (New York: Routledge, 2008); Margaret E. Keck and Kathryn Sikkink, *Activists Beyond Borders: Advocacy Networks in International Politics* (Ithaca, NY: Cornell University Press, 1998); Martha Finnemore, *The Purpose of Intervention: Changing Beliefs About the Use of Force* (Ithaca, NY: Cornell University Press, 2003); Matthew J. Hoffmann, *Ozone Depletion and Climate Change: Constructing a Global Response* (Albany: State University of New York Press, 2005); Emanuel Adler and Michael Barnett, *Security Communities* (Cambridge: Cambridge University Press, 1998).
19. Václav Havel, "Address to U.S. Congress," *Congressional Record*, February 21, 1990, pp. S1313–1315.

PHOTO CREDITS

Credits are listed in order of appearance:

picture-alliance/dpa/Newscom.

Lionel Cironneau/AP Images.

From Westphalia to World War I

World War I: The aftermath of battle

The primary political unit has varied in human history from time to time and from place to place. In isolated, rural, hunter-gatherer societies, small-scale groups such as tribes or even extended family units tended to dominate. With urbanization and the development of more specialized social and economic roles, larger-scale units such as city-states and small kingdoms came to the fore. As societies advanced technologically, organizationally, and militarily, they sometimes exercised dominion over vast areas. The largest contiguous political unit of all time was the Mongol Empire, which at its height in 1279 CE stretched from the Sea of Japan to the Baltic and from the South China Sea to the Persian Gulf. The British Empire in 1922 covered nearly one-quarter of the Earth's surface and ruled over nearly a quarter of the human population. Typically, different political units would dominate in different places at the same time. While Kublai Khan ruled the territorially well-defined Mongol Empire, Europe was a patchwork of feudal kingdoms, bishoprics, principalities, and lesser fiefdoms, and North America was home to mostly nomadic or seminomadic tribes. Only in the twentieth century did a single form of political organization come to dominate the entire globe: namely, the sovereign state. Today, the entire land mass of the planet—with the exception of Antarctica, which by treaty has been off-limits to territorial claims since 1961—is under the jurisdiction of a sovereign state or (as in the case of Taiwan) its functional equivalent. How did this come to be?

While many political units all over the globe throughout history have been well defined territorially, ruled internally, and subservient to no outside authority, the modern sovereign state as we know it, with its specified rights, privileges, and obligations to international society, is a European creation. In fact, one might go so far as to say that it is Europe's most successful export. For hundreds of years after Europe had abandoned feudalism for the Westphalian system, powerful European countries ventured abroad and directly or indirectly ruled virtually the entire world. Countries committed to respecting the autonomy of other polities in their home neighborhood, in other words, very much ignored it elsewhere. In the wake of World War II, European empires gradually collapsed. Nationalist groups worldwide fought for or negotiated formal independence. Though eager to throw off colonial yokes, independence movements were just as eager to adopt the Westphalian model.

The Peace of Westphalia was actually a set of treaties, of which the two most important, the treaties of Osnabrück and Münster (1648), ended the *Thirty Years' War*.[1] While there are no precise figures for casualties, the Thirty Years' War was certainly one of the deadliest in European history.

Most of the destruction occurred in the territory of modern Germany, or what was then called the Holy Roman Empire (about which Voltaire once quipped that it was "neither holy, nor Roman, nor an empire"). There were as many issues and stakes as participants, but one important underlying conflict was religious. The Peace of Westphalia effectively entrenched the principle of *cuius regio, eius religio*, whereby each ruler would have the right to determine the religion of his or her own state. The treaties did not quite amount to a full endorsement of the principle of state sovereignty as we know it today, as they contained rights of intervention to enforce their terms, but, as University of British Columbia political scientist Kalevi Holsti puts it, "[B]y providing a legal basis for the developing territorial particularisms of Europe, and by terminating the vestiges of relations between superiors and inferiors, with authority emanating downward from the Emperor and the Pope, the documents licensed an anarchical dynastic states system and the internal consolidation of its members."[2]

Although political philosophers would later justify the principle of state sovereignty with reference to the rights of political communities to regulate their own affairs according to their own visions of the good life, there is a good case to be made that it was, in fact, appealing primarily because it would empower and enrich rulers. Columbia sociologist Charles Tilly compares the state with a protection racket in which rulers justify extracting "rents" (i.e., surplus funds) from hapless citizens by pleading the necessities of state security.[3] This was also part of the attraction of sovereign statehood for some rapacious Third World leaders during the period after decolonization, several of whom managed to enrich themselves considerably.

The Peace of Westphalia did not eliminate war from Europe, but it did moderate its severity and intensity. The European great powers continued to vie for primacy. The Netherlands enjoyed a brief period of commercial hegemony in the seventeenth century, thanks largely to the efforts of the Dutch East India Company, and were among the first Europeans (along with the Portuguese) to establish a long-lasting imperial presence overseas. France under Louis XIV (1638–1715) attained a degree of preeminence in Europe; succeeded in engineering a centralized, modern bureaucratic state; and colonized much of North America. Britain, which contended with both the Netherlands and France for maritime supremacy (despite its formidable economic and naval power and its astonishing success in acquiring overseas colonial territory, Britain never became a major land power in Europe), gradually established its claim for preeminence in the eighteenth and nineteenth centuries by defeating French forces on the Plains of Abraham in Québec (1759), by defeating the combined French and Spanish fleets in the Battle of Trafalgar (1805), and by helping to defeat Napoleon at the Battle of Waterloo (1815). Despite its embarrassing and costly loss of colonies in the American Revolutionary War, Britain became the world's most powerful country in the nineteenth century because of its early industrialization, its control of the seas, its dominance of capital markets, and the embrace of the pound as the world's reserve currency.

Most of the wars fought in Europe between the Thirty Years' War and the Napoleonic Wars were short, sharp, and geographically limited. They were fought over dynastic issues, territorial disputes, and in some cases merely to prevent certain states from becoming too powerful. In this period, European states did not have wars whose purpose was to rewrite the fundamental rules of the game. Put another way, it was a very stable international system. European leaders did not have revolutionary goals. In the eighteenth century, for example, the basic rule of the game was: Protect the legitimacy of monarchical states—the divine right of rulers—and maintain a balance of power among them (the 1713 *Treaty of Utrecht* referred explicitly to the importance of the balance of power). Consider Frederick the Great of Prussia (1740–1786) and the way he treated his neighbor Maria Theresa (1717–1780) of Austria. In 1740, Frederick decided he wanted Silesia, a province belonging to Maria Theresa. Frederick had no great revolutionary cause, only a simple goal of aggrandizement. He did not try to incite a popular revolution against Maria Theresa by appealing to the people in Silesia to overthrow the German-speaking autocrats of Vienna. After all, Frederick was a German-speaking autocrat in Berlin. He took Silesia because he wanted it and was careful not to do anything else that would damage Austria or the basic principle of monarchical legitimacy.

Compare that to the French Revolution (1789–1799) half a century later, when the prevailing view in France was that all monarchs should be sent to the gallows or the guillotine and that power should emanate from the people. Napoleon spread this revolutionary idea of popular sovereignty throughout Europe, and the Napoleonic Wars (1799–1815) posed an enormous challenge to both the rules of the game and the balance of power. The moderate process and stable balance of the system in the middle of the century changed to a revolutionary process and unstable balance at the end of the century. We refer to changes like the French Revolution as *exogenous* to a structural theory because they cannot be explained inside the theory. This is an example of how a realist structural theory can be supplemented by constructivist work. Constructivism is well suited to explaining phenomena such as the rise of a norm of popular (as opposed to monarchical) sovereignty.

In addition to changing their goals, states can also change their means. The process of a system is also affected by the nature of the instruments actors use. Different means can have stabilizing or destabilizing effects. Some instruments change because of technology. For example, the development of new weapons such as the machine gun made World War I a particularly bloody encounter. Means can also change because of new social organization. In the eighteenth century, Frederick the Great not only had limited goals, he was also limited by his means. He had a mercenary army with limited loyalties and poor logistics. Eighteenth-century armies generally campaigned in the summer, when food was readily available or when the treasury had accumulated enough gold to pay soldiers who were often from the fringes of society. When the food or the gold ran out, the soldiers deserted. The French Revolution changed the social organization of war to what the French called the *levée en masse,* or what we call "conscription" or "the draft." As constructivists point out, soldiers' sense of identity changed. People came to understand themselves as citizens, rallied to the concept of a national homeland, and felt that all should participate. War was no longer a matter among a few thousand mercenaries who campaigned far away; war now involved nearly everyone. This large-scale involvement and mass support overwhelmed the old mercenary infantries. The change in the means available to states also helped change certain processes of the eighteenth-century international system.

MANAGING GREAT POWER CONFLICT: THE BALANCE OF POWER

The European system of sovereign states was stable from Westphalia to the Napoleonic Wars in large part because of the fairly effective operation of the *balance of power*.

What exactly is the balance of power? It is one of the most frequently used concepts in international politics, but it is also one of the most confusing. The term is loosely used to describe and justify all sorts of things. The eighteenth-century British philosopher David Hume characterized the balance of power as a constant rule of prudent politics, but the nineteenth-century British liberal Richard Cobden called it "a chimera—an undescribed, indescribable, incomprehensible nothing."[4] Woodrow Wilson, the American president during World War I, thought the balance of power was an evil principle because it encouraged statesmen to treat countries like cheeses to be cut up for political convenience regardless of the concerns of their peoples.

Wilson also disliked the balance of power because he believed it caused wars. Defenders of balance-of-power policies argue that they produce stability. However, as we have seen, peace and stability are not the same thing. Over the five centuries of the European state system, the great powers were involved in 119 wars. Peace was rare; during three-quarters of the time there was war involving at least one of the great powers. Ten of those wars were large general wars with many of the great powers involved—what we call hegemonic or world wars. Thus if we ask whether the balance of power preserved peace very well over the five centuries of the modern state system, the answer is no.

That is not surprising because states balance power not to preserve peace, but to preserve their independence. The balance of power helps preserve the anarchic system of separate states. Not every state is preserved. For example, at the end of the eighteenth century, Poland was, indeed, cut up like a cheese, with Poland's neighbors—Austria, Prussia, and Russia—all helping themselves to a large slice. More recently, in 1939 Stalin and Hitler made a deal in which they carved up Poland again and gave the Baltic states to the Soviet Union. Thus Lithuania, Latvia, and Estonia spent half a century as Soviet republics until 1991. The balance of power has not preserved peace and has not always preserved the independence of each state, but it has preserved the anarchic state system.

The difficulty of measuring changing power resources is a major problem for leaders trying to assess the balance of power. For analysts of international politics, additional confusion ensues when the same word is used for different things. We must try to separate and clarify the underlying concepts covered by the loose use of the same words. The term *balance of power* commonly refers to at least four different things.

Balances as Distributions of Power

The term *balance of power* can be used, first, simply to describe a distribution of power. If you hear the phrase "the current balance of power," then you are probably hearing someone use the term in this purely descriptive sense. In the 1980s, it was common to hear some Americans argue that if Nicaragua became a communist state, this would change the Cold War balance of power. This might have been true, but it would have done so only marginally, so in the grand scheme of things, it was not a very interesting or important insight. This purely descriptive use of the term can be powerful rhetorically, but it is often of limited use analytically.

A special (and rare) use of the phrase in this sense is to describe a situation in which power is distributed equally. This usage conjures up the image of a set of scales in equilibrium. While some realists argue that the international system is most stable when there is an equal balance of power, others argue the system is most stable when one side has a preponderance of power so the others dare not attack it. This is the view held by proponents of *hegemonic stability theory*. In this view, a strong dominant power is the best guarantee of stability. But according to hegemonic stability theory's first cousin, *hegemonic transition theory*, when the strongest power begins to slip, as it inevitably will, or as a new aspirant for hegemony arises, war is particularly likely. A declining hegemon or states fearing a rising power will take desperate measures to protect their position, while a rising power will gamble to attain hegemony. As we will see later in this chapter, hegemonic transition theory sheds light on the outbreak of World War I. It also helps us make sense of Thucydides' account of the origins of the Peloponnesian War: Sparta's fear of the allegedly growing power of Athens led it to take the bold and risky gamble of supporting Corinth.

We must be cautious about such theories, for they tend to overpredict conflict. In the 1880s, the United States passed Great Britain as the largest economy in the world. In 1895, the United States and Britain disagreed over borders in South America, and it looked as if war might result. There was a rising challenger, a declining hegemon, and a cause of conflict, but you do not read about the great British-American War of 1895 because it did not occur. As Sherlock Holmes pointed out, we can get important clues from dogs that do not bark. In this case, the absence of war leads us to look for other causes. Realists point to the rise of Germany as a more proximate threat to Britain.

Liberals point to the increasingly democratic nature of the two English-speaking countries and to transnational cultural ties between the old leader and the new challenger. The best we can conclude about the balance of power in the first sense of the term is that changes in the distribution of power among leading states may be one factor that helps explain war and instability, but they are clearly not the whole story.

Balance of Power as Policy

The second use of the term *balance of power* refers to a deliberate policy of balancing. Lord Palmerston's dictum that states have no permanent friends or permanent enemies, merely permanent interests, is a view that any strong proponent of balance-of-power politics would hold. Indeed, as British foreign secretary in the mid-1800s, Palmerston pursued balance-of-power politics consistently. When Hitler invaded the Soviet Union in 1941, Prime Minister Winston Churchill (1874–1965) embraced balance-of-power politics as well. Churchill was a strong anticommunist who disliked Soviet leader Josef Stalin, but an alliance with Stalin was vital to prevent Nazi Germany from dominating Europe. "If Hitler invaded Hell," Churchill famously said, "I would make at least a favourable reference to the Devil in the House of Commons."[5]

Leaders who embrace a balance-of-power policy are almost certainly also likely to hold an essentially realist view of international politics. For this reason, the consistent pursuit of a balance-of-power policy is often referred to by the German word *realpolitik*.

A key instrument for attempting to maintain a balance of power is *alliance*. Alliances are agreements that sovereign states enter into with each other in order to ensure their mutual security. As was the case with Britain's alliance with the Soviet Union in World War II, they can be motivated by purely military concerns: Two medium-sized states might decide they will be more secure against threats from a larger state by forming an alliance. Traditionally, military alliances have been one of the focal points of international politics. But states might also ally for nonmilitary reasons. From time to time two or more states may be drawn together into an alliance for economic reasons, or because of ideological or cultural affinity. This is particularly true in those parts of the modern world where purely military concerns are receding, such as in Europe and North America today.

Alliances collapse for as many reasons as they form, but in general states cease to ally when they come to see each other as irrelevant or as threats to their security. That might occur because the regime in one state changes. Before, the two states might have shared a common ideology; now they are opposed. Thus China and the United States were allies when the Nationalists were in power before 1949 and enemies after the Communists came to power in 1949. Of course, there may be other reasons for an alliance to end. One state may grow more powerful. It might view the other state as a rival, while the other state might view it as a threat and look for alliances elsewhere to balance that threat.

Balance of Power as Theory

A third use of the term *balance of power* is to describe a more or less automatic equilibration of power in the international system. This is balance-of-power *theory*.

Balance-of-power theory predicts that states will act to prevent any one state from developing a preponderance of power; or put another way, it predicts that leaders will, as a matter of course, embrace a balance-of-power policy simply because they cannot afford not to. Recall that realists see the Westphalian system as a Hobbesian anarchy in which fear is endemic and trust is in short supply. They see it as a "self-help" system in which the only way to be sure of surviving is to do what one can to prevent any other state or group of states from attaining a preponderance of power. This can be done through internal adjustment (e.g., spending more on the military), external collaboration (e.g., allying with other countries), or both.

In domestic politics, we often see *bandwagoning* instead of balancing: Politicians often flock to a likely winner. Balance-of-power theory, however, predicts that a state will join whoever seems *weaker*, because states will act to keep any one state from becoming preponderant. Bandwagoning in international politics risks one's independence. In 1939 and 1940, the Italian dictator Benito Mussolini joined Hitler's attack on France as a way to get some of the spoils, but Italy became more and more dependent on Germany. That is why a balance-of-power policy says, "Join the weaker side." Balance of power is a policy of helping the underdog because if you help the top dog, it may eventually turn around and eat you.

Balance-of-power theory does not predict that states will make common cause with states that share ideological or cultural characteristics. When Iran and Iraq went to war in the early 1980s, some observers thought all Arab states would support Saddam Hussein's Iraq, a largely Arab and Sunni Muslim state ruled by a secular Ba'ath Party, against Ayatollah Khomeini's Iran, an overwhelmingly Persian theocracy in which the minority Shi'ite version of Islam dominated. But Syria, despite being a Sunni Arab state with a secular Ba'athist leader, supported Iran. Why? Because Syria was worried about the growing regional power of its neighbor Iraq. Syria chose to balance Iraqi power regardless of its ideological preferences. Efforts to use ideology to predict state behavior are often wrong, whereas counterintuitive predictions based on balancing power are often correct.

Of course, there are exceptions. Human behavior is not fully determined. Human beings have choices, and they do not always act as predicted. Certain situations predispose people toward a certain type of behavior, but we cannot always predict the details. If someone shouts "Fire!" in a crowded lecture hall, we could predict that students would run for exits, but not *which* exits. If all choose one exit, the stampede may prevent many from getting out. Theories in international politics often have large exceptions. Even though balance-of-power theory provides a clear way of making predictions in international politics, its record is far from perfect.

Why do countries sometimes eschew balance of power and join the stronger rather than the weaker side, or stand aloof, thus ignoring the risks to their independence? Some countries may see no alternatives or believe they cannot affect the balance. If so, a small country may decide it has to fall within the sphere of influence of a great power while hoping that neutrality will preserve some freedom of action. For example, after World War II Finland was defeated by the Soviet Union and was far from the center of Europe. The Finns felt neutrality was safer than trying to become part of the European balance of power. They were in the Soviet sphere of influence, and the best they could do was bargain away independence in foreign policy for a large degree of control over their domestic affairs.

Another reason that balance-of-power predictions are sometimes wrong has to do with perceptions of threat. For example, a mechanical accounting of the power resources of countries in 1917 would have predicted that the United States would join World War I on the side of Germany because Britain, France, and Russia had 30 percent of the industrial world's resources while Germany and Austria had only 19 percent. This did not happen, in part because the Americans perceived the Germans as militarily stronger and the aggressor in the war.

Perceptions of threat are often influenced by *proximity*. A neighbor may be weak on some absolute global scale, but threatening in its region or local area. Consider Britain and the United States in the 1890s: Britain could have fought, but instead chose to appease the United States. It conceded to the United States on many issues, including the building of the Panama Canal, which allowed America to improve its naval position. One reason is that Britain was more worried about its neighbor Germany than it was about the distant Americans. The United States was larger than Germany, but proximity affected which threat loomed larger in British eyes. Proximity also helps explain the alliances after 1945. The United States was stronger than the Soviet Union, so why didn't Europe and Japan ally with the Soviet Union against the United States? The answer lies partly in the proximity of the threat. From the point of view of Europe and Japan, the Soviets were an immediate threat and the United States was far away. The Europeans and the Japanese called in the distant power to rebalance the situation in their immediate neighborhood. The fact that proximity often affects how threats are perceived qualifies any predictions based on a simple mechanical toting up of power resources.

Another exception to balance-of-power predictions relates to the growing role of economic interdependence in world affairs. According to a balance-of-power policy, France should not wish to see Germany grow, but because of economic integration, German growth stimulates French growth. French politicians are more likely to be reelected when the French economy is growing. Therefore, a policy of trying to hold back German economic growth would be foolish because the French and German economies are so interdependent. In economic considerations, joint gains would often be lost by following too simple a balance-of-power policy.

Finally—contrary to the predictions of balance-of-power theory—ideology sometimes does cause countries to join the top dog rather than the underdog. Even in Thucydides' day, democratic city-states were more likely to align with Athens and oligarchies with Sparta. Britain's appeasement of the United States in the 1890s or the Europeans joining with the Americans in an alliance of democracies after 1945 owed something to the influence of ideology, as well as to the proximity of a threat. But it is easy—and can be dangerous—to overestimate the relevance of ideology. Many Europeans believed that Stalin and Hitler could not come together in 1939 because they were at opposite ends of the ideological spectrum, and yet they did. Likewise, in the 1960s the United States mistakenly assumed that all communist countries represented a united, monolithic threat. A policy based on balance of power would have predicted that China, the Soviet Union, Vietnam, and Cambodia would balance one another, as they eventually did. Had American leaders foreseen this, no doubt they would have found a far less expensive way to pursue stability in East Asia than by committing more than half a million troops to the war in Vietnam.

Balances of Power as Historical Multipolar Systems

The fourth way in which the term *balance of power* is sometimes used is to describe historical cases of multipolarity. The historian Edward Vose Gulick, for example, used the term "the classical balance of power" to refer to eighteenth-century Europe's multipolar system. We often use the phrase "the nineteenth-century balance of power" to refer to the European system between the Napoleonic Wars and World War I. In this sense, a balance of power requires a number of countries that follow a set of rules of the game that are generally understood. Since this use of the term *balance of power* refers to historical systems, we look at the two dimensions of systems, structure and process.

Follow Up

- Edward Vose Gulick, *Europe's Classical Balance of Power* (New York: Norton, 1967).
- William C. Wohlforth, Stuart J. Kaufman, and Richard Little, eds., *The Balance of Power in World History* (New York: Palgrave Macmillan, 2007).

THE NINETEENTH-CENTURY BALANCE-OF-POWER SYSTEM

The nineteenth-century balance-of-power system produced the longest interval without world war in the modern state system: from 1815 to 1914. But it was a dynamic system that was far from entirely peaceful. Changes in its structure and processes were instrumental in bringing about two cataclysmic world wars in 1914 and 1939. We must therefore be careful not to romanticize or oversimplify a complex story. The concepts and distinctions we have discussed to this point can help us navigate the complexity and better understand the nineteenth-century origins of the great twentieth-century conflicts.

Structure

If we look at the structure of the nineteenth-century balance-of-power system as understood by neorealists—that is, as a simple distribution of power—we can identify three distinct periods (see Table 1). The first began with the defeat of Napoleon at Waterloo. Napoleon had tried to establish French hegemony over Europe. His efforts united the other great powers in a coalition that eventually defeated France. Had he succeeded, the European system would have been unipolar. But after Napoleon's defeat in 1815 the Congress of Vienna restored the old multipolar order, with five major powers balancing one another: Britain, Russia, France, Prussia, and Austria. These five powers often shifted alliances to prevent any one of them from dominating the continent. From 1815 to 1870, the European system could be characterized as a "loose multipolarity."

When Germany and Italy unified, Europe now had six major powers. The big change came with the unification of Germany in 1871. Prior to this, "Germany" consisted of 37 states and had been an arena of international politics in which others intervened. After 1871, Germany became a united actor. Furthermore, it was located right in the center of Europe, which had tremendous geopolitical consequences. From a structural perspective, a united Germany could be a problem if it were either too strong or too weak. If Germany were strong enough to defend itself against both Russia and France at the same time, it would also be strong enough to defeat either Russia or France alone; but if Germany were not strong enough to defeat Russia and France simultaneously, it might suffer the same fate as Poland did at the hands of its neighboring great powers: invasion, dismemberment, or domination.

During this second structural phase, German power steadily rose. For a while, Bismarck's brilliant diplomacy prevented a newly unified, rapidly growing German state in the center of Europe from destabilizing the system. But a combination of the growing wariness of Germany in the other capitals of Europe and a series of missteps by Bismarck's successors ushered in the third structural phase. By 1907 the European balance of power had lost all flexibility. Two sets of alliances developed and rigidified: the Triple Entente (Great Britain, France, and Russia) and the Triple Alliance (Germany, Austria-Hungary, and Italy). The

TABLE 1

Structural Changes in the Pre–World War I Balance of Power

1815–1871	Loose Multipolarity
1871–1907	Rise of Germany
1907–1914	Bipolarity of Alliances

polarization of the European balance of power into two tight blocs resulted in an inability to maintain balance, which, as we shall shortly see, contributed significantly to the outbreak of World War I.

Process

We cannot explain structural changes in the European system by looking solely at changes in the distribution of power. *Process*, which classical realists and constructivists emphasize, was crucially important. If we look at the ways in which the system worked, and if we take into account the changes in European culture and ideas that influenced patterns of relations among states, we can distinguish five different phases (see Table 2).

Following Napoleon, European great powers sought to maintain order in part by holding periodic congresses in which they deliberated jointly and attempted to strike agreements that would both preserve the balance of power and stem the revolutionary tide of liberal nationalism. This system came to be known as the *Concert of Europe*. The Concert came into effect at the *Congress of Vienna,* at which the victors of Waterloo brought France back into the fold and agreed on certain rules of the game to equalize the players. From 1815 to 1822 the Concert was active and effective. European states met frequently to deal with disputes and to maintain an equilibrium. They accepted certain interventions to keep governments in power domestically when their replacements might lead to a destabilizing reorientation of policy. From 1822 to 1854 the Concert was less active and somewhat less effective. Ultimately, liberal nationalist revolutions challenged the practices of providing territorial compensation or restoring governments to maintain equilibrium, and the Concert ceased to function. As constructivists point out, the ideas of nationalism became too strong to allow such an easy cutting up of cheeses.

The third period in the nineteenth-century balance-of-power system, from 1854 to 1870, was far less moderate and was marked by five wars. One, the Crimean War, was to some extent a classic balance-of-power war in which France and Britain sought to prevent Russia from gaining at the expense of a declining Ottoman Empire. The other conflicts, however, were related to the unification of Italy and Germany. Political leaders abandoned old rules and began to use nationalism instrumentally. Bismarck, for

TABLE 2

Processes of the Pre–World War I Balance of Power

1815–1822	Concert of Europe
1822–1854	Loose Concert
1854–1871	Nationalism and the Unification of Germany and Italy
1871–1890	Bismarck's Revived Concert
1890–1914	The Loss of Flexibility

example, was not an ideological German nationalist. He was, in fact, a deeply conservative man who wanted Germany united under the Prussian monarchy. But he was quite prepared to use nationalist appeals and to engineer nationalist wars against Denmark, Austria, and France to bring this about. He returned to a more conservative style once he had accomplished his goals.

The fourth period, 1871 to 1890, was the Bismarckian balance of power in which the new Prussian-led Germany played the key role. Bismarck played flexibly with a variety of alliance partners and tried to divert France into imperialistic adventures overseas so as to distract its attention from the provinces of Alsace and Lorraine that it lost to Germany at the conclusion of the Franco-Prussian War. He limited German imperialism in order to keep the balancing act in Europe centered on Berlin. The hallmarks of Bismarck's alliance system were its flexibility and its complexity. The former made the resulting balance-of-power system stable because it allowed for occasional crises or conflicts without causing the whole edifice to crumble. But its complexity was its weakness. Its smooth operation required an expert juggler such as Bismarck who was able to keep several balls in the air. Bismarck's successors were not as gifted. They failed to renew his treaty with Russia, and they mistakenly allowed Britain, France, and Russia to gradually come together. They also failed to put the brakes on Austrian confrontations with Russia over the Balkans. Finally, Germany became involved in overseas imperialism and attempted to challenge Britain's naval supremacy. These policies exacerbated fears of rising German power and further polarized the system.

While each of these five phases has distinct characteristics, the characteristics themselves and the changes from one phase to another were driven by a number of powerful trends that proceeded more or less unabated throughout the entire period, affecting states' goals, the instruments at their disposal for pursuing them, and their incentives for cooperation. The most important of these trends were the growth of liberalism and the growth of nationalism. As a result of these, the state and the ruler gradually ceased being the same. More than a century before Waterloo, Louis XIV had famously said: "*L'état, c'est moi*" ("I am the state")—and no one had contradicted him. By the early nineteenth century, such a claim would have triggered an uproar. Napoleon may have failed to change the *structure* of European politics by failing to establish French hegemony, but he succeeded in changing the *process* by spreading revolutionary ideas across Europe. The Congress of Vienna held these ideas at bay for a while, but the volcanic forces of nationalism and liberalism erupted in the revolutions of 1848, signaling the beginning of the end of monarchical rule.

As the century progressed, both peoples and leaders began to see themselves differently. The nationalist challenge to the legitimacy of dynastic rulers led to some strange alliances that defied the classical balance of power. For example, in 1866, France failed to support Austria when it was attacked by Prussia, a major error from a structural realist point of view. France was

STRUCTURE AND PROCESS

Statesmen regularly judged the European balance to be satisfactory or unsatisfactory on the basis of factors that had little or nothing directly to do with power and its distribution—e.g., the rank and status a state enjoyed, its honor and prestige, whether it was considered worthy of alliance, whether it was allowed a voice in international questions, etc. It helps explain how crises could and did arise when the balance of power was not affected or threatened, but the balance of satisfactions was. It shows how devices other than power-political ones—international laws, Concert practices, alliances used as devices for restraining one's ally—were more common and more useful in promoting and preserving the European equilibrium than power-political ones such as rival alliances or blocking coalitions.

—*Paul Schroeder, "The Nineteenth Century System"*[6]

opposed to Austrian repression of nationalism in the part of Italy that Austria occupied. Bismarck played on the nationalistic views of other German states in unifying Germany under Prussian leadership, but nationalism became a restraint on what could be done later. When Bismarck took Alsace-Lorraine from France in 1871, he created nationalist resentment in France that prevented France and Germany from becoming potential alliance partners in the future. As constructivist approaches point out, the new ideologies changed states' goals and made the process of international politics less moderate over the course of the nineteenth century.

There were also changes in the means. The application of new industrial technology to military purposes produced massively powerful yet inflexible instruments of war. The development of railways made possible moving large numbers of troops from one place to another very quickly, but doing so required precise scheduling, which reduced crisis stability by reducing mobilization options and giving first-movers a crucial advantage in the first few days of war. The development of machine guns, heavy artillery, and trench warfare made a mockery of the idea of short, sharp, limited wars that Bismarck had used so successfully in the 1860s. Changes in technology, just like changes in ideas, altered leaders' perceptions of what was possible and what was desirable. Thus we need to look at both structure and process if we want to understand the changes in the nineteenth-century balance-of-power system that led to World War I.

Follow Up

- Henry A. Kissinger, *A World Restored: Metternich, Castlereagh and the Problems of Peace, 1812–1822* (New York: Grosset & Dunlap, 1964).
- John Lowe, *The Great Powers, Imperialism and the German Problem, 1865–1925* (London and New York: Routledge, 1994), pp. 202–239.

A MODERN SEQUEL

The so-called German problem from the nineteenth century reemerged in debates when East and West Germany were reunified in 1990. At first, Foreign Minister Eduard Shevardnadze of the Soviet Union argued that the reunification of Germany would profoundly destabilize the balance of power in Europe. Leaders once again asked, "How many German-speaking states are consistent with stability in Europe?" Over time, that question has had different answers. As we have seen, the Congress of Vienna in 1815 included thirty-seven German-speaking states. Bismarck felt there should be two, not one. He did not want the Austrians included in his new German empire because he feared they would dilute Prussian control of the new state. Hitler had a different answer: one, which would be the center of a world empire, thus leading to World War II. In 1945, the victorious Allies eventually decided on three: East Germany, West Germany, and Austria. When asked how many Germanys there should be, one Frenchman at the end of World War II allegedly quipped, "I love Germany so much that the more there are, the better."

The decline of Soviet power in Eastern Europe in the late 1980s ended the bipolar structure of postwar politics and made possible Germany's reunification. But reunification created new anxieties about the union of 80 million people with Europe's largest economy located in the heart of the continent. Would Germans search for a new role? Would they again cast about, turn eastward, and then westward? Would they be drawn into the countries to their east where German influence had always been strong? John Mearsheimer, a University of Chicago political scientist, said the answer was "back to the future." He relied on structural realist analysis to reach pessimistic conclusions that the future will be like the past because the structure of the situation is similar to the past.

But things have changed in three ways. At the structural level, the United States is involved in Europe, and the United States is nearly four times the size of the reunified Germany. Structuralists worry that the Americans will not stay involved. With the Cold War over, at some point the Americans may turn isolationist and go home. But there are important nonstructural changes as well. The process of international politics in Europe has been transformed by the development of new institutions that liberals emphasize. The European Union unites Germany and other European states in a way in which they were never tied together before. A third change is not at the system level, but at the domestic level. Constructivists point out that Germany's domestic politics represent a half century of democracy, and changes in popular values have transformed a warfare state into a welfare state. The Germany that caused trouble in the heart of Europe in 1870, 1914, and 1939 was not democratic. Which of these approaches, structural or process or domestic, will best predict the future of Europe? We should pay attention to all three, but thus far predictions based on process and domestic change seemed to have fared best.

CHRONOLOGIES: EUROPE

The Seventeenth Century

1618–1648	Thirty Years' War: conflict between Catholic and Protestant Europe; last of the great religious wars; Germany devastated
1643–1715	Louis XIV, king of France
1648	Peace of Westphalia; end of Thirty Years' War
1649–1660	English king Charles I beheaded; Commonwealth under Oliver Cromwell
1652–1678	Series of Anglo-French and Anglo-Dutch wars for supremacy of the seas
1660	Stuart restoration in England; accession of Charles II
1682–1725	Peter the Great begins "westernization" of Russia
1683	Turkish siege of Vienna repulsed
1685	Louis XIV revokes Edict of Nantes; persecution of French Protestants
1688–1689	Glorious Revolution in England
1688–1697	War of the League of Augsburg; general war against Louis XIV

The Eighteenth Century

1700–1721	Great Northern War: Russia, Poland, and Denmark oppose Swedish supremacy in the Baltic; Russia emerges as a European power
1701–1714	War of the Spanish Succession and the Treaty of Utrecht, which result in the permanent separation of French and Spanish thrones; further decline of French power
1707	Great Britain formed by union of England and Scotland
1740–1748	War of the Austrian Succession
1756–1763	Seven Years' War: Britain and France in colonial wars; France ejected from Canada and India; Britain emerges as world's major colonial power
1775–1783	War of the American Revolution
1789–1799	French Revolution
1799	Coup d'état by Napoleon Bonaparte in France
1799–1815	Napoleonic Wars make France preeminent power on European continent

The Nineteenth Century

1801	United Kingdom formed by union of Great Britain and Ireland
1804–1814	Napoleon I, emperor of France
1806	End of Holy Roman Empire; imperial title renounced by Francis II

(*Continued*)

- 1810 Kingdom of Holland incorporated in French Empire
- 1812 French invasion of Russia; destruction of Napoleon's army
- 1814–1815 Congress of Vienna: monarchies reestablished in Europe
- 1815 Napoleon escapes from Elba but is defeated by British and Prussian armies in the Battle of Waterloo
- 1833–1871 Unification of Germany
- 1837–1901 Victoria, queen of England: period of great industrial expansion and prosperity
- 1848 Revolutions in France, Germany, Hungary, and Bohemia; publication of Karl Marx's *Communist Manifesto*
- 1848–1916 Franz Joseph, emperor of Austria; becomes ruler of the Austro-Hungarian Empire in 1867
- 1852–1870 Napoleon III, emperor of Second French Empire
- 1853–1856 Crimean War: Britain and France support Ottomans in war with Russia
- 1855–1881 Alexander II, tsar of Russia
- 1859–1870 Italian political unification, led by Giuseppe Garibaldi
- 1861 Emancipation of Russian serfs by Tsar Alexander II
- 1862–1890 Otto von Bismarck, premier and chancellor of Germany, forges German Empire
- 1864–1905 Russian expansion in Poland, Balkans, and central Asia
- 1867 Austro-Hungarian Empire founded
- 1870–1871 Franco-Prussian War: German invasion of France; Third French Republic created
- 1870–1914 European imperialism at peak; industrial growth; rise of labor movements and Marxism
- 1871 Paris Commune: Paris, a revolutionary center, establishes own government and wars with national government
- 1878 Congress of Berlin: division of much of Ottoman Empire among Austria, Russia, and Britain
- 1881 Alexander II of Russia assassinated
- 1882 Triple Alliance of Germany, Austria-Hungary, and Italy; renewed in 1907
- 1899–1902 Boer War in South Africa

The First Decade of the Twentieth Century

- 1904 Dual Entente between Britain and France
- 1904–1905 Russo-Japanese War; Russia defeated; Japan emerges as world power
- 1907 Russia joins Britain and France in Triple Entente

THE ORIGINS OF WORLD WAR I

World War I killed more than 15 million people. In one battle, the Somme, 1.3 million were killed and wounded. Compare that to 36,000 casualties when Bismarck defeated Austria in 1866. The United States lost about 55,000 troops in both Korea and Vietnam. World War I was a horrifying war of trenches, barbed wire, machine guns, and artillery that ground up a generation of Europe's youth. It not only destroyed people, it destroyed three European empires: German, Austro-Hungarian, and Russian. Until World War I, the global balance of power was centered in Europe. After World War I, Europe still mattered, but the United States and Japan emerged as major players. World War I also ushered in the Russian Revolution in 1917 and the beginning of the ideological battles that racked the twentieth century.

How could such an event happen? Prince Bernhard von Bülow, the German chancellor from 1900 to 1909, met with his successor, Theobald von Bethmann Hollweg, in the chancellor's palace in Berlin shortly after the war broke out. Here is how von Bülow described what he remembered:

> Bethmann stood in the center of the room; shall I ever forget his face, the look in his eyes? There is a picture by some celebrated English painter, which shows the wretched scapegoat with a look of ineffable anguish in its eyes, such pain as I now saw in Bethmann's. For an instant we neither of us spoke. At last I said to him, "Well, tell me, at least, how it all happened." He raised his long, thin arms to heaven and answered in a dull, exhausted voice: "Oh, if I only knew!" In many later polemics on war guilt I have often wished it had been possible to produce a snapshot of Bethmann Hollweg standing there at the moment he said those words. Such a photograph would have been the best proof that this wretched man had never wanted war.[7]

Generations of historians have examined the origins of World War I and tried to explain why war came. As we will see, it is impossible to isolate one cause, but it is possible to break the question down into distinct levels. At each of these levels, the balance of power—as *a multipolar system* and as the *policy* of separate states and individual leaders—is essential to an understanding of the war's outbreak. As the alliance system became less flexible, the balance of power became less multipolar and the likelihood of war increased.

Three Levels of Analysis

Parts of the answer lie at each of the three levels of analysis. Parsimony suggests we start with the simplest causes, see how much they explain, and go on to more complexity as needed. Thus we look first at the system-level explanations, both the structure and the process; then at the domestic societal level; and finally at the individuals. Then we will use counterfactual thought experiments to see how the pieces fit together to explain World War I.

Serbian nationalist Gavrilo Princip kills Austrian archduke Franz Ferdinand and his wife Sophie, Duchess of Hohenberg, in Sarajevo, June 28, 1914

At the structural level, there were two key elements: the rise of German power and the increased rigidity in the alliance systems. The rise of German power was truly impressive. German heavy industry surpassed that of Great Britain in the 1890s, and the growth of German gross national product at the beginning of the century was twice that of Great Britain's. In the 1860s, Britain had 25 percent of the world's industrial production, but by 1913 its share had shrunk to 10 percent, and Germany's share had risen to 15 percent. Germany transformed some of its industrial strength into military capability, including a massive naval armaments program. A strategic aim of Germany's "Tirpitz Plan" of 1911 was to build the second largest navy in the world, thereby advancing itself as a world power. This expansion alarmed Britain's First Lord of the Admiralty, Winston Churchill. Britain began to fear becoming isolated and worried about how it would defend its far-flung empire. These fears were increased during the Boer War due to German sympathy for the Boers, the Dutch settlers in South Africa, against whom Britain was fighting at the end of the century.

In 1907, Sir Eyre Crowe, permanent secretary of the British Foreign Office, wrote a document famous in the history of British foreign policy, a long memorandum in which he tried to interpret German foreign policy. He concluded that although German policy was vague and confused, Britain clearly could not allow one country to dominate the continent of Europe. Crowe argued that the British response was nearly a law of nature.

Britain's response to Germany's rising power contributed to the second structural cause of the war: the increasing rigidity in the alliance systems in Europe. In 1904, parting from its geographically semi-isolated position as a balancer off the coast of Europe, Britain moved toward an alliance with France. In 1907, the Anglo-French partnership broadened to include Russia (already allied with France) and became known as the Triple Entente. Germany, seeing itself encircled, tightened its relations with Austria-Hungary. As the alliances became more rigid, diplomatic flexibility was lost. The balance of power could no longer operate through the shifting alignments that characterized the balance of power during Bismarck's day. Instead, the major powers wrapped themselves around two poles. The tightening of alliances accentuated the security dilemma that defensive realists emphasize in their analyses.

What about changes in the process? One was the continued rise of nationalism. In Eastern Europe there was a movement calling for all Slavic-speaking peoples to come together. Pan-Slavism threatened both the Ottoman and Austro-Hungarian empires, which each had large Slavic populations. A nationalistic hatred of Slavs arose in Germany. German authors wrote about the inevitability of the Teutonic-Slavic battles, and schoolbooks inflamed nationalist passions. Nationalism proved to be stronger than socialism when it came to bonding working classes together and stronger than the capitalism that bound bankers together. Indeed, it proved stronger than family ties among the monarchs. Just before the war broke out, the kaiser wrote to Russian tsar Nicholas II (1868–1918) and appealed to him to avoid war. He addressed his cousin as "Dear Nicky" and signed it "Yours, Willie." The kaiser hoped that because war was impending over the assassination of a fellow royal family member, the Austrian archduke Franz Ferdinand, the tsar would see things the same way he did. But by then nationalism had overcome any sense of aristocratic or monarchical solidarity, and that family telegram did nothing to prevent war.

A second cause for the loss of moderation in the early twentieth-century balance of power was a rise in complacency about peace. This is an example of the importance of changing ideas that constructivists emphasize. The great powers had not been involved in a war in Europe for 40 years. There had been crises—in Morocco in 1905–1906, in Bosnia in 1908, in Morocco again in 1911, and the Balkan wars in 1912—but they had all been manageable. However, the diplomatic compromises that resolved these conflicts caused frustration. Afterward, there was a tendency to ask, "Why should my side back down? Why didn't we make the other side give up more?" Additionally, there was growing acceptance of social Darwinism. Charles Darwin's ideas of survival of the fittest made good sense as a way of explaining why some genetic traits arise and others disappear in natural species over the course of many generations, but they were misapplied to human society and to unique events. Darwin's ideas were used to justify the view that "the strong *should* prevail." And if the strong should prevail, why worry about peace? Long wars seemed unlikely, and many leaders believed short, decisive wars won by the strong would be a welcome change.

A third contributing factor to the loss of flexibility in the early twentieth-century balance of power was German policy. As Eyre Crowe said, it was vague and confusing. There was a terrible clumsiness about the kaiser's policy of seeking greater power that offensive realists focus upon. The Germans were no different from other colonial powers in having "world ambitions," but they managed to press them forward in a way that antagonized everybody at the same time—just the opposite of the way Bismarck played the system in the 1870s and 1880s. The kaiser focused too much on hard power and neglected soft power. The Germans antagonized the British by starting a naval arms race (Figure 1). They antagonized the Russians over issues in Turkey and the Balkans. They antagonized the French over a protectorate in Morocco. The kaiser tried to shock Britain into a friendship, believing that if he scared Britain enough, it would realize how important Germany was and pursue improved relations. Instead, he scared the British first into the arms of the French, and then into the arms of the Russians. So by 1914, the Germans thought they had to break out of this encirclement and thereby deliberately accepted the risk of war. Thus the rise of nationalism, increased complacency, social Darwinism, and German policy all contributed to the loss of moderation in the international system and helped contribute to the onset of World War I.

The second level of analysis allows us to examine what was happening in domestic society, politics, and government prior to World War I. We can safely reject one explanation at that level: Russian revolutionary Vladimir Lenin's argument that the war was caused by capitalism. In Lenin's view, World War I was simply the final stage of capitalist imperialism. But the war did not arise out of imperialist conflicts on the colonial peripheries, as Lenin had expected. In 1898, Britain and France confronted each other at Fashoda in the Sudan as the British tried to complete a north-south line from South Africa to Egypt, while the French tried to create an east-west line of colonies in Africa. If war had occurred then, it might have fit Lenin's explanation. But, in fact, the war broke out sixteen years later in Europe, and even then bankers and businessmen strongly resisted it. Bankers believed the war would be bad for business. Sir Edward Grey, the British foreign minister, thought he had to follow Eyre Crowe's advice and that Britain had to prevent Germany from gaining mastery of the European balance of power. But Grey also worried about getting the London bankers to go along with declaring war. We can therefore reject the Leninist explanation. But two other domestic causes need to be taken more seriously: the internal crises of the declining Austro-Hungarian and Ottoman empires, and the domestic political situation in Germany.

Both Austria-Hungary and Ottoman Turkey were multinational empires and were therefore threatened by the rise of nationalism. In addition, the Ottoman government was very weak, very corrupt, and an easy target for nationalist groups in the Balkans that wanted to free themselves from centuries of Turkish rule. The Balkan wars of 1912 pushed the Turks out, but in the next year the Balkan states fell to war among themselves while dividing the

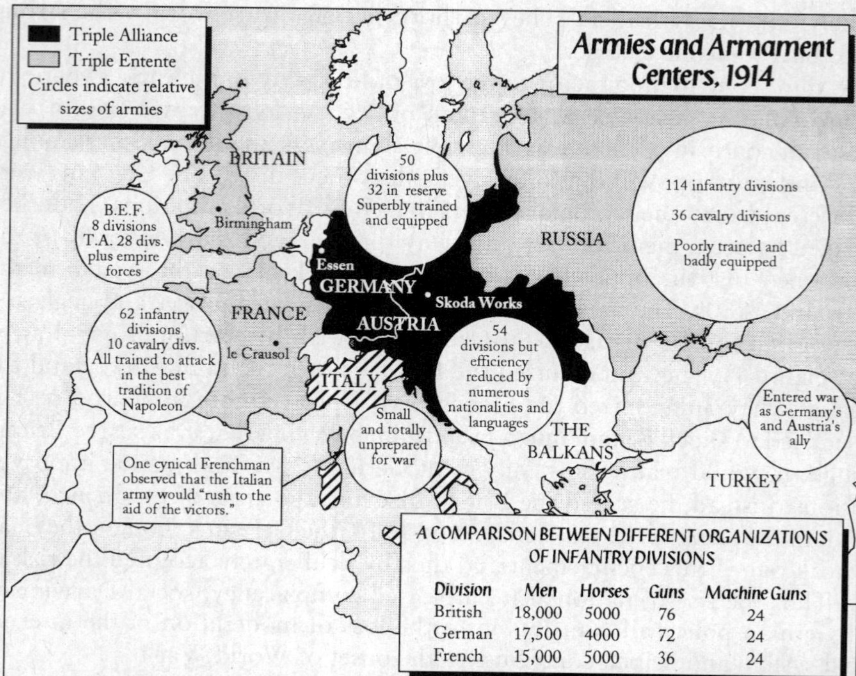

A COMPARISON BETWEEN DIFFERENT ORGANIZATIONS OF INFANTRY DIVISIONS

Division	Men	Horses	Guns	Machine Guns
British	18,000	5000	76	24
German	17,500	4000	72	24
French	15,000	5000	36	24

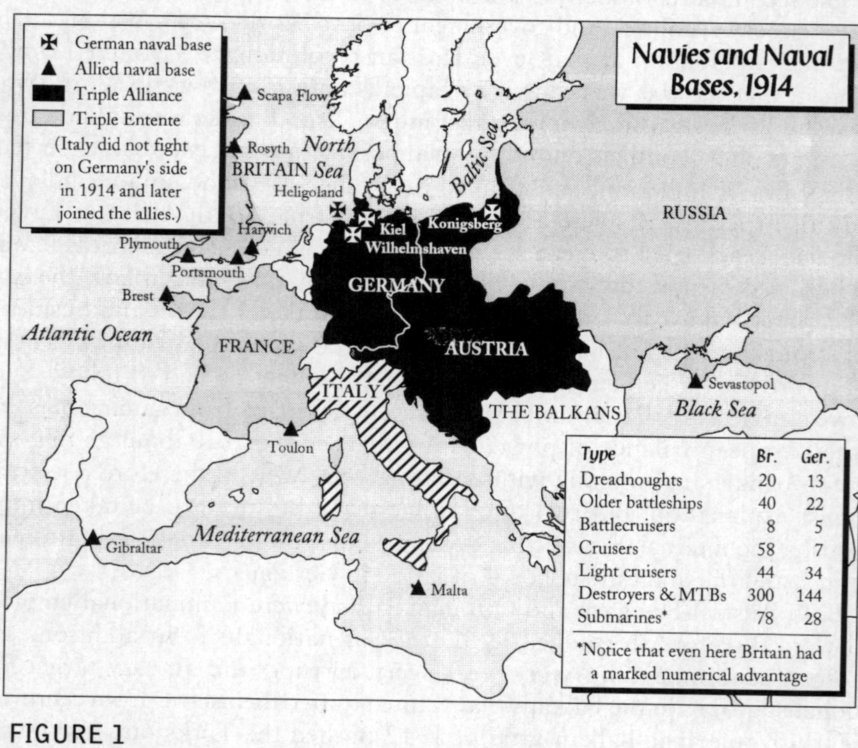

Type	Br.	Ger.
Dreadnoughts	20	13
Older battleships	40	22
Battlecruisers	8	5
Cruisers	58	7
Light cruisers	44	34
Destroyers & MTBs	300	144
Submarines*	78	28

*Notice that even here Britain had a marked numerical advantage

FIGURE 1

The European Balance of Military Power in 1914

THE KAISER'S REACTION TO BRITAIN'S DECLARATION OF WAR

Edward VII [the kaiser's uncle and king of England, 1901–1910] in the grave is still stronger than I, who am alive! And to think there have been people who believed England could be won over or pacified with this or that petty measure!!! . . . Now this whole trickery must be ruthlessly exposed and the mask of Christian pacifism roughly and publicly torn from the face [of Britain], and the pharisaical sham peace put in the pillory!! And our consuls in Turkey and India, agents and so forth, must fire the whole Mohammedan world to fierce revolt against this hateful, lying, unprincipled nation of shopkeepers; for if we are to bleed to death, England will at least lose India.

—*Kaiser Wilhelm II*[9]

spoils. These conflicts whetted the appetite of some Balkan states to fight Austria; if the Turks could be pushed out, then why not the Austrians too?

Serbia took the lead among the Balkan states. Austria feared disintegration from this nationalistic pressure and worried about the loss of status that would result. In the end, Austria went to war against Serbia not because a Serb assassinated its archduke, Franz Ferdinand (1863–1914), but because Austria wanted to weaken Serbia and prevent it from becoming a magnet for nationalism among the Balkan Slavs. General Conrad von Hötzendorf, the Austrian chief of staff in 1914, laid bare his motives very clearly: "For this reason, and not as vengeance for the assassination, Austria-Hungary must draw the sword against Serbia. . . . The monarchy had been seized by the throat and had to choose between allowing itself to be strangled, and making a last effort to prevent its destruction."[8] Disintegration of an empire because of nationalism was the more profound cause of the war; the slain Franz Ferdinand was a pretext.

Another important domestic-level explanation of World War I lay in the politics of Germany. German historian Fritz Fischer and his followers argue that Germany's social problems were a key cause of the war. According to Fischer, Germany's efforts toward world hegemony were an attempt by German elites to distract attention from the poor domestic integration of German society. He notes that Germany was ruled by a domestic coalition of landed aristocrats and some very large industrial capitalists called the Coalition of Rye and Iron. This ruling coalition used expansionist policies to provide foreign adventures instead of domestic reform—circuses in place of bread. They viewed expansionism as an alternative to social democracy. Internal economic and social tensions are not sufficient to explain World War I, but they do help explain one source of the pressure that Germany put on the international system after 1890.

A final domestic-level explanation appeals to the crisis instability of the situation in the summer of 1914. Military leaders in all countries shared a "cult of the offensive" favoring rapid mobilization and deployment, dramatic strategies involving sudden flanking movements of armies or dramatic breakthrough assaults, and freewheeling tactics of maneuver. In fact, as we have seen, the prevailing military technology of the day did not favor the offense, but European leaders believed that it did (a phenomenon we can explain at the individual level of analysis by noting that generals frequently expect the next war to look like the last, and the most recent large-scale European war—the Franco-Prussian War of 1870–1871—was indeed a freewheeling affair). Once the July crisis hit, leaders felt enormous pressure to get in the first blow. Of course, this particular explanation does not help us understand why Europe sat on a powderkeg. It does, however, help us understand why the spark in the Balkans traveled so quickly along the fuse.

What about the first level of analysis, the role of individuals? What distinguished the leadership on the eve of World War I was its mediocrity. The Austro-Hungarian emperor, Franz Joseph (1830–1916), was a tired old man who was putty in the hands of General Conrad and Count Leopold von Berchtold, his duplicitous foreign minister. Ironically, Franz Ferdinand, the crown prince who was assassinated at Sarajevo, would have been a restraining force, for the potential heir had liberal political views. In Russia, Tsar Nicholas II was an isolated autocrat who spent most of his time resisting change at home. He was served by incompetent foreign and defense ministers and was strongly influenced by his sickly and neurotic wife. Most important was Kaiser Wilhelm II (1859–1941), who had a great sense of inferiority. He was a blusterer, a weak man who was extremely emotional. He led Germany into a risky policy without any skill or consistency. As political scientist Richard Ned Lebow puts it:

> [Wilhelm] II did not want war, if only because he did not trust his nerves not to give way under the strain of any really critical situation. The moment there was danger, his majesty would become uncomfortably conscious that he could never lead an army into battle. He was well aware that he was neurasthenic. His more menacing jingo speeches were intended to give the foreigner the impression that here was another Frederick the Great or Napoleon.[10]

It did not help the kaiser to make sound decisions, either, that sycophantic German diplomats were filing overly rosy reports from most other great power capitals to please their vindictive superiors in the foreign ministry.

Personality did make a difference. There was something about the leaders, the kaiser in particular, that made them significant contributory causes of the war. The relationships among some of the systemic, societal, and individual causes are illustrated in Figure 2.

Was War Inevitable?

When several causes exist, each of which is sufficient, we call a situation *overdetermined*. If World War I was overdetermined, does that mean it was inevitable? The answer is no; war was not inevitable until it actually broke out in August 1914. And even then it was not inevitable that four years of carnage had to follow.

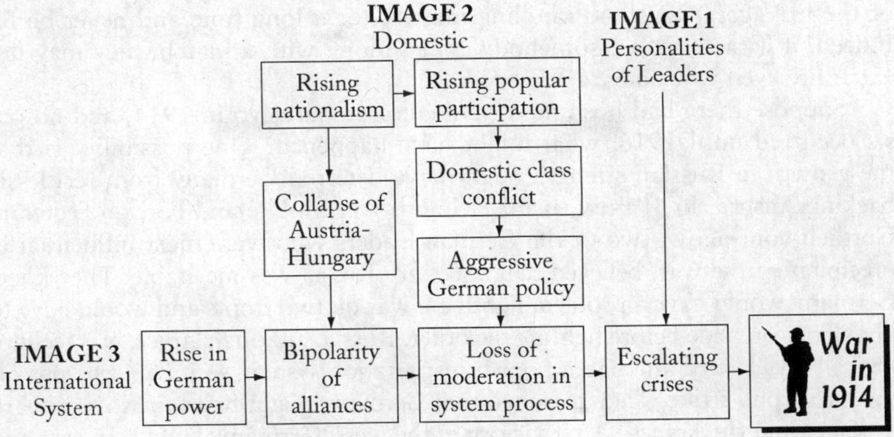

FIGURE 2
Causes of World War I

Let us distinguish three types of causes in terms of their proximity in time to the event we are studying. The most remote are *deep causes*, then come *intermediate causes*, and those immediately before the event are *precipitating causes*. By analogy, ask how the lights came to be on in your room. The precipitating cause is that you flicked the switch, the intermediate cause is that someone wired the building, and the deep cause is that Thomas Edison discovered how to distribute electricity. Another analogy is building a fire: The logs are the deep cause, the kindling and paper are the intermediate cause, and the actual striking of the match is the precipitating cause.

In World War I, the deep causes were changes in the balance of power and certain aspects of the domestic political systems. Especially important reasons were the rise of German strength, the development of a bipolar alliance system, the rise of nationalism and the resultant destruction of two declining empires, and German politics. The intermediate causes were German policy, the rise in complacency about peace, and the personal idiosyncrasies of the leaders. The precipitating cause was the assassination of Franz Ferdinand at Sarajevo by a Serbian terrorist and its rapid escalation owing to acute crisis-instability.

Looking back, things always look inevitable. Indeed, we might say that if the assassination had not occurred, some other precipitating incident would have caused the war. Some say precipitating events are like buses—they come along every ten minutes. Thus the specific event at Sarajevo was not all that important; some incident would probably have occurred sooner or later. This type of argument can be tested by counterfactual history. We can ask, "What if?" and "What might have been?" as we look carefully at the history of the period. What if there had been no assassination in Sarajevo? What if the Social Democrats had come to power in Germany? There is also the issue of probability. The deep and intermediate causes suggested a high probability of war, but a high probability is not the same as inevitability. Using the metaphor of the fire again, logs and kindling may sit for a long time and never be lit. Indeed, if it rains before somebody comes along with a match, they may not catch fire even when a Sarajevo occurs.

Suppose there had been no assassination in Sarajevo in 1914, and no crisis occurred until 1916; what might have happened? One possibility is that the growth in Russian strength might have deterred Germany from recklessly backing Austria. In 1914, General Helmuth von Moltke and Foreign Secretary Gottlieb von Jagow, two of the German leaders who were most influential in precipitating the war, believed that war with Russia was inevitable. They knew Germany would have a problem fighting a war on two fronts and would have to knock out one side before fighting the other. Russia, although larger, was technologically backward and had a poor transportation system, so it could be put off for the second strike. They reasoned that Germany ought first to rush westward to knock out the French. After victory in the west, Germany could turn east and take its time to defeat the Russians. Indeed, that was the Schlieffen Plan (Figure 3), the war plan of the German general staff, which called for a rapid sweep through Belgium (violating Belgian neutrality in the process) to knock out France quickly, and then to turn east.

But this strategy might have become obsolete by 1916 because Russia was using French money to build railroads. In the 1890s it would have taken the Russians two or three months before they could have transported all their troops to the German front, giving Germany ample time to fight France first. By 1910, that time had shrunk to eighteen days, and the German planners knew they no longer had a large margin of safety. By 1916, the margin would have been gone and Germany might have had to drop its two-front strategy. Consequently, some German leaders thought that a war in 1914 was better than a war later. They wanted to seize the crisis to wage and win a preventive war.

If no assassination and crisis had occurred in 1914, and the world had made it to 1916 without a war, it is possible the Germans might have felt deterred, unable to risk a two-front war. They might have been more careful before giving Austria a blank check to deal with Serbia as it liked. Or they might have dropped the Schlieffen Plan and concentrated on a war in the east only. Or they might have come to terms with Great Britain or changed their view that the offense had the advantage in warfare. In summary, in another two years, a variety of changes related to Russian strength might have prevented the war. Without war, German industrial strength would have continued to grow. Ironically, without war, the British historian A. J. P. Taylor has speculated, Germany might have won mastery over Europe. Germany might have become so strong that France and Britain would have been deterred.

We can also raise counterfactuals about what might have happened in Britain's internal affairs if two more years had passed without war. In *The Strange Death of Liberal England*, historian George Dangerfield tells of Britain's domestic turmoil. The Liberal Party was committed to withdrawing British troops from Ireland while the Conservatives, particularly in Northern Ireland, were bitterly opposed. There was a prospect of mutiny in the British army. If the Ulster Revolt had developed, it is quite plausible that Britain would have been so internally preoccupied that it would not have been able to join the coalition with France and Russia. Certainly many historically significant changes could have occurred in two more years of peace.

What Kind of War?

Another set of counterfactuals raises questions about what *kind* of war would have occurred rather than *whether* a war would have occurred. It is true that Germany's policies frightened its neighbors and that Germany in turn was afraid of being encircled by the Triple Entente, so it is reasonable to assume war was more likely than not. But what kind of war? The war did not have to be what we now remember as World War I. Counterfactually, four other wars were possible.

One was a simple local war. Initially, the kaiser expected a replay of the Bosnian crisis of 1908–1909 when the Germans backed the Austrians, and Austria was therefore able to make Russia stand down in the Balkans. On July 5, 1914, the kaiser promised full support to Austria-Hungary. And with that, he went on vacation. When the kaiser returned from his cruise, he found that

Britain's King George V visits his cousin Kaiser Wilhelm II at Potsdam for a wedding a little more than a year before the outbreak of World War I

the Austrians had filled in the blank check he left them by issuing an ultimatum to Serbia. When he realized that, the kaiser made efforts to keep the war from escalating; hence the Willie-Nicky telegrams referred to earlier. If his efforts had been successful, we might today recall not World War I, but merely a relatively minor Austro-Serbian War of August 1914.

A second counterfactual possibility was a one-front war. When the Russians mobilized their troops, the Germans also mobilized. The kaiser asked General von Moltke whether he could limit the preparations to just the eastern front. Moltke replied that it was impossible, because any change in the timetables for assembling the troops and supplies would create a logistical nightmare. He told the kaiser that if he tried to change the plans, he would have a disorganized mass instead of an army. However, after the war, General Hermann von Staab of the railway division of the German army admitted that it might have been possible, after all, to alter the mobilization schedules successfully. Had the kaiser known that and insisted, there might have been a one-front war.

A third counterfactual is to imagine a two-front war without Britain: Germany and Austria versus France and Russia. If the British had not been there to make the difference, Germany might well have won. It is possible that Britain might not have joined if Germany had not invaded Belgium, although Belgium was not the main cause of Britain entering the war. For some people, like Sir Edward Grey and the Foreign Office, the main reason for entering the war was the danger of German control of the Continent. But Britain was a democracy, and the Liberal Party in the Cabinet was split. The left Liberals opposed war, but when Germany swept through Belgium and violated Belgian neutrality, it allowed the prowar Liberals to overcome the reluctance of the antiwar Liberals and to repair the split in the British Cabinet.

Finally, a fourth counterfactual is a war without the United States. By early 1918, Germany might have won the war if the United States had not tipped the military balance by its entry in 1917. One of the reasons the United States became involved was the German submarine campaign against Allied and American shipping. There was also some German clumsiness: Germany sent a message, now known as the Zimmermann telegram, instructing its embassy in Mexico to approach the Mexican government regarding an alliance against the United States. Washington regarded these intercepted instructions as a hostile act. These factors ensured that the United States would enter the war.

Our counterfactual analysis first suggests ways in which the war might not have occurred in 1914, and second, ways in which the war that occurred did not have to become four years of carnage, which destroyed Europe as the heart of the global balance of power. It suggests that World War I was probable, but not inevitable. Human choices mattered.

The Funnel of Choices

History is path dependent. Events close in over time, degrees of freedom are lost, and the probability of war increases. But the funnel of choices available to leaders might open up again, and degrees of freedom could be regained

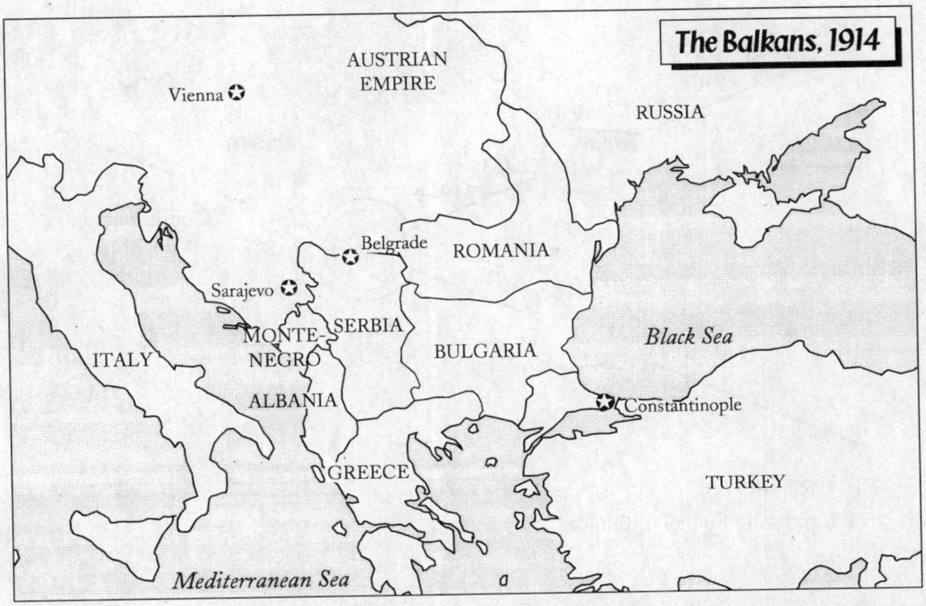

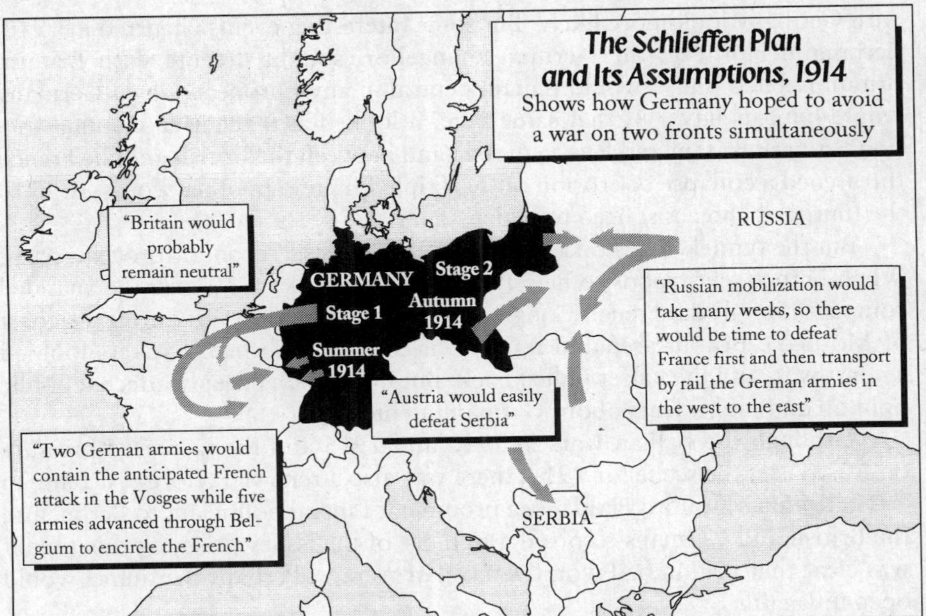

FIGURE 3
Flawed Thinking on the Eve of War

(see Figure 4). If we start in 1898 and ask what was the most likely war in Europe, the answer would have been war between France and Britain, which were eyeball to eyeball in a colonial dispute in Africa. But after the British and French formed the Entente in 1904, a Franco-British war looked less likely. The first Moroccan crisis in 1905 and the Bosnian crisis in 1908 made war

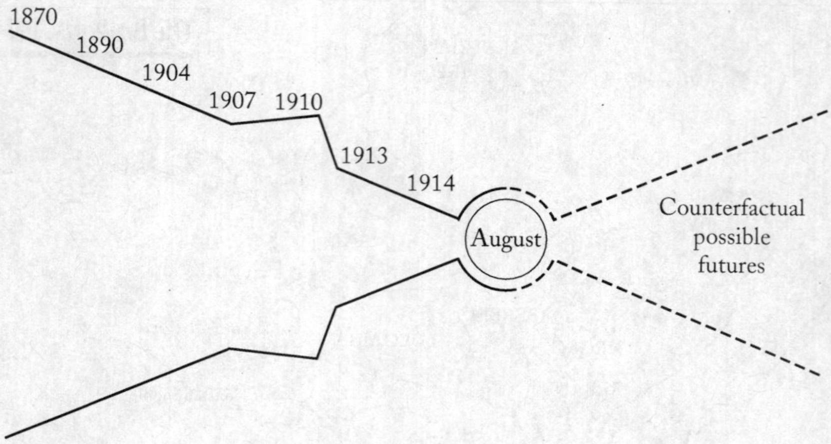

FIGURE 4
The Narrowing Funnel of Choices

with Germany look more likely. But some interesting events occurred in 1910. Bethmann Hollweg, the German chancellor, sought détente with Britain. Britain implied that it would remain neutral in any European war if Germany would limit its navy. At that same time, it looked as if renewed colonial friction between Britain and Russia in Asia and between the British and the French threatened a collapse or erosion of the Triple Entente. In other words, in 1910 the funnel of choices started to widen again.

But the funnel closed once more in 1911 with the second Moroccan crisis. When France sent troops to help the sultan of Morocco, Germany demanded compensation in the French Congo and sent a gunboat to Agadir on the coast of Morocco. Britain prepared its fleet. French and German bankers lobbied against war, and the kaiser pulled back. But these events deeply affected public opinion and raised fears about German intentions.

Although the Balkan wars in 1912 and 1913 and the increased pressure on Austria set the scene for 1914, there was also a renewed effort at détente in 1912. Britain sent Lord Haldane, a prominent Liberal politician, to Berlin, and the British and Germans resolved a number of the issues. Also, by this time it was clear that Britain had won the naval arms race. Perhaps the funnel would open up again.

In June 1914, the feeling that relations were improving was strong enough for Britain to send four of its great dreadnought battleships to Kiel, Germany, for a state visit. If Britain had thought war was about to occur, the last thing it would have done was put four of its prime battleships in an enemy harbor. Clearly, the British were not thinking about war at that point. In fact, on June 28, British and German sailors were walking together along the quay in Kiel when they heard the news that a Serbian terrorist had shot an Austrian archduke in a faraway place called Sarajevo. History has its surprises, and once again, *probable* is not the same as *inevitable*.

Lessons of History Again

Can we draw any lessons from this history? We must be careful about lessons. Analogies can mislead, and many myths have been created about World War I. For example, some say World War I was an accidental war. World War I was not purely accidental. Austria went to war deliberately. And if there was to be a war, Germany preferred a war in 1914 to a war later. There were miscalculations over the length and depth of the war, but that is not the same as an accidental war.

It is also said that the war was caused by the arms race in Europe. But by 1912, the naval arms race was over, and Britain had won. While there was concern in Europe about the growing strength of the armies, the view that the war was precipitated directly by the arms race is too simple.

On the other hand, we can draw some valid warnings from the long slide into World War I. One lesson is to pay attention to the process of a balance-of-power system as well as to its structure or distribution of power. Here the constructivists make an important point that some realists miss. Moderation evolves from the process. Stability is not assured by the distribution of power alone. Another useful lesson is to beware of complacency about peace or believing that the next crisis is going to fit the same pattern as the last crisis: The July crisis of 1914 was supposed to be a repeat of the Bosnian crisis of 1908, though clearly it was not. World War I was supposed to be a repeat of the Franco-Prussian War. In addition, the experience of World War I suggests it is important to have military forces that are stable in crisis, without any feeling that one must use them or lose them. The railway timetables were not the major determinants of World War I, but they did make it more difficult for political leaders to buy time for diplomacy.

Today's world is different from the world of 1914 in two important ways: One is that nuclear weapons have made large-scale wars more dangerous, and the other, as constructivists note, is that the ideology of war, the acceptance of war, is much weaker. In 1914, war was thought to be inevitable, a fatalistic view compounded by the social Darwinist argument that war should be welcome because it would clear the air like a good summer storm. On the eve of World War I that was indeed the mood. Winston Churchill's book *The World Crisis* captures this feeling very well:

> There was a strange temper in the air. Unsatisfied by material prosperity, the nations turned fiercely toward strife, internal or external. National passions, unduly exalted in the decline of religion, burned beneath the surface of nearly every land with fierce, if shrouded, fires. Almost one might think the world wished to suffer. Certainly men were everywhere eager to dare.[11]

They dared and they lost, and that is the lesson of 1914.

Follow Up

- Gordon Martel, *The Origins of the First World War* (New York: Pearson Longman, 2008).
- William Mulligan, *The Origins of the First World War* (Cambridge: Cambridge University Press, 2010).
- Kier A. Lieber, "The New History of World War I and What It Means for International Relations Theory," *International Security* 32:2 (Fall 2007), pp. 155–191.

CHRONOLOGY: THE ROAD TO WORLD WAR I

▪ 1905–1906	First Moroccan crisis: Kaiser visits Tangier as Germany attempts to supplant France; settled to France's satisfaction at the Algeciras Conférence
▪ 1908	Austria proclaims annexation of Bosnia and Herzegovina, Slavic territories it had administered since 1878; Serbia threatens war but is powerless without Russian backing; Germany supports Austria-Hungary, deterring Russia
▪ 1911	Second Moroccan crisis: German gunboat *Panther* appears at Agadir in attempt to force France into colonial concessions in other areas in return for German recognition of French claims in Morocco
▪ 1912	First Balkan War: Bulgaria, Serbia, and Greece defeat Turkey and gain Thrace and Salonika; Austria-Hungary helps create Albania as check to Serbian power
▪ 1913	Second Balkan War: Serbia, Greece, and Romania defeat Bulgaria and gain territory at the latter's expense
▪ 1914	
June 28	Assassination of Austrian archduke Franz Ferdinand and his wife at Sarajevo
July 5	Austria seeks and obtains German backing against Serbia
July 23	Austria sends harsh ultimatum to Serbia
July 25	Serbia rejects some terms of ultimatum; seeks Russian support
July 26	British foreign minister Sir Edward Grey proposes conference to resolve the crisis; Germany and Austria reject proposal
July 28	Austria declares war on Serbia
July 29	Austrian forces bombard Belgrade; Russia mobilizes against Austria
July 30	Russia and Austria order general mobilization; French troops withdraw ten kilometers from German border
July 31	Germany delivers ultimatum to Russia, demanding demobilization; Russia does not reply
August 1	Germany declares war on Russia; British fleet mobilizes; France mobilizes as German forces invade Luxembourg
August 2	Germany demands unimpeded passage through Belgium
August 3	Belgium rejects German ultimatum; Germany declares war on France
August 4	German troops march into Belgium; Britain declares war on Germany

STUDY QUESTIONS

1. Was World War I inevitable? If so, why and when? If not, when and how could it have been avoided?
2. How might you apply Waltz's images to the origins of World War I?
3. Which of the following factors do you consider most significant in explaining the outbreak of World War I?
   a. alliance systems
   b. public opinion
   c. military doctrine or military leadership (specify countries)
   d. political leadership (specify countries)
   e. economic pressures or forces
   f. misperception
   g. other (specify)
4. Thucydides argues that the underlying cause of the Peloponnesian War was the growth of Athenian power and the fear this caused in Sparta. To what extent was World War I caused by the growth of German power and the fear this caused in Britain? Or the growth of Russian power and the fear this caused in Germany?
5. To what extent, if any, was World War I "accidental"? Does it make sense to talk about "accidental" wars? What about "unintended" ones? What kind of war was intended? By whom?
6. What do realist, liberal, and constructivist approaches add to our understanding of the origins of World War I?
7. What are some "lessons" from 1914 that might help policy makers avoid war today?

NOTES

1. The Treaty of the Pyrenees (1659), which ended the war between France and Spain that began in 1635, is often considered part of the overall settlement.
2. Kalevi J. Holsti, *Peace and War: Armed Conflicts and International Order, 1648–1989* (Cambridge: Cambridge University Press, 1991), p. 39.
3. Charles Tilly, "War Making and State Making as Organized Crime," in Peter B. Evans, Dietrich Rueschemeyer, and Theda Skocpol, eds., *Bringing the State Back In* (Cambridge: Cambridge University Press, 1985), pp. 169–191.
4. Richard Cobden, *The Political Writings of Richard Cobden* (London: Unwin, 1903; New York: Kraus Reprint, 1969).
5. Winston Churchill, June 22, 1941, to his private secretary, Sir John Colville, quoted in Robert Rhodes James, ed., *Churchill Speaks: Winston Churchill in Peace and War: Collected Speeches 1897–1963* (New York: Chelsea, 1980).
6. Paul Schroeder, "The Nineteenth Century System: Balance of Power or Political Equilibrium?" *Swords & Ploughshares* 4:1 (October 1989), p. 4.

7. Bernhard von Bülow, *Memoirs of Prince von Bülow 1909–1919* (Boston: Little, Brown, 1932), pp. 165–166.
8. Baron Conrad von Hötzendorf, quoted in Sidney Fay, *The Origins of the World War*, vol. 2 (New York: Macmillan, 1929), pp. 185–186.
9. Kaiser Wilhelm II, quoted in Richard Ned Lebow, *Between Peace and War: The Nature of International Crisis*, (Baltimore: Johns Hopkins University Press, 1981), p. 139.
10. Lebow, *Between Peace and War,* p. 144.
11. Winston Churchill, *The World Crisis* (New York: Scribner's, 1923), p. 188.

PHOTO CREDITS

Credits are listed in order of appearance:

akg-images/Alamy

Hulton Royals Collection/Getty Images

Design Pics/Newscom.

MAP CREDIT

Maps are drawn from Brian Catchpole, *A Map History of the Modern World* (Oxford: Heinemann Publishers, 1982), reprinted with adjustments by permission.

The Failure of Collective Security and World War II

Victorious Allied leaders Georges Clemenceau, Woodrow Wilson, and David Lloyd George shortly before the signing of the Treaty of Versailles, 1919

From Chapter 4 of *Understanding Global Conflict and Cooperation*, Ninth Edition. Joseph S. Nye, Jr., David A. Welch.

THE RISE AND FALL OF COLLECTIVE SECURITY

World War I caused enormous social disruption and shock waves of revulsion at the senseless slaughter (Table 1). Balance-of-power politics was widely blamed for the war. Woodrow Wilson, the American president during World War I, was a classic nineteenth-century liberal who regarded balance-of-power policies as immoral because they violated democratic principles and national self-determination. He argued, "The balance of power is the great game now forever discredited. It's the old and evil order that prevailed before this war. The balance of power is a thing that we can do without in the future."[1]

Wilson had a point, because balance-of-power policies do not give priority to democracy or peace. As we have seen, the balance of power is a way to preserve the sovereign state system. States act to prevent any state from becoming preponderant. The resulting balance of power allows for war or violations of self-determination if that is the only way to preserve independence. However, World War I was so devastating, chaotic, and brutal that many people began to think that war to preserve the balance of power was no longer tolerable. But if the world could not afford a balance-of-power system, what would take its place?

Sovereign states could not be abolished, Wilson admitted, but force could be tamed by law and institutions, as it was at the domestic level. The liberal solution was to develop international institutions analogous to domestic legislatures and courts, so that democratic procedures could be applied at the

TABLE 1

War Deaths, 1914–1918

COUNTRY	DEATHS
Austria-Hungary	1,250,000
Britain (including empire)	900,000
Bulgaria	100,000
France	1,500,000
Germany	1,750,000
Italy	600,000
Romania	300,000
Russia	1,750,000
Serbia	50,000
Turkey	30,000
United States	112,000

international level. Some liberals of the day thought that not only was World War I fought to make the world safe for democracy, but in turn democracy could make the world more peaceful. In January 1918, Wilson issued a *fourteen-point* statement of America's reasons for entering the war. The fourteenth point was the most important. It called for "a general association of nations [he meant states] to be formed under specific covenants for the purpose of affording mutual guarantees of political independence and territorial integrity to great and small states alike." In effect, Wilson wanted to change the international system from one based on balance-of-power politics to another based on collective security.

The League of Nations

Although critics called Wilson a utopian, he believed that organizing international security could be a practical approach to world politics. He knew mere paper agreements and treaties would not be sufficient; organizations and rules were needed to implement the agreements and enforce the rules. This is why Wilson put so much faith in the idea of a *League of Nations*. Moral force was important, but a military force was necessary to back it up. Security had to be a collective responsibility. If all nonaggressive states banded together, Wilson believed, the preponderance of power would be on the side of the Good. International security would be a collective responsibility in which nonaggressive countries would form a coalition against aggressors. Peace would be indivisible.

How could the states bring about such a new system of collective security? First, make aggression illegal and outlaw offensive war. Second, deter aggression by forming a coalition of all nonaggressive states. If all pledged to aid any state that was a victim anywhere in the world, a preponderance of power would exist on the side of the nonaggressive forces. Third, if deterrence failed and aggression occurred, all states would agree to punish the state that committed aggression. This doctrine of *collective security* bore some similarities to balance-of-power policies in that states tried to deter aggression by developing a powerful coalition, and if deterrence failed they were willing to use force.

But there were three important differences between the collective-security and balance-of-power approaches. First, in collective security the focus was on the aggressive policies of a state rather than its capacity. This contrasted with balance-of-power politics, in which alliances were created against any state that was becoming too strong; that is, the focus was on the capacity of states. Second, unlike in a balance-of-power system in which coalitions were formed in advance, coalitions in a collective-security system could not be predetermined because it was not known which states would be aggressors. However, once aggression occurred, all states would band against the aggressor. Third, collective security was designed to be global and universal, with no neutrals or free riders. If too many countries were neutral, the coalition of the Good might appear weak and diminish the coalition's ability to deter or punish the aggressor.

The doctrine of collective security was embodied in the Covenant of the League of Nations, which, in turn, was part of the treaties that ended World

War I. Several of the articles of the League of Nations Covenant were especially noteworthy. In Article 10, states pledged to protect all members against aggression. In Article 11, any war or threat of war was declared to be of concern to all states. In Articles 12 and 15, states agreed to submit their disputes to arbitration and not to go to war until three months after arbitration failed. Article 16, the critical article, said any war disregarding the League of Nations procedures would be regarded as a declaration of war against all the members of the League of Nations. The state that started a war would be immediately subject to economic sanctions, and the Council of the League might recommend further military measures.

This sounds straightforward, but there were ambiguities. All members had to agree to apply collective security. Each state had a veto. When states signed the Covenant they agreed to abide by Article 16, but in practice it was up to each state to decide what kinds of sanctions to apply and how to implement them; they were not bound by any higher authority. Thus, the League of Nations was not a move toward world government in which a higher authority could commit the member states to certain policies. It was not the end of the anarchic system of states, but rather an effort to make the states collectively discipline unruly members.

Collective security implicates two related concepts: *sovereignty* and *international law*. The definition of sovereignty, as we have seen, is very simple: legal supremacy within a given territory. As championed by state moralists and as recognized by the League of Nations, the sovereignty of the state is absolute and inviolable; a state government has full authority within its borders. It can limit that authority only with its own consent—that is, if a government signs a treaty allowing another government to have some influence in its domains, or agreeing to be bound by the decisions of others. These are agreed limitations rather than an infringement of sovereignty. Thus, by signing on to the League of Nations, states would voluntarily give up some sovereignty to the international community in return for the guarantees of collective security and international law.

As understood by Wilson and implied in the League of Nations charter, international law transcended national law and hence sovereignty in particular situations. Ever since the Peace of Westphalia in 1648, a central tenet of international law has been that states are sovereign except when they violate international law, in which case they are subject to punishment. Collective security was to international law what the police are to domestic law. However, international law enjoyed far less acceptance among states than domestic law. Many states refused to be constrained by international law and saw compliance as voluntary rather than mandatory.

The United States and the League of Nations

The unwillingness of some states to relinquish a degree of sovereignty in exchange for collective security lay at the heart of one of the League's most notable weaknesses: the failure of the United States to join its own creation.

The American Senate refused to ratify the Treaty of Versailles, which contained language endorsing the creation of the League of Nations. As a result, the collective-security system had to function without what would have been its biggest player.

Why did the United States hold back when, to a large extent, the League was an American liberal plan to reorder world politics? After World War I, most Americans wanted to return to "normalcy." Many defined "normal" as avoiding involvement in international affairs. Opponents of American involvement in world affairs claimed that the Monroe Doctrine of 1823 limited American interests to the Western Hemisphere, and noted George Washington's warning that the United States should avoid open-ended foreign commitments. The leader of this opposition to the League of Nations, Senator Henry Cabot Lodge of Massachusetts, feared that Article 16 of the Covenant would dilute both American sovereignty and the constitutional power of the Senate to declare war. Lodge suspected the United States might be drawn into distant wars on the basis of the League's decisions to enforce collective security rather than by the Senate's decision or the will of the American people.

The debate between President Wilson and his opponents is sometimes portrayed as a clash between idealism and realism, but it can also be seen as a debate between different forms of American moralism. Wilson's obdurate refusal to negotiate terms with Lodge—one of his more notable character traits, as Alexander and Juliette George point out in their fascinating psychobiography[2]—was part of the problem. But the Senate's resistance reflected a long-standing American attitude toward the balance of power in Europe. Opponents of the League believed that European states pursued immoral policies in the name of the balance of power, and that America should not become an active player in such games. In fact, however, the United States was able to ignore the balance of power in the nineteenth century because Americans were enjoying a free ride behind Britain's fleet. Other European countries could not penetrate the Western Hemisphere to threaten Americans. And though the United States was isolationist toward Europe, it was not at all isolationist when it came to interfering in the affairs of its weak neighbors in Central America, Mexico, or Cuba. At the end of World War I Americans were torn between two forms of moralism, and the isolationist impulse toward the European balance of power won. The result was that the country that had tipped the balance of power in World War I refused to accept responsibility for the postwar order.

The Early Days of the League

What France wanted more than anything else at the end of World War I was a set of military guarantees ensuring that Germany could not rise again. Because the United States would not join the League of Nations, France pressed Britain for a security guarantee and military preparations in case Germany recovered. Britain resisted on the grounds that such an alliance would be against the

A LIBERAL VISION

> My conception of the League of Nations is just this, that it shall operate as the organized moral force of men throughout the world, and that whenever or wherever wrong and aggression are planned or contemplated, this searching light of conscience shall be turned upon them.
>
> *—Woodrow Wilson*[3]

spirit of collective security, because it would identify the aggressor in advance. Moreover, Britain saw France as stronger than Germany and argued there was no need for an alliance, even on traditional balance-of-power terms. Britain said it was important to reintegrate Germany into the international system, just as the Congress of Vienna had brought France back into the Concert of Europe at the end of the Napoleonic Wars in 1815. War passions had abated more quickly in Britain than in France, and the British felt it was time to appease the Germans by bringing them back into the process.

Unmoved by these arguments, France formed alliances with Poland, which had been reborn at the end of World War I, and with the "Little Entente," the new states of Yugoslavia, Czechoslovakia, and Romania, which had emerged out of the former Austro-Hungarian Empire. The French policy fell between two stools: Not only were these alliances against the spirit of collective security, but they did not do very much for France in terms of the balance of power. Poland was on bad terms with its neighbors and, as France's ally, acted as a poor substitute for Russia, which had been ostracized because of the Bolshevik Revolution. The Little Entente states were destabilized by ethnic problems and domestic divisions, and as a result were also feeble allies.

Germany emerged from World War I enormously weakened (Figure 1). It lost 25,000 square miles of territory that had been home to 7 million people. Signed in June 1919, the Treaty of Versailles forced Germany to reduce its army to only 100,000 men and prohibited it from having an air force. The treaty contained the famous "war guilt clause," placing the blame for war solely on Germany. Because the victors believed that Germany was responsible, they argued Germany should pay for its costs. The reparations bill was $33 billion, a sum Germans thought impossibly high given their damaged economic position. When they initially failed to pay, France sent troops to occupy Germany's Ruhr industrial area until they did. After engaging in passive resistance, Germany suffered enormous inflation that wiped out the savings of its middle class. That, in turn, removed one of the sources of internal stability as the Weimar Republic struggled to create democracy.

Italy had never been keen on the Paris peace treaties or the League of Nations. Italy had originally been allied with Germany and Austria-Hungary, but at the beginning of the war, the Italians decided they would get a better payoff from the Allies and switched sides. In the secret Treaty of

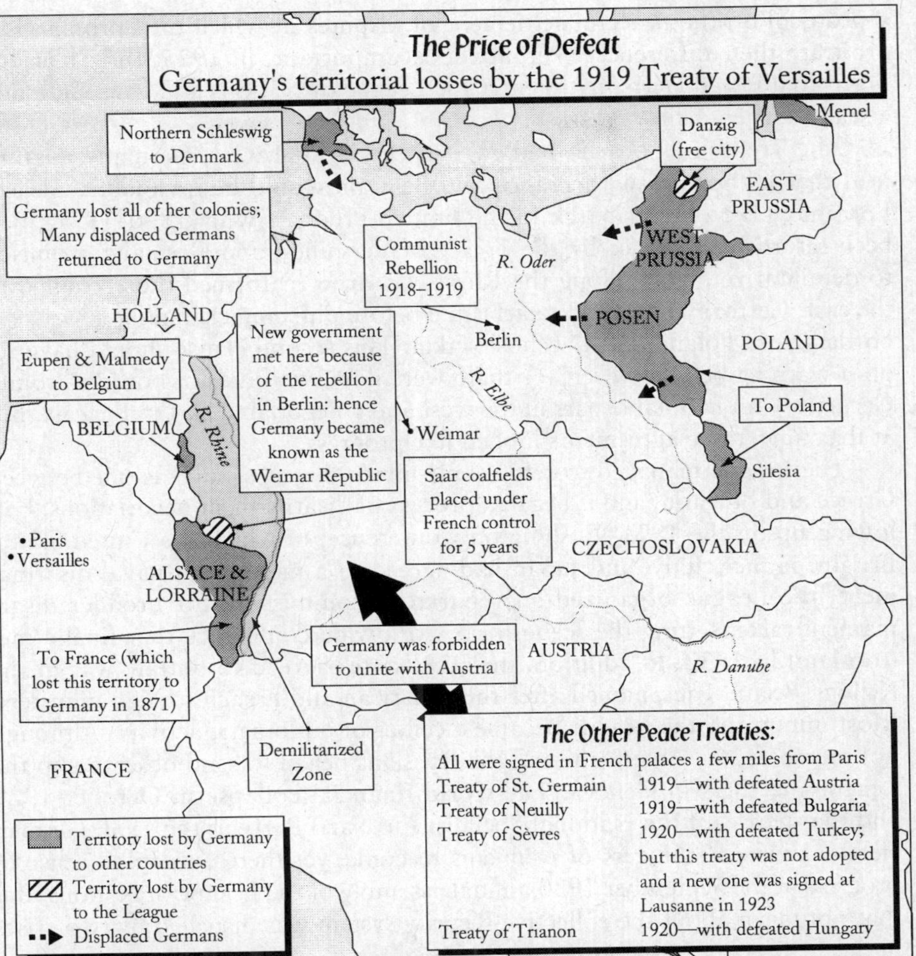

FIGURE 1
Germany's Losses

London signed in 1915, Italy was promised compensation at the expense of the part of the Austro-Hungarian Empire that became postwar Yugoslavia. The Italians expected that these promises would be honored, but Woodrow Wilson objected to such old-fashioned spoils-of-war behavior. In addition, after Benito Mussolini and the fascists took power in 1922, one of their foreign policy aims was to gain glory and finally fulfill the destiny of a new Roman Empire. These goals were inconsistent with the new vision of collective security.

With such a start, it is remarkable the League was able to achieve anything at all. Yet 1924–1930 was a period of relative successes. Plans were made to scale down the reparations Germany had to pay. In 1924, governments signed a protocol on the peaceful settlement of disputes in which they promised to arbitrate their differences. Perhaps most important, in 1925, the Treaty of Locarno allowed Germany to enter the League of Nations and gave Germany a seat on its council.

The Treaty of Locarno had two aspects. In the west, Germany guaranteed that its borders with France and Belgium would be inviolable. Alsace-Lorraine, taken by Bismarck in the Franco-Prussian War (1870–1871), had been returned to France by the Treaty of Versailles, and Germany promised to demilitarize a zone along the Rhine. Locarno reaffirmed those results. In the east, Germany promised to arbitrate before pursuing changes in its eastern borders with Poland and Czechoslovakia. This second clause should have set off a warning bell, however, for there were now two kinds of borders around Germany—an inviolable part in the west and a negotiable part in the east. But at that time, these agreements looked like progress.

The League managed to settle some minor disputes, such as one between Greece and Bulgaria, and it began a process of disarmament negotiations. Following up on the 1921 Washington Conference, in which the United States, Britain, France, Italy, and Japan had agreed to a measure of naval disarmament, the League organized a preparatory commission for broader disarmament talks, setting the scene for a worldwide conference that finally met (too late) in 1932. In addition, in 1928, states agreed to outlaw war in the Kellogg-Briand Pact, named after the American and French foreign ministers. Most important, the League became a center of diplomatic activity. Although not members, the Americans and the Russians began to send observers to the League meetings in Geneva. The world financial collapse in October 1929 and the success of the National Socialist (or Nazi) Party in the 1930 German elections were harbingers of problems to come, yet there was still a sense of progress at the September 1930 annual assembly of the League of Nations. But that optimism about the collective-security system was dispelled by two crises in the 1930s over Manchuria and Ethiopia.

The Manchurian Failure

To understand the Manchurian case, we must understand the situation in Japan. Japan had transformed itself from a potential victim of imperialist aggression in the mid-nineteenth century to a very successful imperialist power by the century's end. Japan defeated Russia in the Russo-Japanese War (1904–1905), colonized Korea in 1910, and joined the Allies in World War I. After the war, Japan sought recognition as a major power. Europeans and Americans resisted. At the Paris peace talks in 1919, the Western governments rejected a Japanese proposal that the Covenant of the League affirm the principle of racial equality. This decision mirrored the domestic political sentiment in the American Congress, which, in the 1920s, passed racist laws excluding Japanese immigrants. Simultaneously, Britain ended its bilateral treaty with Japan. Many Japanese thought the rules were changed just as they were about to enter the club of the great powers.[4]

China was the other actor in the Manchurian crisis. The 1911 revolution led to the fall of the Manchu or Qing dynasty that had ruled China since 1644 and established a republic. But the country quickly fell into chaos as regional civil wars broke out among contending warlords. Manchuria, though part of China, was under the sway of one of these warlords and maintained a quasi-independent status. With Chiang Kai-shek (1887–1975) as chief military adviser to the republic, the Chinese Nationalist movement tried to unify the country and bitterly criticized the unequal treaties that had humiliated and exploited China ever since the end of the imperialist Opium Wars of the nineteenth century. As the Nationalists gained strength in the 1920s, friction with Japan increased, and China declared a boycott against Japanese goods.

Meanwhile, in Japan, military and civilian factions contended for dominance. The global economic crisis that began in the late 1920s left Japan, an island nation, extremely vulnerable. The military cliques gained the upper hand. In September 1931, the Japanese army staged an incident along the Manchurian Railway, where they had had a right to station troops since the Russo-Japanese War. This act of sabotage on the Manchurian Railway provided Japan with a pretext to take over all of Manchuria. Although Japan said its actions were intended to protect the Manchurian Railway, it went further and set up a Japanese-controlled puppet state called Manchukuo, installing China's last Manchu emperor, Pu Yi, as its ruler. China appealed to the League of Nations to condemn Japan's aggression, but Japan prevented passage of a resolution asking it to withdraw its troops. In December 1931, the League agreed to send a committee under the British statesman Victor Bulwer-Lytton to investigate the events in Manchuria. Lord Lytton finally reported to the League in October 1932. His report identified Japan as the aggressor and rejected Japan's pretext as an unjustified intervention. Although his report recommended that the members of the League of Nations not recognize the state of Manchukuo, it did not call for applying Article 16 sanctions against Japan. In February 1933, the Assembly of the League of Nations voted 42 to 1 to accept Lytton's report on the Japanese invasion of Manchuria. The one opposing vote was Japan, which then announced its intention to withdraw from the League of Nations. Overall, the Manchurian case showed the procedures of the League of Nations to be slow, cautious, and totally ineffective. The Manchurian episode tested the League, and it failed.

The Ethiopian Debacle

The last great test of the League of Nations' collective-security system came in Ethiopia in 1935. This time sanctions were applied, but the outcome was again failure. Italy had long planned to annex Ethiopia; not only was it near Italy's colonies in Eritrea on the Red Sea, but the ruling Italian fascists felt affronted that the Ethiopians had defeated an Italian effort to colonize them during the imperialist era in the nineteenth century. Fascist ideologists argued that this historic "wrong" should be rectified. Between 1934 and 1935, Italy provoked incidents on the border between Ethiopia and Eritrea. It did so despite the existence of a peace treaty between Ethiopia and Italy, despite the fact that Italy had signed the Kellogg-Briand Pact outlawing war, and despite its commitment as a member of the League of Nations to arbitrate for three months before doing anything.

In October 1935, Italy invaded Ethiopia. The invasion was a clear-cut case of aggression, and the Council of the League avoided an Italian veto by the procedural device of calling for a special conference to decide what sanctions to impose against Italy. Fifty states attended, and eight days after the invasion the conference recommended to member states that they impose four sanctions: an embargo on the sale of all military goods to Italy; a prohibition against loans to Italy; cessation of imports from Italy; and refusal to sell certain goods that could not be easily bought elsewhere, such as rubber and tin. But three things were missing: Italy was still allowed to buy steel, coal, and oil; diplomatic relations were not broken; and Britain did not close the Suez Canal to Italy, allowing it to continue shipment of materials to Eritrea.

Why didn't the members of the League of Nations do more? There was general optimism that the recommended sanctions would force Italy to withdraw from Ethiopia. Sanctions certainly had an effect on the Italian economy: Italian exports declined by about one-third during the following year, the value of the Italian lira declined, and there were estimates that Italy's gold reserves would be exhausted in nine months. But aside from inflicting economic damage, sanctions did not cause Mussolini to change his policies toward Ethiopia. The anger of Britain and France over Ethiopia was more than offset by their concern for the European balance of power. Britain and France wanted to avoid alienating Italy because Germany, now under Hitler's leadership, was regaining its strength, and Britain and France thought it would be useful to have Italy in a coalition to balance Germany. In 1934, when it looked as though Hitler would annex Austria, Mussolini moved Italian troops to the Austrian border, and Hitler backed down. The British and French therefore hoped Mussolini could be persuaded to join a coalition against Germany.

Traditional diplomats did not fight the League of Nations' collective-security system; they reinterpreted it according to the old balance-of-power approach. From a balance-of-power perspective, the last thing they wanted was to become involved in a distant conflict in Africa when there were pressing problems in the heart of Europe. Distant aggression in Africa, said the traditional realists, was not a threat to European security. Conciliation and negotiation were needed to bring the Italians back into the coalition to balance Germany. Not surprisingly, the British and French began to get cold feet about sanctions. Sir Samuel Hoare and Pierre Laval, the British and French foreign ministers, met in December 1935 and drew up a plan that divided Ethiopia into two parts, one Italian and the other a League of Nations zone. When someone leaked this plan to the press, there was outrage in Britain. Accused of having sold out the League of Nations and collective security, Hoare was forced to resign.

But within three months, British opinion turned again. In March 1936, Hitler denounced the Locarno treaties and marched German troops into the demilitarized Rhineland. Britain and France immediately stopped worrying about Ethiopia. They met with Italy to consult about how to restore the balance of power in Europe. Consequently, the balance of power in Europe prevailed over the application of the collective-security doctrine in Africa. In May 1936, the Italians completed their military victory, and by July the sanctions were removed.

The best line in this tragedy was spoken by the Haitian delegate to the League of Nations: "Great or small, strong or weak, near or far, white or colored, let us never forget that one day we may be somebody's Ethiopia."[5] Within a few years, most European nations fell prey to Hitler's aggression in World War II. The world's first efforts at collective security were a dismal failure.

Follow Up

- George Scott, *The Rise and Fall of the League of Nations* (New York: Macmillan, 1974).
- Graham Ross, *The Great Powers and the Decline of the European States System, 1919–1945* (London: Longman, 1983), pp. 109–126.

THE ORIGINS OF WORLD WAR II

World War II overshadows all other wars in terms of its human costs, estimated to be between 35 and 50 million people. The war was noted for advances in weaponry. Tanks and planes that had just been introduced and played an insignificant role in World War I dominated World War II. Radar played a significant role, for example, in the Battle of Britain, one of the turning points in World War II. And at the end of the war, of course, the atomic bomb ushered in the dawn of the nuclear age.

World War II ended with unconditional surrender. Unlike World War I, the Allies occupied Germany and Japan and transformed their societies during the occupation. The "German problem" was solved for half a century by dividing Germany. World War II also created a *bipolar* world in which the United States and the Soviet Union emerged from the conflict much stronger than the world's former great powers. The war represented the end of Europe as the arbiter of the balance of power. Now Europe became an arena where outsiders contended, somewhat like Germany before 1870. The end of World War II in 1945 created the framework for world order until 1989.

Hitler's War?

World War II (1939–1945) is often called "Hitler's war." While true, this label is too simple. World War II was also old business, Act II of the Great War that ended Europe's hegemony in 1918; the interwar period was only an

Hitler greeted by the Reichstag in 1939

intermission. Hitler wanted war, but not the war we now know as World War II. He wanted a short, sharp war. Another reason it was not simply Hitler's war was the war in the Pacific. Hitler had continually, but unsuccessfully, urged the Japanese to attack the British colony of Singapore or to attack Siberia to divert Soviet troops away from Europe. Japan did neither; it surprised Hitler by attacking the American naval base at Pearl Harbor instead. The war in the Pacific, while part of World War II, had different origins and was more a traditional imperial effort at regional hegemony.

On the other hand, we can go too far in emphasizing other causes. Some historians have nearly exonerated Hitler. A. J. P. Taylor argues that while Hitler was a terrible person and a very unpleasant adventurer, he was merely an opportunist stepping into the power vacuums created by the appeasement policies of the Western democracies. But Taylor goes too far. For example, Hitler's 1924 book, *Mein Kampf*, set forth a vague plan that Taylor dismisses as Hitler's ranting in resentment of the French invasion of the Ruhr. But Hitler wrote another, secret book in 1928 that repeated many of the arguments in

ONE HISTORIAN'S VIEW OF HITLER

Here, it seems to me, is the key to the problem whether Hitler deliberately aimed at war. He did not so much aim at war as expect it to happen, unless he could evade it by some ingenious trick, as he had evaded civil war at home. Those who have evil motives easily attribute them to others; and Hitler expected others to do what he would have done in their place.

—A. J. P. Taylor, *The Origins of the Second World War*[6]

Mein Kampf. Even if it was not a detailed plan, it was a clear indication of what he wanted to do.

Taylor also deals too lightly with the "Hossbach memorandum." Colonel Hossbach, an aide to Hitler, took notes at a meeting at Berchtesgaden in 1937 that detailed Hitler's plan to seize foreign territory by 1943, before Germany's adversaries had fully rearmed. Hitler knew it was important to take opportunities when they arose in the east, and that Austria and Czechoslovakia would be his first targets. Taylor dismisses the importance of this memo by saying it was not an *official* memorandum. Since Taylor wrote, additional evidence has come to light. We know Hitler talked often of this timetable and of these objectives. The Hossbach memorandum generally predicted Hitler's actions.

Hitler's Strategy

Hitler had four options after he came to power in 1933, and he rejected three of them. He could have chosen *passivity*, accepting Germany's weakened international position. He could have tried *enrichment* through economic growth (like Japan after World War II) and led Germany to international influence through industrial expansion. He could have *limited his goals* to revision of the Treaty of Versailles and regained some of Germany's 1918 losses. This option seemed likely even if some other leader had come to power in Germany. By the 1930s, the Western democracies were sensitive to the injustice of blaming Germany for *all* of World War I. But these three strategies were rejected by Hitler, who chose instead an *expansionist strategy* to break out from what he saw as Germany's containment. In his view, Germany, stuck in the middle of Europe, could not live forever encircled. It had to gain land. He would go east for living space, expand his base, and at a later stage go for a larger world role.

Hitler followed this fourth option through four phases. First, he set out to destroy the Versailles framework through a very clever set of diplomatic maneuvers. In October 1933, he withdrew from the League of Nations and from the disarmament conference the League had convened. He blamed the withdrawal on the French, who he said were not willing to cut their forces, thereby making it impossible for Germany to continue in the League or the conference. In January 1934, he signed a treaty with Poland, disrupting the arrangements France had been trying to make with Poland and the smaller Eastern European states through the "Little Entente." In March 1935, Hitler denounced the military clauses of the Versailles treaty, saying Germany would no longer be restricted to an army of 100,000. Instead, he announced plans to triple the army and build an air force.

The British, French, and Italians met at Stresa (in Italy) to respond to Hitler's activities, but before they could reach a consensus, Hitler invited Britain to enter negotiations on a naval treaty. Britain leapt at the opportunity, thereby disrupting any coordinated response from the Stresa meeting. In March 1936, when events in Ethiopia diverted attention from central Europe, Hitler moved his troops into the Rhineland, which had been demilitarized by the Locarno Pact. He blamed France for forcing him to do this, claiming France had destroyed the Locarno treaty by developing an arrangement with the Soviet Union. He dropped hints that he might return to the League of Nations after the other states in Europe accepted his views about the revisions of the Versailles treaty, a clever maneuver that played on guilt and uncertainty in many Western capitals.

The second phase (1936–1940) was Hitler's expansion into the small countries neighboring Germany. In 1936, Hitler outlined a four-year economic plan for a military buildup in order to be ready for war by 1940. He signed the Axis Pact with Italy and an Anti-Comintern Pact with Japan. (Founded by Lenin in 1919 to foment worldwide Bolshevik-style revolution, the Communist International, or Comintern, changed its policy in 1935 under Stalin to support so-called "Popular Front" governments—antifascist coalitions comprised of socialists, anarchists, and "bourgeois parties.") Hitler also intervened on the side of the fascists in their war against a left-wing, democratically elected, popular-front government in Spain. Hitler justified sending troops and bombers to support the fascist general Francisco Franco in the Spanish Civil War (1936–1939) as part of the protection of the West against the threat of Bolshevism. In 1937, Spain became a testing ground for Germany's military muscle when Hitler's pilots bombed defenseless civilian populations and annihilated the Basque city of Guernica, a savage attack immortalized in what many regard as Pablo Picasso's best and most disturbing painting. Despite widespread international outcry, France, Great Britain, and the United States did little or nothing to defend the Spanish Republic. The following year, Chancellor Kurt von Schuschnigg of Austria called for a plebiscite on whether Austria should reunite with Germany, hoping that the Austrian people would vote against it before Hitler forced it upon them. But Hitler intervened. In the 1938 *anschluss* ("coming together"), German troops marched into Vienna, ending Austrian independence.

Czechoslovakia was next. Hitler pressured Czechoslovakia by pushing the issue of national self-determination for the 3 million Germans in the Sudetenland section of Czechoslovakia. This area where Czechoslovakia borders Germany was militarily important because it included the Bohemian mountains, the natural line of defense for Czechoslovakia and the logical place for it to resist a potential German attack. Hitler argued that the post–World War I settlement that put these German-speaking people in Czechoslovakian territory was a violation of their self-determination and another example of the perfidy of the Western countries. He demanded that the German-speaking territory be permitted to leave Czechoslovakia to join the German fatherland. The Czechs became worried and mobilized portions of their reserves. That infuriated Hitler, who vowed to crush Czechoslovakia.

These events also alarmed Britain, which did not want war to break out in Europe. Neville Chamberlain, the British prime minister from 1937 to 1940, made three trips to Germany to try to stave off war. Chamberlain believed it was not possible for Britain to defend Czechoslovakia because of the distance, and because Britain had no troops on the Continent. More important, he did not think Czechoslovakia was worth war, and he knew Britain was not ready for war. As the bombing of Guernica had shown, air power was becoming more significant, fear of bombing campaigns was growing, and Chamberlain realized the British air defense and radar systems were not ready for an air war. (Some British officials also thought that Sudeten Germans had a valid complaint about being forcibly detached from Germany and given to Czechoslovakia after World War I.) For this combination of reasons, Chamberlain met with Hitler at Munich in September 1938 and agreed to the partition of Czechoslovakia, giving the Sudetenland to Germany if Hitler would promise to leave the rest of Czechoslovakia alone. Hitler promised, and Chamberlain returned to Britain claiming that he had saved Czechoslovakia and achieved "peace for our time."

Only six months later, in March 1939, German troops rolled into the rest of Czechoslovakia and took the capital city, Prague. A shocked Britain realized Hitler might seek further conquests and that his next target might be Poland. Divided in the eighteenth century, Poland was re-created as a state after World War I and given a corridor to the port of Danzig on the Baltic Sea, though the area included German-speaking people. Once again, Hitler used the same tactics. He claimed that having German-speaking people inside Polish territory was a violation of self-determination, another example of the perfidy of the Versailles treaty. This time, Britain and France tried to deter Hitler by issuing a guarantee to defend Poland.

Hitler then pulled off a brilliant diplomatic coup. Despite having said he would protect the West against Bolshevism, Hitler suddenly signed a treaty with Stalin in August 1939. The pact gave Hitler a free hand to do what he wanted in the West. It also included a secret protocol for another partition of Poland. Stalin and Hitler each agreed to take a part. Hitler seized his part by starting a war against Poland on September 1, 1939. This time, he was not looking for another Munich agreement in which the British would step in and give him part of Poland in return for promises of moderation.

Phase three of Hitler's strategy was short. Germany achieved military mastery on the Continent in 1940 (Figure 2). After Hitler took Poland, things were temporarily quiet; this period was called the "phony war." Hitler expected Britain to sue for peace. In the spring of 1940, however, Hitler feared Britain would move troops to Norway. He preempted a British landing in Norway by sending his troops there first. Then he launched his blitzkrieg into Holland,

ANOTHER HISTORIAN'S VIEW OF HITLER

The charismatic nature of Hitler's position as Fuhrer—a quasi-messianic personalized form of rule that arose from the desire for national rebirth and unity in a country traumatized by national humiliation and paralyzed by political collapse—could of its essence not settle into "normality" or routine, or sag into more conservative authoritarianism. Visionary goals of national redemption through European domination and racial purification were at the heart of the regime. These meant constant dynamism and self-perpetuating, intensifying radicalism. The longer the regime lasted, the more megalomaniac were its aims, the more boundless its destructiveness. Its gamble for world supremacy meant an alliance against extremely powerful allies. It was a gamble against the odds, in which the regime asked its own destruction and that of Germany itself. This was Nazism's essential irrationality. Hitler's charismatic leadership implied, therefore, not just an unprecedented capacity for destruction, but also an inbuilt tendency for self-destruction. In this sense the suicide of the German dictator on 30 April 1945 was not merely a welcome but also a logical end to the Third Reich.

—*Ian Kershaw, "Hitler and the Nazi Dictatorship"*[9]

Belgium, and France. Sending his tanks through the supposedly impenetrable Ardennes Forest in May 1940, Hitler took the French and British by surprise. He had skirted the Maginot Line of French fortifications that guarded most of the French border with Germany. German forces drove the British troops back to the port of Dunkirk, where they had to leave their equipment and evacuate what was left of the men across the English Channel. Thus, Hitler became master of the European continent west of the Soviet Union through a brilliant set of moves in 1940.

The fourth phase of Hitler's plans, "the phase of overreaching" (1941–1945), unleashed the full-scale war. Hitler had long wanted to move east against the Soviet Union. But he wanted to dispose of Britain first to avoid the possibility of a war on two fronts. If he could gain air supremacy, he could then cross the channel and invade Britain. But Hitler's air force was defeated in the Battle of Britain (July–October 1940). Unable to gain air supremacy, Hitler was faced with a conundrum: Should he put off his plans to attack the Soviet Union?

Hitler decided to attack the Soviet Union even though he had been unable to defeat Britain, thinking he could beat Stalin quickly, and then go at Britain once again. Furthermore, he believed that attacking the Soviet Union would deprive the British of any potential alliance with the Soviet Union. In June 1941, Hitler attacked the Soviet Union, a massive mistake. In December 1941, after the Japanese attacked Pearl Harbor, he made another huge mistake: He declared war on the United States. Hitler probably did this to keep Japan locked into the war, since he had been urging Japan to join him, and he took the occasion to unleash his U-boat campaign against American shipping. In doing so, he also unleashed the global war that ended his Third Reich.

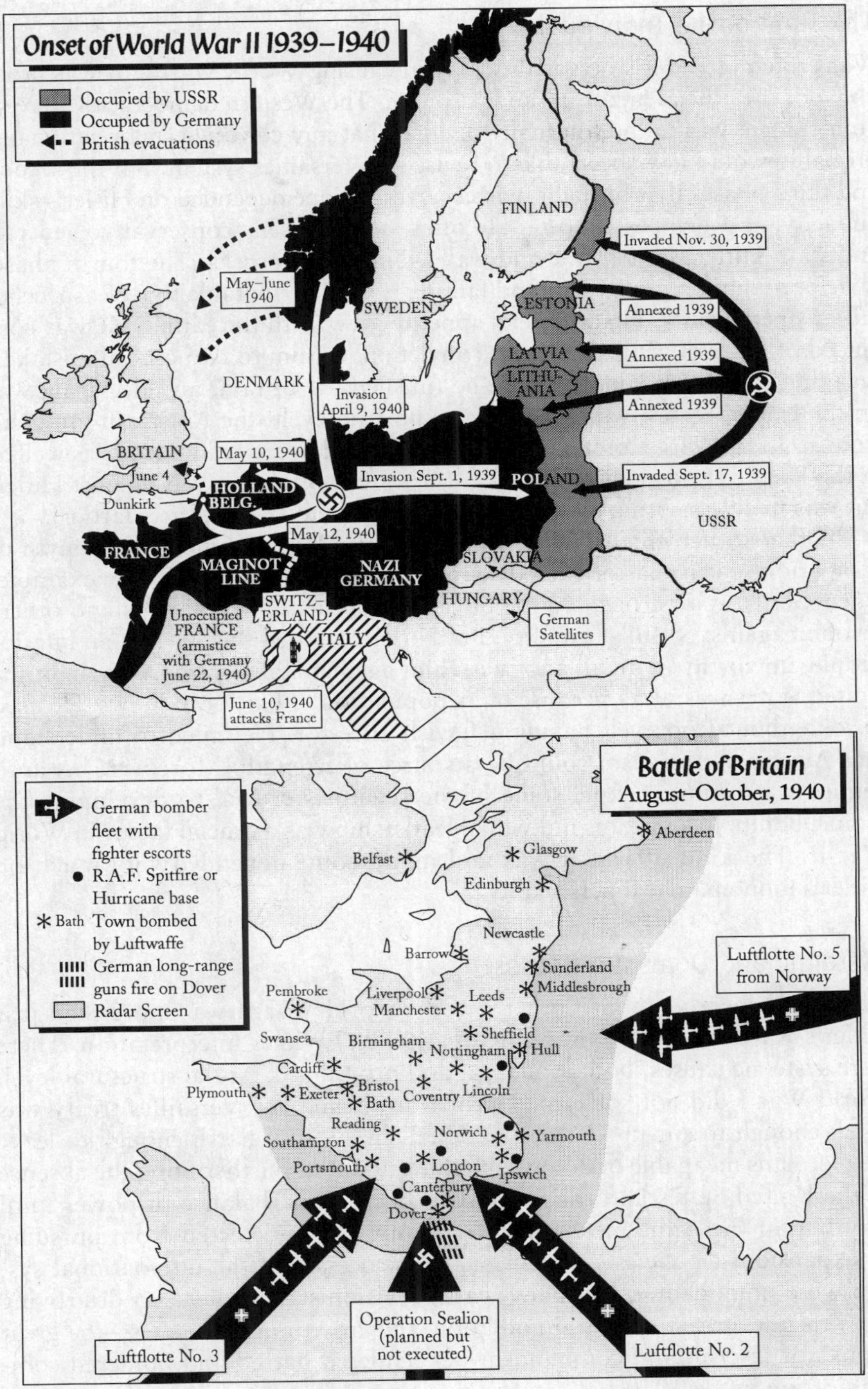

FIGURE 2
Early Stages of World War II

The Role of the Individual

What role did Hitler's personality play in causing World War II? It was probably not the crucial factor in the first phase. The Western democracies were so guilt-ridden, weak, and internally divided that any clever German nationalist probably would have been able to revise the Versailles system. But the second and third phases that brought mastery over Europe depended on Hitler's skill, audacity, and bellicose nature. He often overruled his conservative generals and staff. Hitler wanted war and was willing to take risks. The fourth phase, which brought on global war and failure, is also attributable to two aspects of Hitler's personality. First, Hitler's appetite grew with the eating. He was convinced of his own genius, but that conviction led him to two crucial mistakes: invading the Soviet Union before he finished off Britain; and declaring war on the United States, which gave Franklin Roosevelt, the American president from 1933 to 1945, a pretext to become engaged in a war in Europe as well as in the Pacific (Roosevelt had been eager to join Britain in war against Hitler, but was unable to bring along a wary Congress until after Pearl Harbor).

Hitler's other great flaw was his racist ideology. Promoting the myth of a superior Aryan master race deprived him of critical assets. For example, when Germany first invaded the Soviet Union, many Ukrainians and others revolted against Stalin's brutality. But Hitler regarded the Slavs as an inferior people, unworthy of an alliance with him against Stalin. He also thought the United States was weak because of its population of blacks and Jews. He used to joke about Roosevelt having a Jewish ancestor. He failed to understand that American pluralism could be a source of strength. Moreover, his anti-Semitism led him to expel some of the scientists crucial to developing the atomic bomb. In short, his individual leadership was a crucial factor in World War II. The kind of war it was and its outcome depended very much on Hitler's monomaniacal personality.[8]

Systemic and Domestic Causes

Of course, there were also other causes. World War II was more than just Hitler's war, and that is the value of A. J. P. Taylor's interpretation. There were systemic causes, both structural and procedural. At the structural level, World War I did not solve the German problem. The Versailles treaty was harsh enough to stir up German nationalism, but not harsh enough to leave the Germans incapable of doing something about it. Furthermore, the absence of the United States and the Soviet Union from the balance of power until very late in the game meant that Germany was undeterred from pursuing its expansionist policies. In addition, the processes of the international system were immoderate. Germany was a revisionist state bent on destroying the Versailles treaty system. In addition, the growth of ideologies—the great "isms" of fascism and communism—engendered hatred and hindered communication in the 1930s.

Three domestic-level changes were also particularly important. First, the Western democracies were torn apart by class cleavages and ideological disputes. Coordinated foreign policy making was nearly impossible. For example, when Léon Blum, a French socialist, came to power after 1936, French conservatives used the slogan, "Better Hitler Than Blum." In 1939, the British conservative government sent a mission to Moscow to see whether they could sign a treaty with Stalin, but both the mission and the government were internally divided. Before the British could make up their minds, Hitler had beat them to it. One reason for the delay was the British upper-class reluctance to deal with communists.

A second domestic-level cause of the war was economic collapse. The Great Depression was systemic in the sense that it affected all countries and grew out of the inability of the major capitalist states to establish effective international economic coordination to deal with imbalances in transnational trade and financial flows. But the Depression had powerful effects on domestic politics and class conflict. The enormous amount of unemployment had the political effect of pouring gasoline on a fire: It contributed to the Nazi takeover in Germany and weakened the governments of the Western democracies.

The third domestic cause was the U.S. policy of isolationism. The United States came out of World War I with the world's strongest economy, but it refused to fully accept the responsibilities of that position. In the 1930s, the Great Depression increased internal preoccupation and significantly deepened isolationism. In his first term, President Franklin Roosevelt, along with other Americans, paid little attention to Europe. After his reelection in 1936, Roosevelt began to realize that if Hitler became too strong, he might dominate Europe and eventually threaten the United States. In 1937, Roosevelt began to speak about events in Europe, but the American public did not want to get involved. In 1940, Roosevelt traded destroyers to the British in return for military basing rights in British territories in the Western Hemisphere. In 1941, he persuaded Congress to approve "lend-lease" war supplies to Britain to prevent it from being defeated by Hitler. However, Roosevelt was limited by domestic opinion on how far he could go in resisting Hitler. Only Japan's attack on Pearl Harbor and Hitler's subsequent declaration of war ended America's isolationism.

How do these domestic, personal, and systemic causes fit together? We could say that the deep causes of World War II were systemic—the unfinished business of World War I. The intermediate causes were largely domestic—the social and ideological disruptions that produced Hitler in Germany and the political and economic weaknesses in the democracies. The precipitating cause was Adolf Hitler's strategy for domination (see Figure 3).

HITLER'S VIEW OF HITLER

Now Poland is in the position in which I wanted her. . . . I am only afraid that at the last moment some swine or other will submit to me a plan for mediation.

—Adolf Hitler, August 27, 1939[7]

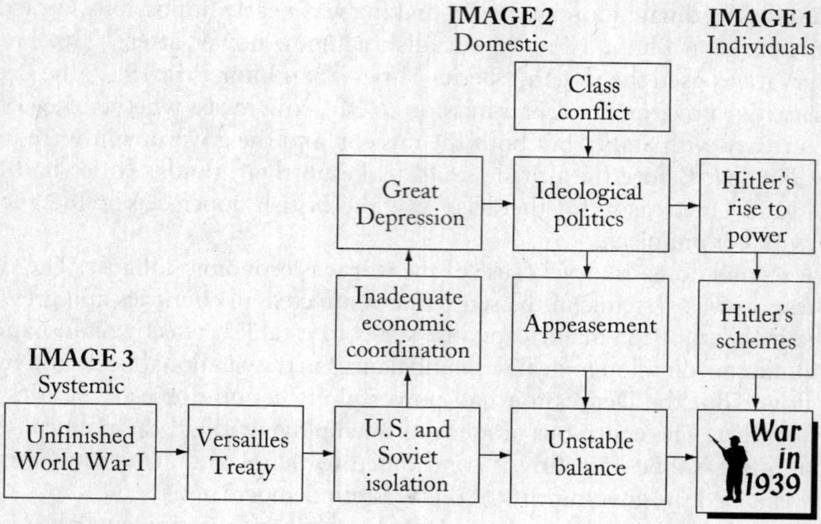

FIGURE 3
Causes of World War II

Was War Inevitable?

Was a second world war inevitable? No, but it became increasingly likely as time passed. In 1926 (after the Locarno treaties), the likelihood diminished, but after the Great Depression in 1929 and Hitler's ascent to power in 1933, the funnel of choices narrowed until the war became global in 1941 (see Figure 4).

The failure of World War I to solve "the German problem" meant there was already in 1918 some probability of a second war. If the Western democracies had chosen to appease Germany in the 1920s and treat it less punitively,

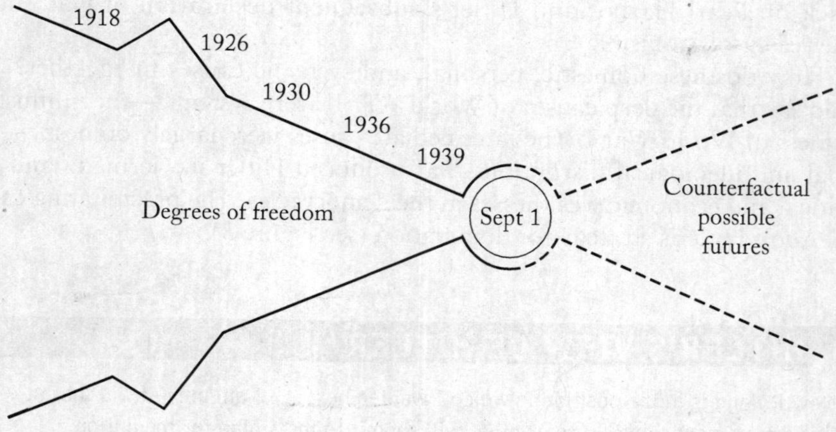

FIGURE 4
Was War Inevitable?

the democratic government of the Weimar Republic might have been preserved. Or, if the United States had ratified the Treaty of Versailles and stayed in Europe to preserve the balance of power (as it did after 1945), Hitler might not have risen to power. There might have been a war in Europe, but not necessarily a world war. In the 1930s, the shock of the economic depression fueled the rise of ideologies that glorified aggression, making war more likely.

Counterfactually, suppose Britain and France had confronted Germany and made an alliance with the Soviet Union early in the 1930s. Or imagine that the United States had joined the League of Nations. Hitler might have been deterred or delayed. He might not have had such dramatic early successes and might have been overthrown by his own generals, who had contemplated such a coup several times and who had repeatedly secretly contacted British officials to warn them of Hitler's warlike intentions and to beg them to do something to stop him.[10] But because these things did not happen, Hitler's personality and strategy became the key precipitating cause. By the late 1930s, once Hitler began to plan war, it became almost inevitable. Even so, some historians believe that if France and Britain had launched an offensive in September 1939, they might have defeated Germany.

The Pacific War

The war in the Pacific had separate origins. Japan's attention was focused on East Asia, and it was not deeply involved in European events. In the 1920s, Japan was far from being a perfect democracy, but it did have a parliamentary system. However, in the 1930s, the military and extreme nationalists gained control of the government. Their policy of imperialist expansion was widely popular. Japan had always worried about maintaining access to the raw materials it had to import to sustain its economy. When the Depression cut Japan's trade, the Japanese feared that if they did not change their situation, they would face a bleak future. Acting as a regional hegemon, Japan tried to create what it called the Greater East Asia Co-Prosperity Sphere (a wonderful euphemism for the conquest of one's neighbors). Japan believed this would allow it to resist threats from Britain and the United States, who were still major naval powers in the Pacific.

Japan first expanded at the expense of China. Japan's brutal war in China brought Japan into diplomatic conflict with the United States, which supported the Chinese Nationalists. After France fell to Hitler in 1940, the Japanese took advantage of the opportunity to extend their control over French Indochina (modern-day Vietnam, Cambodia, and Laos). At this point, the Japanese expansionists had three options. One was to strike westward against the Soviet Union. Since clashes had already occurred between Japanese and Soviet forces along the border in Manchuria, some people thought a Japanese-Soviet war along the Manchurian border was most likely. The second option for the Japanese was to strike south and seize the Dutch East Indies (today's Indonesia), which had the oil Japan needed. Option three was to strike east against the United States, by far the riskiest of the three options.

The attack on Pearl Harbor, December 7, 1941

The Japanese eventually chose both options two and three. On December 7, 1941, they struck east against the United States and south toward Indonesia and the Philippines. While the move south was for raw materials, the attack on the United States is more difficult to explain. Given the disparity in power resources, the Japanese knew they could not ultimately win a war against the United States, but they hoped the surprise attack on Pearl Harbor would so demoralize the United States that full-scale war would never erupt. That was a gross miscalculation on the part of the Japanese, but from the perspective of the Japanese government, it seemed a better risk than the sure defeat they believed would ensue if they did nothing.

By the fall of 1941, Japanese expansionists no longer considered the Soviet Union a viable target. Hitler's attack on the Soviet Union had removed the Soviet threat to Japan. At the same time, the Americans tried to deter the Japanese from striking south by placing an embargo on oil shipments to Japan. As President Roosevelt put it, "The United States would slip a noose around Japan's neck and give it a jerk now and then." Assistant Secretary of State Dean Acheson was quoted at the time as saying this would not lead to war because "no rational Japanese could believe that an attack on us could result in anything but disaster for his country."[11] But the Japanese felt that if they did not go to war with the United States, they would eventually suffer defeat in any case. With 90 percent of their oil imported, they calculated that their navy could not last for even a year if that supply were cut off; therefore, they concluded it was better to go to war than to be slowly strangled.

In addition to restricting Japan's oil supplies, the United States demanded that Japan withdraw from China. The Japanese believed this would cut them off from the area they viewed as their economic hinterland. As a Japanese military officer explained to Emperor Hirohito, the situation was like that of a patient with a serious illness: "An operation, while it might be extremely dangerous, would still offer some hope of saving his life."[12] From their point of view, it was *not* totally irrational for Japan to go to war because it was the least bad of the alternatives they saw. If Germany defeated Britain, and American opinion was discouraged by the suddenness of the attack, a negotiated peace might result. A poorly reasoned form of the Japanese leaders' mood was expressed by Vice Army Chief of Staff Ko Tsukada:

> In general, the prospects if we go to war are not bright. We all wonder if there isn't some way to proceed peacefully. There is no one who is willing to say, "Don't worry, even if the war is prolonged, I will assume all responsibility." On the other hand, it is not possible to maintain the status quo. Hence, one unavoidably reaches the conclusion that we must go to war.[13]

Of course, Japan had the option of reversing its aggression in China and Southeast Asia, but that was unthinkable for the military leaders with their expansionist and bellicose outlook. Thus on December 7, 1941, the Japanese attacked Pearl Harbor (see Figure 5).

What about the three levels of analysis as applied to the Pacific war? The *role of the individual* is certainly less pronounced than it was with Hitler in Europe, but individual policy makers nonetheless influenced the trajectory of events. In Japan, expansionist generals and admirals wanted to increase Japan's regional dominance and actively sought an expanded war: west to China; south to Singapore, Indonesia, and the Philippines; and east to U.S. possessions in the Pacific. Military leaders such as General Hideki Tojo played a leading role in determining government policy. However, Tojo supported policies identical to those of many other high-ranking military and political leaders. While Hitler had military and industrial support in Germany, he made decisions largely on his own. In Japan, there was a greater diffusion of power at the top, and decisions were more the result of consensus among the political and military elite.

The role of the individual was also important for determining U.S. policy. Franklin Roosevelt was willing to impose punitive sanctions in response to Japanese aggression in Southeast Asia, but many in Congress and throughout America were uneasy with Roosevelt's activist and confrontational foreign policy. There was still strong isolationist sentiment in the United States in 1940 and 1941. If an isolationist such as Senator Burton Wheeler of Montana, Senator Gerald Nye of North Dakota, or Senator Hiram Johnson of California had been president, the United States might have tried to appease

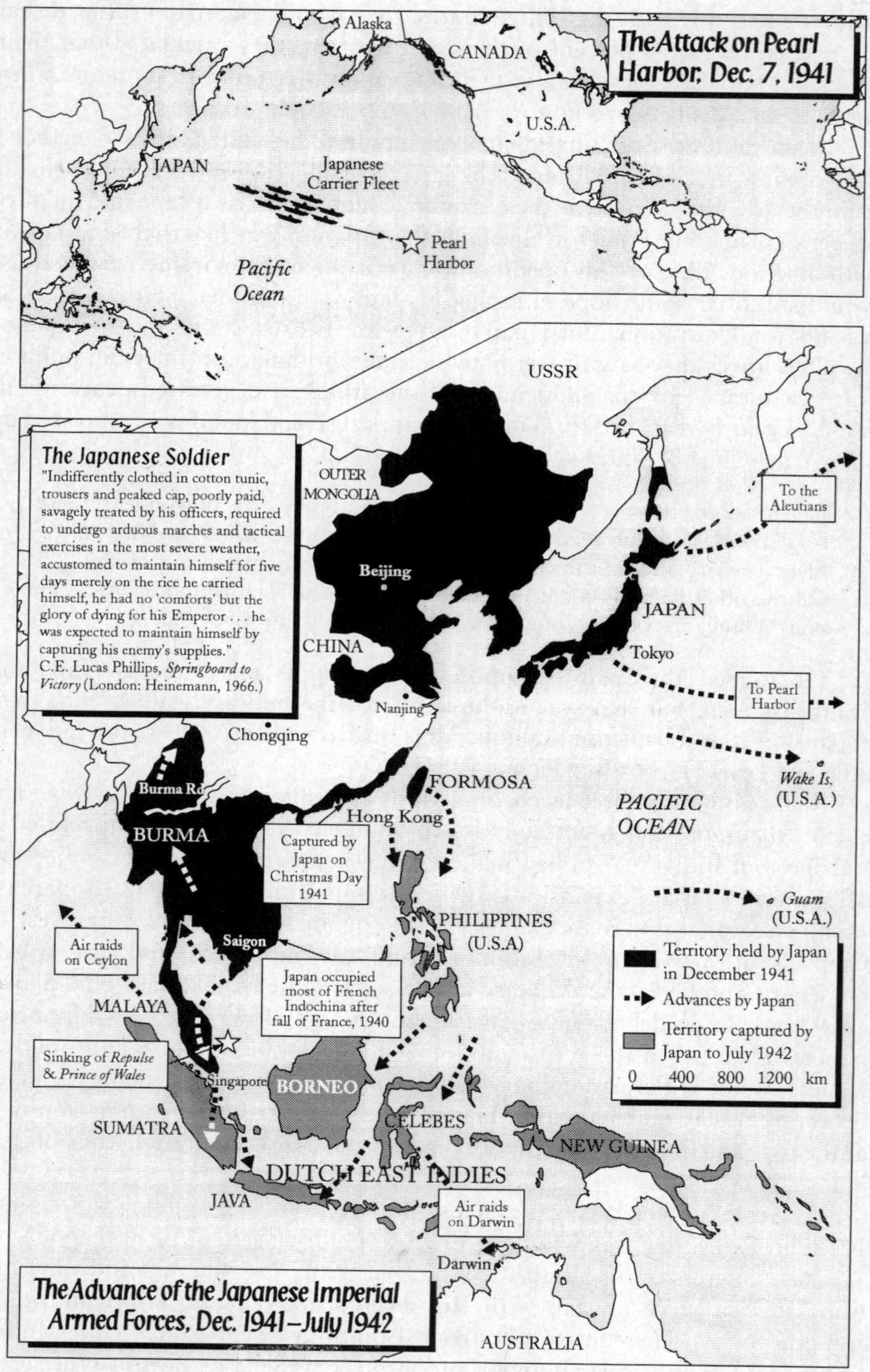

FIGURE 5

World War II in the Pacific

JAPAN'S PREDICAMENT, AS SEEN BY ITS LEADERS

Even if we should make concessions to the United States by giving up part of our national policy for the sake of a temporary peace, the United States, its military position strengthened, is sure to demand more and more concessions on our part; and ultimately our empire will lie prostrate at the feet of the United States.

—Records of Japan's 1941 Policy Conferences

Japanese aggression rather than confront it, and consequently, Japan might never have felt the need to attack the United States. Of course, Japanese aggression would then have been unchecked, and Japan would have established itself as the regional power in the western Pacific.

In terms of *domestic* and *systemic causes,* we have seen how at a domestic level the increased militarism of Japan's government made war more likely. And as with Europe in the 1930s, the economic collapse in both Japan and the United States affected the foreign policies of both countries. Japan became more expansionist, while until 1940 the United States became even more isolated. In addition, the domestic chaos in Nationalist China continued in the 1930s, making it more vulnerable to Japanese expansion. That, in turn, increased the influence of the militarists within Japanese domestic politics. Throughout the interwar period, lingering resentment among the Japanese for the U.S. unwillingness to enshrine the principle of racial equality in the Covenant of the League of Nations poisoned relations between Tokyo and Washington. At the system level, the Treaty of Versailles had left the ambitions of Japan in China unsatisfied, while the economic problems of the 1930s made it more difficult for Japan to obtain the raw materials it needed by trade alone. And the breakdown between 1931 and 1933 of the already weak League of Nations' collective-security system in Asia removed any institutional constraints on Japan's imperial ambitions. Unlike the war in Europe, both the deep and intermediate causes of the war in the Pacific were largely domestic—the shift toward expansion in Japan and toward greater isolationism in the United States, and the chaos of 1930s China. The precipitating causes were Roosevelt's decision to implement a full embargo in July 1941 and the resulting decision of the Japanese military to attack the United States on December 7.

Appeasement and Two Types of War

What lessons can we draw from this? Some say the key lesson of the 1930s is that *appeasement* does not work—indeed, that it is downright evil. But appeasement is not bad per se; it is a classic tool of diplomacy. It is a policy choice to allow for changes in the balance of power that benefit a rival state. Rather than attempting to deter or contain the aggression of adversaries, a state might prefer to allow its adversaries modest gains. On the eve of the

Peloponnesian War, Corinth tried to persuade Athens that it should be allowed to absorb Corcyra. However, Athens refused to appease Corinth and chose instead to fight. Given subsequent events, it is possible that Athens would have done better to appease Corinthian ambitions than to challenge them over Corcyra. Appeasement was used successfully in 1815 when the victorious powers appeased the defeated but still strong France. In the late nineteenth and early twentieth centuries, Britain very effectively appeased the rising United States.[14] We could even argue that appeasement might have been the right policy for the Western Allies to have taken toward Germany in the 1920s, particularly since the British were especially willing to try appeasement when it would satisfy "legitimate grievances" (many in Britain came to have serious moral qualms about the Treaty of Versailles' territorial dismemberment of Germany).[15] One of the great ironies of the interwar period is that the West confronted Germany in the 1920s when it should have been appeased and appeased Germany in the 1930s when it should have been confronted.

Appeasement was the wrong approach to Hitler, but British prime minister Neville Chamberlain was not such a coward as the Munich experience makes him out to be. He wanted to avoid another world war. In July 1938, he said,

> When I think of those four terrible years [1914–1918] and I think of the 7 million young men who were cut off in their prime and 13 million who were maimed and mutilated, the misery and suffering of the mothers and fathers, sons and daughters, I must say that there are no winners in a war, but all losers. It is those thoughts which make me feel that it is my prime duty to strain every nerve to avoid repetition of the Great War in Europe.[16]

Chamberlain's sins were not his intentions, but rather his ignorance and arrogance in failing to appraise the situation properly. And in that failure he was not alone.

World Wars I and II are often cast as two quite different models of war: accidental war versus planned aggression. World War I is sometimes portrayed as an unwanted spiral of hostility. To some extent, it might have been avoided with appeasement, though German demands might not have been easily accommodated. Political scientist David Calleo has argued, "The proper lesson is not so much the need for vigilance against aggressors, but the ruinous consequences of refusing reasonable accommodation of upstarts."[17] World War II, however, was definitely not an unwanted spiral of hostility—it was a failure to deter Hitler's planned aggression. In that sense, the policies appropriate for preventing World Wars I and II were almost opposite. Accommodation of Germany might have helped delay or forestall World War I, and deterrence of Germany might have prevented World War II, but the policies were reversed. In trying to avoid a repetition of World War I, British leaders in the 1930s helped precipitate World War II. At the same time, the efforts of U.S. leaders to deter Japan helped bring on war in the Pacific. Deterrence failed because the Japanese felt cornered in a situation in which the alternative of peace looked worse than risking a war.

Of course, these two models of war are too simple. World War I was not purely accidental, and World War II was not merely the result of Hitler's planned aggression (certainly in the Pacific, it was not the result of Hitler's aggression at all). The ultimate lesson is to be wary of overly simple historical models. Always ask whether a model is true to the facts of history and whether it really fits the current reality. It helps to remember the story of Mark Twain's cat. As Twain pointed out, a cat that sits on a hot stove will not sit on a hot stove again; but neither will it sit on a cold one. It is necessary to know which stoves are cold and which are hot when using historical analogies, or when using World Wars I and II as models for understanding later events.

Follow Up

- A. J. P. Taylor, *The Origins of the Second World War* (London: Hamilton, 1961).
- Alan Bullock, "Hitler and the Origins of the Second World War," in W. R. Louis, ed., *The Origins of the Second World War: A. J. P. Taylor and His Critics* (New York: Wiley, 1972), pp. 117–145.
- Scott Sagan, "The Origins of the Pacific War," *Journal of Interdisciplinary History* 18:4 (Spring 1988), pp. 893–922.

CHRONOLOGY: BETWEEN THE WORLD WARS

▪ 1919	Peace Conference opens at Versailles; adoption of Weimar Constitution
▪ 1920	Creation of the League of Nations
▪ 1921–1922	Washington conference on naval armaments
▪ 1922	Permanent Court of Justice at The Hague established; Treaty of Rapallo between Germany and the Soviet Union; Mussolini assumes power in Italy
▪ 1923	France and Belgium occupy the Ruhr in response to German default on coal deliveries; Nazi Beer Hall *Putsch* aborted
▪ 1924	Dawes Plan for reparations accepted; Geneva Protocol for the peaceful settlement of international disputes adopted
▪ 1925	Locarno Conference and treaties
▪ 1926	Germany admitted to the League of Nations
▪ 1928	Kellogg-Briand Pact signed
▪ 1930	London Naval Conference
▪ 1931	Japanese invasion of Manchuria; failure of the Austrian Credit-Anstalt; Bank of England forced off the gold standard
▪ 1932	Disarmament conference; Lausanne Conference on German reparations

(*Continued*)

- 1933 — Adolf Hitler becomes chancellor of Germany; Reichstag fire; Enabling Act passed establishing Nazi dictatorship; Germany withdraws from the disarmament conference and League of Nations
- 1934 — Soviet Union joins the League of Nations
- 1935 — Germany renounces the disarmament clauses of the Versailles treaty; Franco-Russian alliance formed; Anglo-German naval agreement reached; Italian invasion of Ethiopia; Hoare-Laval Pact
- 1936 — Germany denounces Locarno pacts and reoccupies the Rhineland; Italy wins the war in Ethiopia; League of Nations discredited as a political instrument; Rome-Berlin axis formed; Anti-Comintern Pact formed
- 1936–1939 — Civil war in Spain
- 1937 — Japan launches attacks on Nanjing and other Chinese cities
- 1938 — German invasion and annexation of Austria; Chamberlain meets Hitler at Berchtesgaden, Godesberg, and Munich to resolve the German-Czech crisis; Munich agreement signed
- 1939 — Crisis in Czechoslovakia; Germany occupies all of Czechoslovakia; British and French pledges to Poland and guarantees to Greece and Romania; Italy invades Albania; Russian-German (Molotov–von Ribbentrop) Pact; Germany invades Poland; Britain and France declare war on Germany
- 1940 — Hitler invades Denmark and Norway; Hitler invades the Netherlands, Belgium, Luxembourg, and France; Battle of Britain; Japan occupies French Indochina
- 1941 — Hitler invades the Soviet Union; Japan attacks Pearl Harbor

STUDY QUESTIONS

1. What "lessons" of World War I did policy makers draw at the time? How did it affect their behavior in the interwar period?
2. How did the concept of collective security differ from balance-of-power politics? Is the notion of collective security utopian? If not, how might collective security have worked better during the interwar period?
3. Was World War II inevitable? If so, why, and when? If not, when and how could it have been avoided?
4. To what extent can the outbreak of World War II be attributed to the personalities of the leaders involved?
5. What might be some lessons of the interwar period that might help policy makers avoid war today?
6. Was Japan irrational to attack the United States?

NOTES

1. Woodrow Wilson, quoted in Ray S. Baker and William E. Dodd, eds., *The Public Papers of Woodrow Wilson: War and Peace,* vol. 1 (New York: Harper, 1927), pp. 182–183.
2. Alexander L. George and Juliette L. George, *Woodrow Wilson and Colonel House* (New York: John Day Co., 1956).
3. Woodrow Wilson, quoted in Inis L. Claude, *Power and International Relations* (New York: Random House, 1962), p. 104.
4. In fact, the treaty was superseded by agreements signed at the Washington conference that recognized Japan's great-power status. Britain's decision to terminate the treaty was influenced heavily by the Canadian government's fear that renewal would alienate the United States. Phillips Payson O'Brien, "Britain and the End of the Anglo-Japanese Alliance," in Phillips Payson O'Brien, ed., *The Anglo-Japanese Alliance, 1902–1922* (London: RoutledgeCurzon, 2003), pp. 264–284.
5. Quoted in F. P. Walters, *A History of the League of Nations* (London: Oxford University Press, 1952), p. 653.
6. A. J. P. Taylor, *The Origins of the Second World War,* 2nd ed. (Greenwich: Fawcett, 1961), p. xvi.
7. Adolf Hitler, quoted in Gordon Craig, *Germany, 1866–1945* (New York: Oxford University Press, 1978), p. 712.
8. Hitler has been the subject of numerous biographies and personality studies, and of course any history of World War II will discuss Hitler in detail. Particularly valuable for its insight, and also particularly well written, is a relatively old biography at this point: Alan Bullock, *Hitler: A Study in Tyranny*, abr. ed. (New York: Harper & Row, 1971). The best genuine psychobiography—carefully researched, yet appropriately cautious about the conclusions it draws—is Fritz Redlick, *Hitler: Diagnosis of a Destructive Prophet* (New York: Oxford University Press, 1999).
9. Ian Kershaw, "Hitler and the Nazi Dictatorship," in Mary Fulbrook, ed., *German History Since 1800* (London: Edward Arnold, 1997), p. 336.
10. Bullock, *Hitler*, p. 190; John Toland, *Adolf Hitler* (Garden City, NY: Doubleday, 1976), pp. 467–469; Sidney Aster, *1939: The Making of the Second World War* (New York: Simon and Schuster, 1973), p. 235.
11. Dean Acheson, quoted in Scott Sagan, "The Origins of the Pacific War," in Robert I. Rotberg and Theodore K. Rabb, eds., *The Origin and Prevention of Major Wars* (New York: Cambridge University Press, 1989), pp. 335–336.
12. Sagan, "The Origins of the Pacific War," p. 325.
13. Tsukada, quoted in Scott Sagan, "Deterrence and Decision: An Historical Critique of Modern Deterrence Theory" (Ph.D. thesis, Harvard University, 1983), p. 280.
14. Stephen R. Rock, *Appeasement in International Politics* (Lexington: University Press of Kentucky, 2000), pp. 25–47.

15. Robert J. Caputi, *Neville Chamberlain and Appeasement* (Selinsgrove, PA: Susquehanna University Press, 2000), p. 39.
16. Neville Chamberlain, *In Search of Peace: Speeches 1937–38* (London: Hutchinson, n.d.), p. 59.
17. David P. Calleo, *The German Problem Reconsidered: Germany and the World Order, 1870 to the Present* (Cambridge: Cambridge University Press, 1978), p. 6.

PHOTO CREDITS

Credits are listed in order of appearance:

akg-images/Newscom.

Bettmann/Corbis.

akg-images/Newscom.

MAP CREDIT

Maps are drawn from Brian Catchpole, *A Map History of the Modern World* (Oxford: Heinemann Publishers, 1982), reprinted with adjustments by permission.

The Cold War

Winston Churchill, Franklin Roosevelt, and Josef Stalin at Yalta, 1945

Given its violent first half, a most remarkable feature of the second half of the twentieth century was the absence of World War III. Instead, there was a *cold war,* a period of intense hostility without actual war. The hostility was so intense that many expected armed conflict between the superpowers. Fighting occurred, but it was on the peripheries and not directly between the United States and the Soviet Union. The Cold War lasted four decades, from 1947 to 1989. The height of the Cold War was from 1947 to 1963, when there were few serious negotiations between the United States and the Soviet Union. There were not even any summit meetings between 1945 and 1955. In 1952, George Kennan, the U.S. ambassador in Moscow, compared his isolation in the American embassy to his experience of being interned during World War II in Berlin. The later phases of the Cold War in the 1970s and 1980s were very different. The Americans and Soviets had many contacts, and they constantly negotiated arms control. The end of the Cold War was sudden and surprising, and quickly followed changes in Soviet policies after Mikhail Gorbachev came to power in 1985. Soviet hegemony over Eastern Europe collapsed in 1989, and the Soviet Union itself disintegrated in 1991.

DETERRENCE AND CONTAINMENT

Why did the Cold War not turn hot? There are several possible reasons for this, as we shall shortly see. Because of its unusual trajectory, the Cold War offers a unique perspective on international relations, and it illuminates the dynamics of two foreign policy choices that were made: the choice to *deter* and the choice to *contain.* To deter is to dissuade through fear. Although frequently associated with the Cold War, deterrence was not a new concept in international politics. Throughout history, countries built armies, formed alliances, and issued threats to deter other countries from attacking. During the Cold War and with the advent of nuclear weapons, the superpowers attempted to maintain peace more by dissuading an attack by threatening painful retaliation than by preparing to defend against an attack after it had occurred. Cold War deterrence depended upon the maintenance of large nuclear arsenals, but it was also an extension of balance-of-power logic. Deterrence by nuclear threat was one way each superpower tried to prevent the other from gaining advantage and hence upsetting the balance of power between them. As we shall see, deterrence often aggravated the tension between the United States and the Soviet Union, and it is not necessarily easy to demonstrate that deterrence worked. There is always the danger of spurious causation. If a professor said her lectures kept elephants out of the classroom, it would be difficult to disprove her claim if no elephants ever came to class. We can test such claims by using counterfactuals: How likely is it that elephants would come to class if someone else had been lecturing? Similarly, what provides a better explanation for peace during the Cold War—nuclear deterrence, or an absence of aggressive designs? We knew during the Cold War that the United States had no desire for military conquest, but Americans assumed that the Soviets did. Now that Soviet Cold War archives are open, it appears that Soviet leaders were just as uncertain of American intentions as Americans were of theirs.

Fearing Soviet expansionism, the United States practiced *containment*. This was a specific policy of surrounding the Soviet Union with U.S. allies and U.S. bases, and of promoting a liberal economic and political world order outside of the Soviet sphere of influence. But like deterrence, containment did not originate with the Cold War, even though the term did. Containment has been a tool of foreign policy for centuries. In the eighteenth century, the conservative monarchical states of Europe attempted to contain the ideology of liberty and equality espoused by the French Revolution, and even earlier, the Catholic Church in the Counter-Reformation attempted to contain the spread of the Reformation and the ideals of Martin Luther. There are different forms of containment. It can be offensive or defensive. It can use military power in the form of war or alliances; it can use economic power in the form of trading blocs or sanctions; and it can use soft power in the form of promoting ideas and values. During the Cold War, the United States wavered between an expansive policy of containing communism and a more limited policy of containing the Soviet Union; but throughout it used a combination of hard and soft power resources.

Follow Up

- Alexander L. George and Richard Smoke, *Deterrence in American Foreign Policy* (New York: Columbia University Press, 1974).
- George F. Kennan, "The Sources of Soviet Conduct," *Foreign Affairs* 25:4 (July 1947), pp. 566–582.

EXPLAINING THE COLD WAR

Three Approaches

Who or what caused the Cold War? Almost since it began, those questions have been the subject of fierce debate among scholars and policy makers. There are three main schools of opinion: *traditionalists, revisionists,* and *postrevisionists*.

The *traditionalists* argue that the answer to the question of who started the Cold War is quite simple: Stalin and the Soviet Union. At the end of World War II, American diplomacy was defensive, while the Soviets were aggressive and expansive. The Americans only slowly awoke to the nature of the Soviet threat.

What evidence do the traditionalists cite? Immediately after the war, the United States was proposing a universal world order and collective security through the United Nations. The Soviet Union did not take the United Nations very seriously because it wanted to expand and dominate its own sphere of influence in Eastern Europe. After the war, the United States demobilized its troops, whereas the Soviet Union left large armies in Eastern Europe. The United States recognized Soviet interests; for example, when Roosevelt, Stalin, and Churchill met in February 1945 at Yalta, the Americans went out of their way to accommodate Soviet interests. Stalin, however, did not live up to his agreements, particularly by not allowing free elections in Poland.

Soviet expansionism was further confirmed in the eyes of traditionalists when the Soviet Union was slow to remove its troops from northern Iran after the war. Eventually they were removed, but only under pressure. In 1948, the communists took over the Czechoslovakian government. The Soviet Union blockaded Berlin in 1948 and 1949, trying to squeeze the Western governments out. And in 1950, communist North Korea's armies invaded South Korea. According to the traditionalists, these events gradually awakened the United States to the threat of communist expansionism and launched the Cold War.

The *revisionists,* who wrote primarily in the 1960s and early 1970s, believe the Cold War was caused by American rather than Soviet expansionism. Their evidence is that at the end of World War II, the world was not really bipolar—the Soviets were much weaker than the United States, which was strengthened by the war and had nuclear weapons while the Soviets did not. The Soviet Union lost up to 30 million people, and industrial production was only half its 1939 level. Stalin told American ambassador Averell Harriman in October 1945 that the Soviets would turn inward to repair their domestic damage. What is more, say the revisionists, Stalin's external behavior early in the postwar period was quite moderate: In China, Stalin tried to restrain Mao Zedong's communists from taking power; in the Greek civil war, he tried to restrain the Greek communists; and he allowed noncommunist governments to exist in Hungary, Czechoslovakia, and Finland.

Revisionists come in two varieties that stress the first and second levels of explanation. Level one revisionists stress the importance of individuals and claim that Roosevelt's death in April 1945 was a critical event, because American policy toward the Soviet Union became harsher after President Harry S. Truman took office. In May 1945, the United States so precipitously cut off the lend-lease program of wartime aid that some ships bound for Soviet ports had to turn around in mid-ocean. At the Potsdam Conference near Berlin in July 1945, Truman tried to intimidate Stalin by mentioning the atomic bomb. In the United States, the Democratic Party gradually shifted from the left and center to the right. In 1948, Truman fired Henry Wallace, his secretary of agriculture, who urged better relations with the Soviets. At the same time, James Forrestal, Truman's new secretary of defense, was a strong anticommunist. These revisionists say these personnel changes help explain why the United States became so anti-Soviet.

The level two revisionists have a different answer. They see the problem not in individuals, but in the nature of U.S. capitalism. Gabriel and Joyce Kolko and William A. Williams, for example, argue that the American economy required expansionism and that the United States planned to make the world safe, not for democracy, but for capitalism. American economic hegemony could not tolerate any country that might try to organize an autonomous economic area. American leaders feared a repeat of the 1930s, because without external trade, there would be another Great Depression. According to level two revisionists, the Marshall Plan of aid to Europe was simply a way to expand the American economy. The Soviets were correct to reject it as a threat to their sphere of influence in Eastern Europe. In Williams's words, Americans always favored an open-door policy in the international economy because they expected to walk through it.

The *postrevisionists* of the late 1970s and 1980s, as exemplified by Yale historian John Lewis Gaddis, have yet another explanation that focuses on the structural level. They argue that the traditionalists and revisionists are both wrong because nobody was to blame for starting the Cold War. It was inevitable, or nearly so, because of the bipolar structure of the postwar balance of power. In 1939 there was a multipolar world with seven major powers, but after the destruction wrought by World War II, only two superpowers were left: the United States and the Soviet Union. Bipolarity plus the postwar weakness of the European states created a power vacuum into which the United States and the Soviet Union were drawn. They were bound to come into conflict and therefore, say the postrevisionists, it is pointless to look for blame.

Postrevisionists also note that the Soviets and the Americans had different kinds of goals at the end of the war. The Soviets were more concerned with securing control of territory—both home territory and a buffer sphere of influence—while Americans were primarily interested in setting up a liberal, rule-governed international order. American *milieu goals*, in other words, clashed with the Soviets' tangible possession goals. The United States promoted the global UN system; the Soviets worked to consolidate control of Eastern Europe. But these differences were no reason for Americans to feel sanctimonious, say the postrevisionists, for the United States benefited from the United Nations and, with a majority of allies voting, was not very constrained by it. The Soviets may have had a sphere of influence in Eastern Europe, but the United States also had a sphere of influence in the Western Hemisphere and Western Europe.

The United States and the Soviet Union were both bound to expand, say the postrevisionists, not because of the economic determinism that the revisionists stress, but because of the age-old security dilemma of states in an anarchic system. Neither the Americans nor the Soviets could allow the other to dominate Europe any more than Athens could afford to let the Corinthians gain control of Corcyra's navy. As evidence, postrevisionists cite Stalin's comment to a Yugoslav leader, Milovan Djilas, in 1945: "This war is not as in the past; whoever occupies a territory also imposes on it his own social system. Everyone imposes his own system as far as his army can reach."[1] In other words, in an ideological bipolar world, a powerful state would use its military power within its sphere of influence to reshape other societies in its image in order to ensure its own security. Roosevelt had said something similar to Stalin in the fall of 1944: "In this global war there is literally no question, political or military, in which the United States is not interested."[2] Given this bipolar structure, say the postrevisionists, a spiral of hostility set in: Hard lines in one country bred hard lines in the other. Both began to perceive the enemy as analogous to Hitler in the 1930s. As perceptions became more rigid, the Cold War deepened.

Since the end of the Cold War, a modest flow of documents from formerly inaccessible Soviet archives has given new vigor to the debate over which side started the confrontation. Gaddis, for example, has become increasingly convinced that the Soviet Union was primarily responsible for the onset and the nature of the superpower conflict. He cites the ideological rigidity of Stalin and other Soviet leaders, as well as the Kremlin's equally rigid commitment to maintaining a formal empire in its sphere of influence. Gaddis's move back toward a traditionalist viewpoint has garnered a skeptical reception in some scholarly quarters, guaranteeing that the debate will continue into the foreseeable future.

Roosevelt's Policies

Franklin Roosevelt wanted to avoid the mistakes of World War I, so instead of a Versailles-like peace, he demanded Germany's unconditional surrender. He wanted a liberal trade system to avoid the protectionism that had damaged the world economy in the 1930s and contributed to the onset of war. The United States would avoid its tendency toward isolationism that had been so damaging in the 1930s. It would join a new and stronger League of Nations in the form of a United Nations with a powerful Security Council. Cordell Hull, U.S. secretary of state during most of the war, was a committed Wilsonian, and public opinion in the United States was strongly in favor of the United Nations.

To promote his great design, Roosevelt needed to maintain bipartisan domestic support for his international position. Externally, he needed to reassure Stalin that his security needs would be met by joining the United Nations. Roosevelt has been accused of a naïve approach to postwar planning. His design was not naïve, but some of his tactics were. He placed too much faith in the United Nations, overestimated the likelihood of American isolationism, and, most important, underestimated Stalin. Roosevelt thought he could treat Stalin the way he would treat a fellow American politician, throwing his arm around him, bonding politician to politician. Roosevelt did not fully realize that Stalin, along with his men, was a totalitarian "who in the name of the people, murdered millions of them; who to defend against Hitler, signs a pact with him, divides the spoils of war with him, and like him, expels, exterminates, or enslaves neighboring peoples; who stands aside and fulminates against the democracies as Germany moves west, and then blames them for not helping enough when Hitler moves east."[4]

Roosevelt misinterpreted Stalin, but Roosevelt did not sell out American interests at the Yalta Conference in 1945, as some later claimed. Roosevelt was not naïve in all aspects of his policy. He tried to tie economic aid to political concessions by the Soviets and refused to share the secrets of the atomic bomb with them. He was simply realistic about who would have troops in Eastern Europe at the end of the war, and, therefore, who would have leverage in that region. Roosevelt's mistakes were in thinking that Stalin saw the world his way, that he understood domestic politics in the United States, and that the same American political skills in which a leader blurred differences and appealed to friendship would work in dealing with Stalin.

Stalin's Policies

Stalin's immediate postwar plans were to tighten domestic control. World War II did tremendous damage to the Soviet Union, not just the terrible losses of life and industry already described, but also to the ideology of communism. Many in the Soviet Union collaborated with the Germans because of their deep resentment over the harshness of communist rule. Germany's invasion seriously weakened Stalin's control. Indeed, Stalin had to increase his appeals to Russian nationalism during the war because the weakened communist ideology was insufficient to motivate his people. (In the Soviet Union at the time, and in Russia today, the war is called "The Great Patriotic War.") Stalin's isolationist policy at the end of the war was designed to cut off external influences from Europe and the United States. Stalin used the United States as an objective enemy as a way of cultivating mistrust of outsiders and increasing central control over the Soviet people. But it does not follow that Stalin wanted the Cold War that actually developed.

Stalin preferred some cooperation, especially if it helped him pursue his goals in Eastern Europe and brought him some economic assistance from the United States. As a good communist, he believed the United States would have to give him economic assistance because the capitalist system had to export capital due to insufficient demand at home. Stalin also believed that in ten or fifteen years, the next crisis of the capitalist system would come along, and at that time the Soviet Union would have recovered and be ready to benefit in the inevitable conflict with the capitalists.

In foreign policy terms, Stalin wanted to protect himself at home, as well as maintain the gains the Soviet Union had made in Eastern Europe from the 1939 pact with Hitler. Stalin also wanted to probe soft spots, something better done when there is no crisis. In 1941, Stalin told the British foreign minister, Anthony Eden, that he preferred arithmetic to algebra; in other words, he wanted a practical rather than a theoretical approach. When Winston Churchill proposed a formula on the postwar division of influence in the Balkans—that is, some countries under British control, some under Soviet control, and others 50/50—Stalin was quite receptive to the idea. Some of Stalin's early caution in supporting communist governments right away in China, Czechoslovakia, and Hungary fit quite well with this arithmetic rather than algebraic approach to achieving his objectives. Stalin was a committed communist who, although he saw the world through the lens of communism, often used pragmatic tactics.

Phases of the Conflict

The early stages of the Cold War can be divided into three phases: 1945–1947, the prelude and slide into the Cold War; 1947–1949, the onset of the Cold War; and 1950–1963, the height of the Cold War.

Neither Stalin nor Truman was looking for a cold war. At the end of World War II, Truman sent Roosevelt's former aide Harry Hopkins to Moscow to see if some arrangements could be worked out. Even after the Potsdam Conference, Truman continued to see Stalin as a moderate. Indeed, as late as 1949, he compared Stalin to his old friend Boss Pendergast in Kansas City. In 1946, George Kennan, writing from Moscow as the U.S. embassy's chargé d'affaires, was trying to warn American decision makers about Stalin's true nature and intentions, and Winston Churchill gave a famous speech in Fulton, Missouri, warning that an "iron curtain" was descending across Europe. While Secretary of State James Byrnes was still trying to negotiate a postwar treaty with the Soviets, Truman asked his aide Clark Clifford to prepare a report on what the Soviets were really planning. Clifford talked with a variety of people and concluded that Kennan was right: The Soviets were going to expand whenever they found an inexpensive opportunity. When Truman received the report in December 1946, however, he told Clifford he did not want its results widely known, for he was still trying to follow Roosevelt's great design and had not yet developed a new strategy.

Six issues contributed to the eventual change of American strategy and the onset of the Cold War. One was Soviet actions in Poland and Eastern Europe. Poland, of course, had been one of the precipitating causes of World War II, and Americans believed that Stalin broke a clear commitment to hold free elections in Poland after the war. However, it was not clear what Stalin had agreed to do. When Stalin and Roosevelt met at Tehran in 1943, Roosevelt raised the Polish issue, but he appealed to Stalin in the context of the looming 1944 American election: There were many Polish-American voters, and he needed to tell them there would be elections in Poland after the war. Stalin, who never worried about elections in the Soviet Union, did not take Roosevelt's concerns seriously. The February 1945 Yalta agreement was also somewhat ambiguous, and Stalin stretched the meaning as far as he could by setting up a puppet government in Warsaw after Soviet troops had driven out the Germans. The Americans felt cheated, but Stalin felt the Americans would adjust to the reality that Soviet troops had liberated Poland.

Second, in May 1945, the lend-lease aid program was abruptly stopped, and the economic relationship between the United States and the Soviet Union became strained. The precipitous termination of lend-lease was to some extent a bureaucratic mistake, but the overall situation was not improved when in February 1946 the United States refused Soviet requests for loans. The Soviets interpreted both acts as hostile.

Germany was a third problem. At the Yalta meeting, the Americans and the Soviets agreed that Germany should pay $20 billion in reparations, with half going to the Soviet Union. The details of how and when the payments would be made were not worked out at Yalta, although both sides agreed they would be negotiated later. At the Potsdam meeting in July 1945, the Soviets demanded their $10 billion; furthermore, they wanted it from the western zones of Germany that the Americans, British, and French had occupied. Harry Truman, worried about how Germany would be reconstructed, said that if the Soviets wanted to take $10 billion out of Germany, they should take it out of the eastern zone they occupied; if there was anything left over after the reconstruction of the western side of Germany, he would let the Soviets know. Thus began a series of divisions between the Americans and the Soviets about how to reconstruct Germany. The Americans, along with the British and French, created a single currency in the western zones (the deutsche mark), starting the process of West German integration, which in turn caused the Soviets to tighten control of the eastern zone of Germany.

East Asia was a fourth issue. The Soviets were neutral in the Pacific war until the very last week. Then the Soviets declared war and opportunistically seized from Japan Outer Manchuria, southern Sakhalin Island, and the entire Kurile Island chain. At Potsdam, the Soviets asked for an occupation zone in Japan, like the American occupation zone in Germany. Truman's response was, in effect, that the Soviets arrived at the party late, so they would get no zone. From an American point of view, this seemed perfectly reasonable, but the situation reminded the Soviets of Eastern Europe, where the Americans wanted free elections and influence, but the Soviet armies had arrived there first. So the Soviets saw the Far Eastern situation as analogous to Eastern Europe, while the Americans saw it as one more example of the Soviets pressing for their own expansion.

A fifth issue was the atomic bomb. Roosevelt had decided not to share the secret of the atomic bomb with the Soviet Union. Most historians now agree that Truman dropped the bomb on Hiroshima and Nagasaki primarily to bring a quick end to the war with Japan, not to intimidate the Soviet Union, as some revisionists have claimed. But he did expect the bomb to have some political effects. At the Potsdam meeting, when Truman told Stalin that America had an atomic bomb, Stalin remained poker-faced and seemingly unimpressed. Of course, Stalin already knew about it from his own spies, but his equanimity was a bit of a jolt to the Americans. In 1946, when the United States set forth the Baruch Plan for UN control of nuclear weapons, Stalin rejected it because he wanted to build his own bomb. As he saw it, a bomb under international control would still be an American bomb—for only the Americans knew how to build it. Stalin believed it would be far better for Soviet security to have their own, which they eventually developed in 1949.

The sixth issue concerned countries in the eastern Mediterranean and the Middle East, where the British had been influential before World War II. After the war, several things occurred. First, the Soviets refused to remove their troops from northern Iran in March 1946. The United States supported Iran in a debate within the United Nations. The Soviets eventually moved out, but not without a good deal of bitterness. The Soviet Union also began to put pressure on Turkey, its neighbor to the south, at the same time that the communists seemed to be winning the civil war in Greece. Once again, the West believed the Soviets were attempting to expand.

These six issues were real, though some misperceptions were involved in almost all of them. Could they have been solved by negotiation and appeasement? Would appeasement have worked? Probably not. Kennan argued that Stalin was intent on probing any soft spots. Appeasement would have been interpreted as a soft spot and invited more probing. In June 1946, Maxim Litvinov, the former Soviet foreign minister, warned an American counterpart against any concessions, because the root cause of the tension was "the ideological conception prevailing here that conflict between Communist and capitalist worlds is inevitable." Concessions would merely lead "to the West's being faced, after a more or less short time, with the next series of demands."[5] Appeasement probably would not have worked, but harder bargaining might have limited some of the events that led to the onset of the Cold War. A tactical appeal to Stalin's pragmatism from a firmer American position, plus a willingness to negotiate, might have worked out better in that early period, from 1945–1947.

The second phase, the onset of the Cold War from 1947–1949, followed from the problems in Greece and Turkey (Figure 1). Britain, severely weakened by World War II, felt it could no longer provide security in the eastern Mediterranean. The United States had to decide whether to let a vacuum develop or to replace British power by providing assistance to Greece and Turkey. This involved a considerable break from traditional American foreign policy. Truman was not sure that American public opinion would support such a move. There was still fear that isolationism would be the mainstay of America's postwar foreign policy. Truman asked Senator Arthur Vandenberg, the Republican leader from Michigan, whether the Senate would go along with aiding Greece and Turkey. Vandenberg said Truman would have to "scare the hell out of them" to get congressional support for this break with traditional American policy. Thus, when Truman explained the policy change, he did not talk about the need to maintain a balance of power in the eastern Mediterranean by providing aid to Greece and Turkey. Instead, he talked about the need to protect free people everywhere. This moralistic, ideological explanation for American assistance became known as the Truman Doctrine.

George Kennan, by then back in the State Department, objected to this ideological approach to formulating foreign policy, arguing that it was too open-ended and would get the United States into trouble. Indeed, there were enormous ambiguities in the policy of containment that flowed from the Truman Doctrine. Was the United States interested in containing Soviet power or communist ideology? At the beginning, containing Soviet power and containing communist ideology seemed to be the same, but later in the Cold War when the communist movement split, the ambiguities became important.

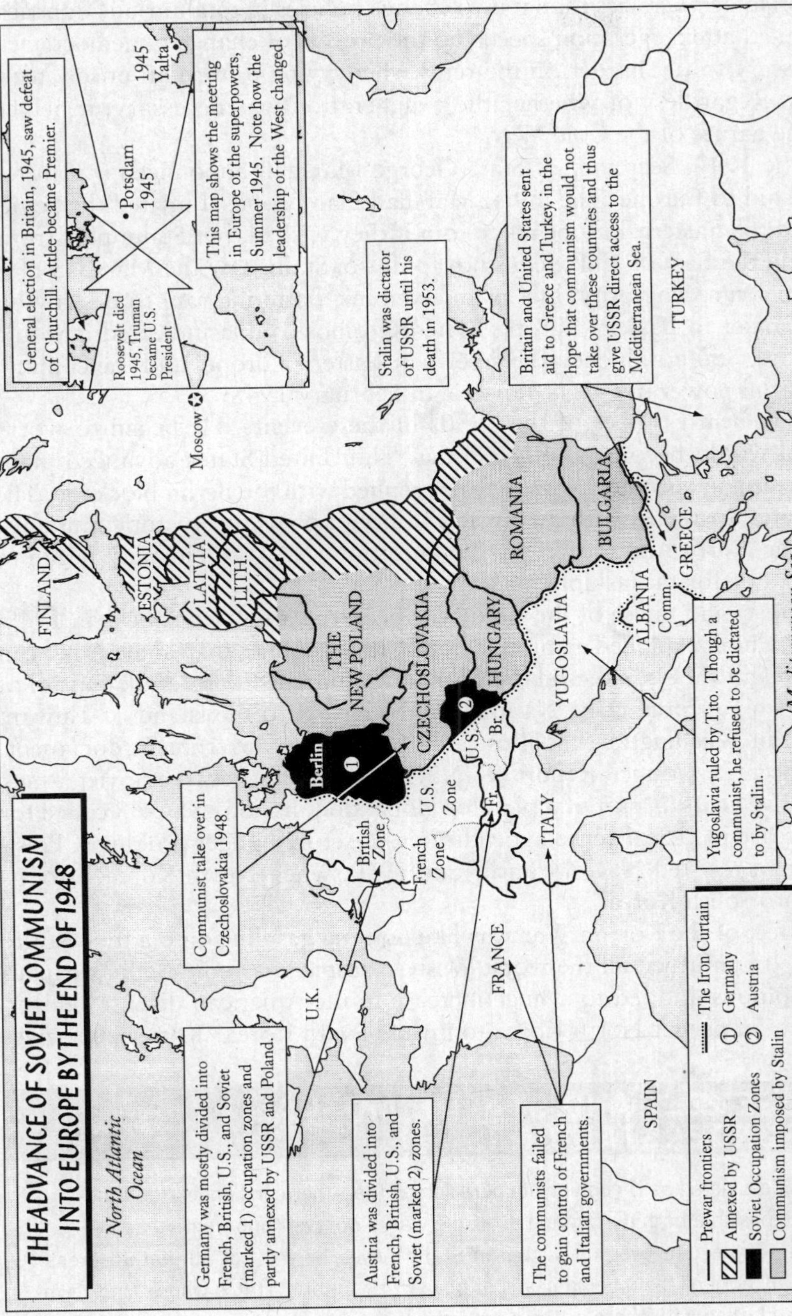

FIGURE 1
The Early Days of the Cold War in Europe

Was Truman wrong to exaggerate the sense of threat and the ideological rationale for the policy change? Some observers feel it is harder to change public opinion in democracies than it is to change policies in totalitarian countries. They argue that exaggeration speeds up the process of change in democracies. It is necessary to tug harder on the reins when trying to turn an unruly team of horses. Regardless of whether the exaggeration was necessary, it helped change the nature of the Cold War.

In June 1947, Secretary of State George Marshall announced a plan for economic aid to Europe. The initial Marshall Plan proposal invited the Soviet Union and the Eastern Europeans to join if they wished, but Stalin put strong pressure on the Eastern Europeans not to do so. Stalin saw the Marshall Plan not as American generosity, but as an economic battering ram to destroy his security barrier in Eastern Europe. When Czechoslovakia indicated it would like U.S. aid, Stalin tightened the screws in Eastern Europe, and the communists took full power in Czechoslovakia in February 1948.

Truman heard echoes of the 1930s in these events. He began to worry that Stalin would become another Hitler. The United States advanced plans for West German currency reform; Stalin replied with the Berlin blockade. The United States answered with an airlift and began plans for an anticommunist alliance, the North Atlantic Treaty Organization (NATO). Hostility began to escalate in a tit-for-tat fashion.

The most rigid phase of the Cold War occurred after two shocks in 1949: The Soviet Union exploded an atomic bomb, much sooner than some American leaders thought they could; and the Chinese Communist Party took control of mainland China, forcing the Nationalists to retreat to the island of Taiwan. The alarm in Washington was illustrated by a secret government document, National Security Council Report 68 (NSC-68), which forecast a Soviet attack in four to five years as part of a plan for global domination. NSC-68 called for a vast increase in U.S. defense expenditures. Beset by budget problems, President Truman resisted NSC-68 until June 1950, when North Korea's troops stormed into South Korea.

The effect of the Korean War was like pouring gasoline onto a modest fire (Figure 2). It confirmed all the worst Western suspicions about Stalin's expansionist ambitions and led to a huge increase in the American defense budget. Why did Stalin permit North Korea to invade South Korea? Khrushchev gives

ROOSEVELT AND STALIN: MUTUAL MISUNDERSTANDINGS

The President acted as if genuine cooperation as the Americans understood the term were possible both during and after the war. Roosevelt apparently had forgotten, if indeed he ever knew, that in Stalin's eyes, he was not all that different from Hitler, both of them being heads of powerful capitalist states whose long-term ambitions clashed with those of the Kremlin.

—*William Taubman, Stalin's American Policy*[3]

an explanation in his memoirs: Kim Il Sung, the North Korean leader, pressed Stalin for the opportunity to unify the peninsula. The United States had said Korea was outside its defense perimeter; Secretary of State Dean Acheson had articulated this position, and the Joint Chiefs of Staff had planned accordingly. To Stalin, Korea looked like a soft spot. But when North Korea actually attacked South Korea, Truman responded in a knee-jerk rather than a calculating way: Truman remembered Hitler moving into the Rhineland and recalled the maxim that aggression must be resisted everywhere. Calculated plans about defense perimeters were overshadowed by the historical analogies triggered by North Korea's invasion. The United States was able to mobilize the UN Security Council to endorse collective security (which was possible because the Soviet Union was then boycotting the Security Council over its failure at that point to give the communist government in Beijing the China seat, instead of the Nationalist government in Taiwan) and sent troops to Korea under the UN flag to push the communists back above the thirty-eighth parallel that bisected the peninsula and had previously divided North and South.

At first, North Korea's armies swept down the peninsula almost to the tip. In September 1950, however, an American amphibious landing at Inchon, halfway up the peninsula, routed the North Koreans. Had the United States stopped there, it could have claimed victory by restoring the preinvasion status quo; but Truman succumbed to domestic pressures to pursue the retreating communist troops north of the thirty-eighth parallel. As the Americans approached the Yalu River, which divides Korea from China, the Chinese communists intervened, pushing the UN troops back to the middle of the peninsula. There the battle stalemated bloodily for three years until a truce was signed in 1953. The United States had become embroiled with China, and communism appeared to be monolithic. At home, the frustrating war led to domestic division and the rise of McCarthyism, named after the harsh and poorly founded accusations of domestic communist subversion made by Senator Joseph McCarthy of Wisconsin. The Cold War blocs tightened and communication nearly ceased.

Inevitability?

Was the onset of the Cold War inevitable? The postrevisionists are correct if we relax the interpretation of inevitability to mean "highly probable." The bipolar structure made it likely that both sides would be sucked into a power

KOREA AND NSC-68

The purpose of NSC-68 was to so bludgeon the mass mind of "top government" that not only could the President make a decision but that the decision could be carried out. Even so, it is doubtful whether anything like what happened in the next few years could have been done had not the Russians been stupid enough to have instigated the attack against South Korea and opened the "hate America" campaign.

—*Secretary of State Dean Acheson, Present at the Creation*[6]

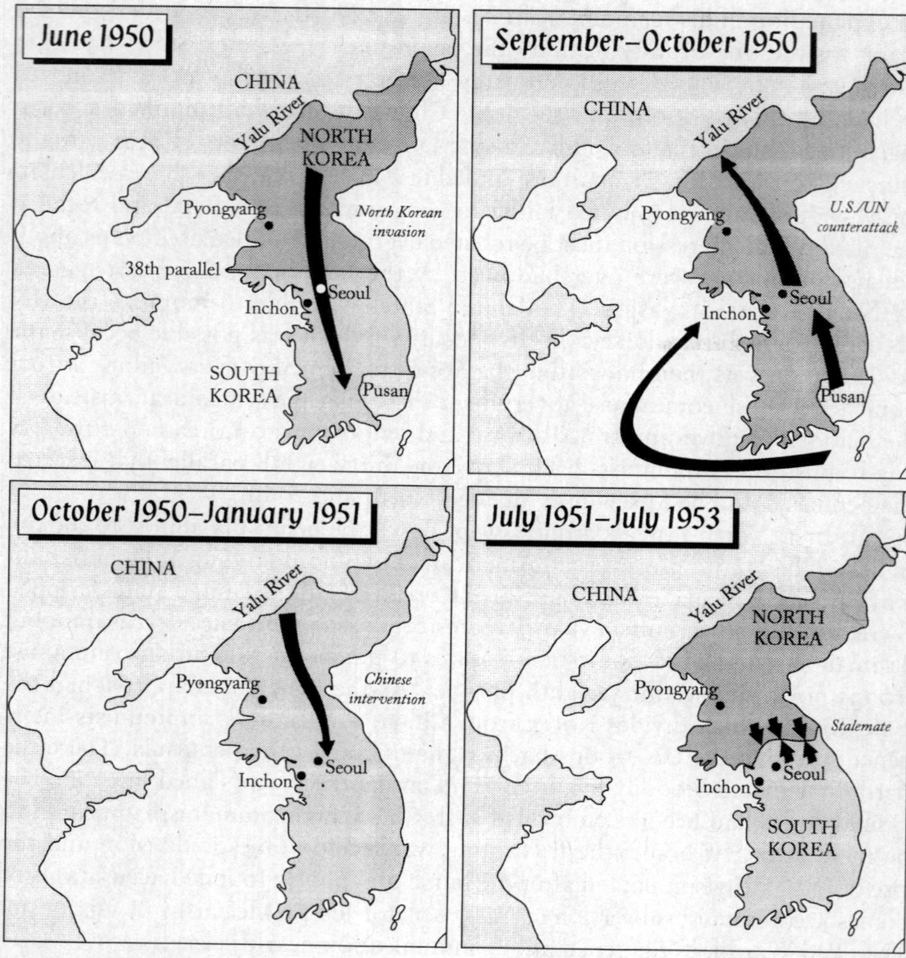

FIGURE 2
The Korean War

vacuum in Europe and find it difficult to disengage. The intense ideological climate hampered the working of the United Nations, restricted clear communication, and contributed to the immoderate process of the international system. Under such systemic conditions, conflicts would have arisen over the six issues just identified, or some others, and proven difficult to resolve.

The postrevisionists rely too heavily, however, on systemic explanation. Perhaps some cold war was inevitable, but its depth was not. After all, there were different degrees of hostility in different phases, and since the bipolarity of the system did not change until 1989, neorealist structural explanations cannot account for the different phases or varying depth of the hostility. That is where individuals and domestic politics matter. Leaders' personalities and the domestic political contexts in which they operated have to be considered to fully understand the Cold War. The revisionists are right to focus on domestic questions, but they are wrong to focus so strongly on economic determinism. More important was the role of ideology and exaggeration in domestic politics. Stalin used ideology because of Soviet domestic problems after the war, and Truman exaggerated the nature of the communist threat in order to rally support for changing American foreign policy. The use of 1930s analogies helped reinforce rigidity on both sides.

Ironically, alternative strategies at different times might have alleviated the depths of hostility. For example, if the United States had followed Kennan's advice and responded more firmly in 1945–1947 and had tried more pragmatic negotiation and communication from 1947–1950, Cold War tensions might not have risen to the extent they did in the early 1950s.

Levels of Analysis

The origins of the Cold War can be characterized in terms of the different images or levels of analysis as illustrated in Figure 3.

In the nineteenth century, Alexis de Tocqueville (1805–1859) predicted that Russia and the United States were bound to become two great continental-scale giants in the world. Realists might thus predict that these two would become locked in some form of conflict. And, of course, in 1917, the Bolshevik

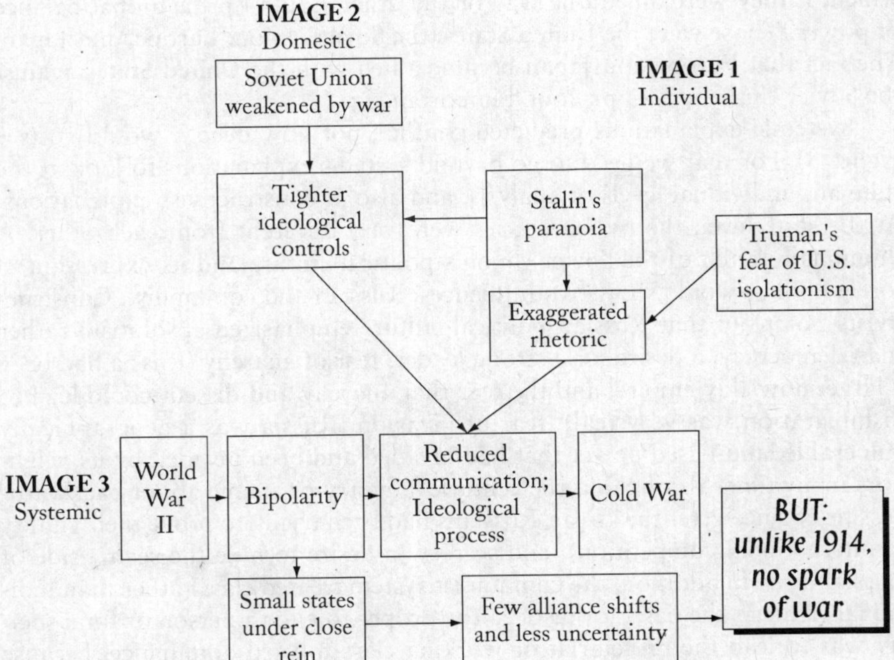

FIGURE 3
Causes of the Cold War

Revolution added an ideological layer to the conflict. When Woodrow Wilson first heard of the Russian Revolution, he congratulated the Russian people for their democratic spirit. But it did not take long before the Americans were accusing the Bolsheviks of regicide, expropriation, and cooperation with Germany in World War I. The United States added a small contingent of troops to an Allied intervention, allegedly to keep the Russians in the war against Germany, but the Soviets saw it as an attempt to strangle communism in its cradle. Despite these differences, the United States and the Soviet Union avoided serious conflict in the interwar period and became allies in the early 1940s. The bipolarity that followed the collapse of all the other great powers in World War II and the resulting power vacuum changed the relationship. Earlier there had been distrust between the two countries, but they distrusted each other at a distance. Before World War II they could avoid each other, but after 1945 they were face to face, Europe was divided, and deep conflict began after 1947. Some people wonder whether the bipolar structure had to have this effect. After all, the Soviet Union was a land-based power, while the United States was a maritime power; why could there not have been a division of labor between the bear and the whale, each staying in its own domain?

The answer is that the key stakes in world politics, the countries that could tip the balance of power, were located on the peripheries of the Soviet Union, particularly Europe and Japan. As George Kennan described the situation after the war, there were four great areas of technological and industrial creativity, which, if they were allied one way or the other, could tip the global balance of power. Those were the United States, the Soviet Union, Europe, and Japan. The fact that Europe and Japan became allied with the United States against the Soviet Union was of profound importance.

Systemic explanations predicted conflict, not how deep it would go (see Figure 3). For that we need to go beyond systems explanations to look at the state and individual levels of analysis, and also at constructivist explanations. At the state level, the two countries were very different from each other. A thumbnail sketch of the Soviet Union's political culture and its expression in foreign policy would show two influences: Russian and communist. Constructivists point out that Russian political culture emphasized absolutism rather than democracy, a desire for a strong leader, fear of anarchy (Russia had been a large, unwieldy empire, and the fear that anarchy and dissent could lead to disintegration was very real), fear of invasion (Russia was a geographically vulnerable land-based power that had invaded and been invaded by its neighbors many times throughout the centuries), worry or shame about backwardness (ever since Peter the Great, Russians had been trying to prove their vitality in international competition), and secrecy (a desire to hide the seamy side of Russian life). In addition, the communist system treated class rather than individual rights as the basis for justice. The proper role for a person or for a society was to lead the proletariat or working class toward dominance, because this was supposed to be the course of history.

The ideological overlay gave an additional outward thrust to traditional Russian imperialism and resulted in a secret and tightly held foreign policy process. It is interesting to note the strengths and weaknesses of that process. The strengths were evident in 1939 when Stalin was able to sign his nonaggression pact with Hitler so quickly. Public opinion did not constrain him, and he did not have to worry about a bureaucracy holding him back. He was free to rush into the pact with Hitler while the British and French were still dithering about whether or not to deal with him. The opposite side of the same coin became evident in 1941, however, when Hitler attacked the Soviet Union. Stalin was unable to believe Hitler would do such a thing and went into a deep depression for more than a week. None of his subordinates dared to fill the leadership vacuum, and the result was a delayed response that proved disastrous for Soviet defenses in the early phases of the war.

In contrast, American political culture emphasized liberal democracy, pluralism, and fragmentation of power. Instead of shame about backwardness, the United States took pride in its technology and expanding economy. For much of its history, the United States had no real fear of invasion because its neighbors were weak (and therefore vulnerable to American invasion); because it was separated from other great powers by two vast oceans; and because the British navy prevented others from projecting influence into the Western Hemisphere. In terms of secrecy, the United States was so open that government documents often reached the press within a matter of days and weeks. Instead of a class basis for conceptions of justice, there was a strong emphasis on individual justice. The foreign policy that resulted from this political culture was moralistic, public, and tended to oscillate between inward and outward orientation. The result was that the American foreign policy process often appeared inconsistent and incoherent. But there was also an opposite side to this coin. The strengths of openness and pluralism often protected the United States from deeper mistakes.

Thus, it is not surprising to constructivists that these two societies, so differently organized and with such different foreign policy processes, would confuse each other. We saw examples of that in the way both Roosevelt and Truman dealt with Stalin in the 1940s. It was difficult for the Americans to understand the Soviet Union during the Cold War, because the Soviet Union was like a black box. American leaders could see what went in and what came out of the box, but not what happened inside. The Americans confused the Soviets as well. The Americans were like a machine that produced so much white noise that it was difficult to hear the true signals clearly. There were too many people saying too many things. Thus, the Soviets were often confused about what the Americans really wanted.

U.S. and Soviet Goals in the Cold War

The Soviets were often accused of being expansionist, of being a revolutionary power rather than a status quo power, but the postrevisionist view is both more subtle and more accurate: The Soviet Union was, in fact, more interested in tangible or possession goals, while the Americans tended to want intangible or milieu goals. We can see this in the demands that Stalin, Churchill, and

Roosevelt brought to the bargaining table at Yalta. Stalin had very clear objectives at Yalta: Germany and Poland. Roosevelt wanted the United Nations and an open international economic system. (Churchill wanted the restoration of France to help balance Soviet power in case the Americans went home!) In some ways, Stalin's postwar goals were classic Russian imperialist goals; he wanted to keep the gains he had made in the treaty with Hitler. His wish list would have been familiar to Peter the Great.

Some Americans thought the Soviets were as expansionist as Hitler in desiring world domination. Others said the Soviets were basically security oriented; their expansion was defensive. There were at least two ways in which Soviet expansionism was not like Hitler's. First, it was not bellicist; the Soviets did not want war. When Hitler invaded Poland, he worried he would be offered another Munich instead of the war he wanted. Another difference was that the Soviet Union was cautiously opportunistic, not recklessly adventuresome. Adventurism was seen as a sin against communism because it might disrupt the natural course of history, which would, in Soviet eyes, result in the inevitable defeat of capitalism. During the Cold War, the Soviet Union was never as bellicose or as reckless as Hitler was.

Nonetheless, there are problems in portraying Soviet behavior as purely defensive. As we know from the Peloponnesian War, it is very hard in a bipolar world to distinguish offense from defense. Certain actions may have defensive motives but may look very threatening to the other side. Moreover, there is a long tradition of defensive expansion, or imperialism. For example, in the nineteenth century, Britain originally went into Egypt to protect the sea routes to India. After it took Egypt, it thought it had to take the Sudan to protect Egypt, and then it had to take Uganda to protect the Sudan. After it took Uganda, Britain had to take Kenya to build a railway to protect Uganda. The appetite grows with the eating as the security dilemma is used to justify further and further expansion. Soviet communism added an ideological motive of freeing working classes in all areas of the world, which further legitimized expansion. In short, the Soviet Union was expansionist during the Cold War, but cautiously and opportunistically so.

What about U.S. goals? During the Cold War, the U.S. government wanted to contain the Soviet Union. Yet the policy of containment involved two large ambiguities. One was the question of the ends: whether to contain Soviet power or to contain communism. The second was a question of means: whether to spend resources to prevent any expansion of Soviet power or just in certain key areas that seemed critical to the balance of power. Those two ambiguities in the ends and means of containment were hotly debated in the period before the Korean War. George Kennan dissented from the rather expansive version of containment that Truman proclaimed. Kennan's idea of containment was akin to classical diplomacy. It involved fewer military means and was more selective. A good example was Yugoslavia, which had a communist totalitarian government under Josip Broz Tito. In 1948, Tito split with Stalin over Soviet efforts to control Yugoslavia's foreign policy, including Belgrade's support for the Greek communists. According to an ideologically

KENNAN'S VIEW OF CONTAINMENT

It would be an exaggeration to say that American behavior unassisted and alone could exercise a power of life and death over the Communist movement and bring about the early fall of Soviet power in Russia. But the United States has it in its power to increase enormously the strains under which Soviet policy must operate, to force upon the Kremlin a far greater degree of moderation and circumspection than it has had to observe in recent years, and in this way to promote tendencies which must eventually find their outlet in either the break-up or the gradual mellowing of Soviet power.

—George Kennan, "The Sources of Soviet Conduct"[7]

driven containment policy, the United States should not have helped Yugoslavia, because it was communist. But in a containment policy driven by balance-of-power considerations, the United States should have helped Yugoslavia as a means of weakening Soviet power. That, in fact, is what the United States did. It provided military aid to a totalitarian communist government, despite the fact that the Truman Doctrine proclaimed the goal of defending free peoples everywhere. The United States did this for balance-of-power reasons, and the policy put a big dent in Soviet power in Europe.

After the Korean War, however, Kennan's approach to containment lost ground. Then it looked as though the NSC-68 predictions of Soviet expansionism had been justified. Communism seemed monolithic after the Chinese entered the Korean War, and the rhetoric of containment emphasized the ideological goal of preventing the spread of communism. In this context, the United States became involved in Vietnam's civil war.

Follow Up

- Robert J. McMahon, *The Cold War: A Very Short Introduction* (New York: Oxford University Press, 2003).
- John Lewis Gaddis, *The Cold War: A New History* (New York: Penguin, 2005).

CONTAINMENT IN ACTION: THE VIETNAM WAR

For nearly two decades (1955–1973), the United States tried to prevent communist control of Vietnam, at a cost of 58,000 American lives, somewhere between 2 and 3 million Vietnamese lives, $600 billion, and domestic turmoil that undercut support for the policy of containment itself. In addition to containing communism in South Vietnam, the United States feared that a defeat might weaken the credibility of its global military commitments, and thus containment in other parts of the world. Under the leadership of Ho Chi Minh, Vietnam successfully fought French efforts to reassert colonial control after World War II, and in 1954 an international conference in Geneva partitioned

AMERICAN INTERVENTION IN VIETNAM

The U.S. sent its troops into Vietnam to reverse the verdict of a local struggle, which meant, in turn, imposing a ghastly cost in death and suffering upon the Vietnamese. As it turned out, the U.S. could not reverse that verdict finally; it could only delay its culmination.

Those of us who opposed American intervention yet did not want a communist victory were in the difficult position of having no happy ending to offer—for the sad reason that no happy ending was possible any longer, if ever it had been. And we were in the difficult position of urging a relatively complex argument at a moment when most Americans, pro- and antiwar, wanted blinding simplicities.

—Irving Howe and Michael Walzer, "Were We Wrong About Vietnam?"[8]

the country into a communist North Vietnam with its capital in Hanoi and a noncommunist South Vietnam with its capital in Saigon (today, Ho Chi Minh City). The Vietnam War began as a civil war between these two governments, with the South Vietnamese government opposing the North's efforts to "unify the country." With the support of the United States, the South successfully blocked a referendum on reunification that had been agreed to at Geneva.

The United States saw the conflict in Cold War terms as aggression by a communist government against a noncommunist government. It feared that if South Vietnam fell, other noncommunist governments in Southeast Asia would topple like a row of dominoes. The North Vietnamese government and its southern allies (the National Liberation Front, or NLF, generally referred to by Americans as the "Viet Cong") viewed the war as a continuation of the struggle against the French for independence and self-determination. After fifteen years of fighting, direct U.S. involvement ended with the signing of a peace treaty in Paris in 1973. The war between the North and South continued until Hanoi succeeded in uniting the country in 1975. But rather than toppling local dominoes, a unified Vietnam wound up fighting with its communist neighbors, Cambodia and China. If the United States had correctly interpreted the conflict as being more about nationalism and self-determination than communism, it might have seen the conflict in terms of the balance of power and used a metaphor of checkers rather than dominoes to guide its policy. Ironically, the communist government of Vietnam enjoys good relations with the United States today.

Motives, Means, and Consequences

Quite apart from the question of whether the Vietnam War was smart, in the light of U.S. objectives, is the question of whether it was moral. What principles can be used to judge the Vietnam War morally? Three dimensions of judgment are related to the just war tradition: motives, means, and consequences. All three are important because judging interventions by one dimension alone may yield an incomplete understanding of the conflict and an ethically problematic judgment.

Good intentions alone do not justify an intervention. The writer Norman Podhoretz argued that the United States was right to intervene in Vietnam because the Americans were trying to save the South Vietnamese from totalitarian rule. Here is an analogy: Suppose a friend offers to drive your child home one night. It is a rainy night; your friend drives too fast and skids off the road, and your daughter is killed. Your friend says, "My intentions were purely good. I wanted to get her home early for a good night's rest before her SATs." You, however, would no doubt be much more concerned with the consequences of your friend's actions, which were clearly the fault of recklessness. Likewise, Podhoretz's argument that the American action in Vietnam was what he called "imprudent but moral" fails to account either for consequences or means. By the same token, consequences alone would not justify intervention. President Lyndon Johnson's national security adviser, Walt Rostow, argued that the Vietnam War was justified because the United States' evident willingness to pay enormous costs in terms of blood and treasure to meet its longstanding commitment to South Vietnam demonstrated American credibility and bolstered deterrence in Western Europe. Even if it were true that the Vietnam War had this effect (many foreign leaders were more puzzled than impressed by the U.S. commitment to South Vietnam), it would be a bit like your friend saying that he deserved nothing but praise for driving your daughter home safely even though the only reason he offered was to avoid his obligation to wash the dishes at home (motives), and even though he ran every red light along the way (means). Finally, means alone do not do the trick. It would be no defense of the Vietnam War if it had been fought strictly legally (which, sadly, was not the case). Your friend would be no worthier of praise if his goal in driving your daughter home was to avoid washing dishes, if he killed three pedestrians en route, yet he obeyed all speed limits and traffic signals. In evaluating interventions, we have to consider motives, means, *and* consequences.

In the Vietnam War, it was not enough that the United States tried to save South Vietnam from the horrors perpetrated by North Vietnamese communists. Even if the cause was just, the means used are a different proposition. Some questions to ask are: Were there alternatives? Was intervention a last resort? Were there efforts to protect innocent life? Was it proportional—did the punishment fit the crime, so to speak—or was it excessive? To what extent was there attention to international multilateral procedures that might have checked the human tendency to weight these considerations in one's own favor? What about the consequences? What about the prospects for success? What about the danger of unintended consequences because a local situation was not well enough understood, because of the difficulty of differentiating between civilians and guerrillas? As obvious as it seems, we must still emphasize the need to be careful about situations where there is enormous complexity and very long causal chains. Motives, means, and consequences must all be considered before judgments can be made.

Consider how the policy of containment led to intervention in Vietnam. As we have seen, in the early stages just after World War II, the issue was whether the United States should step into Britain's place in the eastern Mediterranean to defend Turkey and Greece against possible Soviet encroachment. U.S. policy makers struggled with how to frame this intervention to the American people. Secretary of State George Marshall was quite cautious. Others, such as Undersecretary Dean Acheson and Senator Arthur Vandenberg, pushed for a moral argument to appeal to the American people's belief in a universal right to freedom. Consequently, when President Truman explained his actions in the Truman Doctrine, he talked of protecting free people everywhere.

The diplomat George Kennan, who had warned against Stalin's aggressive plans, became disillusioned as containment became highly ideological. He argued that the United States was trying to contain Soviet power; therefore, anything that balanced Soviet power without intervening directly with American troops was for the good. But those who took the more ideological view said the United States should contain communism directly, through more aggressive means. Over time, the argument for balancing Soviet power gave way to a broader view of containment as keeping the world free from communism. In Vietnam, this view caused leaders to underestimate national differences among communist states. The United States began to think it had to contain Chinese and Soviet power and the spread of communist ideology. By the time the doctrine of containment moved from the eastern Mediterranean in 1947 to Southeast Asia in the 1950s, it had become a justification for an overly ambitious and ill-fated intervention.

Follow Up

- David A. Welch, *Painful Choices: A Theory of Foreign Policy Change* (Princeton, NJ: Princeton University Press, 2005), pp. 117–160.
- Richard J. Regan, *Just War: Principles and Cases* (Washington, DC: Catholic University of America Press, 1996), pp. 136–150.

CHRONOLOGY: AMERICAN INVOLVEMENT IN VIETNAM

▪ 1954	In response to the French defeat at Dien Bien Phu, President Dwight D. Eisenhower articulates the "domino theory," warning that if Vietnam falls to the communists, other states in Southeast Asia will follow
▪ 1956	
Summer	Following French withdrawal, the U.S. Military Assistance Advisor Group begins training South Vietnamese military forces
July	Vietnam fails to hold elections, as required under the Geneva Convention Agreements of 1954
▪ 1961	*By year's end, U.S. assistance to the South exceeds $1 million a day*

(Continued)

January	Soviet premier Nikita Khrushchev announces Soviet support for "wars of national liberation"; North Vietnamese president Ho Chi Minh interprets this as a green light to escalate the communist assault on South Vietnam
May	President John F. Kennedy deploys 400 Green Berets to serve as "advisers" to the South Vietnamese military regarding counterinsurgency warfare
▪ 1963	***As of December 31, roughly 16,000 U.S. military advisers are stationed in Vietnam***
November 1	With the tacit approval of the United States, South Vietnamese troops surround the presidential palace in Saigon; on November 2, President Ngo Dinh Diem is assassinated
November 22–24	Following the assassination of Kennedy, Lyndon Johnson becomes president and says that the United States will "not lose" Vietnam during his administration
▪ 1964	***The cost of U.S. support to the Vietnamese Army exceeds $2 million per day; by December 31, 23,000 U.S. military advisers are deployed to South Vietnam***
August 2	Three North Vietnamese patrol boats open fire on the USS *Maddox* in the Gulf of Tonkin
August 7	Congress overwhelmingly approves the Gulf of Tonkin resolution authorizing Johnson to "take all necessary steps, including the use of armed force, . . . to prevent further aggression"
▪ 1965	***As of January, public support for U.S. involvement in Vietnam is roughly 80 percent; by the end of the year, roughly 184,000 U.S. troops are deployed to Vietnam***
March	Johnson orders the start of Operation Rolling Thunder, a three-year bombing campaign, and authorizes ground combat patrols
December	U.S. secretary of defense Robert McNamara warns Johnson that time favors the North and that U.S. combat deaths could top 1,000 per month; late in the month, the second bombing pause begins
▪ 1966	***As of year's end, roughly 390,000 U.S. military personnel are deployed to Vietnam***
Late January	The U.S. military commences six weeks of "search and destroy" missions to root out the NLF; the U.S. bombing campaign restarts and B-52s are introduced in April
▪ 1967	***U.S. troop levels reach roughly 463,000 by year's end, and combat deaths total roughly 16,000***
November 29	McNamara resigns as secretary of defense, in part because of his increasing discomfort with Johnson's war policies
▪ 1968	***U.S. troop levels rise to 495,000 by year's end; more than 1,000 U.S. troops are killed each month, and the total number of U.S. troops killed in Vietnam tops 30,000***

(*Continued*)

January	The NLF launches the Tet Offensive, a series of attacks against South Vietnamese cities, including Saigon; though U.S. forces defeat the communist insurgents, the size of their offensive causes the American press and public to question optimistic Pentagon claims about the progress of the war; subsequent polls show only 26 percent of Americans support Johnson's war policy
March 31	Johnson announces that he will not seek reelection; additionally, he calls for a partial halt to U.S. bombing and encourages the North Vietnamese to attend peace talks
May 10	The "Paris Peace Talks" begin with the United States represented by Averell Harriman and the North represented by Foreign Minister Xuan Thuy; negotiations between both sides continue on and off for the next five years
November	Richard M. Nixon elected president
▪ 1969	***Total U.S. combat deaths are roughly 40,000***
Late January	Paris Peace Talks resume
March 17	Nixon orders secret bombing campaign against North Vietnamese supply depots in Cambodia
April	U.S. troop levels reach their highest point: 543,400
June	Nixon and Secretary of Defense Melvin Laird announce a U.S. policy of "Vietnamization," by which the United States will begin withdrawing forces and handing over more responsibilities to South Vietnamese troops
▪ 1970	***U.S. troops drop to 280,000 by December 31***
February	Kissinger begins two years of secret talks with North Vietnamese envoy Le Duc Tho
April 30	Nixon announces an expansion of the U.S. war effort into Cambodia
June 24	U.S. Senate votes to repeal the Gulf of Tonkin resolution
December 22	Congress passes the Cooper-Church Amendment, banning the use of defense spending for U.S. military operations in Laos or Cambodia
▪ 1971	***U.S. troop levels decrease to roughly 156,000 by year's end; total combat deaths exceed 45,000***
June 18–22	The U.S. Senate passes a nonbinding resolution calling for the withdrawal of all U.S. forces from Vietnam by year's end
▪ 1972	
April	Nixon orders B-52s to bomb Hanoi and Haiphong, with the intent of pressuring the North to make further concessions at the peace talks
July	Paris Talks resume

(*Continued*)

October	Kissinger announces "peace is at hand" after reaching a broad agreement with Le Duc Tho; South Vietnamese president Nguyen Van Thieu, however, rejects the U.S. proposal that communist forces be permitted to remain in South Vietnam
December	Peace talks collapse after the North balks at dozens of amendments submitted by Thieu; Nixon orders a series of "Christmas bombings" to force the North back to the negotiation table
▪ 1973	***By year's end, all U.S. troops are withdrawn from Vietnam; the combat death toll is 47,424 U.S. military personnel***
January	Kissinger and Le Duc Tho reach a revised agreement, which the U.S. forces Thieu to accept; Thieu calls the agreement "tantamount to surrender"
March 29	The United States completes its military withdrawal from Vietnam
▪ 1974	
December	North Vietnam launches a new offensive against the South, taking the Mekong Delta region; the United States responds diplomatically
▪ 1975	
April 30	As North Vietnamese troops enter Saigon, the last U.S. government personnel evacuate the embassy; within hours, the North declares the end of the Vietnam War

THE REST OF THE COLD WAR

In 1952, Dwight D. Eisenhower was elected president on a campaign pledge to end the Korean War and to roll back communism. The Republican Party argued that containment was a cowardly accommodation to communism: The right approach was to roll it back. Within six months, however, it became clear that rolling back communism would carry too great a risk of nuclear war. After Stalin died in 1953, the frozen relations of the Cold War thawed slightly. In 1955, there was a U.S-Soviet summit in Geneva at which both sides agreed to the establishment of Austria as a neutral state. In 1956, Nikita Khrushchev, now first secretary of the Communist Party of the Soviet Union, gave a secret speech exposing Stalin's crimes to the Twentieth Party Congress. The secret leaked out and contributed to a period of disarray in the Soviet sphere in Eastern Europe. Hungary attempted to revolt, but Khrushchev intervened militarily to keep it in the communist camp.

Khrushchev decided he needed to get the Americans out of Berlin and reach a final settlement of World War II so he could consolidate the Soviet hold on Eastern Europe and begin to take advantage of the decolonization occurring in the Third World. But Khrushchev's style and efforts to negotiate with the United States were reminiscent of the kaiser's style in trying to force the British to bargain before 1914—full of bluster and deception. Efforts to make the United States come to terms had the opposite effect. Khrushchev failed in the Berlin crisis of 1958–1961 and again in the Cuban missile crisis in 1962.

The Soviet Union and the United States came so close to the nuclear brink during the Cuban missile crisis that they scared each other into a new phase in their relationship. From 1963 to 1978, there was a gradual détente, or relaxation of tensions. In the aftermath of the Cuban missile crisis, arms control negotiations produced the Limited Test Ban Treaty that restricted atmospheric nuclear tests in 1963, and the Nuclear Non-Proliferation Treaty in 1968. Trade began to grow gradually, and détente seemed to be expanding. The Vietnam War diverted U.S. attention more to the threat from Chinese communism.

From 1969 to 1974, the Nixon administration used détente as a means to pursue the goals of containment. After the Cuban missile crisis, the Soviets launched a major military buildup and gained parity in nuclear weapons. The Vietnam War led to the American public's disillusionment with Cold War interventions. Nixon's strategy was (1) to negotiate a strategic arms control treaty with the Soviet Union to cap each country's nuclear arsenal at relative parity; (2) to open diplomatic relations with China and thus create a three-way balance of power in Asia (rather than pushing the Soviets and the Chinese together); (3) to increase trade so there would be carrots as well as sticks in the U.S.-Soviet relationship; and (4) to use "linkage" to tie the various parts of the policy together. The high point of détente occurred in 1972 and 1973, but it did not last very long.

The Middle East War of 1973 and Soviet assistance to anti-Western movements in Africa led to bad feelings about who misled whom. American domestic politics contributed to the decline of détente when American legislators such as Senator Henry Jackson tried to link trade with the Soviet Union to human rights issues, such as the treatment of Soviet Jews, rather than to the Soviet Union's international behavior. In 1975, when Portugal decolonized Angola and Mozambique, the Soviet Union provided transport for Cuban troops dispatched by Fidel Castro to help keep communist-oriented governments in power there. In the 1976 presidential campaign, President Gerald Ford never used the word "détente." His successor, Jimmy Carter, tried to continue détente with the Soviet Union during his first two years in office, but the Soviet Union and Cuba became involved in the Ethiopian civil war. The Soviets continued their military buildup, and in December 1979 the Soviet Union delivered the coup de grâce to détente by invading Afghanistan.

Why was there a resurgence in the level of hostility? One argument is that détente was always oversold: Too much was expected of it. More to the point, there were three trends in the 1970s that undercut it. One was the Soviet military buildup, in which the Soviets increased their defense spending by nearly 4 percent annually and introduced new heavy missiles that particularly worried American defense planners. The second was Soviet intervention in Angola, Ethiopia, and Afghanistan. The Soviets thought that these military actions were justified by what they called the changing "correlation of forces" between capitalism and socialism—their belief, in other words, that history was moving in the direction that Marxism-Leninism predicted. Third were changes in American domestic politics: a rightward trend that tore apart the coalition supporting the Democratic Party. The result of the interaction of Soviet acts and U.S. political trends reaffirmed the view that the Cold War persisted and that détente could not last. However, the renewed hostility in the 1980s was *not* a return to the Cold War of the 1950s. There was a return to the rhetoric of the 1950s, but actions were quite different. Even though President Ronald Reagan talked about the Soviet Union as an "evil empire," he pursued arms control agreements. There was increased trade, particularly in grain, and there were constant contacts between Americans and Soviets. The superpowers even evolved certain rules of prudence in their behavior toward each other: no direct wars, no nuclear use, and discussions of arms and the control of nuclear weapons. It was a different kind of cold war in the 1980s than in the 1950s.

The End of the Cold War

When did the Cold War end? Because the origins of the Cold War were very heavily related to the division of Europe by the United States and the Soviet Union, the end of the Cold War might be dated by when the division ended in 1989. When the Soviet Union did not use force to support the communist government in East Germany and the Berlin Wall was breached by jubilant crowds in November 1989, the Cold War could be said to be over.

But why did it end? One argument is that containment worked. George Kennan argued right after World War II that if the United States could prevent the Soviet Union from expanding, there would be no successes to feed the ideology, and gradually Soviet communism would mellow. New ideas would arise, people would realize that communism was not the wave of the future, that history was not on its side. In some larger respect, Kennan was right. American military power helped deter Soviet expansion while the soft power of American culture, values, and ideas eroded communist ideology. But the puzzle of timing remains: Why did the Cold War end in 1989? Why did it last four decades? Why did it take the Soviet Union so long to mellow? Alternatively, why didn't it last another ten years?

Another possible explanation is "imperial overstretch." The Yale historian Paul Kennedy has argued that empires expand until overexpansion saps their empire's internal strength. With more than a quarter of its economy devoted to defense and foreign affairs (compared to 6 percent for the United States in the 1980s), the Soviet Union was overstretched. But Kennedy went on to say that none of the overexpanded multinational empires in history ever retreated to their own ethnic base until they had been defeated or weakened in a great power war. The Soviet Union, however, was not defeated or weakened in a great power war.

A third explanation is that the U.S. military buildup in the 1980s forced the Soviets to surrender in the Cold War. There is some truth to that insofar as President Ronald Reagan's policies dramatized the extent to which the Soviets were imperially overstretched, but it does not really answer the basic question. After all, earlier periods of American military buildup did not have that effect. Why 1989? We must look for deeper causes, because to think that American rhetoric and policy in the 1980s were the prime cause of the Soviet Union's decline may be similar to thinking that the rooster who crows before dawn causes the sun to come up—another example of the fallacy of spurious causal inference.

We can gain more exact insights into the timing of the end of the Cold War by looking at our three types of causes: precipitating, intermediate, and deep. The most important precipitating cause of the end of the Cold War was an individual, Mikhail Gorbachev. He wanted to reform communism, not replace it. However, the reform snowballed into a revolution driven from below rather than controlled from above. In both his domestic and foreign policy, Gorbachev launched a number of actions that accelerated the existing Soviet decline and hastened the end of the Cold War. When he first came to power in 1985, Gorbachev tried to discipline the Soviet people as a way to overcome economic stagnation. When discipline was not enough to solve the problem, he launched the idea of *perestroika*, or "restructuring," but he was unable to restructure from the top because the Soviet bureaucrats kept thwarting his orders. To light a fire under the bureaucrats, he used a strategy of *glasnost*, or open discussion and democratization. Gorbachev believed that airing people's discontent with the way the system was working would put pressure on the bureaucrats and help perestroika work. But once glasnost and democratization let people say what they were thinking and vote on it, many people said, "We want out. There is no new form of Soviet citizen. This is an imperial dynasty, and we

George H. W. Bush, Ronald Reagan, and Mikhail Gorbachev in New York, 1987

do not belong in this empire." Gorbachev unleashed the disintegration of the Soviet Union, which became increasingly evident after a failed coup by hard-liners in August 1991. By December 1991, the Soviet Union ceased to exist.

Gorbachev's foreign policy, which he called "new thinking," also contributed to the end of the Cold War. This policy had two very important elements. One was changing ideas that constructivists emphasize, such as the concept of common security, in which the classical security dilemma is escaped by joining together to provide security. Gorbachev and the people around him said that in a world of increasing interdependence, security was a non-zero-sum game, and all could benefit through cooperation. The existence of the nuclear threat meant all could perish together if the competition got out of hand. Rather than try to build as many nuclear weapons as possible, Gorbachev proclaimed a doctrine of "sufficiency," holding a minimal number for protection. The other dimension of Gorbachev's foreign policy change was his view that expansionism is usually more costly than beneficial. The Soviet control over an empire in Eastern Europe was costing too much and providing too little benefit, and the invasion of Afghanistan had been a costly disaster. It was no longer necessary to impose a communist social system as a way to ensure security on Soviet borders.

Thus, by the summer of 1989, the Eastern Europeans were allowed a greater degree of freedom. Hungary permitted East Germans to escape through its territory into Austria. This exodus of East Germans put enormous pressure on the East German government. Additionally, Eastern European governments no longer had the nerve (or Soviet backing) to put down demonstrations. In November, the Berlin Wall was pierced—a dramatic conclusion to a crescendo of events occurring over a very short period. We can argue that these events stemmed from Gorbachev's miscalculations. He thought communism could be repaired, but in fact, in trying to repair it, he punched a hole in it. And as if through a hole in a dam, the pent-up pressures began to escape, rapidly increasing the opening and causing the entire system to collapse.

That still leaves the question, why 1989? Why under this leader? To some extent, Gorbachev was an accident of history. In the early 1980s, three old Soviet leaders died, one after another. It was not until 1985 that the younger generation—the people who had come up under Khrushchev, the so-called generation of 1956—had their chance. But if the members of the Communist Party Politburo had chosen one of Gorbachev's hard-line competitors in 1985, it is quite plausible that the declining Soviet Union could have held on for another decade. It did not have to collapse so quickly. Gorbachev's personality explains much of the timing.

As for the intermediate causes, Kennan and Kennedy were both on target. Two important intermediate causes were the soft power of liberal ideas, emphasized in constructivist explanations, and imperial overstretch, emphasized by realists. The ideas of openness, democracy, and new thinking that Gorbachev used were Western ideas that had been adopted by the generation of 1956. One of the key architects of perestroika and glasnost, Aleksandr Yakovlev, had been an exchange student in the United States for a year and ambassador to Canada for a decade. He was attracted to Western theories of pluralism. The growth of transnational communications and contacts pierced the Iron Curtain and helped spread Western popular culture and liberal ideas. The demonstrated effect of Western economic success gave them additional appeal. While hard military power deterred Soviet expansionism, soft power ate away the belief in communism behind the Iron Curtain. When the Berlin Wall finally fell in 1989, it did not succumb to an artillery barrage, but to an onslaught of civilian hammers and bulldozers.

As for imperial overstretch, the enormous Soviet defense budget began to affect other aspects of Soviet society. Health care declined and the mortality rate in the Soviet Union increased (the only developed country in which that occurred). Without funds for upkeep, the country's infrastructure began to crumble. Eventually even the military became aware of the tremendous burden caused by imperial overstretch. In 1984, Marshal Nikolai Ogarkov, the Soviet chief of staff, realized the Soviet Union needed a better civilian economic base and more access to Western trade and technology. But during the period of stagnation, the old leaders were unwilling to listen, and Ogarkov was removed from his post.

Thus the intermediate causes of soft power and imperial overstretch are important, though ultimately we must deal with the deep causes, which were the decline of communist ideology (a constructivist explanation) and the failure of the Soviet economy (a realist explanation). Communism's loss of legitimacy over the postwar period was quite dramatic. In the early period, immediately after 1945, communism was widely attractive. Many communists had led the resistance against fascism in Europe, and many people believed that communism was the wave of the future. The Soviet Union gained a great deal of soft power from their communist ideology, but they squandered it. Soviet soft power was progressively undercut by the de-Stalinization in 1956 that exposed his crimes; by the repressions in Hungary in 1956, in Czechoslovakia in 1968, and in Poland in 1981; and by the growing transnational communication of liberal ideas. Although in theory communism aimed to instill a system of class justice, Lenin's heirs maintained domestic power through a brutal state security system involving reform camps, gulags, broad censorship, and the widespread use of informants. The net effect of these repressive measures on the Russian people was a general loss of faith in the system as voiced in the underground protest literature and the rising tide of dissent advanced by human rights activists.

Behind this, there was also decline in the Soviet economy, reflecting the diminished ability of the Soviet central planning system to respond to change in the world economy. Stalin had created a system of centralized economic direction that emphasized heavy smokestack industries. It was very inflexible—all thumbs and no fingers—and tended to stockpile labor rather than transfer it to growing service industries. As the economist Joseph Schumpeter pointed out, capitalism is creative destruction, a way of responding flexibly to major waves of technological change. At the end of the twentieth century, the major technological change of the third industrial revolution was the growing role of information as the scarcest resource in an economy. The Soviet system was particularly inept

EXPLAINING THE COLD WAR FROM INSIDE AND OUT

In contrast to the way most history is written, Cold War historians through the end of the 1980s were working within rather than after the event they were trying to describe. We had no way of knowing the final outcome, and we could determine the motivations of only some—by no means all—of the major players. . . . We know now, to coin a phrase. Or, at least, we know a good deal more than we once did. We will never have the full story: we don't have that for any historical event, no matter how far back in the past. Historians can no more reconstruct what actually happened than maps can replicate what is really there. But we can represent the past, just as cartographers approximate terrain. And with the end of the Cold War and at least the partial opening of documents from the former Soviet Union, Eastern Europe, and China, the fit between our representations and the reality they describe has become a lot closer than it once was.

—*John L. Gaddis, "The New Cold War History"*[9]

at handling information. The deep secrecy of its political system meant that the flow of information was slow and cumbersome. Ronald Reagan's defense buildup added pressure on an already economically stressed political regime.

Soviet goods and services could not keep up to world standards. There was a great deal of turmoil in the world economy at the end of the twentieth century, but the Western economies using market systems were able to transfer labor to services, to reorganize their heavy industries, and to switch to computers. The Soviet Union could not keep up with the changes. For instance, when Gorbachev came to power in 1985, there were 50,000 personal computers in the Soviet Union; in the United States there were 30 million. Four years later, there were about 400,000 personal computers in the Soviet Union, and 40 million in the United States. Market-oriented economies and democracies proved more flexible in responding to technological change than the centralized Soviet system that Stalin created for the smokestack era of the 1930s. According to one Soviet economist, by the late 1980s, only 8 percent of Soviet industry was competitive at world standards. It is difficult to remain a superpower when 92 percent of your industry is subpar.

The end of the Cold War was one of the great transformative events of the twentieth century. It was equivalent to World War II in its effects on the structure of the international system, but it occurred without war.

Following the breakup of the Soviet Union, Russia has undergone a significant transformation. Renouncing the planned economy of the Soviet state, post–Cold War Russia tentatively embarked on a path of democratization and economic liberalization. That road has been fraught with peril, however. Following the advice of the International Monetary Fund, the Russian government at first embraced economic "shock therapy" as a way of making the transition from economic autocracy to liberal democracy. Yet shock therapy so disrupted Russian society that it was quickly shelved in favor of a more gradualist approach. As the economic situation deteriorated, Russian nationalism was rejuvenated.

Theorists such as Michael Doyle, hypothesizing that liberal democracies do not fight wars with one another, have concluded that if Russia makes a successful transition to democracy, it will bode well for international peace. It remains to be seen whether Russian foreign policy will fit the model of the democratic peace, or whether a resurgence of Russian authoritarianism and nationalism will challenge the United States and Western Europe.

Regardless of what the future holds, one major puzzle remains. Just as important as the question of why the Cold War ended is the question of why it did not turn hot. Why did the Cold War last so long without a "hot war" erupting between the two superpowers? Why did it not result in World War III?

The Role of Nuclear Weapons: Physics and Politics

Some analysts believe that advanced developed societies learned from the lessons of World War I and World War II and simply outgrew war. Others believe that the "long peace" in the second half of the twentieth century stemmed from the limited expansionist goals of the superpowers. Still others credit what they consider the inherent stability of pure bipolarity in which two states (not two tight alliances) are dominant. But for most analysts, the largest part of the answer lies in the special nature of nuclear weapons and nuclear deterrence.

The enormous destructive power of nuclear weapons is almost beyond comprehension. A 1-megaton nuclear explosion can create temperatures of 100 million degrees Celsius—four to five times the temperature in the center of the sun. The bomb dropped on Hiroshima in 1945 was relatively small, about the equivalent of 15,000 tons of TNT. Today's missiles can carry 100 times that explosive power or more. In fact, all the explosive power used in World War II could fit in one 3-megaton bomb, and that one bomb could fit in the nose cone of one large intercontinental missile. By the 1980s, the United States and the Soviet Union together had thousands of nuclear weapons (see Figure 4).

Some physical effects of nuclear explosions are uncertain. For example, the theory of nuclear winter holds that a nuclear war would kick so much dust and ash into the atmosphere that it would block sunlight, preventing most plants from photosynthesizing, and leading to mass extinctions and the destruction of human civilization. A National Academy of Sciences study reported that nuclear winter is possible, but highly uncertain. Much would depend on whether the weapons were aimed at cities rather than at other weapons. Burning cities would generate an enormous amount of smoke that would block a great deal of sunlight, but it is uncertain how long the smoke would stay aloft. If the bombs exploded in the Northern Hemisphere, would the smoke travel to the Southern Hemisphere? Some skeptics argue that the worst result would not be nuclear winter, but nuclear autumn—a faint consolation. The certainty is that a large-scale nuclear war would destroy civilization as we know it, at least in the Northern Hemisphere. In their 1983 report on nuclear weapons,

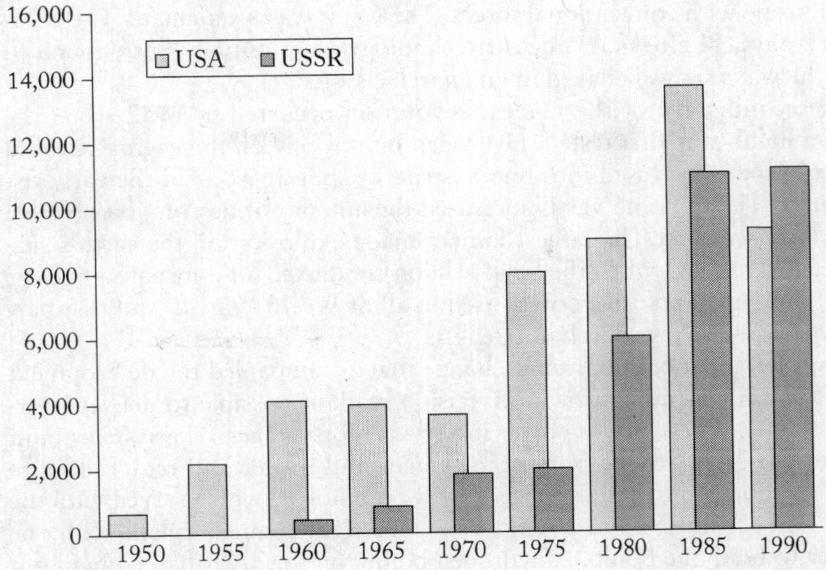

FIGURE 4
U.S. and Soviet strategic nuclear weapons

the American Catholic bishops engaged in only slight hyperbole when they said, "We are the first generation since Genesis with the capability of destroying God's creation."[10]

Nuclear weapons changed the nature of warfare, but they did not change the basic way in which the world is organized. The world of anarchic states with no higher government above them continued in the nuclear age. In 1946, when the United States proposed the Baruch Plan to establish international control of nuclear weapons, the Soviet Union viewed it as just another American plot. After this failure, Albert Einstein lamented that everything changed except our thinking. Perhaps apocryphally, he is supposed to have said that "physics is easier than politics."

There are both military and political reasons why nuclear weapons did not have a more dramatic effect right after 1945. For one thing, the early atomic weapon did not do as much damage as the most deadly uses of mass conventional weapons. The firebombing of Tokyo in March 1945 killed more people than did the nuclear bombing of Hiroshima. Of course, the Hiroshima raid involved a single B-29 bomber, whereas the Tokyo raid involved 279. But at first there were very few nuclear weapons in the U.S. arsenal. The United States had only two in 1947, and fifty in 1948.

The emerging U.S.-Soviet rivalry also slowed change in political thinking. The Soviet Union mistrusted the United Nations and saw it as too reliant on the United States. The United States could not coerce the Soviets into cooperation because Europe was a hostage between the Soviets and the Americans. If the United States threatened nuclear attack, the Soviets could threaten to invade Europe with conventional forces. The result was a stalemate. The revolutionary physical effects of nuclear technology were initially not enough to change the ways states behaved in an anarchic system.

The second stage of the nuclear revolution occurred in 1952 when the hydrogen bomb was first tested. Hydrogen bombs rely on the energy released when two atoms are fused into one, instead of split apart as in the early fission bombs. The H-bomb vastly increased the amount of destruction possible with a single weapon. The largest human-made explosion on the earth's surface occurred in 1961 when the Soviet Union conducted a 60-megaton nuclear test—20 times the explosive power used in all of World War II. And that particular weapon was tested at half strength.

Ironically, the more important change that accompanied the development of the H-bomb was miniaturization. Fusion made it possible to deliver enormous amounts of destructive power in very small packages. The systems built to deliver the early atomic bombs got bigger and bigger and required more space as the bombs increased in size. The B-36 bomber, which served with the U.S. Air Force from 1948 to 1958, was a huge eight-engine airplane with one big cavity to hold one bomb. A hydrogen bomb, on the other hand, could put the same potential destruction in a much smaller space. Once that destructive power was mounted in the nose cone of a ballistic missile, an intercontinental nuclear war could occur with only thirty minutes' warning, compared to the eight hours it took a B-36 to fly the same distance.

The increased destructiveness of hydrogen bombs also dramatized the consequences of nuclear war. No longer could warfare be considered merely

The Convair B-36 (right) and the Boeing B-29 (left), which dropped atomic bombs on Hiroshima and Nagasaki

an extension of politics by other means. Karl von Clausewitz (1780–1831), a nineteenth-century Prussian general and military theorist, said war is a political act, and therefore absolute war is an absurdity. The enormous destructive power of nuclear weapons meant there was now a disproportion between the military means and virtually all the political ends a country might seek. This disjunction between ends and means caused a paralysis in the use of the ultimate force in most situations. Nuclear weapons have not been used since 1945. Nuclear weaponry is muscle-bound. It is too powerful, and thus disproportionate to any meaningful political goal.

The H-bomb had five significant political effects, even though it did not reorganize the anarchic way in which the world goes about its business. First, it revived the concept of limited war. The first half of the twentieth century saw a change from the limited wars of the nineteenth century to the two world wars, which took tens of millions of lives. At mid-century, analysts were referring to the twentieth century as "the century of total war." But war in the second half of the century was more like the old wars of the eighteenth and nineteenth centuries. For instance, though the Korean and Vietnam wars each cost more than 55,000 American deaths (combat and noncombat), they remained limited in scope and scale. In Vietnam and Afghanistan, the United States and the Soviet Union each accepted defeat rather than use their ultimate weapon.

Second, crises replaced wars as moments of truth. In the past, war was the time when all the cards were face up on the table. But in the nuclear age, war is too devastating and the old moments of truth are too dangerous. The Berlin crises, the Cuban missile crisis, and the Middle East crises of the early 1970s played the functional equivalent of war in this sense, providing glimpses into the true correlation of forces in military power. Third, nuclear weapons made deterrence (dissuasion through fear) the key strategy. It was now critical to organize military might to produce fear in advance so an attack would be deterred. In World War II, the United States relied on its ability to mobilize and gradually build a war machine after the war started, but that mobilization approach no longer worked when a nuclear war could be over in a matter of hours.

A fourth political effect was the development of a de facto regime of superpower prudence. The two superpowers, despite their bitter ideological differences, developed one key common interest: avoiding nuclear war. During the Cold War, the United States and the Soviet Union engaged in proxy or indirect peripheral wars, but in no case did the two countries go head to head. In addition, the two sides developed spheres of influence. While the Americans talked about rolling back communism in Eastern Europe in the 1950s, in practice, when the Hungarians revolted against their Soviet rulers in 1956, the United States did not rush in to help them, fearing nuclear war. Similarly, with the exception of Cuba, the Soviets were relatively careful about incursions into the Western Hemisphere. Both countries adhered to a developing norm of nonuse of nuclear weapons. Finally, the superpowers learned to communicate. After the Cuban missile crisis, Washington and Moscow developed a "hotline" (initially a teletype connection) to allow virtually instantaneous communication between Soviet and American leaders. Simultaneously, the codification of a number of arms control treaties, starting with the Limited Test Ban Treaty in 1963, and frequent arms control negotiations became a way to discuss stability.

Fifth, nuclear weapons in general, and the H-bomb in particular, were seen by most officials as unusable in time of war. It was not purely a matter of the destructive potential of the H-bomb. A stigma gradually came to be attached to the use of nuclear weaponry that did not similarly apply to conventional weaponry. By the late 1960s, in fact, engineers and scientists had managed to shrink the size and "yield" (destructive blast) of nuclear weapons so greatly that some—nuclear mines and nuclear demolition charges, for example—could have been used by the United States in Vietnam and the Gulf War or by the Soviet Union in Afghanistan without causing much more destruction than conventional weapons. Yet both Americans and Soviets refrained from using smaller-yield nuclear weapons in favor of conventional ones. In part, they feared that using any nuclear weapon, no matter how small, would open the window to using other nuclear weapons, and that risk was simply unacceptable.

There was yet another dimension to the reluctance to use nuclear weapons. Ever since the first bomb was dropped by the United States on Hiroshima, there was a lingering sense that nuclear weapons were immoral—that they went beyond the realm of what was acceptable in war. Though that normative restraint is hard to measure, it clearly suffused the debates over nuclear weapons and was one reason for the unwillingness of states to use them.

Balance of Terror

Nuclear weapons produced a peculiar form of the balance of power that was sometimes called the "balance of terror." Tests of nuclear strength were more psychological than physical. Both sides followed a policy of preventing preponderance by the other, but the result was different from previous systems. Unlike the nineteenth-century balance-of-power system in which five great powers shifted alliances, the Cold War balance was very clearly organized around two very large states, each capable of destroying the other in a matter of minutes.

The problems raised by the classical security dilemma were not ended by the terror of nuclear weapons, but the superpowers acted prudently despite their ideological differences. Their prudence was similar to the effects of the constant communications that occurred in managing the multipolar nineteenth-century balance of power. At the same time, the superpowers tried to calculate balances of force, just as in the days when statesmen compared provinces, infantry, and artillery.

The nuclear balance of terror coincided with a period of bipolarity. Recall that some neorealists, such as Kenneth Waltz, define bipolarity as a situation in which two large states have nearly all the power. That type of pure bipolarity is rare. More often bipolarity has occurred in history when alliances tighten so much that flexibility is lost, as happened in the Peloponnesian War. Even though they were independent city-states, the alliances around Athens and around Sparta coalesced tightly into a bipolar situation. Similarly, on the eve of World War I the alliance systems became tightly bound into bipolarity.

Waltz argued that bipolarity can be stable because it simplifies communication and calculations: When you only have one other great power to pay particularly close attention to, you can monitor the balance very closely. On the other hand, bipolar systems lack flexibility and magnify the importance of marginal conflicts such as the Vietnam War—and without other significant countries to throw their weight into the balance on the weaker side, if one side begins to outstrip the other, the balance can break down entirely. As we have seen, the conventional wisdom in the past was that bipolarity either erodes or explodes. If so, why did bipolarity not explode after World War II?

Perhaps the prudence produced by nuclear weapons provided the answer, and the stability that Waltz attributed to pure bipolarity was really the result of the bomb. The very terror of nuclear weapons may have helped produce stability through the "crystal ball effect." Imagine that in August 1914 the kaiser, the tsar, and the emperor of Austria-Hungary looked into a crystal ball and saw a picture of 1918. They would have seen that war would cost them their thrones, that their empires would be dismembered, and that millions of their people would be killed. Would they still have gone to war? Probably not. Knowledge of the physical effects of nuclear weapons may be similar to the effect of giving leaders in the post-1945 period a crystal ball. Because few or no political goals would be proportionate to such destruction, they would not want to take great risks. Of course, crystal balls can be shattered by accidents and by miscalculations, but the analogy suggests why the combination of bipolarity and nuclear weapons produced the longest period of peace between the central powers since the beginning of the modern state system. (The previous record was 1871–1914.)

Problems of Nuclear Deterrence

Nuclear deterrence is a subset of general deterrence, but the peculiar qualities of nuclear weapons changed how the superpowers approached international relations during the Cold War. Nuclear deterrence encourages the reasoning, "If you attack me, I may not be able to prevent your attack, but I can retaliate so powerfully that you will not want to attack in the first place." Nuclear weapons thus put a new twist on an old concept.

One way to assess the efficacy of nuclear deterrence is by counterfactual analysis. How likely was it that the Cold War would have turned hot in the absence of nuclear weapons? The political scientist John Mueller argues that nuclear weapons were irrelevant; they were no more than the rooster crowing. He argues that the peoples of Europe had been turning away from war as a policy instrument ever since the horrors of World War I. The cause of peace was the increased recognition of the horror of war, at least in the developed world. According to Mueller, Hitler was an aberration, a rare person who had not learned the lessons of World War I and was still willing to go to war. After World War II, the general revulsion toward war returned more strongly than before. Most analysts, however, believe nuclear weapons had a lot to do with

NUCLEAR WEAPONS AND THE VIETNAM WAR

When President Kennedy made the first decision to increase significantly the American military presence in 1962–63, . . . he had in mind two things: What would have happened if Khrushchev had not believed him in the Berlin crisis of 1961–62, and what would have happened if Khrushchev [had not believed him] in the Cuban Missile Crisis of 1962?

I think we made a mistake in concluding that the Chinese would probably not intervene in the Korean War in 1950, and that influenced the American decision not to invade North Vietnam. The military said they did not think China would come in, but if it did, it would lead to nuclear war, and that decided that.

—*Secretary of State Dean Rusk*[11]

avoiding World War III. Crises over Berlin, Cuba, and perhaps the Middle East might have spiraled out of control without the prudence instilled by the crystal ball effect of nuclear weapons.

That raises a number of questions. One is, what deters? Effective deterrence requires both the capability to do damage and a credible threat that the weapons will be used. Credibility depends on the stakes involved in a conflict. For example, an American threat to bomb Moscow in retaliation for a nuclear attack was probably credible. But suppose the United States had threatened to bomb Moscow in 1980 if the Soviets did not withdraw their troops from Afghanistan. The United States certainly had the capability, but the threat would not have been credible because the stakes were too low, and the Soviets could easily have threatened in return to bomb Washington. So deterrence is related not just to capability, but also to credibility.

The problem of credibility leads to a distinction between deterring threats against one's homeland and extending deterrence to cover an ally. For example, the United States could not stop the Soviet Union from invading Afghanistan by nuclear deterrence, but for the four decades of the Cold War, it threatened to use nuclear weapons if the Soviet Union invaded the NATO countries of Western Europe. Thus, to look for the effects of nuclear weapons in extending deterrence and averting war, we must look at major crises in which the stakes were high.

Can history answer these questions about the effect of nuclear weapons? Not completely, but it can help. From 1945 to 1949, the United States alone had nuclear weapons but did not use them. So there was some self-restraint even before mutual nuclear deterrence. This was due in part to the small size of U.S. arsenals, a lack of understanding of these new weapons, and the American fear that the Soviets would capture all of Europe with their massive conventional forces. By the 1950s, both the United States and the Soviet Union had nuclear weapons, and American leaders considered their use in several crises. Nuclear weapons were not used in the Korean War or in 1954 and 1958 when the Chinese communists mobilized forces and threatened to invade territory held by the Nationalists based in Taiwan. Presidents Truman and Eisenhower vetoed the use of nuclear weapons for several reasons. In the Korean War, it was not clear that dropping a nuclear weapon would stop the Chinese, and the United States was concerned about the Soviet response. There was always the danger that the threats might escalate and the Soviets might use a nuclear weapon to help their Chinese ally. So even though the Americans had a larger nuclear arsenal, there was the danger of escalating to a wider war involving more than just Korea and China.

In addition, ethics and public opinion played a role. In the 1950s, U.S. government estimates of the number of citizens who would be killed by a nuclear attack were so high that the idea was put aside. When asked about using nuclear weapons, President Eisenhower said, "We can't use those awful things against Asians for the second time in less than ten years. My God!"[12] Even though the United States had more nuclear weapons than the Soviet Union in the 1950s, a combination of factors persuaded the Americans not to use them.

The Cuban Missile Crisis

The key case in nuclear deterrence in the Cold War was the Cuban missile crisis of October 1962, triggered by Khrushchev's attempt to sneak strategic nuclear missiles into Cuba. This thirteen-day period was the closest the world

THE "GRAVEST ISSUES"

By mid-October 1962, the Cold War had intensified in unforeseen ways. Cuba, which had long been a virtual colony of the United States, had recently moved into the Soviet orbit. In late September, U.S. newspapers had begun reporting shipments of Soviet weapons to Cuba. President John F. Kennedy told the American public that, to the best of his understanding, these weapons were defensive, not offensive. Soviet Premier Nikita Khrushchev had given him absolute assurances that this was the case. "Were it to be otherwise," Kennedy said, "the gravest issues would arise."

Shortly before 9:00 A.M. on Tuesday, October 16, Kennedy's Assistant for National Security Affairs, McGeorge Bundy, brought to his bedroom photographs showing that the "gravest issues" had indeed arisen. Taken from very high altitude by a U-2 reconnaissance plane, these photographs showed the Soviets in Cuba setting up nuclear-armed ballistic missiles targeted on cities in the continental United States.

For Kennedy, the presence of these missiles was intolerable. So was the fact that Khrushchev had lied to him. For the next 13 days, Kennedy and a circle of advisers debated how to cope with the challenge. They knew that one possible outcome was nuclear war, and during their discussions Kennedy's civil defense expert offered the chilling information that the U.S. population was frighteningly vulnerable.

—*Ernest May and Philip Zelikow, The Kennedy Tapes*[13]

has ever come to nuclear war. If a total outsider, a "man from Mars," had looked at the situation, he would have seen that the United States had a massive superiority in nuclear weaponry. The Soviets had a mere handful of strategic missiles that could have reached the United States.[14] If President Kennedy considered Khrushchev's gambit so utterly unacceptable, why didn't he order an attack on the Soviet missile sites in Cuba, most of which were still under construction when discovered, and all of which were relatively vulnerable? The answer was that Kennedy was not willing to run the risk of even one or two of the Soviet missiles escaping destruction and being fired at an American city. In addition, as the crisis unfolded, both Kennedy and Khrushchev learned how little they could actually control the potentially disastrous actions of their own military organizations, which were on high alert and ready to fight at a moment's notice. What they did not know would have frightened them even more.[15] Khrushchev expressed the fear very powerfully in a letter to Kennedy near the climax of the crisis: "[W]e and you ought not now to pull on the ends of the rope in which you have tied the knot of war," he wrote, "because the more the two of us pull, the tighter that knot will be tied. And a moment may come when that knot will be tied so tight that even he who tied it will not have the strength to untie it, and then it will be necessary to cut that knot. And what that would mean is not for me to explain to you, because you yourself understand perfectly of what terrible forces our countries dispose."[16]

Twenty-five years after the event, a group of Harvard scholars organized a conference with Americans who had been members of President Kennedy's Executive Committee of the National Security Council, the first of six such meetings that ultimately included both Soviets and Cubans. One of the most striking differences among the participants was their willingness to take risks. That in turn depended on how likely each thought were the prospects of nuclear war. Robert McNamara, Kennedy's secretary of defense, became more cautious as the crisis unfolded. At the time, he thought the probability of nuclear war in the Cuban missile crisis might be one chance out of fifty (though later he rated the risks much higher after he learned in the 1990s that the Soviets had delivered both strategic and tactical nuclear weapons to Cuba). Douglas Dillon, who was the secretary of the treasury, said he thought the risks of nuclear war were about zero. He did not see how the situation could possibly progress to nuclear war and as a result was willing to push the Soviets harder and to take more risks than was McNamara. General Maxwell Taylor, the chairman of the Joint Chiefs of Staff, also thought the risk of nuclear war was low, and he complained that the United States let the Soviet Union off too easily. He argued that Kennedy could have pushed much harder and should have demanded the removal of Cuba's president, Fidel Castro. General Taylor said, "I was so sure we had 'em over a barrel, I never worried much about the final outcome."[17] But the risks of losing control weighed heavily on President Kennedy, who took a very cautious position—indeed, more prudent than some of his advisers would have liked. The moral of the story is that a little nuclear deterrence can go a long way. This has been called *finite* or *existential deterrence*. It is clear that such nuclear deterrence made a difference in the Cuban missile crisis.

Nonetheless, it is difficult to attribute the whole outcome of the crisis to the nuclear component. The public consensus was that the United States won. But the question of how much the United States won and why it won is overdetermined. There are at least three possible explanations. One view is that because the United States had more nuclear weapons than the Soviet Union, the Soviets gave in. A second explanation adds the importance of the relative stakes of the two superpowers in the crisis. Cuba was in America's backyard, but a distant gamble for the Soviets. Third, Cuba's proximity to the United States meant that the Americans could bring overwhelming conventional forces to bear. An American naval blockade and the possibility of an American invasion of Cuba also played a role. The psychological burden was on the Soviets because higher stakes and readily available conventional forces bolstered the credibility of the American threat.

Kennedy and Khrushchev meeting in Vienna in 1961

Finally, although the Cuban missile crisis was widely considered an American victory at the time—because Khrushchev publicly agreed to reverse his nuclear deployment—it was, in fact, something of a compromise. The Americans had three options in the Cuban missile crisis. One was a shoot-out, that is, to bomb the missile sites; the second was a squeeze-out by blockading Cuba to persuade the Soviets to take the missiles out; the third was a buyout by offering to trade something the Soviets wanted, such as removal of American missiles from Turkey. For a long time, the participants did not say much about the buyout aspects of the solution, but it came to light many years after the crisis that Kennedy made a quiet promise to remove obsolete U.S. missiles from Turkey in return for the withdrawal of Soviet missiles from Cuba. We can conclude that nuclear deterrence mattered in the crisis, and that the nuclear dimension certainly figured in Kennedy's thinking. On the other hand, the number of weapons was less important. It was not the ratio of nuclear weapons that mattered so much as the fear that even a few nuclear weapons could wreak such devastation.

Moral Issues

After the Cuban missile crisis there was a relative easing of the tension in the Cold War—almost as if the United States and the Soviet Union had stumbled to the brink of a cliff, looked over, and pulled back. In 1963, a hotline allowing direct communication between Washington and Moscow was created, an arms control treaty limiting atmospheric nuclear tests was signed, Kennedy announced the United States would be willing to trade more with the Soviet Union, and there was some relaxation of tension. Through the late 1960s, the United States was preoccupied with the Vietnam War, yet there were still arms control efforts. Intense fear of nuclear war returned after the Soviet Union invaded Afghanistan in 1979. During "the little cold war" from 1980 to 1985, strategic arms limitation talks stalled, rhetoric became particularly harsh, and military budgets and the number of nuclear weapons increased on both sides. President Ronald Reagan talked about fighting and "winning" a nuclear war, and peace groups pressed for first a freeze, and then ultimately the abolition, of nuclear weapons.

In the climate of heightened anxiety, many people asked a basic question: Is nuclear deterrence moral? War theory argues that certain conditions must be met in making moral judgments. Self-defense is usually regarded as a just cause, but the means and consequences by which a war is fought are equally important. In terms of the means, civilians must be distinguished from combatants; in terms of consequences, there has to be some proportionality—some relationship between the value of the ends and the cost of the means.

Could nuclear war possibly fit the just war model? Technically, it could. Low-yield nuclear artillery shells or depth charges might be used against radar systems, submarines, ships at sea, or deep underground command bunkers without being dramatically different in their effects from similar conventional

LEARNING FROM HISTORY

In 1962 President Kennedy insisted that each member of the National Security Council read Barbara Tuchman's *The Guns of August*. The book is the story of how the nations of Europe inadvertently blundered into World War I. The author begins by quoting Bismarck's comment that "some damned foolish thing in the Balkans" would ignite the next war. She then related the series of steps—following the assassination on June 28, 1914, of the Austrian heir apparent, Archduke Franz Ferdinand, by Serbian nationalists—each small and insignificant in itself, that led to the most appalling military conflict in the history of the world. Time and again, at the brink of hostilities, the chiefs of state tried to pull back, but the momentum of events dragged them forward.

President Kennedy reminded us of the 1914 conversation between two German chancellors on the origins of that war. One asked, "How did it happen?" and his successor replied, "Ah, if we only knew." It was Kennedy's way of stressing the constant danger of miscalculation.

—*Robert McNamara, Blundering into Disaster*[18]

weapons. In that case, we could discriminate between combatants and non-combatants and keep the effects relatively limited. If the fighting stopped there, we could fit nuclear weapons within just war theory. But would fighting stop there, or would it escalate? Escalation is the great risk, for what could be worth a hundred million lives or the fate of the Earth?

During the Cold War, some people answered, "It's better to be Red than dead." But that may have been the wrong way to pose the question. Alternatively, we might ask, is it ever justifiable to run a small risk of a large calamity? During the Cuban missile crisis, John Kennedy was reputed to have said he thought the chances of war were "between one out of three and even."[19] And there was a risk of nuclear escalation as well. Was he justified in taking such a risk? We can ask the counterfactual: If Kennedy had not been willing to take the risk in Cuba, would Khrushchev have tried something even more dangerous? What if a Soviet success had led to a later nuclear crisis, or an even larger conventional war—for example, over Berlin?

Nuclear weapons probably played a significant role in preventing the Cold War from turning hot. During the 1980s, the American Association of Catholic Bishops said that nuclear deterrence could be justified on a conditional basis as a tolerable interim measure until something better was developed. But how long is the interim? So long as nuclear knowledge exists, some degree of nuclear deterrence will exist. Although the weapons induced prudence during the Cold War, complacency is a danger. It took the United States and the Soviet Union some time to learn how to control nuclear weapons, and it is far from clear that such control systems will exist among new nuclear states such as North Korea, and possibly Iran. Moreover, terrorist groups might have no use for controls.

Concern about the proliferation of nuclear weapons continues. While 189 states have signed the Nuclear Non-Proliferation Treaty, India and Pakistan exploded weapons in 1998, followed by North Korea—a signatory, no less—in 2006. Countries such as Iraq, Iran, and Libya also pursued nuclear weapons despite having signed the treaty. Also of concern is the spread of unconventional arsenals such as biological and chemical weapons. Libya and Iraq, for example, constructed chemical weapons facilities, and Iraq used them in its war with Iran (1980–1988). After the Gulf War in 1991, UN inspectors uncovered and destroyed major Iraqi nuclear, biological, and chemical weapons programs. The fear that such programs could be reconstituted was one of the causes of the Iraq War in 2003. Newspaper accounts of nuclear material making its way out of the former Soviet Union and into the international black market demonstrate that these weapons can still cause tension and bring countries to the brink of war. In 2004, it was disclosed that a Pakistani nuclear scientist, A. Q. Khan, had sold nuclear secrets to a number of countries, including Libya, Iran, and North Korea. Moreover, the reports that terrorist groups such as the Japanese Aum Shinrikyo cult and Osama bin Laden's al Qaeda network were investigating the production of nuclear and biological weapons indicate that they may someday become available to nonstate actors as well.

The continued international worry about weapons of mass destruction has both a moral and a realist dimension. The moral opprobrium against nuclear weapons is shared not just by states that do not have the capacity or desire to make such weapons, but even by states that continue to have them, such as the United States, Britain, France, and Russia. Chemical and biological weapons have been condemned since World War I, when the use of mustard gas led to a widespread outcry. The realist dimension is simple: Weapons of mass destruction carry great risk of escalation and enormous potential for devastation. Whenever these weapons are present, the dynamics of conflict change. Weak states with nuclear or unconventional weapons are better able to threaten strong states, while strong states with these weapons can more effectively threaten and deter adversaries. At the same time, the risk that these devices will be used if a crisis spins out of control raises the level of tension, whether between the United States and North Korea, India and Pakistan, or Israel and Iran. And the threat of use by terrorists adds a chilling dimension in which deterrence is not a sufficient response. The Cold War may be over, but the era of weapons of mass destruction is not.

Follow Up

- Richard Ned Lebow and Thomas Risse-Kappen, eds., *International Relations Theory and the End of the Cold War* (New York: Columbia University Press, 1995).
- T. V. Paul, *The Tradition of Non-Use of Nuclear Weapons* (Stanford, CA: Stanford University Press, 2009), pp. 1–123.
- Don Munton and David A. Welch, *The Cuban Missile Crisis: A Concise History* (New York: Oxford University Press, 2011).
- Joseph S. Nye, Jr., *Nuclear Ethics* (New York: Free Press, 1986).

CHRONOLOGY: THE COLD WAR YEARS

▪ 1943	Tehran meeting among Stalin, Churchill, and Roosevelt
▪ 1944	
July	Bretton Woods Conference: Creation of International Monetary Fund and World Bank
August	Dumbarton Oaks Conference: Creation of United Nations
October	Moscow meeting between Churchill and Stalin: Spheres of influence plan for the Balkans
▪ 1945	
February	Yalta Conference among Stalin, Churchill, and Roosevelt
April	Roosevelt dies
May	Germany surrenders
April–June	San Francisco Conference; UN Charter drafted
July	First test of A-bomb; Potsdam Conference: Truman, Churchill/ Attlee, Stalin
August	Hiroshima and Nagasaki destroyed by A-bombs; the Soviet Union enters war in Asia; Japan surrenders
▪ 1946	Churchill's Iron Curtain speech; resumption of Greek civil war
▪ 1947	
March	Truman Doctrine announced
June	Marshall Plan announced
October	Creation of Cominform by Moscow
▪ 1948	
February	Coup by Czech Communist Party
March	Partial blockade of Berlin begins
June	Berlin airlift begins; Yugoslavia ousted from Cominform
November	Truman reelected president
▪ 1949	
April	North Atlantic Treaty signed in Washington
May	End of the Berlin blockade
August	Soviet Union explodes first A-bomb
September	Federal Republic of Germany (West Germany) created
October	People's Republic of China proclaimed; German Democratic Republic (East Germany) proclaimed
▪ 1950	
February	Sino-Soviet pact signed in Moscow
April	NSC-68 drafted
June	Beginning of Korean War
▪ 1952	First U.S. H-bomb exploded; Eisenhower elected president; Dulles becomes secretary of state
▪ 1953	
March	Death of Stalin
June	East Berlin uprising

(*Continued*)

July	Armistice in Korea
August	First Soviet H-bomb test
September	Khrushchev becomes first secretary of Soviet Communist Party
▪ 1954	Chinese bombardment of Quemoy and Matsu
▪ 1955	West Germany admitted to NATO; Warsaw Pact signed; Austrian State Treaty signed; Austria neutralized
▪ 1956	
February	Khrushchev denounces Stalin at Twentieth Party Congress
June	Poznan uprising in Poland
October	Start of Hungarian uprising
November	Soviet Union intervenes in Hungary
▪ 1957	
August	Launching of first Soviet ICBM
October	Sputnik satellite launched
▪ 1958	
February	Launching of first U.S. satellite
August	China threatens Taiwan
▪ 1959	
January	Victory of Fidel Castro in Cuba
September	Khrushchev visits United States
▪ 1960	
February	First French A-bomb test
May	American U-2 shot down over Soviet Union; Paris summit fails
▪ 1961	
April	Failure of Bay of Pigs landing in Cuba
June	Khrushchev and Kennedy meet in Vienna
August	Building of the Berlin Wall
October	Incidents at Checkpoint Charlie in Berlin; tensions increase
▪ 1962	
October	Cuban missile crisis
▪ 1963	
June	Kennedy visits Berlin, declares "*Ich bin ein Berliner*" ("I am a Berliner") as a gesture of solidarity
October	Kennedy signs Limited Test Ban Treaty; Soviet Union, United States, and United Kingdom outlaw tests in the atmosphere, underwater, and in space
November	Kennedy assassinated; Johnson sworn into office
▪ 1964	
August	Tonkin Gulf Resolution passes Congress, escalating U.S. involvement in Vietnam
October	Khrushchev ousted, replaced by Brezhnev and Kosygin
November	China detonates first atomic bomb

(*Continued*)

▪ 1966	
March	Anti–Vietnam War rallies held in United States and Europe
April	Beginning of Chinese Cultural Revolution
▪ 1967	
January	United States, Soviet Union, and 60 other countries agree to Outer Space Treaty limiting military uses of space
June	China explodes first H-bomb
▪ 1968	
January	Prague Spring reforms begin in Czechoslovakia; Tet Offensive in Vietnam
July	Treaty on the Non-Proliferation of Nuclear Weapons (NPT) by United States, Soviet Union, and 58 other countries
August	Soviet invasion of Czechoslovakia
November	Nixon elected president
December	U.S. forces reach peak of 543,400 in Vietnam
▪ 1969	Strategic Arms Limitation Talks (SALT) begin between United States and Soviet Union
▪ 1970	
February	Paris Peace Talks begin between United States and North Vietnam
April	U.S. troops invade Cambodia; four U.S. college students killed by National Guard at Kent State University at antiwar rally
▪ 1971	People's Republic of China joins United Nations
▪ 1972	
February	Nixon visits China
May	SALT I signed, freezing number of ICBMs and SLBMs in place for five years
▪ 1973	
January	Paris Accords establish cease-fire and political settlement of Vietnam War
May	East and West Germany establish formal diplomatic relations
September	Chilean socialist government of Salvador Allende overthrown in U.S.-backed military coup
October	Yom Kippur War between Israel and Arab states; United States and Soviet Union nearly drawn into conflict; Arab oil embargo against the United States that lasts until March 1974
▪ 1974	Nixon resigns over Watergate; Gerald Ford sworn in as president
▪ 1975	
April	United States leaves Vietnam after fall of Saigon
July	U.S. and Soviet astronauts link up in space; United States and Soviet Union sign Helsinki Accords, pledging acceptance of European borders and protection for human rights
▪ 1976	Jimmy Carter elected president

(*Continued*)

▪ 1979	
January	United States and People's Republic of China establish full diplomatic relations
June	SALT II agreement limiting long-range missiles and bombers signed by Carter and Brezhnev
July	Sandinista forces overthrow Somoza dictatorship in Nicaragua
December	Soviet Union invades Afghanistan; United States imposes sanctions and announces intention to boycott Moscow Olympics
▪ 1980	Carter Doctrine states that Persian Gulf is a vital U.S. interest
▪ 1981	
January	Lech Walesa leads Polish Solidarity union in illegal strike; Ronald Reagan inaugurated
December	Martial law imposed in Poland
▪ 1982	Reagan outlines Strategic Arms Reduction Treaty (START) to reduce ICBMs and number of strategic nuclear weapons on both sides
▪ 1983	
March	Reagan proposes Strategic Defense Initiative (SDI), popularly called "Star Wars," to develop missile defense technology
November	United States begins deployment of INF Pershing II missiles in West Germany
▪ 1985	Mikhail Gorbachev becomes Soviet general secretary; Nuclear and Space Talks (NST) open in Geneva, based on START model
▪ 1986	
October	At Reykjavik Summit Reagan refuses Gorbachev's proposal to make significant arms reductions if United States gives up SDI
November	Secret funding of Nicaraguan contras through arms sales to Iran becomes public
▪ 1987	At Washington Summit Reagan and Gorbachev agree to eliminate INF and work toward completing a START agreement
▪ 1988	
April	Soviet Union agrees to withdraw from Afghanistan by February 1989
June	Gorbachev tells Communist Party leaders that elements of communist doctrine must change
August	Cuba withdraws troops from Angola
November	George H. W. Bush elected president
▪ 1989	
June	Chinese army assaults prodemocracy demonstrators in Tiananmen Square

(*Continued*)

November	Berlin Wall falls; thousands of East Germans cross to Western side
▪ 1990	
May–June	Washington Summit between Bush and Gorbachev
October	Germany reunifies
November	Treaty of Conventional Armed Forces in Europe cuts size of land armies
December	Lech Walesa elected president of Poland
▪ 1991	
July	Bush and Gorbachev sign START, pledge to destroy thousands of nuclear weapons
August	Coup against Gorbachev fails, but power flows to Russian president Boris Yeltsin
September	All SAC bombers, tankers, and Minuteman II ICBMs taken off alert
December	Soviet Union dissolves; United States recognizes Armenia, Belarus, Kazakhstan, Kyrgyzstan, Russia, and Ukraine

STUDY QUESTIONS

1. When did the Cold War begin? When did it end? Why? What do realist, liberal, and constructivist approaches contribute to your answers?
2. Was the Cold War inevitable? If so, why and when? If not, when and how could it have been avoided?
3. Why were leaders unable to restore a nineteenth-century-style Concert system after World War II? What sort of system evolved?
4. How important were first- and second-image considerations in the development of the Cold War? What were the views of American and European leaders on the Soviet Union and its international ambitions? What were Soviet views of the United States and the rest of the West?
5. Some historians argue that the real question is not why the Cold War occurred, but why it did not escalate into a "hot" war. Do you agree? Why didn't a hot war begin?
6. What is "containment"? How did this American policy emerge, and how was it implemented? What were Soviet responses?
7. How are nuclear weapons different from conventional weapons? Has the advent of nuclear weapons fundamentally changed the way countries behave?
8. Is Mueller correct that nuclear weapons are not the cause of the obsolescence of major wars among developed states? What other factors does he consider?
9. Is nuclear deterrence morally defensible? Or, in the words of one theorist, is it morally analogous to tying infants to the front bumpers of automobiles to prevent traffic accidents on Memorial Day? Might some strategies of deterrence be more ethical than others?

10. What is the significance of nuclear weapons to international relations apart from nuclear deterrence? How useful are they?
11. Why did the Cold War end? What roles did hard and soft power play?

NOTES

1. Milovan Djilas, *Conversations with Stalin,* trans. Michael B. Petrovich (San Diego: Harcourt Brace Jovanovich, 1962), p. 114.
2. Ralph B. Levering, *The Cold War, 1945–1972* (Arlington Heights, IL: Harlan Davidson, 1982), p. 15.
3. William Taubman, *Stalin's American Policy* (New York: Norton, 1982), p. 36.
4. John Lewis Gaddis, *We Now Know: Rethinking Cold War History* (Oxford: Oxford University Press, 1997), pp. 23–24.
5. Ibid., p. 24.
6. Dean Acheson, *Present at the Creation* (New York: Norton, 1969), p. 375.
7. George Kennan, "The Sources of Soviet Conduct," *Foreign Affairs* 25:4 (July 1947), p. 581.
8. Irving Howe and Michael Walzer, "Were We Wrong About Vietnam?" *The New Republic*, August 18, 1979, p. 18.
9. John L. Gaddis, "The New Cold War History," *Foreign Policy Research Institute Footnotes* 5:5 (June 1998).
10. United States Catholic Conference, "The Challenge of Peace: God's Promise and Our Response," *Origins* 13:1 (May 19, 1983), p. 1.
11. Quoted in *The New York Times,* April 30, 1985, p. 6.
12. Stephen E. Ambrose, *Eisenhower* (New York: Simon & Schuster, 1983), p. 184.
13. Ernest R. May and Philip D. Zelikow, eds., *The Kennedy Tapes: Inside the White House During the Cuban Missile Crisis* (Cambridge, MA: Belknap & Harvard University Press, 1997), p. 1.
14. The intelligence available to the CIA in September 1961 suggested that the Soviets had somewhere between 10 and 25 intercontinental ballistic missile (ICBM) launchers. Jeffrey Richelson, *The Wizards of Langley: Inside the CIA's Directorate of Science and Technology* (Boulder, CO: Westview Press, 2001), p. 28.
15. Among the sobering events at the height of the crisis were, on the American side, a reconnaissance plane accidentally straying into Soviet airspace; a Titan ICBM being launched from California according to its preplanned flight-test schedule; a Minuteman ICBM crew in Montana hot-wiring their launch control system; and a training tape mistakenly feeding into radar monitors in New Jersey indicating a Soviet nuclear missile attack. On the Soviet side, a submarine commander, mistakenly thinking war had already broken out, ordered his nuclear torpedo armed and fired (an order countermanded by the submarine's cooler-headed political officer); and the shooting down of an American reconnaissance

plane over Cuba in violation of standing orders. Don Munton and David A. Welch, *The Cuban Missile Crisis: A Concise History*, 2nd ed. (New York: Oxford University Press, 2011), pp. 99–100. See also Michael Dobbs, *One Minute to Midnight: Kennedy, Khrushchev, and Castro on the Brink of Nuclear War* (New York: Knopf, 2008), passim.

16. May and Zelikow, *The Kennedy Tapes*, p. 299.
17. James Blight and David Welch, *On the Brink: Americans and Soviets Reexamine the Cuban Missile Crisis* (New York: Hill & Wang, 1989), p. 80.
18. Robert McNamara, *Blundering into Disaster: Surviving the First Century of the Nuclear Age* (New York: Pantheon, 1986), p. 14.
19. Theodore C. Sorensen, *Kennedy* (New York: Harper & Row, 1965), p. 705.

PHOTO CREDITS

Credits are listed in order of appearance:

Tass Photos/Newscom.

Bettmann/Corbis.

Air Force Historical Research Agency/
Maxwell Air Force Base, Montgomery, AL.

Bettmann/Corbis.

BOX CREDITS

Credits are listed in order of appearance:

Excerpted from George Kennan, "The Sources of Soviet Conduct," *Foreign Affairs*, 25: 4 (July 1947), p. 581. Reprinted by permission of *Foreign Affairs*, July 1947. Copyright 1947 by the Council on Foreign Relations, Inc.

"American Intervention in Vietnam": Excerpted from Irving Hower and Michael Walzer, "Were We Wrong About Vietnam?" *The New Republic*, August 18, 1979, p. 18. Reprinted by permission of *The New Republic*. Copyright 1979, The New Republic Inc.

MAP CREDITS

Credits are listed in order of appearance:

Map is original to this chapter.

Map is drawn from Brian Catchpole, *A Map History of the Modern World* (Oxford: Heinemann Publishers, 1982), reprinted with adjustments by permission.

Post–Cold War Cooperation, Conflict, Flashpoints

Post–Cold War Cooperation, Conflict, Flashpoints

Chinese PLA (Peoples Liberation Army) soldiers for UN peacekeeping missions learn to deal with mines during a training session in Luzhou city, southwest Chinas Sichuan province.

MANAGING CONFLICT

Conflict marks all aspects of our social lives. Any time two or more people have different preferences, there is a potential conflict. If you want to watch *Law & Order* and your sister wants to watch *CSI*, then, unless you have two television sets, you have a conflict. The overwhelming majority of conflicts in life are resolved peacefully. Very few escalate to violence. In some cases, conflicts are resolved by one party winning and another losing. If your parents tell you that you must let your sister watch *CSI*, she has won and you have lost. You may not be happy about it, but you are unlikely to fetch a gun and start shooting.

Another way of resolving conflict is to compromise in which you get some—but not all—of what you want. If you and your sister both want the last piece of cake, one solution is to cut it in half. This may work with cake, but it does not work very well with television dramas. You and your sister are both likely to think that half a piece of cake is better than none, but half an episode of *Law & Order* is completely unsatisfying.

When your parents tell you to let your sister watch *CSI*, they may soften the blow by promising that you will get your way next time. If so, they would be managing the conflict by invoking a norm of turn-taking, a form of reciprocity. This move effectively embeds a single instance of winner/loser conflict resolution into a broader pattern of compromise. Over time, you and your sister will share the time slot. If you are like most people, this will soothe the sting of defeat. It will also make you more likely to respect your parents' authority, since they are being reasonable and fair. A third way of resolving conflict is for someone to persuade either party or both to change their preferences. Your father may inform you that tonight's episode of *Law & Order* is a rerun that you have already seen. Your mother may offer to pay if you both go out for ice cream instead of watching TV.

Notice the variety in these scenarios not only in the solutions, but also in the conflict management strategies. By simply ordering you to defer to your sister, you parents leveraged their authority, which is a right to rule. By proposing a norm of turn-taking, they leveraged your sense of fairness and promoted a norm. By telling you about the rerun, your father wielded soft power by altering your preferences through novel relevant information. By offering to buy you ice cream, your mother wielded hard power in the form of a material incentive.

Peaceful conflict management of this kind requires mutual *cooperation*, which the dictionary defines as "working or acting together." Cooperation does not normally come naturally. Someone, or something, must usually arrange it.

Take, for example, the marines who raised the U.S. flag atop Mount Suribachi during the battle for Iwo Jima in 1945. No doubt the senior officer present told the others what to do. Some of them might have preferred to do something else. If left to their own devices, people often simply assert their own preferences (exceptions are societies that have very strong norms of deference to others). It is doubtful the flag would have been raised at all if this had been the case. *Harmony* is a situation in which people share the same preference and everyone can be happy at once. Harmony is nice, and most people experience it at least some of the time in all aspects of their lives, too; but we often don't even notice it, because it does not present us with a problem to solve.

Not all solutions or strategies of conflict management are available at all times, or effective in all cases. Much depends upon the nature of the "good" at stake. Economists distinguish between four main types of goods:

- "Private goods" are *excludable:* it is possible to prevent others from getting them. There is also *rivalry* for private goods. If you have one, it means that no one else can have it. Your car is a private good. If you have the keys (and a decent antitheft system), you can prevent others from driving it, and if you are driving it, others can't.
- "Public goods" are nonexcludable and nonrivalrous: There is no way of preventing others from enjoying them, and if you have some, it does not effectively diminish what is available for the benefit of others. Clean air is a public good: It is virtually impossible to prevent people from breathing the same air you do, and your breathing it does not reduce the ability of others to breathe it as well.
- "Club goods" are excludable and nonrivalrous. These include such things as satellite television signals. In contrast to conventional radio signals, satellite TV broadcasts are encrypted, and you can prevent people from watching by controlling access to the set-top boxes that decrypt them. But anyone with a decoder can watch. Your decoding the signal doesn't weaken it for others.
- "Common goods" are nonexcludable and rivalrous. These include such things as wild fish and game. You can't stop people from fishing, but if you catch a fish, no one else can catch it—unless you are fishing purely for sport and throw it back, in which case you have turned that particular fish into a public good!

Different kinds of goods pose different problems for cooperation. A classic problem of cooperation concerning public goods, for example, is underprovision: Since everyone can benefit from a public good, no one has a strong incentive to shoulder the cost of providing it. Roads, for example, are public goods. Most drivers would be willing in principle to chip in voluntarily for the cost of building and maintaining roads, but there would always be people who sought a "free ride." Studies show that the amount of money that would be available for roads if the entire budget came from voluntary donations would be nowhere near what was needed, so governments resort to taxes and/or tolls.

A classic cooperation problem involving common goods is called the "tragedy of the commons." The North Atlantic cod fishing industry collapsed in the 1990s in part because, since every individual trawler captain had a financial incentive to catch as many fish as possible, fishing fleets caught cod faster than the fish could reproduce.

Cooperation is required to decide how to allocate and safeguard the use of private goods and club goods as well. Your car is only really *your* car against the backdrop of a complex social, legal, and economic system that makes possible things such as financing, licensing, registration, and law enforcement (to defend your right to ownership). Someone had to mark out a particular part of the electromagnetic spectrum for the use of satellite TV and prevent someone else from trying to broadcast at that frequency. The same can be said of radio signals in a sense. The signals may be public goods, but the radio spectrum is not: It is a private good. You can prevent people from using it at all, and if someone broadcasts at a particular frequency, no one else within range can broadcast at that frequency at the same time.

As we can see, cooperation is essential to ensure that people can benefit from goods of any kind. The above examples demonstrate that many of the most effective solutions to cooperation problems involve rules and norms, often created and enforced by governments (or other authorities, such as parents, associations, and clubs). In fact, governments sometimes use their powers to ensure that goods don't migrate from one category to another. MP3 music files, for example, are in a certain sense natural public goods: With online file sharing, it is almost impossible to prevent people from getting them, and the fact that one person downloads an MP3 file does not prevent another from downloading it also. But if music were a true public good, performers and composers would be unable to earn a living from music because of the free-rider problem. So governments try to enforce intellectual property rights by passing laws against file sharing, and increasingly they go after people who illegally share files. In the summer of 2009, a Boston University graduate student was ordered to pay four record labels $675,000 for downloading and sharing music by groups such as Green Day and Nirvana.

One of the great differences between international politics and domestic politics is precisely that there is no higher authority than states, which means that a large number of mechanisms for solving problems of international cooperation are simply not available. This does not make international cooperation impossible, but it does complicate it. Green Day and Nirvana can get the U.S. government to prosecute people in the United States who illegally share music, but Washington cannot arrest, try, and punish someone who shares files from his home computer in Shanghai. Instead, American officials must try to persuade the government of China to pass and enforce intellectual property rights laws. As a sovereign state, China has a perfect right to decide whether or not to do so, though it must consider issues of international trade reciprocity if it refuses.

Interestingly, while international cooperation is generally more difficult than domestic cooperation, most international conflicts are also resolved peacefully. Relatively few escalate to violence. When attempts to resolve them fail, the most common outcome is either a standoff or further efforts to find agreeable solutions. During the Cold War, most people did not notice this, because the Cold War itself was such a preoccupation. Even so, there was remarkably little Cold War violence, at least when seen against the background of the levels of destruction of which the superpowers were capable. Most Cold War violence took place on the so-called periphery and involved Cold War "proxies" (Soviet or American client regimes, liberation movements, and militias or irregular forces of various kinds). Even though there were many unresolved East-West conflicts, most of them were nothing more than standoffs that gradually came to be managed through broader and deeper cooperative agreements, either formal (such as arms control treaties) or informal (various "security regimes").

International Law and Organization

Two of the primary vehicles for managing conflict and promoting cooperation in world politics are international law and organization. We have already encountered these many times in the course of our exploration thus far, but it is worth examining them more closely here because many heralded the end of the Cold War as an opportunity at last to realize the Wilsonian dream of a world governed more effectively and more reliably by means of both. One could say that new Wilsonians expected constructivist processes of socialization and norm-promotion to overcome realist obstacles to liberal ideals. Arguably, the world is a more orderly place today precisely because of progress in international governance and the deepening and thickening of norms of peaceful conflict resolution. But the most optimistic neo-Wilsonians have been disappointed thus far; the world is not as peaceful, not as stable, and not as safe as they had hoped it would be by now. At the same time, however, the pessimists who confidently predicted that the enduring logic of realism would simply give rise to some new dominant axis of enmity that would frustrate any progress whatsoever have been proven wrong as well.

People sometimes have problems understanding international law and organization because they use a domestic analogy. But international organization is not like domestic government, and international law is not like domestic law. International organizations do not act as an incipient world government for two reasons. First, the sovereignty of member states is protected in the charters of most international organizations. The United Nations is the closest thing we have to a world government, because of its near-universal membership and its exceptionally broad mandate and agenda, but Article 2.7 of the UN Charter says: "Nothing in the Charter shall authorize the United Nations to intervene in matters within domestic jurisdiction." In other words, the organization is not an effort to replace states.

The other reason that international organization is not incipient world government is because of its weakness. There is an international judiciary in the form of the *International Court of Justice (ICJ),* which consists of fifteen judges elected for nine-year terms by the United Nations, but the International Court of Justice is not a world supreme court. States may refuse its jurisdiction, and a state may refuse to accept its judgments, even if the state has accepted the court's jurisdiction. In the 1980s, for example, the Reagan administration refused to accept an ICJ ruling that the United States had acted illegally in mining the harbors of Nicaragua.

If we imagine the UN General Assembly as the equivalent of Congress, it is a very strange kind of legislature. It is based on the principle of one state, one vote, but that principle reflects neither democracy nor power relations in the world. Democracy rests on the principle of one person, one vote. In the UN General Assembly, the Maldive Islands with almost 400,000 people in the southern Indian Ocean has one vote and China, a country with more than 1.3 billion people, has one vote. That means a Maldive Islander has more than 3,000 times the voting power of a Chinese in the UN General Assembly, which does not fit well with the democratic criteria for legislatures. Nor is it a very good reflection of power, because the Maldive Islands has the same vote in the General Assembly as the United States or India or China. So there is an oddity about the General Assembly that makes states unwilling to have it pass binding legislation. UN General Assembly resolutions are just that: resolutions, not laws.

Finally, we might imagine that the secretary-general of the United Nations is the incipient new president of the world. But that is also misleading. The secretary-general is a weak executive, more secretary than general. If the secretary-general has power, it is more like the soft power of a pope than the combination of hard and soft power a president possesses. Trying to understand international organizations by analogy to domestic government is a sure way to get the wrong set of answers. They are better understood as frameworks by which states arrange coordination and cooperation.

International law is not like domestic law in various important ways. Domestic law is the product of legislatures and customs, sometimes called common law. Domestic law involves provisions for enforcement, adjudication by individuals (you can go to a court yourself and bring suit), and orderly revision by legislation. Public international law is similar in the sense that it consists of treaties, which are agreements among states, and customs, which are the generally accepted practices of states. But it differs dramatically in enforcement and adjudication. On enforcement, there is no executive to make a state accept a court decision. International politics is a self-help system. In the classic ways of international law, enforcement was sometimes provided by the great powers. For example, in the Law of the Sea, a custom developed that a state could claim a three-mile jurisdiction out into the oceans. In the nineteenth century, when Uruguay claimed broader territorial seas to protect the fisheries off its coasts, Britain, the greatest naval power of the day, sent gunboats within three miles of the coast. In the 1980s, when Libya attempted to claim the Gulf of Sidra as territorial water, the United States, then and still the greatest naval power in the world, sent in the Sixth Fleet. You might ask, "Who enforced the law against Britain or the United

States if they violated the law?" The answer is that enforcement in a self-help system is a one-way street.

Adjudication in international law is by states, not by individuals (though the European Court at Strasbourg is a regional exception). Instead of any of the world's billions of citizens bringing cases to the international court, only states can bring cases, and they are unlikely to bring cases unless they want to get them off their docket or think they have a reasonable chance of winning. Thus the court has had relatively few cases. In the 1990s, special tribunals were established to try war criminals from the Bosnian and Rwandan conflicts, and in 2002 a large number of states established an *International Criminal Court* to try war criminals and genocidaires if their national governments failed to try them. However, a number of significant states, including the United States and China, refused to ratify the treaty because they felt it infringed on their sovereignty. In addition, there are problems about how customary rules should be interpreted even when a principle is agreed on. Take the principle of expropriation. It is accepted that a state can nationalize a corporation from another country that operates on its territory, but it must pay compensation for what the corporation is worth. But who is to say what is just compensation? Many of the less developed countries have argued that low compensation is adequate; rich countries usually want higher levels.

Finally, even when the UN General Assembly has passed resolutions, there is a good deal of ambiguity about what they mean. They are not binding legislation. The only area in the UN Charter in which a state must legally accept a decision is Chapter VII, which deals with threats to peace, breaches of the peace, and acts of aggression. If the Security Council (not the General Assembly) finds that there has been an act of aggression or threats to peace warranting sanctions, then member states are bound to apply the sanctions. That is what happened in 1990 when Iraq invaded Kuwait, and in 2001 after the United States was the target of transnational terrorist attacks.

The other way in which new law is sometimes created is through large intergovernmental conferences that negotiate draft treaties for governments to sign. Such conferences are often very large and unwieldy. For example, in the 1970s the Law of the Sea Conference involved more than a hundred participating states trying to draft principles for a twelve-mile territorial sea, an exclusive economic zone for fisheries out to 200 miles, and designating the minerals on the bottom of the ocean as the common heritage of all. The trouble was that some states agreed to only parts of the text, leaving the outcome unclear in international law. Nonetheless, in 1995, when the United States wanted to resist possible Chinese claims to the seas around the Spratly Islands, it appealed to the international Law of the Sea.

International law basically reflects the fragmented nature of international politics. The weak sense of community means there is less willingness to obey or restrain oneself out of a sense of obligation or acceptance of authority. The absence of a common executive with a monopoly on the legitimate use of force means that sovereign states are in the realms of self-help, force, and survival. And when matters of survival come up, law usually takes second place.

Predictability and Legitimacy

Nonetheless, international law and organization are an important part of political reality because they affect the way states behave. States have an interest in international law for two reasons: predictability and legitimacy.

States, like people, are involved in conflicts with each other all the time. The vast range of international transactions, both public and private, includes trade, tourism, diplomatic missions, and contacts among peoples across national boundaries. As interdependence grows, those contacts grow and there are increasing opportunities for friction. International law allows governments to avoid conflict at a high level when such friction arises. For example, if an American tourist is arrested for smuggling drugs in Mexico, if a British ship collides with a Norwegian ship in the North Sea, or if a Japanese firm claims that an Indian company has infringed its patents, the governments may not want to spoil their other relations over these private conflicts. Handling such issues by international law and agreed principles depoliticizes them and makes them predictable. Predictability is necessary for transactions to flourish and for the orderly handling of the conflicts that inevitably accompany them.

Legitimacy is a second reason why governments have an interest in international law. Politics is not merely a struggle for physical power, but also a contest over legitimacy. As we have seen, power and legitimacy are not antithetical, but complementary. Humans are neither purely moral nor totally cynical. It is a political fact that the belief in right and wrong helps move people to act, and therefore legitimacy is a source of power. If a state's acts are perceived as illegitimate, the costs of a policy will be higher because compliance will be lower. States appeal to international law and organization to legitimize their own policies or delegitimize others, and that often shapes their tactics and outcomes. Legitimacy enhances a state's soft power.

In major conflicts of interest, international law may not always restrain states, but it often helps shape the flow of policy. Law is part of the power struggle. Cynics may say these are just games that lawyers play; but the fact that governments find it important to make legal arguments or to take the resolutions of international organizations into account shows they are not completely insignificant. To put it in an aphorism: "When claims to virtue are made by vice, then at least we know virtue has a price." Simply put, governments may be trapped by their own legal excuses.

An example is UN Security Council Resolution 242. Passed at the end of the 1967 Middle East War, it called for a return to prewar boundaries. Over the years, it had the effect of denying the legitimacy of the Israeli occupation of the territories it captured during that war. That put Israel on the defensive in the United Nations. The Arab states lost the war, but were nonetheless able to put pressure on Israel. In 1976, when the Arab coalition tried to expel

Israel from the United Nations, the United States spent a good deal of political capital lobbying before the General Assembly to prevent Israel's expulsion, another indication that symbols of legitimacy in international organizations are part of a power struggle.

When vital issues of survival are at stake, a state will use its most effective form of power, which is military force. And that may explain the limited success of efforts of international law and organization to deal with the use of force. It is one thing to handle drug smuggling, collision of ships at sea, or patent infringement by international law; it is another to put the survival of one's country at risk by obeying international law. That was the problem with collective security in the 1930s, but a modified form of collective security was re-created in the UN charter.

The United Nations: Collective Security and Peacekeeping

The classical balance of power did not make war illegal. The use of military force was accepted, and it often ensured the stability of the system. During the nineteenth century, with changes in technology making war more destructive, and with the rise of democracy and peace movements, there were several efforts to organize states against war. Twenty-six states held a peace conference at The Hague in 1899. In 1907, another Hague conference was attended by 44 states. The approach taken in these conferences was very legalistic. The conferees tried to persuade all states to sign treaties of arbitration so disputes would be handled by arbitration rather than force. They also tried to codify rules of war in case arbitration did not work.

As we have seen, after World War I the League of Nations was an attempt to develop a coalition of states that would deter and punish aggressors. In the eyes of Woodrow Wilson and those who thought as he did, World War I had been largely an accidental and unnecessary war caused by the balance of power, and such wars could be prevented by an alliance of all states for collective security. If the League of Nations was designed to prevent another World War I, the United Nations was designed in 1943–1945 to prevent a repeat of World War II. Forty-nine states met in San Francisco in 1945 to sign a charter that included innovations to repair the deficiencies of the League. Unlike the balance-of-power system of the nineteenth century, the offensive use of force was now illegal for any state that signed the UN charter, with three exceptions: Any use of force had to be for either self-defense, collective self-defense, or collective security.

The designers of the UN also created a Security Council composed of five permanent members and a rotating pool of nonpermanent members. The Security Council can be seen as a nineteenth-century balance-of-power mechanism integrated into the collective security framework of the UN. The Security Council can pass binding resolutions under Chapter VII of the charter. If the five great power policemen do not agree, they each have a veto, which is like a fuse box in a house lighting system. The UN's founders felt that it was preferable to allow the great powers each to have a veto that makes the lights go out rather than have the house burn down in the form of a war against one or two recalcitrant great powers.

During the Cold War, the UN collective security system only worked once: in the Korean War—and it only worked then because the Soviet Union was boycotting the Security Council over the fact that the Nationalist government in Taiwan, rather than the Communist government in Beijing, was occupying the China seat. For most of the Cold War, the great powers could not agree on what counted as a legitimate use of force. They also experienced great difficulty trying to define aggression. For example, how should one weigh covert infiltration against forces crossing a border first? In 1956 Israel suffered from covert attacks by Egyptian-backed guerrillas, yet Israeli conventional forces crossed the border into Egypt first. Depending on which side you favored, you took a different view regarding who was the aggressor in this case. For two decades during the Cold War, UN committees tried to define aggression. They came up with a vague and generally ineffective rule: A list of acts of aggression was followed by the proviso that the Security Council could determine that other acts also constituted aggression. Even when armed force had been used, the Security Council could choose not to declare that there had been any aggression. So as far as the United Nations was concerned, aggression was committed when the Security Council said it was. Everything depended on a consensus in the Security Council, and that was rare during the Cold War.

The impasse over collective security gave rise to the concept of UN preventive diplomacy and *peacekeeping* forces. Rather than identifying and punishing the aggressor, which is the basic concept of collective security, the United Nations would assemble independent forces and interpose them between the warring powers. The model was developed during the Suez Canal crisis of 1956.

In July 1956, President Gamal Abdel Nasser of Egypt nationalized the Suez Canal (Figure 1). Sir Anthony Eden, the British prime minister, saw this as a major threat to Britain. He regarded Nasser as a new Hitler, and he drew analogies to the 1930s. He worried about the fact that Nasser had accepted Soviet arms. Britain worked up a secret plan with France and Israel: Israel would attack Egypt, which had been sending guerrillas across the Israeli border, whereupon France and Britain would "intervene" to restore peace, occupying the Suez Canal in the process. The UN Security Council debated a resolution calling for a cease-fire, which Britain and France vetoed. They wanted their intervention to continue long enough to destabilize Nasser.

Dag Hammarskjöld, the UN secretary-general, working with Canadian secretary of state for external affairs Lester Pearson, devised a plan to separate the Israelis and the Egyptians by inserting a UN peacekeeping force. A resolution in the General Assembly, where there was no veto, authorized a UN force in the Sinai region. The United States did not support its European allies, worrying that their intervention would antagonize Arab nationalists and increase the opportunities for the Soviet Union in the Middle East. On November 15, the first United Nations Emergency Force (UNEF) deployed into the Sinai between Egyptian and Israeli forces, and later in December, the United Nations took on the task of clearing the ships that had been sunk in the canal.

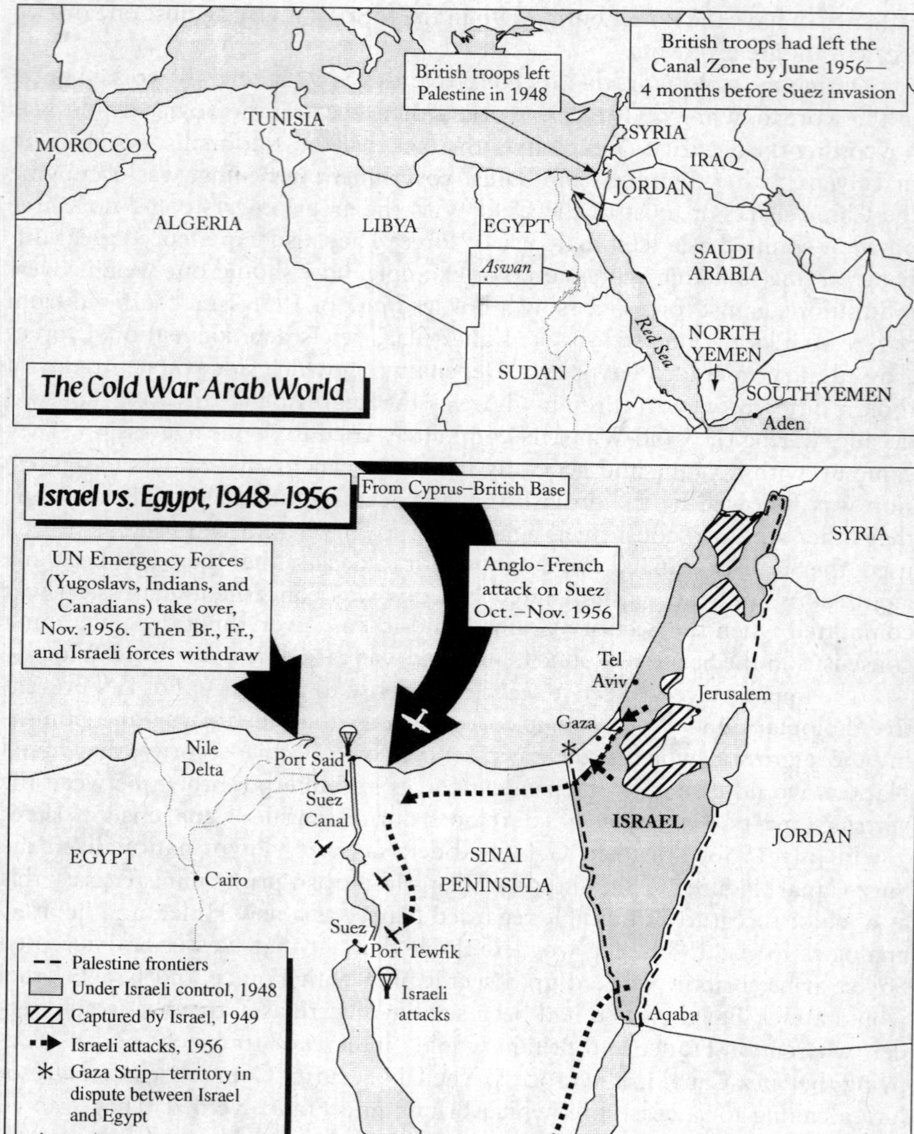

FIGURE 1

The Suez Crisis and the Birth of Peacekeeping

UNEF served as a model for dozens of "blue helmet" peacekeeping missions, and in 1992 the UN created a Department of Peacekeeping Operations (DPKO) to oversee them. At present there are 14 UN peacekeeping operations on four continents. Nearly 100,000 troops from 114 countries participate. The total number of PKOs to date is 64, with a total budget of almost $70 billion. Peacekeeping is an excellent example of a function that the UN invented for itself—but that the UN's founders never imagined. In contrast, the total number of collective security operations to date—which the UN's founders imagined would be among its principal activities—is two (Korea in 1950, Kuwait in 1991).

Thus even though the Cold War prevented the United Nations from implementing the formal doctrine of collective security, it did not prevent the innovation of using international forces to keep two sides apart. In collective security, if a state crosses a line, all the others are to unite against it and push it back. In peacekeeping, if a state crosses a line, the United Nations steps in and holds the parties apart without judging who is right or wrong. During the Cold War, one of the basic principles of UN peacekeeping was that the forces always came from small states, not from the Soviet Union or the United States, so that the great powers would be kept out of direct conflict. Preventive diplomacy and peacekeeping were important innovations that still play significant roles in regulating international conflicts. But they are not collective security, and today many peacekeepers are trying to separate parties in internal conflicts.

Iraq's 1990 invasion of Kuwait was the first post–Cold War crisis. Since the Soviet Union and China did not exercise their vetoes, UN collective security was used for the first time in forty years. There were three reasons for this remarkable resurrection. First, Iraq committed an extraordinarily clear-cut aggression, very much like the 1930s, which reminded leaders of that failure of collective security. The second reason was the feeling that if UN collective security failed in such a clear case, it would not be a principle for order in a post–Cold War world. Third, the small states in the United Nations supported

A LETTER TO PRESIDENT DWIGHT D. EISENHOWER

In the nineteen-thirties Hitler established his position by a series of carefully planned movements. These began with occupation of the Rhineland and were followed by successive acts of aggression against Austria, Czechoslovakia, Poland and the West. His actions were tolerated and excused by the majority of the population of Western Europe. . . .

Similarly the seizure of the Suez Canal is, we are convinced, the opening gambit in a planned campaign designed by Nasser to expel all Western influence and interests from Arab countries. He believes that if he can get away with this, and if he can successfully defy eighteen nations, his prestige in Arabia will be so great that he will be able to mount revolutions of young officers in Saudi Arabia, Jordan, Syria and Iraq. (We know that he is already preparing a revolution in Iraq, which is most stable and progressive.) These new Governments will in effect be Egyptian satellites if not Russian ones. They will have to place their united oil resources under the control of a United Arabia led by Egypt and under Russian influence. When that moment comes Nasser can deny oil to Western Europe and we here shall be at his mercy.

—British Prime Minister Anthony Eden, 1956[1]

the action because most of them were fragile and had disputable postcolonial boundaries. The arguments Saddam Hussein used to justify his invasion of Kuwait threatened most of the other small states as well. To paraphrase the Haitian delegate to the League of Nations, they did not want to become someone else's Kuwait.

Will UN collective security be a basis for a new world order? Only rarely. The permanent members of the Security Council, for example, were not able to agree on resolutions to authorize either the Kosovo or Iraq wars in 1999 and 2003. There are important problems. First, the UN system works best when there is clear-cut aggression; it is much more difficult to apply in civil wars. Second, collective security will work if there is no veto, but if the United States, Russia, China, Britain, or France cannot reach agreement, collective security will be hamstrung once more. Moreover, in 1945, UN collective security was not designed to be applicable against the five great powers with vetoes in the Security Council. Third, collective security works when UN member states provide the necessary financial and military resources, but it is difficult to imagine collective security working if the states with large military forces do not contribute. Collective security was a miserable failure in the 1930s, was put on ice during the Cold War, and then, like Lazarus, rose from the dead in the Persian Gulf in 1990. But it was only a minor miracle, for collective security is only part of what will be needed for world order in the future.

The United Nations has political effects, even when collective security cannot be applied, because the presumption against force written into the UN charter places the burden of proof on those who want to use force. As constructivists note, such changes in normative ideas about the use of force affect states' soft power. In addition, the Security Council provides an important forum for the discussion of international violence, dramatizing the practice of collective concern and directing attention to important matters in times of crisis. It sometimes crystallizes viewpoints, raising the costs of aggressive uses of force, and acts as a safety valve for diplomacy. Finally, the role of the UN peacekeeping forces is limited but useful. These trip wires and buffer zones are devices that states have found to be in their interests again and again.

With the end of the Cold War came more opportunities for the United Nations. The United Nations played a role in the decolonization of Namibia, in monitoring human rights in El Salvador, in the elections in Nicaragua, in the administration in Cambodia, in addition to overseeing peacekeeping forces. Its recent peacekeeping record is mixed. UN peacekeepers helped in Haiti and Cambodia in the 1990s, but failed to prevent genocide in Rwanda and Sudan or to stop civil war in Angola, and in Bosnia had to be replaced by a stronger North Atlantic Treaty Organization (NATO) force. Sometimes it is difficult even to assess success or failure. UN peacekeepers have certainly helped prevent bloodshed between Greek and Turkish Cypriots, but critics of the Cyprus mission argue that the seemingly open-ended commitment (blue helmets have been on the ground since 1964) has actually impeded progress toward a negotiated reunification of the country. It seems that neutral interposition of troops does not always work well in ethnic conflicts. Indeed, some political scientists argue that neutral interventions may lengthen the duration of civil wars, causing greater bloodshed and loss of life. On the other hand, the UN still plays an important legitimizing role. The failure of the United States and Britain to obtain a Security Council resolution explicitly authorizing their use of force in 2003, for example, greatly increased the cost of their occupation of Iraq.[2] In addition, the UN continues to invent new roles for itself. One good example is *peacebuilding*, illustrated by the United Nations Integrated Mission in Timor-Leste (UNMIT). Through a complex sixteen-point mandate involving a wide variety of social, political, economic, and security tasks, UNMIT is attempting to help Timor-Leste build the capacity for, and cultivate a climate conducive to, a stable, independent, democratic state. "Peace support operations" of this kind were never envisaged by the drafters of the UN Charter in San Francisco, but are an increasingly important component of the UN's contribution to managing conflict. Even though the original doctrines of collective security do not fit as neatly as once thought, it would be a mistake to dismiss international law and the United Nations. They are part of the political reality of the anarchic state system. It is a mistake to be too cynical or too naïve about international law and organization. States do not live by law alone, but they do not live completely without it.

At the beginning of the twenty-first century, the UN is clearly not the "parliament of humankind" that some of its founders hoped for when it was created in 1945. With an annual regular budget of roughly $4 billion a year and a central staff of 14,000 members, the organization has fewer resources than many towns and cities. Even when the special budget for peacekeeping operations (roughly $3 billion) and the annual budgets of all the specialized agencies and development funds are added together, the total comes to around $12 billion, or about 2 percent of what the United States spends on defense. The budget for human rights activities is smaller than that of the Zurich Opera House, and the budget of the UN's World Health Organization is similar to that of one large university hospital system.[3]

Many observers have called for the reform of UN institutions. The fifteen members of the Security Council have the legal power to authorize the use of force, and five permanent members (China, the United States, Russia, Britain, and France) have had veto power since 1945. In 2005, a "High-Level Panel" appointed by Secretary-General Kofi Annan suggested enlarging the Council to 24 members and adding India, Brazil, Japan, and Germany as permanent members. The plan failed, however, when China objected to Japan's inclusion, regional rivals raised objections, and African states demanded more seats. The panel made a number of other useful suggestions for reform, including a Peacebuilding Commission to oversee the reconstruction of failed states, revision of the Human Rights Commission to exclude states that violate human rights, clearer criteria for preemptive use of force and humanitarian intervention, and an agreed definition of terrorism. Except for a small Peacebuilding Commission and a modest new Human Rights Council, the member states were reluctant to implement these recommendations.

The UN remains an assembly of 193 sovereign states trying through diplomacy to find a common denominator for dealing with international problems while protecting their national interests. Yet it also represents a central point for focusing on issues of security, international development, humanitarian assistance, environmental degradation, drugs, transnational crime, health and diseases, and global common spaces that require international collaboration. Despite its flaws, it remains the only universal organization that creates a focal point for international diplomacy. It is sometimes said that if the UN did not exist, it would have to be invented. Given the diversity of cultures and national interests in the world today, it is not clear that it could be.

Follow Up

- Robert O. Keohane, *After Hegemony: Cooperation and Discord in the World Political Economy* (Princeton, NJ: Princeton University Press, 1984).
- Linda M. Fasulo, *An Insider's Guide to the UN*, 2nd ed. (New Haven: Yale University Press, 2009), pp. 1–89.

INTRASTATE CONFLICT

Major war became less likely after the end of the Cold War, but regional and domestic conflicts persist, and there will always be pressures for outside states and international institutions to intervene. Of the 116 conflicts that occurred between the end of the Cold War and the beginning of the twenty-first century, 89 were purely intrastate (civil wars) and another 20 were intrastate with foreign intervention.[4] More than 80 state actors were involved, as well as two regional organizations and more than 200 nongovernmental parties.[5] Many of these intrastate conflicts are *ethnic* or *communal wars*—wars in which belligerents define themselves in part along cultural lines such as language, religion, or similar characteristics. Others are revolutionary wars in which the combatants divide along ideological lines. Some of the worst conflicts are deliberately fueled by governments; in other cases, governments find themselves powerless to stop them. The carnage can be extreme. Since the Second World War, more than 100,000 people have died in countries such as Afghanistan, Angola, Burundi, Indonesia, Iraq, Liberia, Rwanda, Sierra Leone, Sudan, Uganda, and Yugoslavia. More than a million have died in Cambodia, China, the Democratic Republic of the Congo (DRC), Ethiopia, and Nigeria.

Most intrastate wars occur where established mechanisms for mediating conflicts break down. The inability of governments to mediate conflict frequently occurs in the aftermath of collapsed empires, such as the European colonial empires in Africa or the Soviet Empire in the Caucasus and Central Asia. Such "failed states" either never had a strong government or their governments were undermined by economic conditions, loss of legitimacy, or outside intervention. Thus, even though the end of the bipolar Cold War conflict led to the withdrawal of foreign troops from Afghanistan, Cambodia, Angola, and Somalia, intrastate war continued. And in the former Yugoslavia, which held together to preserve its independence in a bipolar world, the death of President Tito and the end of the Cold War weakened the ability of the central government to mediate ethnic conflicts.

Constructivists point out that ethnicity is not an immutable fact that inevitably leads to war. It is socially constructed in the sense that symbols, myths, and memories can be altered over time. For example, in Rwanda, which suffered a genocide in 1994, people spoke the same language and had the same skin color, but there were economic class differences between the Tutsi people, who had migrated into the area with a cattle-based culture centuries earlier, and the larger number of agricultural Hutu people. Over time, intermarriage and social change had blurred some of the distinctions, but they were reinforced during colonial rule. In the 1994 genocide in which 750,000 Tutsis were killed, many Hutus who urged moderation or who appeared to be Tutsi were also murdered.

The breakup of the former federation of Yugoslavia in 1991 also led to ethnic conflicts. Some of the worst fighting occurred between Serbs, Croats, and Muslims in Bosnia, the most heterogeneous of the Yugoslav republics. When Slovenia and Croatia declared independence from Yugoslavia in the summer of 1991, ethnic Serbs and Croats began fighting. The UN imposed an arms embargo on all members of the former Yugoslav Republic. In the following year, Bosnia-Herzegovina (44 percent Muslim, 31 percent Serbian, 17 percent Croatian) declared independence and was recognized by the West. Within Bosnia, Bosnian Serbs declared an independent Serbian Republic and war erupted as ethnic tensions exploded. In 1992 and 1993 there were reports of "ethnic cleansing" or expulsions of Muslims in Bosnia. Moreover, Serb forces blocked UN humanitarian convoys intended to protect Muslims. The Serbs also rejected a division of Bosnia along ethnic lines as Croatians switched from fighting against the Serbs to fighting Muslims. In 1994, Bosnian government forces received NATO support in their battle with Serb forces. The fighting continued in 1995 as Serbs massacred 6,000 Muslims in Srebrenica and the Croatian army forced Serbs in Krajina to flee in a massive ethnic-cleansing operation. Later in the year, Bosnia, Serbia, and Croatia signed the Dayton Peace Accord to end the war in Bosnia, and NATO peacekeeping forces were sent there.

In 1998, Serbian president Slobodan Milošević sent troops to quell unrest in the province of Kosovo. A guerrilla war with the Kosovo Liberation Army ensued and in September, Milošević faced a NATO ultimatum to either stop the crackdown on Kosovar Albanians or to expect airstrikes. In 1999, NATO bombed Yugoslavia for 78 days, which created a massive refugee crisis. As a result of the airstrikes, Milošević withdrew troops from Kosovo and was indicted as a war criminal by a special UN tribunal. Following an election in 2000 and huge protests against Milošević, he stepped down. One year later, Milošević was arrested and handed over to The Hague tribunal. Milošević's trial started in 2002, but was never concluded as he died of natural causes in his prison cell four years later. Final status issues remain unresolved in the Balkans, and international peacekeepers continue to be deployed there.

But one can also regard the conflict in the former Yugoslavia as one between rural areas where old identities and myths were strongest, and urban communities where many people had intermarried and come to identify themselves as "Yugoslavs" rather than as Croats, Serbs, or Muslims. Once Yugoslavia collapsed and fighting broke out, some of these people had new identities thrust upon them. As one man said in 1993, "All my life I considered myself a Yugoslav, not a Muslim. Now I am a Muslim because that has been forced upon me." Some theorists attribute ethnic conflicts to deep and ancient hatreds or grand clashes of civilizations, but the ethnic distinctions are better described by Sigmund Freud's term "the narcissism of minor differences."

> When I asked a Bosnian Croat military commander during a battle in Mostar how he knew whom to shoot, since people on the street looked so similar, his reply was that before the war, you would have to know their name, but now uniforms made it easy.
>
> —Joseph S. Nye, Jr.

Why do people kill over minor differences? Most often they do not. Humans always differentiate themselves into groups, and sometimes the differences are accompanied by prejudice and hatred. But such differences rarely lead to large-scale violence. While no two conflicts are exactly the same, a common dynamic is that ethnic symbols and myths create divisions; economic rivalries or the weakening of state authority create fears for group survival. Elites or leaders then mobilize support by appealing to ethnic symbols, and any number of events (such as Bosnia's declaration of independence in 1992 or the death of Rwanda's president in an April 1993 plane crash) can spark the fighting.

Political scientist John Mueller stresses the role of violent groups who achieve their ends by manipulating ethnic myths and fears. In his view, the entire concept of "ethnic warfare" is misguided because it implies a Hobbesian war of all against all, whereas so-called ethnic conflicts are "waged by small groups of combatants, groups that purport to fight and kill in the name of some larger entity."[6] Mueller argues that the minority that resorts to violence destroys the space for the moderate middle, and pathological and criminal elements thrive in the resulting chaos. Stuart Kaufman emphasizes the role of symbolic politics. Political entrepreneurs and extremist groups use the emotional power of ethnic symbols to reconstruct the larger group's preferences. The classic security dilemma arises among rational actors when lack of trust and inability to enforce agreements under anarchic conditions causes serious conflicts to erupt. But in Kaufman's view, many ethnic conflicts "erupted because one or both sides preferred conflict to cooperation."[7] In failed states such as Sierra Leone and Liberia, uneducated and unemployed young men developed a vested economic interest in looting and plundering. In addition to the problem that rational actors face in the structural conditions of anarchy, the security dilemmas involved in the early stages of ethnic conflict often grow out of the manipulation of emotional symbols by those who prefer and profit from violence.

Intervention and Sovereignty

Where failed states exist or genocide is threatened, some analysts believe outsiders should ignore sovereignty and intervene for humanitarian purposes. In 2005, the United Nations High-Level Panel on Threats, Challenges and

Changes endorsed the "norm that there is a collective international responsibility to protect . . . civilians from the effects of war and human rights abuses." According to the UN panel, this responsibility is "exercisable by the Security Council, authorizing military intervention as a last resort, in the event of genocide and other large-scale killing, ethnic cleansing or serious violations of humanitarian law which sovereign Governments have proved powerless or unwilling to prevent."

Intervention is a confusing concept, partly because the word is both descriptive and normative. It not only describes what is happening, but it also casts value judgments. Thus discussions of intervention often involve moral issues. Nonintervention in the internal affairs of sovereign states is a basic norm of international law. Nonintervention is a powerful norm because it affects both order and justice. Order sets a limit on chaos. International anarchy—the absence of a higher government—is not the same as chaos if basic principles are observed. Sovereignty and nonintervention are two principles that provide order in an anarchic world system. At the same time, nonintervention affects justice. States are communities of people who deserve the right to develop a common life within their own boundaries. Outsiders should respect their sovereignty and territorial integrity. But not all recognized states fit this ideal. Sovereignty is a concept that has been applied to many states where it fits poorly. For example, group and clan fighting meant that no government was effectively in control in Sierra Leone, Liberia, or Somalia at the beginning of the twenty-first century. Even children were pressed into battle. Thus there is often a tension between justice and order that leads to inconsistencies about whether to intervene.

Defining Intervention

In its broadest definition, *intervention* refers to external actions that influence the domestic affairs of another sovereign state. Some analysts use the term more narrowly to refer to *forcible* interference in the domestic affairs of another state. The narrow definition is merely one end of a spectrum of influences ranging from low coercion to high coercion (see Figure 2). At the low end of the scale, intervention may be simply a speech designed to influence domestic politics in

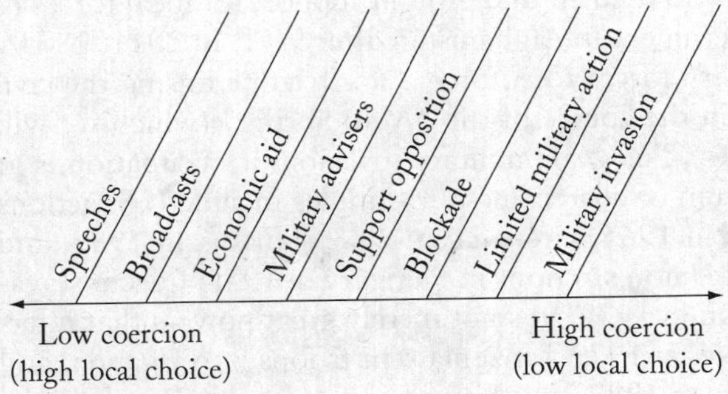

FIGURE 2
Defining Intervention

another state. For example, in 1990 President George H. W. Bush appealed to the Iraqi people to overthrow Saddam Hussein, and in 1999, Saddam appealed to the peoples of several Arab states to overthrow their leaders. Such speeches are designed to interfere in the domestic politics of another state—almost always without much effect. In the 1980s, the U.S. government established Radio Martí to broadcast its messages against Fidel Castro in Cuba, but Castro was still in power at the turn of the new century.

Economic assistance can also influence the domestic affairs of another country. For example, during the Cold War U.S. economic aid to El Salvador and Soviet aid to Cuba were designed to influence domestic affairs in those states. Though a form of illegal economic assistance, bribing high-level foreign officials can induce them to pursue a third party's preferred policies. During the Cold War, American and Soviet intelligence agencies often poured resources into foreign elections in an attempt to engineer a favorable outcome. Similarly, in the 1970s, the government of South Korea spent a great deal of money to help elect U.S. politicians who were more favorable to its interests.

A little further along the spectrum of coercion is the provision of military advisers. In the late 1950s, during the early days of the Vietnam War, the United States began its intervention first with economic and later with military assistance. Similarly, the Soviet Union and Cuba provided military aid and advisers to Nicaragua and other "client" states. Another form of intervention is support for the opposition. For example, in the early 1970s, the United States channeled money to the opponents of Salvador Allende, the democratically elected president of Chile, and at various times the Soviet Union channeled money to peace groups in Western European countries. More recently, the United States has provided financial assistance to nascent democratic movements in several former Soviet bloc countries, including Ukraine; Syria has been heavily involved in Lebanon; and Venezuela has used its oil wealth to influence elections in Latin American countries.

Toward the coercive end of the spectrum is limited military action. For example, in the 1980s the United States bombed Libya in response to its support of terrorism. In 1998, the United States launched cruise missile attacks into Sudan and Afghanistan in reprisal for terrorist attacks against American embassies in East Africa. It also used air and ground support for local forces to overthrow the Taliban government in Afghanistan after 9/11. In 2011, 18 UN members contributed military forces to enforce a no-fly zone during the civil war that erupted in Libya in the course of the "Arab Spring" (which we will discuss in more detail below). Full-scale military invasion or occupation is at the upper end of the spectrum of coerciveness. Examples include U.S. actions in the Dominican Republic in 1965, Grenada in 1983, Panama in 1989, and Iraq in 2003; and the Soviet Union's actions in Hungary in 1956, Czechoslovakia in 1968, and Afghanistan in 1979. It is not merely great powers that intervene with force. For example, in 1979 Tanzania sent troops into Uganda, and Vietnam invaded Cambodia. In 1997, tiny Rwanda intervened militarily in the affairs of its troubled larger neighbor, the DRC, and Ethiopia sent troops into Somalia in 2007. Some interventions are multilateral, but often one state takes the lead. For example, the United States led the 1995 UN intervention in Haiti and NATO's 1999 intervention in Kosovo, and Nigeria led a group of West African states that intervened in Liberia and Sierra Leone in the 1990s.

The broad definition of intervention therefore includes the whole range of behavior, from not very coercive to highly coercive. The degree of coercion involved in intervention is important because it relates to the degree of choice that the local people have, and thus the degree of outside curtailment of local autonomy.

Judging Intervention

For skeptics, moral judgments do not matter, but realists, cosmopolitans, and state moralists have different views of intervention. For realists, the key values in international politics are order and peace, and the key institution is the balance of power; they believe that intervention can be justified when it is necessary to maintain the balance of power and to maintain order. This approach to intervention was utilized throughout the Cold War by both superpowers in order to maintain their two respective spheres of influence: the American sphere in the Western Hemisphere, and the Soviet sphere in Eastern Europe. For example, in 1965 the United States intervened in the Dominican Republic and in the 1980s in Central America on the grounds that there should be no more communist governments in the Western Hemisphere, and the Soviet Union intervened to preserve communist governments in Eastern Europe. The Soviets articulated a right to intervention in 1968 with the Brezhnev Doctrine, which claimed that they had a right to intervene to preserve socialism in their sphere of influence. Realists might justify such interventions on the grounds that they preserved order and prevented the possibility of misunderstandings and miscalculations that might escalate to war, particularly nuclear war.

In contrast, cosmopolitans value justice. For them, the key international institution is a society of individuals. Therefore, intervention can be justified if it promotes individual justice and human rights; it is permissible to intervene on the side of the "good." But how is "good" to be defined? During the Cold War, liberal cosmopolitans argued that intervention was justified against right-wing regimes such as the dictatorship of Ferdinand Marcos in the Philippines (1965–1986) or the apartheid regime in South Africa (1948–1990), while conservative cosmopolitans said that intervention was justified against left-wing governments. In the 1980s, some Americans proclaimed a Reagan Doctrine when defending the United States' right to intervene against the Sandinista government in Nicaragua and against the communist governments in Angola and Mozambique because of their violation of democratic rights. In the 1990s, with the end of the Cold War, cosmopolitans urged humanitarian intervention in Somalia (1992) to halt widespread starvation, in Haiti (1994) to restore a democratically elected leader to power, in Bosnia (1995) to stop a civil war, and in Kosovo (1999) to stop "ethnic cleansing" triggered by the government of Slobodan Milošević in Serbia. Similarly, they called for U.S. intervention in conflicts in Liberia (2003) and the Darfur region of Sudan (2008). What cosmopolitans, left and right, share is the view that intervention is justified if it promotes individual justice and human rights.

For state moralists, the key value in international politics is the autonomy of the state and its people. The key institution is a society of states with certain rules and international law. Of these precepts, the most important is nonintervention in the sovereign territory of another state. Consequently, state moralists believe that intervention is justified only to defend a state's territorial integrity or to defend its sovereignty against external aggression. However, the real world is sometimes more complicated. External aggression is often ambiguous. For example, in June 1967, Israel preemptively attacked Egypt in response to its decision to deny Israel access to vital shipping lanes and mass troops along its border. Who was the aggressor, the Egyptians who massed their forces on the border and appeared to be preparing an attack on Israel, or the Israelis who struck just before the Egyptians could attack?

Exceptions to the Rule of Nonintervention

In *Just and Unjust Wars,* Michael Walzer, a political scientist who presents the state moralist position, discusses four situations that could morally justify war or military intervention in the absence of overt aggression. The first exception to a strict rule is preemptive intervention, exemplified by the Israeli attack in 1967. If there is a clear and serious threat to a state's territorial integrity and political sovereignty, it must act right away or it will have no chance to act later. But the threat must be imminent. Such an argument would not justify, for example, the 1979 Soviet intervention in Afghanistan. There is a distinction between preemptive wars and preventive wars. A *preemptive strike* occurs when war is imminent. A *preventive war* occurs when leaders believe merely that war is better now than later. As we have seen, views regarding preventive war influenced the German general staff in 1914, which feared that if Germany waited until 1916 to launch a war, Russia would be too strong for the Schlieffen Plan to work. Walzer's first exception to nonintervention would not have allowed a preventive war because there was no clear and present danger to Germany. Many other things might have changed the situation between 1914 and 1916. During the buildup to the 2003 Iraq War, U.S. officials blurred this classic distinction by claiming that a preventive strike against Iraq was preemptive even though the threat of an Iraqi attack against the United States or its allies was not imminent.

The second exception to the strict rule against intervention occurs when intervention is needed to balance a prior intervention. This rule goes back to John Stuart Mill and the nineteenth-century liberal view that a "people" has the right to determine its own fate. If an intervention prevents local people from determining their own fate, a counterintervention nullifying the first intervention can be justified because it restores the people's right to decide. Mill's argument permits intervention only as far as it counterbalances a prior intervention; more than that is not justifiable. The overriding principle is to allow the local people to solve their own problems. The United States sometimes used this as a justification for its involvement in Vietnam. In 1979, China intervened in Vietnam by crossing the border, but China pulled its troops back within a few weeks. China argued that it was countering Vietnam's intervention in Cambodia.

The third exception to the rule against intervention is when it is necessary to rescue people who are threatened with massacre. If such people are not saved from total destruction, there is no point to nonintervention as a sign of respect for their autonomy or rights. In 1979, Tanzania invaded Uganda when a dictatorial leader was slaughtering large numbers of people, and it justified its intervention as rescuing people threatened by massacre. Vietnam used a similar justification for its invasion of Cambodia. Still, massacres or genocide do not necessarily lead states or the international community to intervene. Note the reluctance of the United States to send troops to Rwanda in 1994, to Bosnia between 1992 and 1995, to Liberia in 1996, to Sierra Leone in 1999, and to the DRC in 2003. In 2005, the UN General Assembly passed a resolution accepting a responsibility to protect people suffering from avoidable catastrophe, but humanitarian intervention remains contentious. In the troubled Darfur region of Sudan, for example, support for a military intervention to stop the killing of various ethnic groups was limited to a modest peacekeeping operation.

The fourth exception to nonintervention is the right to assist secessionist movements when they have demonstrated their representative character. In other words, if a group of people within a country has clearly demonstrated that it wants to be a separate country, it is legitimate to assist its secession because doing so helps the group pool its rights and develop its autonomy. But when does a secessionist movement become worthy of assistance? Is their success the way to judge their worthiness? Part of Mill's argument was that to have a legitimate claim, a people must be able to seek its own salvation and fight for its own freedom. Such a view is consistent, at least, with the principle of nonintervention and a society of states, but it is deficient as a moral principle because it suggests that might makes right.

Problems of Self-Determination

A major problem of intervention on behalf of secessionist movements is defining a "people." Who shares a common life? How do outsiders know whether a people really agreed to pool their rights in a single community or state? *Self-determination* is the right of a people to decide their own political fate, and most commonly it expresses itself in the desire to form a state. This is an important principle, but there is always the question of who determines. Consider Somalia, whose people, unlike many other African states, had roughly the same linguistic and ethnic background. Neighboring Kenya was formed by colonial rule from dozens of different peoples or tribes, with different linguistic backgrounds and customs. Part of northern Kenya was inhabited by

Somalis. Somalia said the principle of national self-determination should allow the Somalis in the northeastern part of Kenya and the Somalis in the southern part of Ethiopia to secede because they were one Somali nation. Kenya and Ethiopia refused, saying they were still in the process of building multinational states. The result was a number of wars in northeast Africa over the Somali nationalist question. The ironic sequel was that Somalia itself later fragmented in a civil war among its clans and warlord leaders.

Voting does not always solve problems of self-determination. First, there is the question of where one votes. Take the question of Ireland. For many years, Catholics objected that if a vote were held within the political area of Northern Ireland, the two-thirds Protestant majority would rule. Protestants replied that if a vote were held within the geographical area of the entire island, the two-thirds Catholic majority would rule. Eventually, after decades of strife, outside mediation helped. But this still does not address the question of when one votes. In the 1960s, the Somalis wanted to vote right away; Kenya wanted to wait 40 or 50 years while it went about its nation-building, or reshaping tribal identities into a Kenyan identity.

Does secession harm those left behind? What about the resources the secessionists take with them, or the disruption they create in the country they leave? For example, after the dismantlement of the Austrian Empire in 1918, the Sudetenland was incorporated into Czechoslovakia even though the people spoke German. After the Munich Agreement in 1938, the Sudeten Germans seceded from Czechoslovakia and joined Germany, but that meant the mountainous frontier went under German control, which was a terrible loss for Czech defenses. Was it right to allow self-determination for the Sudeten Germans, even if it meant stripping Czechoslovakia of its military defenses? When eastern Nigeria decided it wanted to secede and form the state of Biafra in the 1960s, other Nigerians resisted in part because Biafra had most of Nigeria's oil. They argued that the oil belonged to all the people of Nigeria, not just the eastern area. Indonesia has made the same argument about secessionist demands in its oil-rich province of Aceh.

After 1989, the issue of self-determination became acute in Eastern Europe and the former Soviet Union. Throughout the former Soviet Union, different ethnic groups claimed the right of self-determination, just as many of them had done between 1917 and 1920. In the Caucasus region, Azerbaijanis, Armenians, Georgians, Abkhazians, and Chechens all demanded states on the basis of self-determination.

As we have seen, in the former state of Yugoslavia, different ethnic and religious groups seceded and claimed self-determination. The Slovenes, Serbs, and Croats managed to carve out independent republics in the early 1990s, but the Muslims in Bosnia-Herzegovina were less successful. The war in Bosnia was devastating for the civilian population, and war-crimes tribunals were convened in The Hague, starting in 1996, to convict those responsible for the massacres. Yet for much of the conflict, the United Nations, NATO, and the European Union were divided over how to respond. Part of what made the war in Bosnia so complicated for the international community was the problem of assessing how much of the fighting could be attributed to tensions among Bosnian Croats, Serbs, and Muslims and how much of the violence was caused by Serbia's intervention. If it was not simple aggression by Serbia, then the only grounds for intervention would be to prevent a massacre. As with Rwanda, the international community was united in its condemnation of the Balkan violence, but was unable to agree on effective joint action until late in the conflict, in 1995, when a NATO peacekeeping force was sent to the troubled area.

Self-determination turns out to be an ambiguous moral principle. Woodrow Wilson thought it would solve problems in central Europe in 1919, but it created as many as it solved. Adolf Hitler used the principle to undermine fragile states in the 1930s. With less than 10 percent of the world's states being relatively homogeneous, it is clear that treating self-determination as a primary rather than secondary moral principle could have disastrous consequences for many parts of the world.

The best hope for the future is to ask *what* is being determined as well as *who* determines it. In situations where groups have difficulties living together, it may be possible to allow a degree of autonomy in the determination of internal affairs. Internal self-determination could allow degrees of cultural, economic, and political autonomy similar to that which exists in countries such as Switzerland or Belgium. Where such loosening of the bonds is still not enough, it may be possible in some cases to arrange an amicable divorce, as happened when Czechoslovakia peacefully divided into two sovereign countries—the Czech Republic and Slovakia—on January 1, 1993. But absolute demands for self-determination are more likely to become a source of violence unless handled extremely carefully.

In conclusion, although the simple absolute principle of nonintervention is frequently breached in practice, the norm of nonintervention remains important. Exceptions to nonintervention must be judged on a case-by-case basis by looking at the motives, means, and consequences. The same principles can be applied to the Iraq War, as we will see shortly.

Genocide and the "Responsibility to Protect"

We noted that sovereign statehood requires the recognition of others. In this respect, the Westphalian system of sovereign states resembles a club: You can only be a member if other members of the club agree to your membership. Since the seventeenth century, membership criteria have evolved. Sovereignty used to represent more of a barrier to outside interference than it does today. Increasingly, members of the international community require that governments meet certain standards of behavior within their borders before they will agree to respect the principle of nonintervention. As the Report of the International Commission on Intervention and State Sovereignty put it, "State sovereignty implies responsibility, and the primary responsibility for the protection of its people lies with the state itself." In practical terms, "Where a population is suffering serious harm, as a result of internal war, insurgency, repression or state failure, and the state in question is unwilling or unable to halt or avert it, the principle of nonintervention yields to the international responsibility to protect."[8]

As so often happens with major normative shifts in world politics, the Responsibility to Protect (R2P) was in large part a reaction to prior failure. The fact that the international community stood idly by while genocide unfolded in Rwanda and intervened only belatedly in Yugoslavia prompted a genuine sense of shame. In this respect it resembled the Convention on the Prevention and Punishment of the Crime of Genocide (colloquially known as the "Genocide Convention"), adopted by the UN General Assembly in December 1948—a sincere reaction to the world's failure to stand up to Hitler and prevent the Holocaust. But although the doctrine of R2P is relatively young, it and the Genocide Convention have had eerily similar fates. Indeed, arguably, all such well-meaning attempts to internationalize responsibility for peace, justice, and security—the League of Nations and the 1928 Kellogg-Briand Treaty outlawing war both come to mind—have run into a powerful set of obstacles: power politics, self-interest, and free rider problems. States are generally reluctant to take on stronger states. Sometimes powerful states see an overriding interest in preventing the international community from interfering in the domestic affairs of allies, clients, or satellites. Often states are wary of setting a precedent that could be used against themselves by too readily agreeing to authorize intervention elsewhere. And peace, justice, and security are, in a sense, public goods: Since they benefit everyone, every state has an incentive to let other states shoulder the cost of providing them.

The Convention on the Prevention and Punishment of the Crime of Genocide illustrates all of these problems, and more. Article 2 of the Convention counts as genocide "any of the following acts committed with intent to destroy, in whole or in part, a national, ethnical, racial or religious group, as such: (a) Killing members of the group; (b) Causing serious bodily or mental harm to members of the group; (c) Deliberately inflicting on the group conditions of life calculated to bring about its physical destruction in whole or in part; (d) Imposing measures intended to prevent births within the group; (e) Forcibly transferring children of the group to another group."[9] The definition itself provides ample opportunity for the international community to justify inaction in the face of atrocity. For example, perpetrators and their apologists can argue that victims are targeted for political reasons, not for their national, ethnic, racial, or religious identities. They can argue that the dead and displaced are "collateral damage" rather than victims of intentional efforts to destroy the groups to which they belong. They can argue that "in whole or in part" means all or virtually all members of a group, not just a portion of it, even if that portion numbers in the hundreds of thousands. Even when a case fits a highly restrictive interpretation of the definition, the international community may consider intervention impractical or premature in the light of ongoing diplomatic efforts. The result is that more than 40 years passed between the adoption of the Convention and the first prosecutions under it, and all international prosecutions have taken place in the context of ad hoc tribunals. That the tribunals have brought charges of genocide at all is certainly an important marker of progress, as is the fact that the judgments themselves have broadened and refined the definition of genocide; rape, for example, is now legally considered a form of genocide under certain circumstances. But progress has been painfully slow.

R2P was a deliberate attempt to address some of these flaws. It asserts a positive and proactive obligation to intervene to deal with "mass atrocity" (including, but not limited to, genocide as understood by the Convention). Yet despite early enthusiasm for the doctrine, it has had very little impact on intrastate violence thus far.

The conflict in Darfur was an early acid test of R2P, and not a very encouraging one. Since its outbreak in 2003, as many as 450,000 civilians may have been killed in ethnic conflict in this westernmost province of Sudan (estimates vary widely; official Sudanese government figures put the number at fewer than 20,000). Most of the deaths have been at the hands of the Janjaweed militia, which operates on behalf of the government of Sudan, despite the government's claims to the contrary. So far, the United States is the only permanent member of the UN Security Council that has been willing to call the conflict a genocide (many states are reluctant to do so precisely because doing so triggers an obligation to act). The international community's only muscular response was to dispatch an African Union peacekeeping force that was inadequately manned, armed, trained, and led, and that even lacked a mandate to protect civilians. Contrary to popular belief, R2P always envisaged military intervention as a last resort, but critics argued that if Darfur did not galvanize decisive international action, it is difficult to know what might.

More encouraging was the international intervention in the 2011 Libyan civil war, which broke out when frustration with the autocratic regime of Muammar Gaddafi boiled over into armed revolt. Opponents of the regime secured control of much of the eastern part of the country, as well as pockets in the west, prompting the Gaddafi regime to go on the offensive. With unchallenged air supremacy, superior armor, and evident willingness to target civilians supporting the opposition, Gaddafi's onslaught seemed to herald a bloodbath. In an unusual display of swiftness and solidarity, the UN Security Council passed Resolution 1973, imposing a no-fly zone for the purpose of protecting civilians—the first decisive implementation of the doctrine of R2P.

Whether Resolution 1973 represents a sea change in the international community's willingness to put muscle behind R2P remains to be seen. While it did justify foreign military intervention in the form of aerial combat missions, and while these missions did succeed in largely destroying Gaddafi's air force, it explicitly prohibited the deployment of foreign soldiers on the ground, and in that sense represented a half measure. By some accounts, too, the speed with which the Security Council passed Resolution 1973 did not reflect enthusiasm for R2P so much as the fear of certain members (primarily China and Russia) that if they did not agree to a no-fly zone, further bloodshed would result in calls for more robust forms of intervention, including "boots on the ground"—measures that they would prefer not to be seen vetoing, but which their own sensitivities about foreign intervention would not allow them easily to approve. Indeed, Russia and China both later expressed concerns about "mission creep"—the use of ground-attack aircraft to strike armored columns, logistical facilities, command and control sites, and even Gaddafi's compound—which seemed to go well beyond the mandate to impose a no-fly zone.

Normative change in world politics is rarely smooth, and rarely linear. It may be that the next time a brutal authoritarian regime targets its own people, the international community may underreact. But the Libyan civil war implies this much, at least: No longer can it be said that the doctrine of R2P is nothing more than a "responsibility to protest."

Follow Up

- Michael Walzer, *Just and Unjust Wars: A Moral Argument with Historical Illustrations* (New York: Basic Books, 2006), pp. 86–108.
- Gareth J. Evans, *The Responsibility to Protect: Ending Mass Atrocity Crimes Once and for All* (Washington, D.C.: Brookings Institution Press, 2008).

INTERSTATE CONFLICT: CURRENT FLASHPOINTS

It is notoriously difficult to measure the level of armed conflict in the world, but several important facts seem reasonably clear. The first is that intrastate war has been a greater cause of death, destruction, and displacement than has interstate war since World War II. During the Cold War, intrastate war became more and more of a problem, while the frequency and severity of interstate war actually slightly declined. If we look solely at the post–Cold War period, intrastate war has declined rather dramatically, though it still represents a much larger problem than interstate war, which has actually slightly increased, but from a very low level. The Center for Systemic Peace, affiliated with the Center for Global Policy at George Mason University, uses a "summed war magnitude score" to represent these trends, as shown in Figure 3.

Ohio State University political scientist John Mueller has argued that major interstate war has become "obsolescent."[10] If by this we mean that it is increasingly difficult to imagine a cost-benefit calculation justifying a major interstate war, then Mueller is probably correct. The states that are capable of waging major wars are all either developed countries with enormous stakes in a peaceful, well-regulated international order that have at their disposal a wide array of conflict management tools, or rapidly developing countries (such as China) who eagerly seek to take their place among this select group. But history shows that wars sometimes break out for reasons that are difficult to explain in traditional cost-benefit terms. Accidents, misperceptions, and inadvertent actions have all played important roles in triggering wars from time to time. History also shows that states sometimes wage war for reasons that do not seem entirely instrumentally rational, but that reflect powerful commitments to symbols, ideals, or other intangible considerations. So while we should take heart from the fact that the world has done a relatively good job

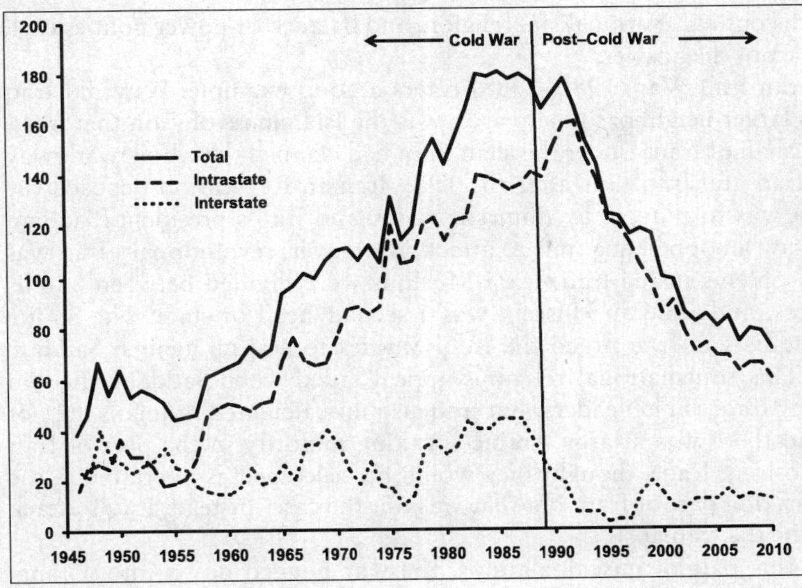

FIGURE 3
Summed War Magnitude Scores
Source: Centre for Systemic Peace. http://www.systemicpeace.org/conflict.htm

of wrestling the problem of interstate war to the ground, we should be wary of declaring victory over the problem—particularly since a number of countries that have ongoing serious disputes with neighbors have at their disposal significant nuclear arsenals.

Interstate war is not equally likely everywhere. Many would consider it virtually impossible in the "islands of peace" known as security communities: Western Europe, Scandinavia, North America, and Australasia. In still other parts of the world, such as parts of sub-Saharan Africa, states are so weak, fractured, or racked with intrastate violence already that interstate war is hardly a pressing problem. Where interstate war remains acutely dangerous are in the various "flashpoints" where well-armed states with longstanding grievances confront each other, and where international crises have the potential to escalate to nuclear war. For reasons that are not entirely clear, these flashpoints dot the southern and eastern rim of Asia—Iran, Kashmir, the South China Sea, the Taiwan Strait, and the Korean peninsula—but the Middle East is the most complex and has the longest history.

The Middle East

Torn by strife for the last half century, the Middle East has been the stage for, perhaps, the world's most notorious regional conflicts. It best fits the realist view of international politics, but despite this, it is also an area where international law and organization have played significant roles. What is the cause of so much conflict? Nationalism, religion, and balance-of-power politics each provide part of the answer.

The Iran-Iraq War (1980–1988) offers a good example. Why did Iraq invade its larger neighbor? One reason was the Islamic revolution that overthrew the shah of Iran. Under the shah, Iran had claimed the whole waterway between Iran and Iraq. But after the 1979 Iranian Revolution deposed the shah, Iran was torn apart by domestic strife, and Iraq's president, Saddam Hussein, saw an opportune time to attack. Moreover, revolutionary Iran was causing problems inside Iraq. Iraqi Muslims were divided between Sunnis and Shi'ites, and Saddam Hussein was a secular head of state. The Shi'ite fundamentalists in Iran urged the Iraqi Shi'ites to rise up against Saddam Hussein. This transnational religious appeal failed when Saddam Hussein killed many Iraqi Shi'ite leaders. But Iraq also miscalculated. Iranians are not Arabs, and there was a large Arabic-speaking minority in the part of Iran adjacent to Iraq. Iraqis thought they would be welcomed as liberators in the Arabic-speaking part of Iran, but that was not the case. Instead, Iraq's attack helped unite the Iranians.

After this pair of miscalculations, the war bogged down into a long, drawn-out affair, instead of the short, profitable war Saddam Hussein had intended. Iraq decided it wanted to withdraw, but Iran refused to let go. Having been attacked, it was not going to let Iraq decide when to quit. The ayatollah Khomeini, spiritual leader of Iran, said Iran would not end the war until the downfall of Saddam Hussein. For most of the decade, the rest of the world looked on. Conservative Arab countries such as Saudi Arabia and Jordan supported Iraq against Iran because they were more afraid of Iranian revolutionary power. But, as we have seen, Arab Syria, a secular and radical regime in many ways similar to Iraq, supported Iran for balance-of-power reasons. Damascus was worried about the rising strength of its neighbor Iraq, rather than more distant Iran.

Outsiders also took sides. The United States, worried about the growth of Iranian power, provided covert assistance to Iraq. Israel secretly shipped U.S.-built weapons to Iran, even though fundamentalists in Iran were calling for the destruction of Israel. Israel's covert weapons assistance can be explained by balance-of-power considerations. Israel feared both Iraq and Iran, but Iraq was a closer threat, and on the principle of "the enemy of my enemy is my friend," Israel provided assistance to Iran. So a war that started from miscalculations rooted in religion, nationalism, and ambition was expanded by balance-of-power concerns into an intractable, nearly decade-long conflict.

How does nationalism cause war? Nationalism is not merely a descriptive term, it is also prescriptive. When words are both descriptive and prescriptive, they become political words used in struggles for power. Nationalism has become a crucial source of state legitimacy in the modern world. Therefore, claims to nationhood become powerful instruments. If a people can get others to accept its claim to be a nation, it can claim national rights and use such claims as weapons against its enemies. For example, in the 1970s the Arab states successfully lobbied in the UN General Assembly to pass a resolution that labeled Zionism as racism. Their intent was to deprive Israel of the legitimacy of calling itself a nation. To be a racist is bad; to be a nation is good. To argue that Israel was not a nation was to use words as weapons that would deprive Israel of legitimacy and weaken its soft power.

The analytic problem with the argument was that religion can be a basis of national identity. It is also true that a religious basis can make it more difficult for minorities outside the religion to share the national identity. Life can be more difficult for Muslims in Israel than for Jews, just as daily life can be more trying for Hindus in Pakistan than for Muslims. But it does not follow from the fact that a people uses religion to call itself a nation that the state is racist. The UN General Assembly finally annulled the resolution by a second vote in 1991.

In the eighteenth century, nationalism was not all that important. Why have claims to nationalism become so important now? After all, as constructivists showed, humans are capable of multiple crosscutting loyalties—above and below the state level—and these loyalties can change. Loyalties tend to change when the usual patterns of life are disrupted. The idea of the nation often starts among the most disrupted, with people who are marginal figures in their own cultures and less certain about their identity. These are often people who are jolted out of normal patterns, who start to ask questions. National claims often start with intellectuals or with deviant religious groups. For example, the early Arab nationalists in the nineteenth century were often Christians rather than Muslims. Gradually their concern about a new identity developed broader support as industry and urbanization disrupted the traditional patterns and loyalties of rural societies.

The disruptions that mobilize people for new identities can come from internal or external forces. Modern nationalism was greatly stimulated by the French Revolution. The rise of the middle class disrupted traditional political and social patterns. Rising political groups no longer wanted the state of France to be defined by the king but to be defined in terms of the nation, all the people. And externally, as Napoleon's armies marched across Europe, they disrupted society and mobilized nationalist feelings among German-speaking peoples and other groups. By the middle of the century, there was widening support for the idea that each nation should have a state. This ideal culminated in the unifications of Germany and Italy. Ironically, Bismarck was a conservative who did not try to unite all German speakers, only those he could control for the Prussian crown. Nonetheless, he harnessed nationalism for his purposes, and the unifications of Germany and Italy became models of success.

World War II weakened the European colonial empires, and decolonization was one of the major movements in Asia and Africa over the next three decades. The metropolitan societies had been weakened by the war itself, and elites in the colonized areas began to use the idea of nationalism against the crumbling European empires. But if the nineteenth-century model of states based on language and ethnicity had been used to organize the postcolonial world, it would have led to thousands of mini-states in Africa and many parts of Asia. Instead, the postcolonial elites asserted the right of the state to make a nation, just the opposite of the nineteenth-century pattern. The local leaders argued that they needed to use the state machinery the colonists had established—the budget, the police, the civil service—to shape a nation out of smaller tribal groups. The same ideology of nationalism came to be used to justify two things that are almost the opposite of each other—nation makes state or state makes nation—because *nationalism* is a political word with an instrumental use. In that sense, national identities are socially constructed. (Even in the seemingly classic "nation makes state" case of France, the state used education and police to bring laggard regions such as Brittany into line.)

In the early romantic days of colonial liberation movements, there was often a successful blurring of these differences in "pan" movements. Europe in the nineteenth and early twentieth centuries saw the rise of pan-Slavism, claiming a common identity of all Slavic-speaking peoples. The modern Middle East saw pan-Arabism, and Africa, pan-Africanism. Early opponents of alien rule argued that since colonized people all suffered alike from the external colonizers, they should form pan-African or pan-Arab nations. But when it came to the actual business of governing, as opposed to liberating or resisting colonialism, the business of government required the instruments of state such as budgets, police, and civil service. And those instruments existed not on a "pan" basis, but on the basis of the artificial boundaries created by colonial rule. So, as the romanticism gradually wore away, identity based on the state began to replace that of the "pan" movements. Nonetheless, the romanticism of the "pan" movements often lingered on as a disruptive force.

The Middle East has often seen appeals to pan-Arabism and odd situations in which countries suddenly announce that they are forming a union, as Egypt and Syria did in forming the United Arab Republic in 1958, or countries as disparate as Libya and Morocco did in 1989. Over time, however, the forces of the state have prevailed over these pan-nationalist movements. But the gradual process is far from complete. Much of the postcolonial world saw enormous disruption of the normal patterns of life because of economic change and modern communications. Political leaders tried to control this postcolonial discontent. Some used national appeals, some used pan-Arab appeals, and others used fundamentalist religious appeals, all contributing to the complexity of the forces that create conflict in regions such as the Middle East. The failure of states in the region to modernize effectively explains why some of their citizens turned toward the fundamentalism and terrorism promoted by the al Qaeda network.

Arab-Israeli Conflict The Arab-Israeli conflict has produced eight wars between two groups of people asserting different national identities, but claiming the same postage-stamp-size piece of land. The Israeli claim dates to biblical times when the area was controlled by Jews before the Romans asserted their authority in the first century BCE. In modern historical times, Israelis have pointed to several events tied to World Wars I and II to justify the existence of Israel. During World War I, the British issued the Balfour Declaration,

TOWARD A PARTITION OF PALESTINE

His Majesty's Government views with favour the establishment in Palestine of a national home for the Jewish people, and will use their best endeavours to facilitate the achievement of this object, it being clearly understood that nothing shall be done which may prejudice the civil and religious rights of existing, non-Jewish communities in Palestine, or the rights and political status enjoyed by Jews in any other country.

—*The Balfour Declaration, November 2, 1917*

a letter written by the British government to Lord Rothschild of the British Zionist Federation promising that the British government would work for a Jewish homeland in Palestine. After World War II, Israelis argue, the horrors of Hitler's Holocaust proved the need for a Jewish state. In 1948, Jewish settlers were willing to accept a partition of Palestine, but the Arab people in the area were not. The United Nations recognized the new Jewish state, but the Israelis had to fight to preserve it from concerted Arab attack. This, the Israelis say, is the historical origin and justification of the state of Israel.

The Palestinian Arabs respond that they also have lived in the area for many centuries. At the time of World War I, when the Balfour Declaration was issued, 90 percent of the people living in the area of Palestine were Arabs. Indeed, as late as 1932, 80 percent of the people were Arabs. They argue that Britain had no right to make a promise to the Jews at the Arabs' expense. What is more, the Arabs continue, the Holocaust may have been one of history's greatest sins, but it was committed by Europeans. Why should Arabs have to pay for it?

Both sides have valid points. In World War I, the area that is now Palestine was ruled by the Turks, and the Ottoman Empire was allied with Germany. After Turkey's defeat, its empire was dismembered, and its Arab territories became mandates under the League of Nations. France governed Syria and Lebanon; Britain called the area it controlled between the Jordan River and the Mediterranean "Palestine," and the area it governed across the Jordan River "Trans-Jordan."

In the 1920s, Jewish immigration to Palestine increased slowly, but in the 1930s, after the rise of Hitler and intensified anti-Semitism in Europe, it began to increase rapidly. By 1936, nearly 40 percent of Palestine was Jewish, and the influx led the Arab residents to riot. The British established a royal commission that recommended partition into two states. In May 1939, with World War II looming, Britain needed Arab support against Hitler's Germany, so Britain promised the Arabs it would restrict Jewish immigration. But restriction was hard to enforce after the war. Because of the Holocaust, many in Europe were sympathetic to the idea of a Jewish homeland, and there was a good deal of smuggling of Jewish refugees. In addition, some of the Jewish settlers in Palestine engaged in terrorist acts against their British rulers. Britain, meanwhile, was so financially and politically exhausted from World War II and the decolonization of India that it announced in the fall of 1947 that, come May 1948, it would turn Palestine over to the United Nations.

In 1947, the United Nations recommended a partition of Palestine. Ironically, it would have been better for the Arabs if they had accepted the UN partition plan, but instead they rejected it. That led to outbreaks of local fighting. In May 1948 Israel declared itself independent, and Israel's Arab neighbors attacked to try to reverse the partition. The first war lasted for eight months of on-and-off fighting. Even though the Arabs outnumbered the Israelis 40 to 1, they were poorly organized and hampered by disunity. After a cease-fire and UN mediation, Jordan controlled the area called the West Bank and Egypt controlled Gaza, but most of the rest of the Palestinian mandate was controlled by the Israelis—more than they would have had if the Arabs had accepted the 1947 UN plan.

The war produced a flood of Palestinian refugees, a sense of humiliation among many Arabs, and broad resistance to any idea of permanent peace. The Arabs did not want to accept the outcome of the war because they did not want to legitimize Israel. They believed time was on their side. Arab leaders fostered pan-Arab feelings and the belief that they could destroy Israel in another war. King Abdullah of Jordan was assassinated when he tried to sign a separate peace treaty with Israel in 1951, further decreasing the likelihood of a peaceful settlement between the Arab states and the new Israeli government.

The second Arab-Israeli war occurred in 1956. In 1952, Nasser and other young nationalist officers overthrew King Farouk of Egypt and seized power. They soon received arms from the Soviet Union and maneuvered to gain control of the Suez Canal, a vital commercial shipping channel linking Europe and Asia. Egypt harassed Israel with a series of guerrilla attacks. Britain and France, angry about the canal and worried about Nasser dominating the Middle East, colluded with Israel to attack Egypt. However, the United States refused to help Britain, and the war was stopped by a UN resolution and peacekeeping force that was inserted to keep the sides apart. But there was still no peace treaty.

The third war, the Six-Day War of June 1967, was the most important because it resulted in the primary current territorial issue. Nasser and the Palestinians continued to harass the Israelis with guerrilla attacks, and Egypt closed the Straits of Tiran, which cut off Israeli shipping from the Red Sea. Nasser was not quite ready for war, but he saw the prospect of a Syrian-Israeli war looming and thought he would do well to join. Nasser asked the United Nations to remove its peacekeeping forces from his border. Israel, watching Nasser prepare for war, decided not to wait, but to preempt Egypt's likely attack. The Israelis caught the Egyptian air force on the ground and went on to capture not only the whole Sinai Peninsula, but also the Golan Heights from Syria and the West Bank from Jordan (See Figure 4).

At that point the superpowers stepped in to press the two sides to accept a cease-fire. In November 1967, the UN Security Council passed Resolution 242, which said Israel should withdraw from occupied lands in exchange for peace and recognition. But Resolution 242 contained some deliberate

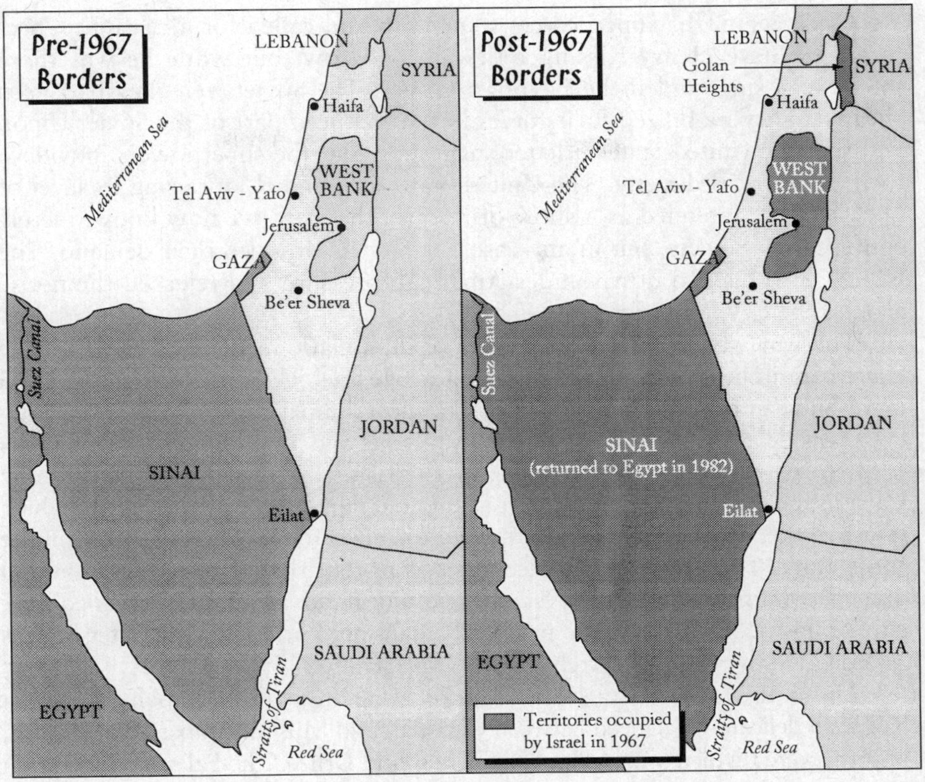

FIGURE 4
Israel's Borders Pre- and Post-1967

ambiguities. Some of the several language versions of the resolution said just "territories," not *all* territories, implying that some land might not have to be returned. It was also ambiguous about the status of the Palestinians, who were not recognized as a nation but were described as refugees. Again, the basic issue was not settled.

The fourth war, the War of Attrition, was a more modest affair. In 1969–1970, Nasser, with support from the Soviet Union, organized crossings of the Suez Canal and other harassments. These provoked an air war in which Israeli and Egyptian pilots fought a number of air battles. Eventually the air war tapered off into a stalemate.

The fifth war was the Yom Kippur War of October 1973. After Nasser died, he was succeeded by Anwar Sadat, who realized that Egypt could not destroy Israel. He decided that some psychological victory was necessary before he could make any conciliatory moves toward peace. Sadat decided to attack across the Suez Canal but not to try to recapture all of the Sinai Peninsula. Sadat colluded with the Syrians and achieved an effective surprise. In the first stages, the war went well for the Egyptians, but the Israelis vigorously counterattacked.

Once again, the superpowers stepped in and called for a cease-fire. Secretary of State Henry Kissinger flew to Moscow, but while he was there the Israelis surrounded the Egyptian armies. The Soviets felt they had been cheated. They mobilized their forces in the southern part of the Soviet Union and sent the United States a letter suggesting that the superpowers introduce their own forces directly. The United States responded by raising its level of nuclear alert. Intended as a show of resolve, the alert, we now know, merely confused the Soviets. But in any case, the Soviets dropped their demand. The Israelis also backed down under American pressure and released the noose around the Egyptian army.

The war was followed by a series of diplomatic maneuvers in which the United States negotiated a partial pullback by Israel. UN observers were placed in the Sinai and on the Golan Heights. The most dramatic result of the war, however, was delayed. In 1977, Sadat went to Israel and announced that Egypt was ready to negotiate a separate peace. In 1978 and 1979, with President Jimmy Carter's mediation, Israel and Egypt negotiated the Camp David Accords, which returned the Sinai to Egypt and provided for talks about local autonomy in the West Bank. The Camp David Accords meant that the largest Arab state had quit the coalition confronting Israel. Egyptian nationalism had prevailed over pan-Arabism. Sadat broke the pan-Arab coalition, but a few years later he was assassinated by religious extremists who objected to his policy.

The sixth war was Israel's invasion of Lebanon in 1982. Initially, Lebanon had been delicately balanced between Christian and Muslim Arabs. The Muslims, in turn, were divided among Sunnis, Shi'ites, and Druze. The Palestine Liberation Organization (PLO) was a major presence in Lebanon, and the Christians were also split into factions. Lebanon was once cited as a haven of stability in the Middle East, the one area of true pluralism and diversity, but as Lebanon began to break apart into civil war, it presented increasing opportunities for outside intervention. Syria began to impose order in the north, and in 1978 Israel went into southern Lebanon as far as the Litani River.

In June 1982, Israeli defense minister Ariel Sharon decided to go further. At first he said Israel would go only 25 miles into Lebanon to protect the northern parts of Israel from attacks launched from Lebanese soil, but in fact Israeli troops besieged Beirut for ten weeks, forcing the PLO to evacuate. A Lebanese Christian leader, Bashir Gemayel, signed a peace treaty with Israel, but was assassinated shortly thereafter, and the treaty collapsed, pitching Lebanon into further chaos. In 1985, the Israelis withdrew from most of Lebanon except for a buffer zone in the south, which they finally evacuated in 2000. But in 2007, Israel and the Lebanese political and paramilitary organization Hezbollah ("Party of God," backed by Syria and Iran) fought yet another war in Lebanon—the seventh in the series—and in 2008 Israel took on another Palestinian group, the fundamentalist Hamas ("Islamic Resistance Movement"), in an eighth war in Gaza.

The violent recent history of the Middle East shows how regional conflicts based on ethnicity, religion, and nationalism can become embittered and difficult to resolve. Hard-liners reinforce each other. Arab governments were slow to make peace because they did not want to legitimize Israel, and in their rejection they reinforced the domestic position of those Israelis who did not want to make peace with the Arabs. The extremists formed a de facto transnational coalition that made it very difficult for moderates who wanted to find a compromise. In 1973 and 1977 Sadat took risks, but he eventually paid for them with his life. A decade later, Israeli prime minister Yitzhak Rabin also took risks for peace and was assassinated by a Jewish religious extremist. In such a world of extremes, trust and cooperation are difficult, particularly when the conflict is over a private good such as territory, which is excludable and rivalrous.

During the bipolar Cold War era, wars in the Middle East tended to be short, in part because the superpower role was so prominent. On the one hand, each superpower supported its clients, but when it looked as if the clients might pull the superpowers toward the nuclear brink, they pulled their clients back. The pressures for cease-fires came from outside. In 1956, the pressure came from the United States via the United Nations; in 1967, the United States and the Soviet Union used their hotline to arrange a cease-fire; in 1973, the United States and the Soviet Union stepped in; and in 1982, the United States pressed Israel to draw back from Lebanon. While in many instances the Cold War exacerbated regional conflicts, it also placed a safety net underneath them.

In the Arab-Israeli conflict, we see the same pattern that we can observe on a global scale: a shift over time from interstate to intrastate war, from regular military combat to irregular (insurgency and counterinsurgency) combat. The last major war between the Israel armed forces and the armed forces of neighboring state took place nearly 30 years ago. But there has been no true peace in the region. In the past decade alone, more than 8,000 Palestinians and Israelis have died as a result of political violence in Israel and the occupied territories (see Figure 5)—more than twice the U.S. toll in Iraq since 2003. More Palestinians than Israelis have died, owing to the superior organization and firepower of the Israeli Defense Forces (IDF), but both sides are vulnerable. The weaker side in an *asymmetrical* conflict often resorts to unconventional means of inflicting harm, and indeed Palestinians have often resorted to using tactics such as suicide bombings, particularly during the Second Intifada ("Uprising"). More than 500 people, mostly Israeli civilians, died in 140 suicide attacks between 2000 and 2007. The deadliest year was 2002, with 55 attacks killing 220 people, prompting calls to complete a physical barrier to prevent attackers from Palestinian-controlled areas from crossing into Israel proper and into Israeli settlements in the occupied territories. The barrier, which Israelis often refer to as "the security fence" and which Palestinians often refer to as "the Apartheid Wall," was effective in stemming suicide attacks, but caused enormous hardship for Palestinians who travel back and forth between their homes on one side and their jobs on the other. The barrier is controversial as well because it does not always follow the 1949 armistice line, or "Green Line," considered by most of the international community to demarcate Israel's legitimate border: Roughly 12 percent of the West Bank falls on the Israeli side.

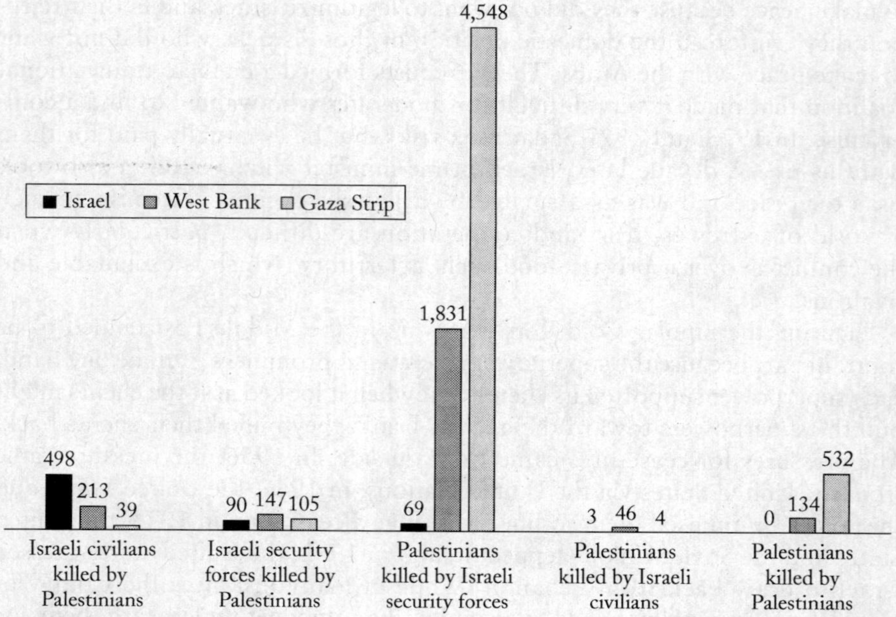

FIGURE 5

Israeli and Palestinian fatalities, 9/29/2001–5/31/2011

Source: B'Tselem, http://old.btselem.org/statistics/english/Casualties.asp

The seeming intractability of the Arab-Israeli conflict is largely a function of the fact that it is a conflict over a private good—namely, territory. Sovereignty is an absolute concept, and territoriality is an essential characteristic of a sovereign state. While some states (and many nonstate actors, such as Hamas) do not recognize Israel's right to exist, most states do, and Israel is a member of the UN. As of yet, however, there is no Palestinian equivalent. As time goes by, more and more people arrive at the conclusion that the only prospect for lasting peace lies in a "two-state" solution.

While a two-state solution is not quite within reach, several developments suggest that it may yet be possible. Perhaps the most significant of these was the Oslo Accords, which resulted in the Declaration of Principles signed in Washington, D.C., in September 1993 between the PLO and the government of Yitzhak Rabin, and that led to series of agreements for the withdrawal of Israeli troops from the Gaza Strip and from Palestinian towns and villages in the West Bank. As a result of these negotiations, Israel recognized the PLO as the legitimate voice of the Palestinian people, and a new Palestinian Authority began to take over the reins of local autonomy, including policing. At the same time, King Hussein of Jordan negotiated a peace treaty with the Rabin government, signed in Washington in 1994.

In a significant unofficial effort, Israeli and Palestinian negotiators met in Geneva in 2003 to work out a model for a more comprehensive peace deal. Known as the Geneva Accord, this informal agreement followed the outlines of various earlier proposals, but went even further by resolving the difficult questions of the status of Jerusalem, Israeli settlements, and the limited Palestinian "right of return" for the families of refugees who had fled in 1948. While the Geneva Accord carried no legal standing, it demonstrated that knowledgeable, concerned parties on both sides could agree on even the toughest issues. U.S. secretary of state Colin Powell met with the accord negotiators despite strong protests from the Israeli government. As more than one observer noted, the episode showed that it was easier to identify a solution to the Israel-Palestine conflict than to identify a way to get there.

Since the death of PLO leader Yasir Arafat in November 2004, progress has been stalled in part by deep fissures within the Palestinian community. Not long after Prime Minister Ariel Sharon withdrew Israeli forces from Gaza in the summer of 2005, Hamas began to filled the vacuum, splitting the leadership of Palestinians into two camps—an increasingly pragmatic Palestinian Authority in the West Bank led by Mahmoud Abbas, Arafat's successor as leader of Fatah, and a militantly inflexible Hamas government in Gaza. Twice Fatah and Hamas have attempted to heal their breach: once in 2007, and again in 2011. The former attempt was short-lived; the fate of the latter remains to be seen. But it is clear that the existence of both pragmatic and doctrinaire voices vying to control the vision for a Palestinian state makes progress toward a two-state solution difficult.

What would it take to solve the Arab-Israeli conflict? Israel craves above all recognition of its right to exist behind secure borders as a Jewish state (de facto, if not de jure; Israel has no formal constitution, and its basic laws

Israeli prime minister Benjamin Netanyahu meets Palestinian president Mahmoud Abbas for talks in Washington with U.S. secretary of state Hillary Clinton, September 2010

nowhere actually define Israel as a Jewish state). Exactly what borders would be acceptable is a matter of great internal debate. Israel also insists upon retaining Jerusalem as its capital, with full control of the sites in the Old City that are holy to Judaism. Palestinians claim at a minimum a right of return for the descendants and remaining first-generation refugees forced to flee their homes and villages as a result of the 1948 and 1967 wars, and insist that Jerusalem should be the capital of Palestine. They also insist upon full control of the Old City's sites that are holy to Islam—some of which directly about Jewish holy sites. Creative solutions may well be possible for issues such as Jerusalem and the holy sites, such as shared or overlapping sovereignty (in effect transforming private goods into jointly managed common goods), but only if moderates on both sides prevail.

For a genuinely durable peace, Israel would have to resolve its longstanding dispute with Syria over the Golan Heights, occupied by Israel since 1967; work out acceptable terms for Israeli settlers in the West Bank and Gaza; and negotiate long-term sharing and management of scarce water resources with Syria, Jordan, and the Palestinians—all against the backdrop of decades of grievance and mistrust. Small wonder that the Arab-Israeli conflict has proven to be one of the world's least tractable!

Conflict in the Persian Gulf, 1991 and 2003 We saw that external powers were sometimes involved in the Arab-Israeli conflict, but most often participating not directly and officially. While the United States backed Israel and the Soviet Union assisted Arab states during the Cold War, they stopped short of getting immediately entangled in the hostilities for two reasons. First, neither superpower was willing to get drawn into a conflict that might have ended in nuclear war. Second, the United States was reluctant to wage a major war abroad as memories of Vietnam had not yet faded. Similarly, the Soviet Union had already been fighting a costly war in Afghanistan since the late 1970s. However, with the end of the Cold War and the demise of the Soviet Union, major military involvement in the Middle East became a new pattern (see Figure 6).

The first Persian Gulf crisis started on August 2, 1990, when Saddam Hussein invaded Kuwait. Iraq had always claimed that Kuwait was an artificial creation of the colonial era and should not be a separate state. In 1961, it tried to take over Kuwait but was deterred by Britain. However, as we have seen, the idea that colonial boundaries are meaningless promised to create enormous havoc in other regions of the postcolonial world, which may explain why so many countries in the United Nations rejected the Iraqi reasoning.

In any case, there were deeper economic and political reasons. Iraq had been economically devastated by its eight-year war with Iran. It had an \$80 billion debt, which was increasing at the rate of \$10 billion every year. At the same time, Iraq sat next to a proverbial gold mine—Kuwait—with enormous oil surpluses and a small population. In addition, Iraq was angry with Kuwait over Kuwait's oil policy. Iraq argued that Kuwait ignored OPEC guidelines for oil production and that every dollar reduction in the price of a barrel of oil cost Iraq \$1 billion per year. Capturing Kuwait, therefore, looked like a solution to Iraq's economic problems.

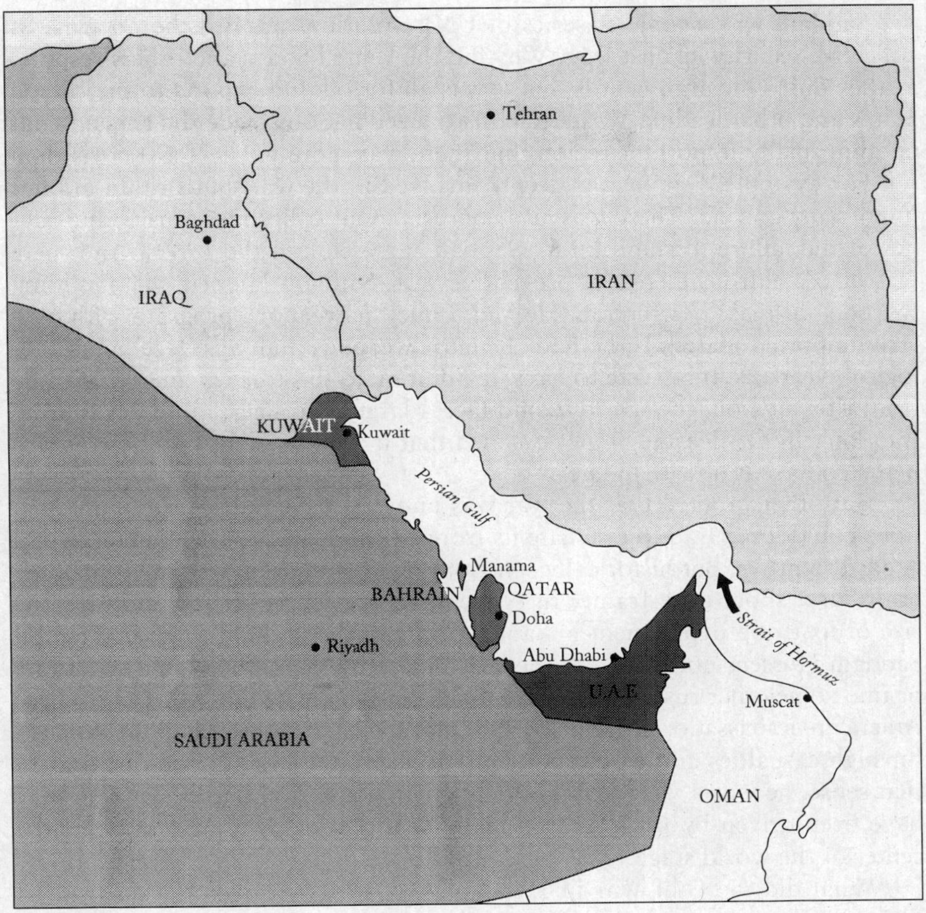

FIGURE 6
The Persian Gulf

Politically, Saddam Hussein was worried about the security of Iraq. He believed that everybody was out to undercut his country. After all, in 1981 the Israelis had bombed his nuclear research reactor, and with the decline of the Soviet Union, it looked as though the United States and Israel were becoming ever more powerful. In a speech in Amman, Jordan, in February 1990, Saddam said the Soviet Union was in decline and could no longer counter the Americans and the Israelis. Saddam believed he would have to do it himself. He undertook a number of actions designed to test the Americans. Ironically, the United States was trying to appease Saddam Hussein, to bring him back into the community of responsible states, and to use Iraq as an effective balance to Iranian power in the region. The inconsistency of American policy misled Saddam Hussein, and he believed he could get away with the invasion of Kuwait without suffering serious reprisals.

Saddam was wrong. A series of UN resolutions applied the doctrine of collective security against Iraq. Why did the United States and others respond as they did? One argument is that it was all for oil. Oil exports to the United States and other leading Western industrialized nations made the Persian Gulf an abnormally important region, but there was more to the 1990 crisis than oil. For example, Britain was deeply involved in the war, but Britain did not import any gulf oil. There was also concern about collective security and echoes of the failure to stand up to German aggression in the 1930s. And there was also a third dimension: preventive war. Saddam Hussein was building weapons of mass destruction. He had a nuclear weapons program with covertly imported materials; he had chemical weapons and was developing biological weapons. If he were to have, in addition to this, the revenues that came from Kuwait's oil, the world would face a larger, stronger, more devastating Iraq later in the decade. Some reasoned that if there were to be a war, it was better to have it now than later.

But others argued that the war was unnecessary because economic sanctions could force Iraq to evacuate its troops from Kuwait. The counterfactual is hard to prove, but historically sanctions have rarely achieved their intended effect in a short time frame. In November, the United States doubled the size of its troop deployment in Saudi Arabia in the prelude to war. Why did Saddam Hussein not escape at the last minute by saying he would withdraw or find some other ruse? Partly, his miscalculation seemed to be, as he told the American ambassador in August 1990, that the United States had no stomach for high casualties and would not commit itself to a long, drawn-out war. In that sense, he was a victim of the Vietnam analogy. And partly, Saddam may have been driven by pride and an inability to back down after being at the center of the world stage.

What did the Gulf War in 1991 solve? It briefly revived the doctrine of UN collective security, but as we have seen, questions exist about how typical this regional conflict was. The cease-fire set a precedent whereby UN inspectors visited Iraq and destroyed its nuclear and chemical facilities. But it left Saddam Hussein in place. President George H. W. Bush decided not to occupy Baghdad because he thought Saddam Hussein might be removed by his own people, and he was concerned that neither the American public nor the UN coalition would tolerate a costly occupation.

A decade later, the new president, George W. Bush, initially promoted a realist foreign policy agenda that emphasized the importance of great power relations with China and Russia. Bush criticized Clinton's involvement in the Middle East peace process and made it clear that he would take a hands-off approach to the conflict. Eight months later, after 9/11, Bush's foreign policy dramatically shifted. Fighting terrorism became the administration's focus.

In Afghanistan, in October through December 2001, American air power and Special Forces initially helped turn the tide in the civil war. The American military intervention allowed the Northern Alliance to overthrow the fundamentalist Taliban government that had provided sanctuaries to Osama bin Laden and his al Qaeda terrorist network, the perpetrators of the September 11 terrorist attacks on New York and Washington. The American action was widely supported by NATO allies and legitimized by a UN resolution.

In 2002, however, the Bush administration decided to go to war against Iraq and international support began to fade. In terms of the distinction drawn earlier in this chapter, the United States called its actions against Iraq "preemptive," but many countries saw the United States' proposed invasion as a "preventive" war of choice because the threat posed by Iraq was not imminent. In September 2002, following a speech in which Bush called on the UN to enforce previous Security Council resolutions against Iraq, the United States obtained a UN Security Council resolution demanding that Saddam Hussein cooperate fully with international inspectors to prove that he was complying with resolutions passed a decade earlier assuring that he had given up his nuclear, biological, and chemical weapons programs. Saddam allowed inspectors to return to Iraq for the first time in four years; simultaneously, the United States moved forward with a large buildup of troops in neighboring Kuwait and Qatar, and Congress passed a resolution authorizing the use of force against Saddam Hussein. In December 2002 and again in February 2003, the inspectors reported partial but not total compliance and asked for more time to complete their task. Concerned about the approach of hot weather and the readiness of its forces, the Bush administration felt that another delay would cause its efforts to lose momentum. After failing to obtain a second Security Council resolution authorizing an attack against Iraq, the United States, Great Britain, and a small coalition argued that the earlier resolutions provided a legal basis for action, and invaded Iraq in March 2003. Within three and a half weeks, Baghdad was occupied and Saddam had fled.

But winning the war proved much easier than winning the peace. While the occupation was initially welcomed in some of the Shi'a and Kurdish areas of the country, many of the former Sunni ruling groups and some Shi'a formed an insurgency against the occupation. They were aided by foreign terrorists, such as the Jordanian-born al Qaeda operative Abu Musab al-Zarqawi, who crossed into Iraq and sought to continue their radical jihad against the United States. The Bush administration had not planned for enough troops to manage the looting that followed the collapse of Saddam's regime, or the insurgency that followed the invasion. The ensuing violence slowed reconstruction efforts that could have helped generate popular support and soft power. Additionally, the failure to obtain a second UN resolution meant that many countries believed that the invasion lacked legitimacy. As a result, their participation in the reconstruction effort was limited.

The costs of the war for American soft power were compounded when inspectors failed to find any weapons of mass destruction after the war. Two of the three reasons given for the war before the invasion—Saddam's weapons of mass destruction and an alleged connection between Saddam and the events of 9/11—turned out to be based on false intelligence and political exaggeration. That left the third cause: the hope that removing Saddam's brutal dictatorship would lead to a democratic Iraq, which would begin a democratic transformation of the Middle East. Three rounds of national elections were successfully held in Iraq in 2005, but as we saw earlier, elections are not sufficient to produce a liberal democracy where societies are divided along ethnic and religious lines, institutions are weak, and there is little sense of overarching community that makes minorities willing to acquiesce in the rule of the majority. While it may take a decade or more to judge the final effects of the Iraq War, polls showed that many Americans came to believe that the costs had outweighed the benefits. Whatever the original intentions, the failure to plan carefully for appropriate means contributed to negative consequences. In early 2007, the Bush administration changed its strategy due to widespread chaos and bloodshed in Iraq, but also as a result of mounting political and popular pressure within the United States. The so-called "Surge Strategy" led to an additional 22,000 soldiers being deployed to serve in Iraq and led to some military improvement in countering the insurgency in 2008, but not to the political compromises necessary to prevent violence among the major factions. Still, by 2009 levels of violence had dropped to the point where President Obama felt comfortable enough to begin withdrawing U.S. forces from urban areas, reducing the total number of troops in Iraq, and shifting focus to the ongoing multinational battle against the resurgence of the Taliban in Afghanistan.

The Middle East illustrates the same dynamics of the individual, the state, and the international system that we have seen in other conflicts. Individuals such as Arafat, Rabin, Sharon, Sadat, King Hussein, and Saddam Hussein determined whether there would be war or peace. Terrorists and assassins also played key roles. The states of the region frequently acted in a manner consonant with the realist model—competing for power and security—but international law and organizations have helped shape the political struggles, as have individual and nonstate actors. Issues such as religion, ethnicity, economic underdevelopment, and population pressures continue to make Middle Eastern politics volatile. Throughout the region, autocratic governments are faced with fundamentalist challenges to their authority, and many of these threaten to explode into civil war, as they have in Algeria and the Sudan. We can expect further conflict in the Middle East.

CHRONOLOGY: CONFLICT IN THE MIDDLE EAST

- 1897 Publication of Theodor Herzl's *The Jewish State;* First World Zionist Congress meets
- 1915 McMahon-Hussein agreements leading to Arab revolt against Turks in return for British assurances on independent Arab state
- 1916 Sykes-Picot agreement secretly establishing Anglo-French spheres of influence in the Middle East
- 1917 Balfour Declaration stating that the British government favored "the establishment in Palestine of a national home for the Jewish people . . . it being understood that nothing shall be done which may prejudice the civil and religious rights of existing non-Jewish communities in Palestine"

(*Continued*)

- 1922 Great Britain given the Palestine Mandate by the League of Nations
- 1936 Formation of Arab High Committee with aim of uniting all Arabs in opposition to Jewish claims
- 1937 Palestinian Arab revolt against British authority; Peel Commission report proposes partition into three states: one Arab, one Jewish, and a British-administered territory; scheme adopted by the World Zionist Congress and rejected by the Pan-Arab Congress
- 1939 British White Paper calls for independent Palestine in ten years
- 1945 Egypt, Iraq, Jordan, Lebanon, Saudi Arabia, and Yemen create the Arab League
- 1947 British government refers Palestine dispute to the United Nations; UN General Assembly votes for partition of Palestine into Jewish and Arab states with Jerusalem under UN trusteeship; UN partition plan accepted by Jews but rejected by Arabs
- 1948 Fighting between Arabs and Jews in Palestine; British mandate ends; Jewish provisional government under David Ben-Gurion proclaims the state of Israel; Israel recognized by the United States and the Soviet Union
- 1948–1949 War between Israel and the Arab League
- 1949 Israel admitted to the United Nations
- 1952 Free Officer revolt led by Gamal Abdel Nasser in Egypt
- 1955 Soviet-Egyptian arms deal concluded; Baghdad Pact created with Great Britain, Iran, Iraq, Turkey, and Pakistan as members
- 1956 Suez crisis: Israeli forces invade the Sinai; Britain and France bomb and land paratroopers in the Suez Canal zone
- 1957 Eisenhower Doctrine: President granted congressional authority for U.S. intervention in event of communist aggression in the Middle East
- 1958 Antimonarchical revolt in Iraq; crisis in Lebanon and Jordan; American Marines land in Beirut
- 1964 Formation of the Palestine Liberation Organization (PLO)
- 1967 Six-Day War: Israel occupies the Sinai, Gaza Strip, West Bank, and the Golan Heights; adoption of UN Resolution 242 calling for Israeli withdrawal from occupied Arab lands in return for peace within negotiated permanent borders; Palestinian demands referred to only as the "refugee" problem
- 1969 War of Attrition
- 1970 "Black September" in Jordan: Jordanian army expels Palestinian commandos from Jordan; death of Nasser: Anwar Sadat becomes Egyptian president
- 1973 Yom Kippur War: Egypt and Syria launch surprise attack against Israel
- 1973–1974 Arab oil embargo
- 1974 Military disengagement accords between Israel and Egypt and Syria

(*Continued*)

- 1975 Sinai Agreement between Israel and Egypt permits reopening of Suez Canal
- 1977 Egypt's Sadat becomes first Arab head of state to recognize Israel and to address Israeli Knesset in Jerusalem
- 1978 Camp David Summit with Carter, Begin, and Sadat
- 1979 Climax of Iranian revolution: Shah forced into exile, Ayatollah Khomeini returns to Tehran as new Iranian leader; Egyptian-Israeli peace treaty signed in Washington, D.C.; American embassy overrun by Iranians and staff taken hostage; Soviet forces invade Afghanistan
- 1980 Carter Doctrine: United States will use force to counter Soviet aggression in the Persian Gulf region; Iraqi forces invade Iranian territory; beginning of Iran-Iraq War
- 1981 Israeli aircraft destroy Iraq's Osirak nuclear research reactor; Sadat assassinated in Cairo
- 1982 Israeli forces invade Lebanon
- 1983 Multinational peacekeeping force arrives in Beirut; attacks against American embassy and Marine barracks
- 1987 Beginning of Palestinian uprising (*intifada*) in Gaza Strip and West Bank
- 1988 Jordan's King Hussein renounces Jordanian sovereignty over West Bank; PLO declares independent Palestinian states on West Bank and Gaza
- 1990 Iraq invades Kuwait; UN Security Council votes sanctions
- 1991 Iraq expelled from Kuwait in Gulf War
- 1991–1992 Arab-Israeli peace talks in Madrid and Washington, D.C.
- 1993 Oslo negotiations and Declaration of Principles between Israel and the PLO
- 1994 Jordanian-Israeli peace treaty signed in Washington, D.C.; PLO-Israeli agreement for Palestinian control of Gaza and Jericho
- 1995 Yitzhak Rabin assassinated in Tel Aviv
- 1996 Likud leader Benjamin Netanyahu elected prime minister after terrorist bombings in Israeli cities undermines support for Shimon Peres, Rabin's Labor successor
- 1997 Israel cedes 80 percent of West Bank town of Hebron to Palestinians
- 1998 United States brokers Israeli-PLO Wye River Accords, which cede additional 13 percent of West Bank to Palestinians; U.S. president Clinton addresses Palestinian Assembly in Gaza
- 1999 Death of Jordan's King Hussein; Labor leader Ehud Barak elected Israeli prime minister
- 2000 Camp David negotiations fail; Second Intifada begins
- 2001 Ariel Sharon elected Israeli prime minister
- 2002 Israel reoccupies towns in West Bank and Gaza and begins construction of security barrier between the West Bank and Israel; UN Security Council demands Israel withdraw from Palestinian towns

(*Continued*)

- 2003 The United States, the European Union, Russia, and the UN release a three-phase "road map" calling for an independent Palestinian state and full peace by 2005; Arafat appoints Mahmoud Abbas (also known as Abu Mazen) prime minister; Abbas, Sharon, and President George W. Bush meet in Jordan for peace talks (June); Abbas resigns after cease-fire collapses and talks break down; the United States invades Iraq (March), defeating Saddam Hussein in three weeks; Saddam captured (December)
- 2004 Death of Arafat; Abbas becomes president of the Palestinian Authority
- 2005 Israel withdraws from Gaza
- 2006 Sharon incapacitated by a major stroke; Hamas wins Palestinian election; Second Lebanon War; Saddam tried, convicted, and hanged
- 2007 Israel bombs a Syrian nuclear facility; Middle East peace conference at Annapolis, MD (November); military clashes between Fatah and Hamas end with Hamas retaining complete control of Gaza: Fatah is forced out of Gaza; U.S. "Surge" in Iraq
- 2008 Israel closes border crossings to Gaza; Israel and Hamas agree to six-month cease-fire; Israel reopens borders only to close them in retaliation for Islamic Jihad attacks; Israel launches massive air raid on Gaza eight days after cease-fire expires
- 2009 Israel launches ground incursion into Gaza; Israel and Hamas declare unilateral cease-fires and claim victory; Likud leader Benjamin Netanyahu sworn in as prime minister; Netanyahu visits United States, where President Obama publicly announces the need for Palestinian statehood and for a halt on settlement construction; Netanyahu conditionally accepts two-state solution; U.S. forces begin withdrawing from Iraqi cities and handing over security tasks to Iraqi police; U.S. troops begin to deploy in force in Afghanistan
- 2010 U.S. combat mission in Iraq ends
- 2011 "Arab Spring" revolts in Tunisia, Egypt, Yemen, Syria, Libya; protests in Algeria, Bahrain, Jordan, Morocco, Oman, Saudi Arabia; Tunisian President Ben Ali and Egyptian President Hosni Mubarak ousted; Libyan civil war; Fatah-Hamas Reconciliation Agreement; Muammar Gaddafi killed; Yemeni president Saleh steps down

A Nuclear Iran?

Moving east, the next serious flashpoint is Iran, though less because of an ongoing dispute than a potential future conflict over Iran's nuclear ambitions.

With a population of more than 77 million people (behind only Egypt and Turkey in the region) and a land mass second only to Saudi Arabia, Iran is naturally a country of consequence, and it could potentially become the most powerful country in the Middle East. First, Iran is poised strategically along the eastern shore of the Persian Gulf and dominates the narrow Strait of Hormuz, through which all sea traffic in and out of the gulf must pass. Second, it has massive proven oil reserves—10 percent of the world's total, behind only Saudi Arabia and Canada. Third, Iran has an energetic ballistic missile program and is in principle capable of striking targets virtually anywhere in the Middle East.

Long recognized as an important country, Iran enjoyed decades of Western patronage following World War II. Shah Mohammed Reza Pahlavi enjoyed very high levels of U.S. aid and investment and proved a loyal anticommunist ally. In 1951, however, a reformist, Dr. Mohammed Mossadegh, was elected prime minister and nationalized Iran's oil reserves. Alarmed, Britain and the United States engineered his ouster, after which the shah ruled in an increasingly autocratic fashion. In 1979 the shah was toppled in an Islamic revolution, and Ayatollah Ruhollah Musavi Khomeini became Iran's supreme leader. Relations with the United States deteriorated spectacularly when Iranian students took over the U.S. embassy in Tehran, holding 52 hostages for more than a year. Partly in response to these dramatic developments, the United States tacitly supported Saddam Hussein's war against Iran. This, coupled with American support for Israel and the willingness of Washington to allow the deposed shah to seek medical treatment in the United States, earned America the moniker "The Great Satan" in Iran.

The unusual hostility of Iran toward both the United States and Israel has been a concern for three decades. During most of this time, Iran had an active nuclear program, officially for peaceful civilian purposes. But the election of the fiercely anti-Israeli and anti-American Mahmoud Ahmadinejad as president in 2005 set off alarm bells. While the intelligence on Iran's nuclear program has been less than fully satisfactory, the United States and most governments in Europe have sought to curb Iran's nuclear ambitions through negotiations and sanctions.

It is too early to know whether Iran's nuclear ambitions will wane or come to a head in the form of a major international crisis, but the Western response has been to seek to leverage a mixture of hard and soft power. The hard power comes in the form of deterrent threats, economic sanctions, and promises of rewards for good behavior. The soft power comes in the form of attempting to attract an Iranian people growing weary of heavy-handed clerical rule. Barack Obama sought to open avenues of contact and communication by promising in the 2008 presidential election to talk to Iranian leaders "without preconditions." Apparently popular in Iran, Obama's olive branch made life difficult for Tehran, undercutting as it did the excuse the so-called American threat gave the Iranian regime for resisting reform. Massive street protests against Ahmadinejad's disputed June 2009 electoral victory over moderate reformist candidate for president Mir-Hossein Mousavi may be evidence of the soft power of liberal democratic ideals—assisted in part by soft-power Western technology such as Psiphon, a software program that enabled ordinary Iranians to bypass official filters and access foreign news about the protests. The successful suppression of the "Green Revolution," however, led in the short-term to renewed Iranian defiance of the international community's concerns about its nuclear program, and to new assertiveness in Iranian foreign policy, including an unprecedented transit of the Suez Canal of an Iranian frigate and supply ship in 2011, which Israel interpreted as a major provocation.

CHRONOLOGY: IRAN'S NUCLEAR PROGRAM

- 1957 Iran and the United States sign civil nuclear cooperation agreement under U.S. Atoms for Peace program; the United States lends several kilograms of enriched uranium to Iran
- 1963 Iran signs and ratifies Partial Nuclear Test Ban Treaty
- 1967 Tehran Nuclear Research Centre built; the United States supplies 5.54 kg of enriched uranium
- 1968 Iran signs and ratifies Nuclear Non-Proliferation Treaty
- 1969 White House extends 1957 Iran-U.S. Agreement for Cooperation Concerning Civil Uses of Atomic Energy for another decade
- 1975 German Kraftwerk Union begins construction on two nuclear reactors at Bushehr
- 1979 Islamic Revolution topples the Shah; construction on Bushehr reactors is suspended; the United States withdraws support for Iranian nuclear program and stops supply of highly enriched uranium; Iranian nuclear progress slows dramatically until late 1980s
- 1984 Iran-Iraq war; Bushehr nuclear reactors repeatedly bombed by Iraqis
- 1989 Death of Ayatollah Khomeini; Ayatollah Khamenei begins to rebuild nuclear program
- 2002 Russian specialists begin reconstructing nuclear reactor at Bushehr despite international objections
- 2003 Iran announces the existence of nuclear facilities at Natanz, invites IAEA inspection; shortly afterwards Iran removes IAEA cameras from its facilities; France, Germany, U.K. (EU3) begin negotiating with Iran to prevent nuclear weapons development
- 2004 IAEA adopts resolution on Iran's failure to suspend enrichment program; Iran and EU3 reach a deal, Iran promises to suspend most uranium enrichment
- 2005 Iran notifies IAEA that it intends to resume uranium conversion and removes IAEA seals from some plants; Iran maintains nuclear activities are for peaceful purposes only; Mahmoud Ahmadinejad becomes president
- 2006 U.S. director of national intelligence John Negroponte tells Senate Select Committee on Intelligence that Iran will be capable of producing a nuclear weapon within ten years; Ahmadinejad announces that Iran has successfully enriched uranium at Natanz; the United States offers to join European negotiations over Iranian nuclear program if Iran suspends all processing and enrichment; UN Security Council adopts Resolution 1696 under Chapter VII of the UN Charter—the first legally binding resolution against Iran includes threat of sanctions; Ahmadinejad formally opens heavy-water production facility at Arak; Iranian Foreign Ministry spokesperson announces Tehran's willingness to negotiate with the United States on regional issues at Washington's invitation; IAEA discovers new traces of uranium in Iranian facilities and concludes they cannot ensure Iranian compliance without improved transparency and cooperation from Iran

(*Continued*)

- 2007 IAEA cuts almost half of its aid to Iran as part of second round of UN sanctions
- 2008 Security Council adopts Resolution 1803 imposing sanctions on banking and the importation of some dual-use items; presidential candidate Barack Obama offers to talk to Iranian leaders "without preconditions"
- 2009 Massive street protests in Iran after Ahmadinejad declared victory in June elections over reformist candidate Mir-Hossein Mousavi; at G8 summit, President Obama promises "consequences" if there is no progress in negotiations
- 2010 UN Security Council imposes fourth round of sanctions on Iran; United States and Israel suspected of creating "Stuxnet" computer worm that damages Siemens control systems used in nuclear centrifuges
- 2011 IAEA claims that it has evidence that Iran has conducted work on triggers for nuclear weapons; Darioush Rezai-Nejad, an Iranian nuclear scientist, gunned down in Tehran by gunmen on motorcycles

India and Pakistan

Still further east is the site of one of the most hotly contested territorial disputes in the world today: the Kashmir conflict. There are three main protagonists—India, Pakistan, and China—but the most dangerous axis of conflict is between the former two.

When Britain withdrew from South Asia in 1947, it divided the territory it had governed into two states. Predominantly Hindu areas were to become India; predominantly Muslim areas were to become Pakistan (East Pakistan in the area of the Ganges River delta; West Pakistan in the Indus River watershed between Afghanistan and Iran on the West and India on the east). The criteria for partition were less than fully clear, however, and certain territories became subjects of dispute. Chief among these was Kashmir, a "princely state" in the remote mountainous northwest of the Indian subcontinent. Previously semi-autonomous, Kashmir was reluctant to accede to either state. The First Indo-Pakistani War (1947–1948) was fought over control of Kashmir, but left India and Pakistan each in possession of only part of it. China controlled a portion as well: the high, remote, virtually unpopulated Aksai Chin, over which China and India fought a brief war in 1962 that resulted in a decisive Indian defeat.

The Second Indo-Pakistani War, also fought over Kashmir, broke out in 1965. In this instance India's tepid military response to Pakistani incursions in a disputed portion of the Indian state of Gujarat encouraged the Pakistani military to believe that it could wrest control of Indian-occupied Kashmir. Pakistan overplayed its hand, however, and India responded forcefully, even going so far as to launch military operations into Pakistani territory in the Punjab. After the UN Security Council called for a cease-fire, hostilities ended and the two countries agreed to meet to negotiate a settlement to the conflict, but ultimately failed to do so. The Third Indo-Pakistani War (1971) was the deadliest. Some 9,000 Pakistani soldiers were killed, as well as 2,500 Indians.

In contrast to the first two, however, it was not fought over Kashmir. It began as a domestic Pakistani dispute and ultimately resulted in East Pakistan seceding to become the state of Bangladesh.

What makes the conflict between India and Pakistan so dangerous today is the fact that both countries now have nuclear arsenals. India developed nuclear weapons first, successfully conducting a "peaceful nuclear explosion" in 1974 intended primarily as a deterrent signal to China, with whom India had ongoing, if stable, territorial disputes. Prime Minister Indira Gandhi did not "weaponize" India's nuclear capability at the time, however. Pakistan began its nuclear weapons program in 1972, in response to its defeat in the Third Indo-Pakistani War, but did not acquire the capability to build a nuclear weapon until the late 1980s. Pakistan first tested nuclear weapons in 1998 immediately following a series of Indian nuclear tests, the motivation for which remains somewhat unclear: Indian prime minister Atal Bihari Vajpayee may have been attempting to send a deterrent signal to both China (at that time undergoing a nuclear modernization program) and Pakistan (whose nuclear ambitions were known and which had recently successfully tested a long-range missile); he may have been keen to develop some useful payload for India's own long-range missiles; or he may simply have sought to assert India's claim to great power status. Some combination of motivations is entirely plausible as well. Pakistan's response was very clearly deterrent in nature. Its tests were hasty and unimpressive.

Several additional factors render the ongoing Indo-Pakistani rivalry particularly worrisome. One is that the two countries have a long history of misperceptions and misjudgments leading to conflict. In one case, the 1999 Kargil confrontation, the two countries found themselves in direct conflict even after their nuclear tests. In this instance, in other words, Indian and Pakistani nuclear weapons proved to be of little deterrent value. Another worrisome consideration is that, while India's nuclear arsenal appears to be under relatively secure civilian control, Pakistan's is under military control, and the Pakistani military is highly politicized and known for its risk-taking. Third, Pakistan does not have a culture or a history of responsible nuclear stewardship. Pakistan's chief nuclear scientist, A. Q. Khan, was at the hub of a major international proliferation network linking Pakistan to Libya, Iran, and North Korea, and he may well have done more harm to the global cause of nonproliferation than any individual on the planet. Fourth, while India is a relatively stable democracy, Pakistan is not, and significant elements within Pakistan are sympathetic to radical Islam. Most analysts believe that the most plausible way in which a terrorist group such as the al Qaeda network might get its hands on a nuclear weapon, unlikely though this might be, would be a diversion from the Pakistani nuclear arsenal.

The international response to India and Pakistan's ascendancy to the nuclear club has been energetic if somewhat contradictory. Both countries were roundly condemned and initially sanctioned for violating a growing norm of nonproliferation (though not for violating the 1968 Treaty on the Non-Proliferation of Nuclear Weapons [NPT], which neither had signed). Yet both were ultimately richly rewarded for their transgressions. President George W. Bush made a deal with Indian prime minister Manmohan Singh in March 2006 granting India an exemption from American laws prohibiting the sale of U.S. nuclear technology to nonsignatories of the NPT in return for India's agreement to open up its civilian nuclear facilities to international inspection. The United States has lavished Pakistan with military and economic aid intended to shore up its secular democracy and help it fight Islamic insurgents. No doubt the United States (and possibly others) have tried to provide the Indian and Pakistani militaries with technology intended to help safeguard against the accidental or unintended use of nuclear weapons. But without a durable, permanent solution to the Kashmir problem, the possibility of an Indo-Pakistani nuclear war can never be dismissed.

CHRONOLOGY: THE KASHMIR CONFLICT

- **1947** India granted independence from Britain, partitioned into India and Pakistan; territory of Jammu and Kashmir remains in dispute; war breaks out between India and Pakistan; Maharaja of Kashmir controversially accedes to India in return for military assistance against Pakistani infiltrators
- **1949** Fighting between India and Pakistan ends on January 1; Line of Control established
- **1962** Sino-Indian War
- **1965** Pakistan launches covert military offensive into Indian-held Kashmir; Second Indo-Pakistani War; three weeks into the fighting, UN-brokered cease-fire is signed
- **1971** East Pakistan demands independence; Pakistan erupts into civil war; India invades East Pakistan to stem the flood of refugees into India; East Pakistan declared the sovereign state of Bangladesh
- **1972** Simla Agreement signed by India and Pakistan: both sides commit to peaceful negotiations
- **1974** Pakistan officially recognizes Bangladesh as an independent state; India detonates a "peaceful" nuclear device
- **1989** Armed resistance to Indian rule begins in Kashmir valley: some groups demand independence for Jammu and Kashmir, others accession to Pakistan
- **1992** Pakistan declares that it has acquired the scientific capability required to build nuclear weapons (after having acquired it de facto in the late 1980s)
- **1998** India conducts underground nuclear tests near Pakistani border; Pakistan retaliates with nuclear tests; the United States imposes sanctions against both countries
- **1999** Pakistani-backed forces cross the Line of Control into Indian territory at Kargil; India launches retaliatory air strikes; General Pervez Musharraf overthrows Pakistani government in military coup

(Continued)

- 2001 Militants attack Kashmiri assembly in Srinagar, killing 38; unidentified men attack Indian parliament in New Delhi, killing 14; India deploys troops to Kashmir in Operation Parakram; both sides escalate military presence in Kashmir
- 2002 After months of intermittent violence, India and Pakistan begin to demobilize
- 2003 India and Pakistan sign cease-fire agreement and restore diplomatic ties; Delhi-Lahore bus service resumes, helping to defuse tensions
- 2006 President George W. Bush signs law permitting civilian nuclear cooperation with India in return for international inspections of Indian civilian nuclear facilities

The South China Sea

Moving still further east, the next significant international flashpoint is the South China Sea. Bordered on the north by China, on the east by the Philippines, on the west by Vietnam, and on the south by Malaysia and Brunei, the South China Sea is an area of enormous strategic and economic importance. One-third of the world's commercial shipping passes through it. Almost 8 percent of the world's fish are caught in it. It is also home to perhaps as much as an entire year's worth of global oil and natural gas consumption.

The danger of international conflict in the South China Sea is significant, for three reasons. First, it is riddled with small islands, reefs, and atolls whose ownership is contested. These territorial disputes are the basis for overlapping claims to maritime space by all five littoral states (plus Taiwan). Indeed, China and Taiwan claim virtually the entire area. Second, the countries involved in these disputes have demonstrated a willingness to back up their claims with force. Third, there is ample opportunity for significant misperceptions or misjudgments that could lead to unintended conflict. Of particular concern is uncertainty over the role of the United States in any serious regional clash. While the U.S. government has stated that it does not take sides in the territorial disputes, it regards the sea as international waters under the Law of the Sea Treaty and will keep important international sea lanes open. It also has treaty obligations to the Philippines and cordial relations with Vietnam that might incline one or both of these countries to misjudge the level of U.S. support they might enjoy in a conflict with China and lead them to overplay their hand. China, for its part, may underestimate the willingness of Washington to resist Chinese attempts to become the dominant naval power in the region—an objective articulated by strategists in the People's Liberation Army (PLA). Countries other than China, moreover, may misjudge the degree to which Chinese policy is formulated in Beijing. There is evidence to suggest that the PLA Navy is in the driver's seat on the South China Sea issue.

Aware that the South China Sea is a powder keg, in 2002 China and ASEAN negotiated a Declaration of Conduct in the South China Sea, which, while not solving any of the territorial or maritime disputes, called upon claimants to settle them peacefully through negotiation and to refrain from actions that would complicate or escalate them. But with China becoming a more assertive naval power, and with global oil and gas prices on the rise, it remains an open question whether conflict or cooperation will prevail in this particularly important corner of the world.

CHRONOLOGY: THE SOUTH CHINA SEA

- 1976 China seizes the Paracel Islands from Vietnam
- 1988 Johnson Reef skirmish between China and Vietnam (Spratly Islands): 70 Vietnamese sailors killed
- 1992 Vietnam accuses China of occupying Da Lac Reef
- 1995 China occupies Philippine-claimed Mischief Reef
- 1996 Three Chinese vessels engage in a 90-minute gun battle with a Philippine patrol boat
- 1998 Philippine navy arrests Chinese fishermen near Scarborough Shoal; Vietnamese soldiers fire on Philippine fishing boat near Pigeon Reef
- 2002 China and ASEAN adopt the Declaration on the Conduct of Parties on the South China Sea, to pave the way for possible commercial cooperation
- 2003 Vietnam challenges Chinese ban on fishing in the South China Sea and asserts claims to Spratly and Paracel Islands
- 2005 Chinese, Vietnamese, and Philippine oil companies sign a deal to jointly protect oil and gas resources in the South China Sea
- 2007 Anti-China demonstrations occur in Hanoi after reports that China has consolidated its administrative rights over the South China Sea, calling it the "Sansha" administrative area
- 2009 Five Chinese vessels confront a U.S. research ship in the South China Sea, renewing American concerns about freedom of navigation; Vietnam and Malaysia jointly claim an extended continental shelf, prompting China and the Philippines to protest
- 2010 Secretary of State Hillary Rodham Clinton declares at an ASEAN Regional Forum in Hanoi that the peaceful resolution of competing sovereignty claims to the South China Sea is a U.S. "national interest," prompting Chinese foreign minister Yang Jiechi to describe Clinton's comments as "an attack on China"
- 2011 Tensions escalate as the Philippines, Vietnam, and China step up efforts to buttress their claims; U.S. secretary of defense Robert Gates warns "there will be clashes" unless multilateral mechanisms are strengthened; Vietnam holds live-fire drills in the South China Sea; anti-China protests break out in Hanoi; the United States and Vietnam issue joint call for freedom of navigation and a rejection of the use of force to resolve disputes; Washington calls on China to cool tensions and reiterates its commitment to defend the Philippines, prompting China to demand that the United States stay out of its regional disputes; the U.S. Senate unanimously passes a resolution condemning China's use of force in the South China Sea and urging a peaceful, multilateral solution, rebuffed by China; U.S., Japanese, and Australian navies conduct exercises in the South China Sea; United States and Vietnam announce naval exchanges

The Taiwan Strait

Another important flashpoint is the Taiwan Strait, separating mainland China from Taiwan. China considers Taiwan a renegade province and adamantly insists on the "One China" principle. However, Taiwan has been a thriving sovereign state in all but name since Chinese Nationalist forces fled in the face of Mao Zedong's communist troops as they swept the mainland at the close of World War II. Since both the Chinese Communist Party (CCP) and Nationalist president Chiang Kai-shek's Kuomintang (KMT) both claimed to be the legitimate ruling party of all of China during most of the postwar period, the One China principle itself was never under serious contention, merely the question of who rightly claimed to represent it. The China seat at the United Nations was originally held by Taiwan, formally known as the Republic of China (ROC). But General Assembly Resolution 2758, passed on October 25, 1971, withdrew recognition of the ROC as the sole legitimate government of China, and the PRC took its place at the UN shortly thereafter.

Despite the fact that no Taiwanese government has unilaterally declared independence, Taiwan has actively sought international recognition over the years, and since 1991 has repeatedly, though unsuccessfully, applied for UN membership.

Three times in the postwar period serious international crises have erupted in the Taiwan Strait. In 1954–1955, Communist forces sought to dislodge Nationalist forces from a series of small islands close to the mainland. They succeeded in overrunning a few islands, but concentrated most of their effort on Quemoy and Matsu, which suffered heavy artillery bombardment but did not fall. The PRC renewed its bombardment of Quemoy and Matsu in 1958, again unsuccessfully. In the third Taiwan Strait crisis (1995–1996), the PRC launched a series of missiles into waters near Taiwan intended to intimidate Taiwanese voters in the lead-up to the 1996 presidential election. Beijing had become convinced that KMT president Lee Teng-hui, if reelected, would abandon the One China principle and declare independence unilaterally. These fears proved unfounded, but the PRC's actions backfired, and Lee was reelected with a strong majority.

In all three crises, the United States has stood firm in its support of Taiwan. During the first two, the United States—but not the PRC—was a nuclear-armed state and held the upper hand. During the third, both were nuclear powers, but the United States was by far the more capable and could count on controlling the seas in the event of a major war. The PRC's options were severely limited.

The Taiwan Strait remains dangerous because the status of Taiwan is still unresolved. While in recent years no Taiwanese government has asserted a unilateral declaration of independence (UDI), surveys indicate that the commitment to the One China principle is weakening among the Taiwanese. The One China principle is still very powerful on the mainland, where secession is unacceptable. Beijing fears that to allow Taiwan formally to secede would be to legitimize secessionist movements in Tibet or Xinjiang, and to undermine the CCP as the sole legitimate ruler of China. Rather than allow Taiwan to secede, Beijing is likely to use force, and this could lead to conflict with the United States. Thus, ironically, Washington and Beijing share a strong interest in attempting to prevent a Taiwanese UDI. The United States has urged no use of force by Beijing, no declaration of independence by Taipei, and negotiations within that framework.

In recent years, cross-strait relations have improved dramatically. In his 2008 inaugural address, Taiwanese president Ma Ying-jeou promised to follow a policy of "no reunification, no independence, and no war." Ma's critics in Taiwan often voice the concern that he means only the last two, and officials in Beijing have certainly been willing to try to woo Taiwanese with increased trade, investment, and travel. Accordingly, the threat of conflict appears to have receded, at least for the time being. Nonetheless, the Taiwan Strait could become dangerous once again if American, Chinese, or Taiwanese leaders underestimate each other's resolve and overplay their hands in a future confrontation.

CHRONOLOGY: THE TAIWAN STRAIT

- 1945 Japan returns territory of Taiwan to China at end of World War II
- 1949 Mao Zedong's Chinese Communist Party (CCP) declares victory over U.S.-backed Chinese Nationalist Kuomintang; Chiang Kai-shek flees to Taiwan (then called Formosa) with Nationalist supporters and establishes "provisional" capital; the United States recognizes Chiang as legitimate Chinese leader
- 1950 U.S. president Harry S. Truman claims the United States will not become involved in conflict between Communists and Nationalists, even if People's Republic of China (PRC) attacks the Republic of China (ROC); Korean war breaks out; Truman declares Formosa Strait neutral waters, sends Seventh Fleet into the Strait, effectively putting Taiwan under American protection
- 1953 Dwight D. Eisenhower inaugurated as U.S. president: withdraws U.S. naval blockade from Taiwan Strait
- 1954 Nationalists send troops to islands Quemoy and Matsu; PRC shells Quemoy and Matsu; Eisenhower rejects Joint Chiefs' recommendation to commit U.S. troops or use nuclear weapons; the United States and ROC sign mutual defense treaty, understood as U.S. pledge to aid Taiwan in the event of PRC attack
- 1955 PRC seizes Yijiangshan Islands; fighting continues along Chinese mainland and on Matsu and Quemoy; Congress approves Formosa Resolution, authorizing use of U.S. forces to defend Taiwan against armed attack; U.S. secretary of state John Foster Dulles publicly admits that the United States is considering a nuclear strike against mainland China; PRC announces willingness to negotiate; cease-fire agreed

(Continued)

- 1958 China shells islands of Quemoy and Matsu; Eisenhower sends U.S. naval contingent to the Taiwan Strait; facing a military stalemate, PRC and ROC agree to a cease-fire; message to the Compatriots in Taiwan issued by Defense Minister Peng Dehuai (actually drafted by Mao Zedong), calling for peaceful solution to the Taiwan issue and for Chinese unity in the face of "the American plot to divide China"; Dulles and Chiang Kai-shek issue a joint communiqué reaffirming their mutual support and intent to refrain from using military means to take back mainland China
- 1971 U.S. Ping-Pong team receives unexpected invitation to visit China while in Japan at World Table Tennis Championships, symbolic of thawing U.S.-PRC relationship; ROC expelled from China's UN seat, replaced by PRC
- 1972 Informal relationship between the United States and PRC established by Nixon's visit to mainland China; Shanghai communiqué issued stating "there is but one China and . . . Taiwan is a part of China"
- 1979 Formal diplomatic ties established between the United States and PRC; mutual defense treaty signed in 1954 with Taiwan terminated; President Jimmy Carter signs the Taiwan Relations Act declaring U.S. commitment to Taiwan's security to reassure ROC
- 1982 The United States and China issue third joint communiqué; the United States declares intent to reduce arms sales to Taiwan
- 1987 Taiwan lifts martial law after 38 years; flow of goods and people between Taiwan and mainland China increases
- 1988 Native Taiwanese Lee Teng-hui assumes presidency of Taiwan and intensifies the pace of democratic reform
- 1989 Tiananmen Square crackdown in mainland China strains U.S.-Chinese relations
- 1995 Lee Teng-hui visits the United States to make a speech at his alma mater, Cornell University; the United States forced to reverse policy and issue travel visa to Lee; Chinese ambassador to the United States recalled in protest; PRC conducts missile tests near ROC-held Pengchiayu Island, mobilizes forces in Fujian; PRC conducts second set of missile tests, live ammunition exercises, and naval exercises; the United States sends USS *Nimitz* through Taiwan Strait—the first U.S. military presence in the Strait since 1976
- 1996 President Clinton deploys the USS *Independence* carrier battle group to waters near Taiwan; PRC announces intent to complete live-fire exercises near Penghu; the United States deploys USS *Nimitz* carrier group to waters near Taiwan; China completes third set of missile tests preceding March 23 Taiwanese presidential election, announces simulated amphibious assault for March 18–25; PRC's attempt at intimidating Taiwanese voters backfires, Lee reelected with 54 percent majority; the United States increases military sales to ROC
- 2000 The U.S. House of Representatives passes the Taiwan Security Enhancement Act, prompting strong Chinese protest

(*Continued*)

- 2001 President Bush approves the largest sale of arms to Taiwan in a decade
- 2002 Taiwanese National Defense Report calls for enhanced confidence-building measures across the Strait
- 2005 At a Security Consultative Committee meeting in Washington, the United States and Japan declare "the peaceful resolution of issues concerning the Taiwan Strait through dialogue" and increased military transparency in China to be among their common strategic objectives, eliciting a strong condemnation from the Chinese Foreign Ministry that Beijing "resolutely opposes the United States and Japan in issuing any bilateral document concerning China's Taiwan, which meddles in the internal affairs of China, and hurts China's sovereignty"; China passes an "Anti-Secession Law" requiring China to prevent a Taiwanese declaration of independence
- 2008 Ma Ying-jeou elected president of Taiwan

North Korea

The last flashpoint we will examine is the Korean peninsula. Korea has been divided since World War II into a communist north (the Democratic People's Republic of Korea, or DPRK) and a capitalist south (the Republic of Korea, or ROK). North Korean leader Kim Il Sung launched a surprise invasion of South Korea in 1950 that prompted the United Nations' very first collective-security action, made possible by a Soviet boycott of the Security Council over the UN's failure to allow Beijing to occupy the China seat (a mistake the Soviet Union would never make again). An American-led UN force pushed North Korean forces almost all the way to the Yalu River, North Korea's border with China, prompting intervention by the PRC to keep the United States at bay. Eventually the war stalemated close to the 38th parallel, the prewar border. Although the belligerents never formally concluded a peace, the border today between North and South Korea falls along the 1953 cease-fire line, known as the demilitarized zone (DMZ), which is a narrow strip of land that serves as a buffer zone between North and South Korean forces. Despite its name, the concentration of soldiers on either side of the DMZ is so great that it is in reality the most heavily militarized border in the world.

In economic terms, North Korea has languished. Isolated and underdeveloped, its infrastructure crumbling, its people malnourished, it is the world's last remaining genuinely totalitarian state. Since the regime devotes an enormous proportion of the country's resources to the military and state security, little remains for genuine economic development. Meanwhile, South Korea has thrived. It is now a wealthy liberal democratic state that enjoys all the benefits of being fully integrated into the world economy.

Why should an impoverished, underdeveloped DPRK represent such a serious regional security threat? The answer is twofold. First, North Korean policy has traditionally been erratic, unpredictable, and aggressive. Not only did North Korea launch a quixotic attack on South Korea in 1950, North Korean agents have staged a bewildering array of bizarre operations over the years whose purpose is often difficult to divine. These include bombings, hijackings, successful and attempted assassinations, and—perhaps most puzzling—abductions of Japanese citizens from beaches near their homes. In 1968, North Korea captured an American intelligence ship in international waters, the USS *Pueblo*, torturing and starving the crew before releasing them after the United States offered an apology for spying (today the ship is a floating museum in Pyongyang). In 2009 North Korea arrested, tried, and sentenced two American journalists to hard labor for allegedly spying along the Chinese border. Although they were eventually released following a diplomatic mission by former U.S. president Bill Clinton, the incident served as a reminder that North Korea remains unpredictable.

Second, North Korea has nuclear weapons and an active missile program. North Korea's nuclear tests in 2006 and 2009 were unimpressive in military terms—so much so that in both instances Western intelligence communities debated whether North Korea had successfully detonated nuclear weapons at all. Its missile tests have also been failures more often than not. Yet North Korea's willingness to conduct provocative tests is a worrisome sign, because it may indicate irrationality or desperation. It is impossible to know how best to deal with North Korea without having a sense of what North Korea wants and why it does what it does.

For the most part, North Korean policy has been mysterious. The only patterns that seem tolerably clear are that North Korea will do something provocative when it feels ignored or under serious economic strain, and that it will make commitments and keep them only as long as it takes to bilk the international community out of valuable resources. But the 2009 nuclear test illustrates the predicament facing foreign leaders attempting to deal with the North Korean "threat": It was equally plausibly a sign of aggressiveness and confidence; of weakness and desperation; of a desire to project an image of self-reliance (in keeping with the prevailing domestic Juche ideology); of a need for attention; of a desire to be taken seriously; of petulance; or of a behind-the-scenes struggle over leadership succession. When a country is erratic, unpredictable, and mysterious, it is difficult to know how to manage the crises that its actions trigger.

In six rounds of "Six-Party Talks" between 2003 and 2009, the United States, China, Russia, South Korea, and Japan sought to address North Korea's security concerns in return for verifiable denuclearization. In the course of these, North Korea managed to extract from its interlocutors food aid, energy aid, and technical assistance of various kinds, in return for nothing more than unfulfilled promises.

North Korea is today a veritable international pariah. Arguably, it is equally a threat to regional security whether it lashes out against its neighbors military or implodes economically. It is without doubt one of the most challenging interstate conflict management problems facing the world today.

CHRONOLOGY: NORTH KOREA

- 1945 World War II ends with Japanese unconditional surrender, liberating Korea from Japanese rule; Potsdam Conference cements multinational trusteeship of Korea; U.S. State Department issues General Order No. 1, dividing Korea along 38th parallel
- 1948 Democratic People's Republic of Korea established north of 38th parallel under rule of Kim Il Sung
- 1950 North Korean troops invade South Korea, triggering Korean War
- 1953 Korean War ends in signing of temporary Armistice Agreement still in effect today; North Korea accepts aid from Soviet Union and China
- 1956 North Korea, China, and Soviet Union begin to engage in joint nuclear research projects
- 1967 Yongbyon nuclear research reactor, 100 kilometres from Pyongyang, becomes active
- 1977 North Korea signs Type 66 agreement with IAEA, subjecting Yongbyon reactor to international scrutiny
- 1984 North Korea tests Scud-B missile
- 1985 North Korea signs Nuclear Non-Proliferation Treaty; United States claims North Korea is constructing a second secret nuclear reactor at Yongbyon giving North Korea complete fuel cycle required for weapons production
- 1989 North Korea tests long-range Scud-C missile
- 1991 United States withdraws nuclear weapons from South Korea; North and South Korea sign Joint Declaration on the Denuclearization of the Korean Peninsula, banning nuclear weapons and calling for international inspections
- 1992 North Korea signs IAEA Full Scope Safeguards Agreement, granting IAEA monitors access to all nuclear facilities
- 1993 North Korea test-fires Nodong I Missile with a range of 900 kilometers; Pyongyang threatens to withdraw from NPT and bars international monitors; IAEA director Hans Blix announces IAEA can no longer meaningfully guarantee absence of North Korean nuclear weapons
- 1994 United States and North Korea sign Agreed Framework, committing United States to supply light-water reactors and alternative energy sources if North Korea shuts down Yongbyon plutonium reactor
- 1998 North Korea launches Taepodong I missile with a range of up to 2,000 km
- 2002 President Bush names North Korea as part of the "Axis of Evil" in his State of the Union address
- 2003 North Korea announces intent to withdraw from NPT; North Korea signals willingness to forego insistence on bilateral talks with United States and engage in multiparty talks; first round of Six-Party Talks begins

(*Continued*)

- 2005 North Korea suspends participation in Six-Party Talks indefinitely in reaction to perceived U.S. bullying; North Korea and United States issue joint statement: United States commits not to attack North Korea in exchange for North Korea rejoining the NPT and ceasing nuclear activities; North Korea issues statement claiming it will not scrap its nuclear program until given a civilian nuclear reactor
- 2006 North Korea detonates nuclear device; UN Security Council passes Resolution 1718 under Chapter VII imposing commercial and economic sanctions; North Korean plutonium stockpiles estimated sufficient for four to thirteen nuclear weapons
- 2007 Round Five of Six-Party Talks concludes with agreement that North Korea will shut down Yongbyon reactor and allow IAEA inspections in exchange for aid and normalization of relations with United States
- 2008 North Korea hands over 60-page review of nuclear capabilities for international inspection; United States removes North Korea from list of state sponsors of terrorism
- 2009 North Korea launches "satellite" believed to be Taepodong-2 ICBM despite international pressure, but launch fails; UN Security Council expresses intent to strengthen sanctions; North Korea expels nuclear inspectors, withdraws from Six-Party Talks; North Korea tests second nuclear device
- 2010 46 sailors die when the South Korean corvette *Cheonan* explodes and sinks, possibly as a result of a North Korean torpedo attack; two soldiers killed and dozens injured in North Korean artillery bombardment of Yeonpyeong Island; Kim Jong-il's son Kim Jong-un named a four-star general and given high-ranking political positions, signaling the beginning of a third-generation power transition

Follow Up

- Ian J. Bickerton and Carla L. Klausner, *A History of the Arab-Israeli Conflict* (Boston: Prentice Hall, 2010).
- F. Gregory Gause III, *The International Relations of the Persian Gulf* (Cambridge: Cambridge University Press, 2010).
- S. Paul Kapur, *Dangerous Deterrent: Nuclear Weapons Proliferation and Conflict in South Asia* (Stanford, CA: Stanford University Press, 2007).
- Lynn E. Davis, Jeffrey Martini, Alireza Nader, Dalia Dassa Kaye, James T. Quinlivan, and Paul Steinberg, *Iran's Nuclear Future: Critical U.S. Policy Choices* (Santa Monica, CA: RAND, 2011).
- Rosemary Foot, "Modes of Regional Conflict Management: Comparing Security Cooperation in the Korean Peninsula, China-Taiwan, and the South China Sea," *Reassessing Security Cooperation in the Asia-Pacific: Competition, Congruence, and Transformation* (Cambridge, MA: MIT Press, 2007), pp. 93–112.
- David A. Welch, "Lessons of the Cuban Missile Crisis for Nuclear Crisis Management and Their Implications for U.S.-Chinese Relations," in Christopher Twomey, ed., *Perspectives on Sino-American Strategic Nuclear Issues* (London: Palgrave Macmillan, 2008), pp. 13–38.

STUDY QUESTIONS

1. What is ethnic conflict? When is it likely to occur?
2. When is intervention justified? Is self-determination always a justification? What are the limits of humanitarian intervention?
3. Is there a difference between international law and morality? How important is international law?
4. What are the respective claims of the Palestinians and the Israelis to the territory Israel now controls? Which group has a better argument, in your opinion, or are they equally valid?
5. What was the UN Palestine partition proposal? Why did the Arabs reject this plan?
6. What were the causes of the Middle East wars of 1956, 1967, 1973, and 1982? Were they inevitable? If so, when and why? Is another Arab-Israeli war inevitable?
7. The 1967 war yielded the present configuration of the Arab-Israeli dispute. What happened in that war? What was the famous Security Council Resolution 242?
8. Sadat claimed that he had to go to war in 1973 to go to peace with Israel afterward. Assess this argument. What parallels can you draw between Nasser's success in 1956 and Sadat's in 1973?
9. How did the 1991 Gulf War and the 2003 Iraq War differ? What reasons were given for each war? What is the difference between preemptive and preventive war?
10. What do realism, liberalism, and constructivism each contribute to your understanding of each of the flashpoints examined in this chapter?
11. What kinds of goods (public, private, club, or common) are at stake in the Middle East, Iran, Kashmir, the South China Sea, the Taiwan Strait, and the Korean peninsula? How do the different types of goods complicate conflict management in each case?
12. Which interstate flashpoint is the most dangerous in the world today? Why?

NOTES

1. Anthony Eden, quoted in Robert R. Bowie, *Suez 1956* (New York: Oxford University Press, 1974), p. 124.
2. "Binding the Colossus," *The Economist,* November 22, 2003, pp. 25–26.
3. Linda Fasulo, *An Insider's Guide to the UN* (New Haven, CT: Yale University Press, 2004), p. 115.
4. Mikael Eriksson and Peter Wallensteen, "Armed Conflict, 1989–2003," *Journal of Peace Research* 41:5 (September 2004), p. 626.
5. Peter Wallensteen and Margareta Sollenberg, "Armed Conflict 1989–2000," report no. 60, in Margareta Sollenberg, ed., *States in Armed Conflict 2000* (Uppsala, Sweden: Uppsala University, Department of Peace and Conflict Research, 2001), pp. 10–12.

6. John Mueller, "The Banality of Ethnic War," *International Security* 25:1 (Summer 2000), p. 42.
7. Stuart Kaufman, *Modern Hatreds* (Ithaca, NY: Cornell University Press, 2001), p. 220.
8. International Commission on Intervention and State Sovereignty, *The Responsibility to Protect: Report of the International Commission on Intervention and State Sovereignty* (Ottawa: International Development Research Centre, 2001), p. XI.
9. http://www.hrweb.org/legal/genocide.html.
10. John Mueller, *Retreat from Doomsday: The Obsolescence of Major War* (New York: Basic Books, 1989).

PHOTO CREDITS

Credits are listed in order of appearance:

Imaginechina via AP Images

Jewel Samad/AFP/Getty Images/Newscom.

MAP CREDITS

Credits are listed in order of appearance:

Map is drawn from Brian Catchpole, *A Map History of the Modern World* (Oxford: Heinemann Publishers, 1982), reprinted with adjustments by permission.

Maps are original to this chapter.

Globalization and Interdependence

Globalization and Interdependence

Shipping containers at the port of Singapore

With the end of the Cold War in 1989, a number of observers argued that economic issues would become more central in world politics. Networks of economic interdependence that span the globe have increased as costs of communication and transportation have declined and shrunk the effects of distance. The role of markets has also increased as a result of new information and transportation technologies, as well as changed attitudes about the role of governments and states. Nearly half of all industrial output today is produced by multinational enterprises whose decisions about where to locate factories have a powerful effect on domestic economies and politics. As the economist Dani Rodrik points out, globalization is "exposing a deep fault line between groups who have the skills and mobility to flourish in global markets" and those who don't, "such as workers, pensioners, and environmentalists, with governments stuck in the middle."[1] Some theorists see a new competition—"geoeconomics"—replacing geopolitics and predict that economic sanctions and embargoes will become the key instruments of international politics.

It is important to keep these changes in perspective. Realists remind us that security can be taken for granted in peaceful times, but all markets operate within a political framework. Global markets depend on an international structure of power. Security is like oxygen: easy to take for granted until you begin to miss it, and then you can think about nothing else. Similarly, economic sanctions have been popular instruments because they avoid the use of force, but their effectiveness is mixed. Studies suggest they have achieved their intended effects in fewer than half of the cases in which they have been tried. Multilateral sanctions were one factor in ending apartheid in South Africa and putting pressure on Serbia and Libya in the 1990s, but they failed to oust Iraqi troops from Kuwait or return an elected president to power even in a poor country such as Haiti. Moreover, globalization and economic interdependence were already growing rapidly when states followed relatively liberal policies toward trade, investment, and migration in the nineteenth century. This did not stop two world wars and an economic depression in the first half of the twentieth century from occurring and interrupting elements of these long-term trends.

THE DIMENSIONS OF GLOBALIZATION

Globalization—defined as worldwide networks of interdependence—does not imply universality. For example, at the beginning of the twenty-first century, half of the American population used the Internet, compared to less than

1 percent of the population of South Asia. Most people in the world today do not have telephones. Even in an era of cheap cell phones, hundreds of millions of people live as peasants in remote villages with only slight connections to world markets or the global flow of ideas. Indeed, globalization is accompanied by increasing gaps, in many respects, between the rich and the poor. It does not imply either homogenization or equity.

Even among rich countries, there is a lot less globalization than meets the eye. A truly globalized world market would mean free flows of goods, people, and capital, and similar interest rates everywhere. In fact, we have a long way to go. For example, even in North America, Toronto trades ten times as much with Vancouver as with Seattle, though the distance is the same and tariffs are minimal. Globalization has made national boundaries more porous, but not irrelevant. Nor does globalization mean the creation of a universal community. In social terms, contacts among people with different religious beliefs and other deeply held values have often led to conflict: witness the great crusades of medieval times (the eleventh through the thirteenth centuries) or the current notion of the United States as "the Great Satan" held by some Islamic fundamentalists in the Middle East. Clearly, in social as well as economic terms, homogenization does not follow necessarily from globalization.

Globalization has a number of dimensions, though all too often economists write as if it and the world economy were one and the same. But other forms of globalization also have significant effects on our daily lives. The oldest form of globalization is environmental. For example, the first recorded smallpox epidemic began in Egypt in 1350 BCE. It reached China in 49 CE; Europe after 700; the Americas in 1520; and Australia in 1789. The bubonic plague, or "Black Death," originated in Asia, but it spread to Europe in the fourteenth century, where it killed a quarter to a third of the population. Europeans carried diseases to the Americas in the fifteenth and sixteenth centuries that destroyed up to 95 percent of the indigenous population. In 1918, a flu pandemic caused by a bird virus killed some 40 million people around the world, far more than died in World War I during the previous four years. Some scientists today predict a repeat of an avian flu pandemic. Since 1973, 30 previously unknown infectious diseases have emerged, and other familiar diseases have spread geographically in new drug-resistant forms. In the 20 years after HIV/AIDS was identified in the 1980s, it killed 20 million people and infected another 40 million around the world. The spread of foreign species of flora and fauna to new areas has wiped out native species and may result in economic losses of several hundred billion dollars a year.

On the other hand, not all effects of environmental globalization are adverse. For instance, both Europe and Asia benefited from the importation of such New World crops as the potato, corn, and the tomato, and the "green revolution" agricultural technology of the past few decades has helped poor farmers throughout the world.

Global climate change will affect the lives of people everywhere. There is now virtual consensus in the scientific community that most of the warming observed over the last fifty years is attributable to human activities, and average global temperatures in the twenty-first century are projected to increase between 2.5 and 10 degrees Fahrenheit. The result could be more severe variations in climate, with too much water in some regions and not enough in others. The effects in North America will include stronger storms, hurricanes, floods, droughts, and landslides. Rising temperatures have lengthened the freeze-free season in many regions and led to a 10 percent decrease in global snow cover since the 1960s. Glaciers and ice caps are melting. The rate at which the sea level rose in the last century was ten times faster than the average rate over the last three millennia. As Harvard scientist James McCarthy notes, "What is different now is that Earth is populated with 6 billion [now 7 billion] people and the natural and human systems that provide us with food, fuel, and fiber are strongly influenced by climate."[2] As climate change accelerates, "future change may not occur as smoothly as it has in the past." It does not matter whether carbon dioxide is pumped into the atmosphere from China or the United States; it still warms the planet.

Military globalization consists of networks of interdependence in which force, or the threat of force, is employed. The world wars of the twentieth century are a case in point. During the Cold War, the global strategic interdependence between the United States and the Soviet Union was acute and well recognized. Not only did it produce world-straddling alliances, but either side could have used intercontinental missiles to destroy the other within the space of 30 minutes. It was distinctive not because it was totally new, but because the scale and speed of the potential conflict arising from military interdependence were so enormous. Today, al Qaeda and other transnational actors have formed global networks of operatives, challenging conventional approaches to national defense in what has been called asymmetrical warfare.

Social globalization is the spread of peoples, cultures, images, and ideas. Migration is a concrete example. In the nineteenth century, some 80 million people crossed oceans to new homes—far more than in the eighteenth century. At the beginning of the twenty-first century, 32 million residents of the United States (11.5 percent of the population) were foreign-born. In addition, some 30 million visitors (students, businesspeople, tourists) enter the country each year. Ideas are an equally important aspect of social globalization. Four great religions of the world—Buddhism, Judaism, Christianity, and Islam—have spread across great distances over the last two millennia, as has the scientific method and the Enlightenment worldview over the past few centuries. Political globalization (a part of social globalization) is manifest in the spread of constitutional arrangements, the increase in the number of countries that have become democratic, and the development of international rules and institutions. Those who think it is meaningless to speak of an international community ignore the importance of the global spread of political ideas. As constructivists point out, the antislavery movement in the nineteenth century, anticolonialism after World War II, and the environmental and feminist movements today have had profound effects on world politics. Of course, the world is a long way from a global community replacing people's loyalties to clans, tribes, and states, but such transnational political ideas affect how states construct their national goals and how they use their soft power.

What's New about Twenty-First Century Globalization?

While globalization has been going on for centuries, its contemporary form is "thicker and quicker." Globalization today is different from that of the nineteenth century, when European imperialism provided much of its political structure, and higher transport and communications costs meant fewer people were involved directly with people and ideas from other cultures. But many of the most important differences are closely related to the information revolution. As the columnist Thomas Friedman argues, contemporary globalization goes "farther, faster, cheaper, and deeper."[3]

Economists use the term *network effects* to refer to situations in which a product becomes more valuable once many other people also use it. One telephone is useless, but its value increases as the network grows. This is why the Internet is causing such rapid change. Social networking sites such as Facebook, Twitter, and LinkedIn have burgeoned. The Nobel Prize–winning economist Joseph Stiglitz argues that a knowledge-based economy generates "powerful spillover effects, often spreading like fire and triggering further innovation and setting off chain reactions of new inventions. . . . But goods—as opposed to knowledge—do not always spread like fire."[4] Moreover, as interdependence has become thicker and quicker, the relationships among different networks have become more important. There are more interconnections among the networks. As a result, "system effects"—by which small perturbations in one area can spread throughout a whole system—become more important.

As government officials fashion foreign policies, they encounter the increasing thickness of globalism—the density of the networks of interdependence—which means that the effects of events in one geographical area, or the economic or ecological dimension, can have profound effects in other geographical areas, on the military or social dimensions. These international networks are increasingly complex, and their effects are therefore increasingly unpredictable. Moreover, in human systems, people are often hard at work trying to outwit each other, to gain an economic, social, or military advantage precisely by acting in an unpredictable way. As a result, globalization is accompanied by pervasive uncertainty. There will be continual competition between, on the one hand, increased complexity and uncertainty in global relationships and, on the other, efforts by governments, corporations, and others to comprehend them and manipulate them to their benefit. Frequent financial crises or sharp increases in unemployment could lead to popular movements to limit interdependence.

Quickness also adds to uncertainty and the difficulties of shaping policy responses. As mentioned, modern globalization operates at a much more rapid pace than its earlier forms. Smallpox took nearly three millennia to spread to all inhabited continents, finally reaching Australia in 1789. HIV took less than three decades to spread from Africa all around the world. And to switch to a metaphorical virus, in 2000 the "love bug" computer virus, invented by hackers in the Philippines, needed only three days to straddle the globe. From three millennia to three decades to three days—that is the measure of the quickening of globalization.

Direct public participation in global affairs has also increased in rich countries. Ordinary people invest in foreign mutual funds, gamble on offshore Internet sites, and travel and sample exotic cuisine that used to be the preserve of the rich. Friedman termed this change the *democratization* of technology, finance, and information because diminished costs have made what were previously luxuries available to a much broader range of society. *Democratization* is not quite the right word, however, because in markets, money votes, and people start out with unequal stakes. There is no equality, for example, in capital markets, despite the new financial instruments that permit more people to participate. A million dollars or more is often the entry price for large hedge fund investors. *Pluralization* might be a more accurate description of this trend, suggesting the vast increase in the number and variety of participants in global networks. In 1914, according to the English economist John Maynard Keynes, "The inhabitant of London could order by telephone, sipping his morning tea in bed, the various products of the whole earth, in such quantity as he might see fit, and reasonably expect their early delivery upon his doorstep."[5] But Keynes's Englishman had to be wealthy to be a global consumer. Today, supermarkets and Internet retailers extend that capacity to the vast majority of people in postindustrial societies.

This dramatic expansion of transnational channels and contacts at intercontinental distances means that more policies are up for grabs internationally, including regulations and practices—ranging from pharmaceutical testing to accounting and product standards to banking regulation—that were formerly regarded as the prerogatives of national governments.

What the information revolution has added to contemporary globalization is a quickness and thickness in the network of interconnections that makes it more complex. But such "thick globalism" is not uniform: It varies by region and locality, and by issue.

Political Reactions to Globalization

Domestic politics channel responses to change. Some countries imitate success, as exemplified by democratizing capitalist societies from South Korea to Eastern Europe. Some accommodate change in distinctive and ingenious ways. For instance, small European states such as the Netherlands, Denmark, Norway, and Sweden have maintained relatively large governments and emphasized compensation for disadvantaged sectors, while the Anglo-American industrialized countries have, in general, emphasized markets, competition, and deregulation. Capitalism is far from monolithic, with significant differences between Europe, Japan, and the United States. There is more than one way to respond to global markets and to run a capitalist economy. There is even variation within countries. The United States used to have one of the world's most freewheeling financial systems, but when the subprime mortgage crisis became critical in 2008 and such seemingly unshakeable pillars of the U.S. financial industry as Bear Stearns and Lehman Brothers collapsed, it triggered a worldwide recession (precisely because of globalization) that forced several countries, including the United States, to intervene. Washington's response—spending billions of dollars to stimulate the economy, taking ownership stakes in firms such as General Motors that were considered too big to be allowed to fail completely, even capping executive compensation packages in some cases—has taken American capitalism back to the more assertive government intervention of the 1930s New Deal era.

In other societies, such as Iran, Afghanistan, and Sudan, conservative groups have resisted globalization strongly, even violently. Reactions to globalization help stimulate fundamentalism. Domestic institutions and divisions—economic or ethnic—can lead to domestic conflict, which can reformulate ethnic and political identities in profound and often unanticipated ways. Political elites in Bosnia appealed to traditional identities of people in rural areas to overwhelm and dissolve the cosmopolitan identities that had begun to develop in the cities, with devastating results. And Iran has seen struggles between Islamic fundamentalists and their more liberal opponents—who are also Islamic, but more sympathetic to Western ideas.

Rising inequality was a major cause of the political reactions that halted a previous wave of economic globalization early in the twentieth century. The recent period of globalization, like the half century before World War I, has also been associated with increasing inequality among and within some countries. The ratio of incomes of the 20 percent of people in the world living in the richest countries, compared to the 20 percent living in the poorest countries, increased from 30 to 1 in 1960 to 74 to 1 in 1997. By comparison, it increased between 1870 and 1913 from 7 to 1 to 11 to 1. In any case, inequality can have political effects even if it is not increasing. According to the economist Robert Wade, "The result is a lot of angry young people, to whom new information technologies have given the means to threaten the stability of the societies they live in and even to threaten social stability in countries of the wealthy zone."[6] As increasing flows of information make people more aware of inequality, it is not surprising that some choose to protest, as we recently saw with the worldwide "Occupy" movement.

The political consequences of these shifts in inequality are complex, but the economic historian Karl Polanyi argued powerfully in his classic study *The Great Transformation* that the market forces unleashed by the Industrial Revolution and globalization in the nineteenth century produced not only great economic gains, but also great social disruptions and political reactions. There is no *automatic* relationship between inequality and political reaction, but the former can give rise to the latter. Particularly when inequality is combined with instability, such as financial crises and recessions that throw people out of work, such reactions could eventually lead to restrictions on the pace of globalization of the world economy.

Protests against globalization are, in part, a reaction to the changes produced by *economic interdependence*. From an economist's view, imperfect markets are inefficient, but from a political view, some imperfections in international markets can be considered "useful inefficiencies" because they slow down and buffer political change. As globalization removes such inefficiencies, it becomes the political prisoner of its economic successes. In addition, as global networks become more complex, there are more linkages among issues that can create friction.

Power and Globalization

Liberals sometimes suggest that globalization means peace and cooperation, but unfortunately it is not that simple. Struggles over power go on, even in a globalized world. Because the coalitions are more complex and different forms of power are used, the conflicts are often like playing chess on several boards at the same time. Conflicts in the twenty-first century involve *both* guns and butter. The Chinese leader Mao Zedong once said that power grows out of the barrel of a gun. After the oil crisis of 1973, the world was reminded that power can also grow out of a barrel of oil—as we shall see shortly.

Follow Up

- Manfred B. Steger, *Globalization: A Very Short Introduction* (Oxford: Oxford University Press, 2009).
- Dani Rodrik, *The Globalization Paradox: Democracy and the Future of the World Economy* (New York: W. W. Norton & Co., 2011).

THE CONCEPT OF INTERDEPENDENCE

Interdependence is often a fuzzy term used in a variety of conflicting ways, like other political words such as *nationalism*, *imperialism*, and *globalization*. (Indeed, as we have seen, globalization is the subset of interdependence that occurs at global distances.) Leaders and analysts have different motives when they use political words. The leader wants as many people marching behind his or her banner as possible. Political leaders blur meanings and try to create a connotation of a common good: "We are all in the same boat together; therefore, we must cooperate; therefore, follow me." The analyst, on the other hand, makes distinctions to understand the world better. He or she distinguishes questions of *good* and *bad* from *more* and *less*. The analyst may note that the boat we are all in may be heading for one person's port but not another's, or that one person is doing all the rowing while another steers or has a free ride.

As an analytical word, *interdependence* refers to situations in which actors or events in different parts of a system affect each other. Simply put, interdependence means mutual dependence. Such a situation is neither good nor bad in itself, and there can be more or less of it. In personal relations, interdependence is summed up by the marriage vow in which each partner is interdependent with another "for richer, for poorer, for better, or for worse." And interdependence among countries sometimes means richer, sometimes poorer, sometimes for better, sometimes for worse. In the eighteenth century, Jean-Jacques Rousseau pointed out that along with interdependence comes friction and conflict. His "solution" was isolation and separation. But this is seldom possible in a globalized world. When countries try isolation, as with the cases of North Korea and Myanmar (formerly Burma), it comes at enormous economic cost. It is not easy for countries to divorce the rest of the world.

Sources of Interdependence

Four distinctions illuminate the dimensions of interdependence: its sources, benefits, relative costs, and symmetry. Interdependence can originate in physical (natural) or social (economic, political, or perceptual) phenomena. Both are usually present at the same time. The distinction helps clarify the degree of choice in situations of reciprocal or mutual dependence.

Military interdependence is the mutual dependence that arises from military competition. There is a physical aspect in the weaponry, especially dramatic since the development of nuclear weapons and the resulting possibility of mutually assured destruction. However, an important element of perception is also involved in interdependence, and a change in perception or policy can reduce the intensity of the military interdependence. Americans lost little sleep over the existence of British nuclear weapons during the Cold War because there was no perception that those weapons would ever detonate on American soil. Similarly, Westerners slept a bit easier in the late 1980s after Gorbachev announced his "new thinking" in Soviet foreign policy. It was not so much the number of Soviet weapons that made the difference, but the change in the perception of Soviet hostility or intent. Indeed, American public anxiety about the Soviet nuclear arsenal virtually evaporated after the final collapse of the Soviet Union, despite the fact that at the twentieth century's close thousands of poorly guarded Soviet warheads seemed potentially to be at risk of falling into the hands of terrorists or "rogue" states such as Iran and North Korea.

Generally speaking, economic interdependence is similar to military interdependence in that it is the stuff of traditional international politics and has significant social, especially perceptual, aspects. Economic interdependence involves policy choices about values and costs. For example, in the early 1970s there was concern that the world's population was outstripping global food supplies. Many countries were buying American grain, which in turn drove up the price of food in American supermarkets. A loaf of bread cost more in the United States because the Indian monsoons failed and because the Soviet Union mishandled its harvest. In 1973, in an effort to prevent price rises at home, the United States decided to stop exporting soybeans to Japan. As a result, Japan invested in soybean production in Brazil. A few years later, when supply and demand were better equilibrated, U.S. farmers greatly

ECOLOGICAL INTERDEPENDENCE

Interdependence forces us to understand that today's challenges represent not just a dilemma for us [in our own country], but a shared dilemma for everybody. The environment brings that into a very tangible focus: there's no such thing as a stable climate for one country or one continent unless the climate is stable for everybody. Climate security is a global public good.

—John Ashton, UK Special Representative for Climate Change, September 27, 2006[7]

regretted that embargo because the Japanese were buying their soybeans from a cheaper source in Brazil. Similarly, in 2008, as rich countries devoted more cropland to producing ethanol fuel, food prices rose globally. Social choices as well as physical shortages affect economic interdependence in the long run. It is always worth considering the long-term perspective when making short-term choices.

Benefits of Interdependence

The benefits of interdependence are sometimes expressed as *zero-sum* and *nonzero-sum*. In a zero-sum situation, your loss is my gain and vice versa. In a *positive-sum* situation, we both gain; in a *negative-sum* situation, we both lose. Dividing a pie is zero-sum, baking a larger pie is positive-sum, and dropping it on the floor is negative-sum. Both zero-sum and nonzero-sum aspects are present in mutual dependence.

Some liberal economists tend to think of interdependence only in terms of joint gain, that is, positive-sum situations in which everyone benefits and everyone is better off. Failure to pay attention to the inequality of benefits and the conflicts that arise over the distribution of relative gains causes such analysts to miss the political aspects of interdependence. Both sides can gain from trade—for example, if Japan and South Korea trade computers and smart phones—but how will the gains from trade be distributed? Even if Japan and South Korea are both better off, is Japan a lot better off and South Korea only a little better off, or vice versa? The distribution of benefits—who gets how much of the joint gain—is a zero-sum situation in which one side's gain is the other's loss. The result is that there is almost always some political conflict in economic interdependence. Even when there is a larger pie, people can fight over who gets the biggest slices.

Some liberal analysts mistakenly think that as globalization makes the world more interdependent, cooperation will replace competition. Their reason is that interdependence creates joint benefits, and those joint benefits encourage cooperation. That is true, but economic interdependence can also be used as a weapon—witness the use of trade sanctions against Serbia, Iraq, and Libya. Indeed, economic interdependence can be more usable than force in some cases because it may have more subtle gradations. And in some circumstances, states are less interested in their absolute gain from interdependence than in how the relatively greater gains of their rivals might be used to hurt them.

Some analysts believe that traditional world politics was always zero-sum. But that is misleading about the past. Traditional international politics could be positive-sum, depending on the actors' intentions. It made a difference, for example, whether Bismarck or Hitler was in charge in Germany. If one party sought aggrandizement, as Hitler did, then politics was indeed zero-sum—one side's gain was another's loss. But if all parties wanted stability, there could be joint gain in the balance of power. Conversely, the politics of economic globalization has competitive zero-sum aspects as well as cooperative positive-sum aspects.

In the politics of interdependence, the distinction between what is domestic and what is foreign becomes blurred. For example, the soybean situation mentioned earlier involved the domestic issue of controlling inflation at home, as well as American relations with Japan and Brazil. In the late 1990s, on the other hand, an Asian financial crisis depressed world commodity prices, which helped the American economy continue to grow without encountering inflationary pressures. In 2005, when U.S. secretary of the treasury John Snow visited China, he pleaded with the Chinese to increase consumer credit because the United States saw it "as going directly to the thing we have most on our minds—the global imbalances." Chinese leaders replied that the Americans "need to get their own house in order by reducing their fiscal deficits."[8] Were Snow and his Chinese counterparts commenting on domestic or foreign policy?

Or, to take another example, after Iran's 1979 revolution curtailed oil production, the American government urged citizens to cut their energy consumption by driving 55 miles per hour and turning down thermostats. Was that a domestic or a foreign policy issue? Some social scientists have taken to calling such issues "intermestic"—international *and* domestic at the same time.

Interdependence also affects domestic politics in a different way. In 1890, a French politician concerned with relative economic gains pursued a policy of holding Germany back. Today a policy of slowing economic growth in Germany is not good for France. Economic interdependence between France and Germany means that the best predictor of whether France is better off economically is when Germany is growing economically. Now with the two countries sharing a common currency, it is in the self-interest of the French politicians that Germany does well economically and vice versa. The classical balance-of-power theory, which predicts that one country will act only to keep the other down lest the other gain preponderance, is not valid. In economic interdependence, states are interested in absolute gains as well as gains relative to other states.

Costs of Interdependence

The costs of interdependence can involve short-run sensitivity or long-term vulnerability. *Sensitivity* refers to the amount and pace of the effects of dependence; that is, how quickly does change in one part of the system bring about change in another part? For example, in 1987, the New York stock market crashed suddenly because of foreigners' anxieties about U.S. interest rates and what might happen to the price of bonds and stocks. It all happened very quickly; the market was extremely sensitive to the withdrawal of foreign funds. In 1998, weakness in emerging markets in Asia had a contagious effect that undercut geographically distant emerging markets in Russia and Brazil. In 2008, the mortgage finance problem in the United States affected housing prices in other countries and eventually helped to trigger a global recession in 2009.

A high level of sensitivity, however, is not the same as a high level of vulnerability. *Vulnerability* refers to the relative costs of changing the structure of a system of interdependence. It is the cost of escaping from the system or of changing the rules of the game. The less vulnerable of two countries is not necessarily the less sensitive, but the one for whom adjustment is less costly. During the 1973 oil crisis, the United States depended on imported energy for only about 16 percent of its total energy uses. On the other hand, in 1973 Japan depended about 95 percent on imported energy. The United States was sensitive to the Arab oil boycott insofar as prices shot up in 1973, but it was not as vulnerable as Japan was. In 1998, the United States was sensitive but not vulnerable to East Asian economic conditions. The financial crisis there cut half a percent off the U.S. growth rate, but with a booming economy the United States could afford it. Indonesia, on the other hand, was both sensitive and vulnerable to changes in global trade and investment patterns. Its economy suffered severely and that, in turn, led to internal political conflict and a change of government.

Vulnerability is a matter of degree. When the shah of Iran was overthrown in 1979, Iranian oil production was disrupted at a time when demand was high and markets were already tight. The loss of Iran's oil caused the total amount of oil on the world markets to drop by about 5 percent. Markets were sensitive, and shortages of supply caused a rapid increase in oil prices. But Americans could reduce 5 percent of their energy consumption simply by turning down their thermostats and by driving on the highways at 55 rather than 60 miles per hour. It appears that the United States was sensitive but not very vulnerable if it could avoid damage by making such simple adjustments.

Vulnerability, however, depends on more than aggregate measures. It also depends on whether a society is capable of responding quickly to change. For example, the United States was less adept at responding to changes in the oil markets than Japan. Furthermore, private actors, large corporations, and speculators may each look at a market situation and decide to hoard supplies because they think shortages are going to grow worse. Their actions will drive the price even higher because it will make the shortages greater and put more demand on the market. Thus, degrees of vulnerability are not quite as simple as they first look.

Vulnerability also depends on whether substitutes are available and whether there are diverse sources of supply. In 1970, Lester Brown of the World Watch Institute expressed alarm about the increasing dependence of the United States on imported raw materials, and therefore its vulnerability.

SENSITIVITY INTERDEPENDENCE

> We had begun to forget the danger of contagion and the speed with which [a financial crisis] takes place when it does occur. The current developments which began in a relatively minor segment of the financial market, the sub-prime mortgage segment [in the United States in 2007], have spread far and wide across continents.
>
> *—Rakesh Mohan, Deputy Governor, Reserve Bank of India, September 20, 2007*[10]

Of thirteen basic industrial raw materials, the United States was dependent on imports for nearly 90 percent of aluminum, chromium, manganese, and nickel. He predicted that by 1985 the United States would be dependent on imports in ten of the basic thirteen.[9] He thought this would lead to a dramatic increase in U.S. vulnerability as well as a drastic increase in strength for the less developed countries that produced those raw materials.

But in the 1980s, raw materials prices went down, not up. What happened to his prediction? In judging vulnerability, Brown failed to consider the alternative sources of raw materials and the diversity of sources of supply that prevented producers from jacking up prices artificially. Moreover, technology improves. Yesterday's waste may become a new resource, and miniaturization reduces inputs. Companies now mine discarded tailings because new technology has made it possible to extract copper from ore that was considered depleted waste years ago. Today's reduced use of copper is also due to the introduction of fiber-optic cables made from silicon, whose basic origin is sand. Far less copper was required to manufacture a state-of-the-art computer in 2010 than in 1980, because it is so much smaller and lighter. Thus projections of U.S. vulnerability to shortages of raw materials were inaccurate because technology and alternatives were not adequately considered.

Some analysts refer to advanced economies today as information-based in the sense that computers, communications, and the Internet are becoming dominant factors in economic growth. Such economies are sometimes called "lightweight" economies because the value of information embedded in products is often far greater than the value of the raw materials involved. Such changes further depreciate the value of raw materials in world politics. One of the few exceptions is oil, which still plays a significant role in most advanced economies, particularly for transportation. This in turn contributes to the strategic significance of the Persian Gulf, where a large portion of the world's currently known oil reserves are located.

Symmetry of Interdependence

Symmetry refers to situations of relatively balanced versus unbalanced dependence. Being less dependent can be a source of power. If two parties are interdependent but one is less dependent than the other, the less dependent party has a

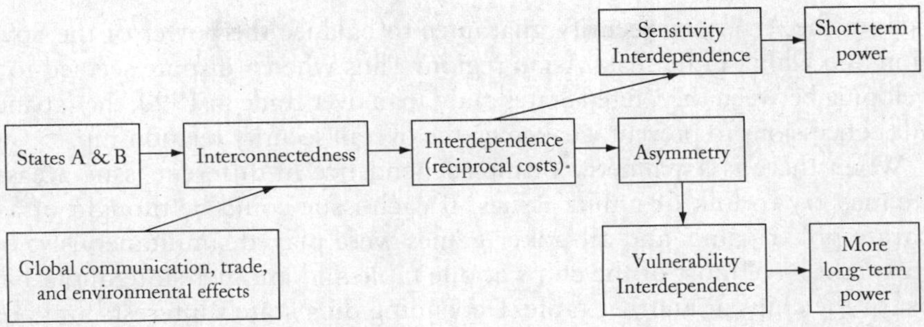

FIGURE 1
The Asymmetric Nature of Interdependence

source of power as long as both value the interdependent relationship. Manipulating the asymmetries of interdependence can be a source of power in international politics. Analysts who say that interdependence occurs only in situations of equal dependence define away the most interesting political behavior. Such perfect symmetry is quite rare; so are cases of complete imbalance in which one side is totally dependent and the other is not dependent at all. Asymmetry is at the heart of the politics of interdependence (see Figure 1).

Asymmetry often varies according to different issues. In the 1980s, when President Reagan cut taxes and raised expenditures, the United States became dependent on imported Japanese capital to balance its federal government budget. Some argued that this gave Japan tremendous power over the United States. But the other side of the coin was that Japan would hurt itself as well as the United States if it stopped lending to the United States. Japanese investors who already had large stakes in the United States would have found their investments devalued by the damage done to the American economy if Japan suddenly stopped lending. Moreover, Japan's economy was a little more than half the size of the American economy, and that meant that the Japanese needed the American market for their exports far more than vice versa (although both needed each other, and both benefited from the interdependence). A similar relationship has developed today between the United States and China. America accepts Chinese imports, and China holds American dollars and bonds, in effect making a loan to the United States. While China could threaten to sell its holdings of dollars and damage the American economy, a weakened American economy would mean a smaller market for Chinese exports, and the American government might respond with tariffs against Chinese goods. Neither side is in a hurry to break the symmetry of their vulnerability interdependence. In 2010, some Chinese generals suggested a massive sale of dollars to punish the United States for its arms sales to Taiwan, but top leaders refused. They knew that if China tried to bring the United States to its knees by dumping dollars, it would bring itself to its knees as well.

Moreover, security was often linked to other issues in the U.S.-Japanese relationship. After World War II, Japan followed the policy of a trading state and did not develop a large military capability or acquire nuclear weapons. It relied on the American security guarantee to balance the power of the Soviet Union and China in the East Asian region. Thus when a dispute seemed to be developing between the United States and Japan over trade in 1990, the Japanese made concessions to prevent weakening the overall security relationship.

When there is asymmetry of interdependence in different issue areas, a state may try to link or unlink issues. If each issue could be thought of as a separate poker game, and all poker games were played simultaneously, one state might have most of the chips at one table and another state might have most of the chips at another table. Depending on a state's interests and position, it might want to keep the games separate or create linkages between the tables. Therefore, much of the political conflict over interdependence involves the creation or prevention of linkage. States want to manipulate interdependence in areas in which they are strong and avoid being manipulated in areas in which they are relatively weak. Economic sanctions are often an example of such linkage. For example, in 1996 the United States threatened sanctions against foreign companies that invested in Iran, but when faced with European threats of retaliation through other linkages, the United States backed down.

By setting agendas and defining issue areas, international institutions often set the rules for the trade-offs in interdependent relationships. States try to use international institutions to set the rules that affect the transfer of chips among tables. Ironically, international institutions can benefit the weaker players by keeping some of the conflicts in which the poorer states are relatively better endowed separated from the military table, where strong states dominate. The danger remains, however, that some players will be strong enough to overturn one or more of the tables. With separate institutions for money, shipping, pollution, and trade, if the militarily strong players are beaten too badly, there is a danger they may try to kick over the other tables. Yet when the United States and Europe were beaten at the oil table in 1973, they did not use their preponderant military force to kick over the oil table because, a complex web of linkages held them back.

The largest state does not always win in the manipulation of economic interdependence. If a smaller or weaker state has a greater concern about an issue, it may do quite well. For instance, because the United States accounts for roughly three-quarters of Canada's foreign trade while Canada accounts for about one-quarter of U.S. foreign trade, Canada is more dependent on the United States than vice versa. Nonetheless, Canada often prevailed in a number of disputes with the United States because Canada was willing to threaten retaliatory actions such as tariffs and restrictions that deterred the United States. The Canadians would have suffered much more than the United States if their actions had led to a full dispute, but Canada felt it was better to risk occasional retaliation than to agree to rules that would *always* make it lose. Indeed, when it came to setting rules, the fact that Canada had more to lose meant that it was motivated to negotiate more effectively and often came away from the bargaining table with the better end of the deal.[11] Deterrence via manipulation of economic interdependence is somewhat like nuclear deterrence in that it rests on a capability for effective damage and credible intentions. Small states can often use their greater intensity and greater credibility to overcome their relative vulnerability in asymmetrical interdependence.

A natural outgrowth of rising interdependence is the proliferation of trade pacts. The European Union is the most sophisticated of these agreements and requires its member states to relax not just some economic sovereignty, but political sovereignty as well. In 1994, the United States, Mexico, and Canada ratified the *North American Free Trade Agreement (NAFTA)*. For Mexico and Canada, NAFTA was appealing because it bound their economies more tightly to the larger U.S. economy and, in so doing, increased their access to U.S. markets and their ability to export their products to the United States. For the United States, NAFTA expanded the realm of U.S. exports and made it easier for U.S. companies to do business in Canada and Mexico.

Regional pacts such as NAFTA may increase interdependence and lessen the asymmetry in a relationship. By agreeing to intertwine its economy with that of Mexico, the United States assumed some of the liabilities of the Mexican economy along with the benefits of easier access. When the value of the Mexican peso plummeted, the Clinton administration rushed in early 1995 to shore up the flagging currency and assembled a multibillion-dollar aid package. At a time when the U.S. Congress was deadlocked over increased domestic spending for services such as health care, the administration saw little choice but to rescue the peso. With greater interdependence, even strong countries can find themselves sensitive to economic developments beyond their borders. In 1997, when Southeast Asia suffered its financial crisis, the United States was less vulnerable than in the Mexican case and responded primarily through multilateral institutions. Nevertheless, fears of an economic domino effect in which collapse of some developing economies would undermine confidence in others meant that the United States and other advanced economies could not continue to stand idly by.

Leadership and Institutions in the World Economy

By and large, the rules of the international economy reflect the policies of the largest states (Figure 2). In the nineteenth century, Great Britain was the strongest of the major world economies. In the monetary area, the Bank of England adhered to the gold standard, which set a stable framework for world money. Britain also enforced freedom of the seas for navigation and commerce, and provided a large open market for world trade until 1932. After World War I, Britain was severely weakened by its fight against the kaiser's Germany. The United States became the world's largest economy, but it turned away from international affairs in the 1930s. The largest player in the world economy behaved as if it could still take a free ride rather than provide the leadership its size implied. Some economists believe that the Great Depression of the 1930s was aggravated by bad monetary policy and lack of American leadership. Britain was too weak to maintain an open international economy, and the United States was not living up to its new responsibilities.

MAJOR INTERNATIONAL ECONOMIC INSTITUTIONS

International Monetary Fund (IMF)

Location: Washington, DC
Founded: 1945, as a result of the International Monetary and Financial Conference held at Bretton Woods, NH, in 1944
Members: 187 countries
Staff: Approx. 2,500 from 160 countries
Assets: $376 billion USD

Organizational Structure:

- Board of Governors, with one representative from each member, which meets annually
- International Monetary and Finance Committee, consisting of 24 members, which meets twice a year
- Executive Board, consisting of 24 members, which carries out daily business of the IMF

System of Voting: Majority—Weighted based on size of membership quota (payment)

Primary Goals:

- Promoting international monetary cooperation
- Facilitating the expansion and balanced growth of international trade
- Promoting exchange stability
- Assisting in the establishment of a multilateral system of payments
- Making its resources available (under adequate safeguards) to members experiencing balance-of-payments difficulties

The World Bank

Location: Washington, DC
Founded: 1945, as a result of the International Monetary and Financial Conference held at Bretton Woods, NH, in 1944
Members: 187 countries
Staff: More than 10,000 from 160 countries
Budget: $44.2 billion USD in commitments; $28.9 billion gross disbursements

Organizational Structure:

- Board of Governors, with one representative from each member, which meets annually
- President from the largest shareholder (the United States) elected to a renewable five-year term and responsible for overseeing the Board of Directors
- Board of Directors consisting of 24 members who meet twice weekly
- Executive Directors carry out daily operations and decision making

System of Voting: Majority—Weighted based on size of each member's economy

Subagencies:

- International Bank for Reconstruction and Development
- International Development Association
- International Finance Corporation
- Multilateral Investment Guarantee Agency
- International Center for the Settlement of Investment Disputes

Primary Goals:

- Reducing poverty through efforts to promote economic growth and employment
- Debt relief for developing and least developed countries
- Improving the quality of governance and capacity of governing institutions
- Reducing the spread of diseases, including HIV/AIDS and malaria
- Increasing child access to primary education
- Reducing environmental degradation

(continued)

FIGURE 2

Overview of Major International Economic Institutions

The World Trade Organization (WTO)

Location: Geneva, Switzerland
Founded: 1995, as a result of the Uruguay Round of multilateral trade negotiations (formerly known as Generalized Agreement on Tariffs and Trade [GATT] which entered force in 1948)
Members: 153 member countries, 31 observer countries
Staff: 629 (Secretariat Staff)
Budget: 196 million CHF (approx. $264 million USD)

Organizational Structure:

- General Council, with one representative from each member, which convenes several times a year to negotiate agreements; also convenes as the Dispute Settlement Body and Trade Policy Review Body
- Appellate Body, consisting of seven permanent members who hear disputes referred to it by the Dispute Settlement Body (i.e. General Council)
- Secretariat, led by a Secretary, which has no formal decision-making powers and thus works to facilitate the daily business of the General Council and various subcommittees

System of Voting: Consensus based—One member, one vote

Primary Goals:

- Administering WTO trade agreements
- Providing a forum for multilateral trade negotiations
- Handling trade disputes
- Monitoring national trade policies
- Providing technical assistance and training to developing countries
- Cooperating with other international development organizations

Organization for Economic Cooperation and Development (OECD)

Location: Paris, France
Founded: 1960, as an economic counterpart to NATO; was preceded by the Organization for European Economic Cooperation founded after World War II to coordinate the Marshall Plan
Members: 34 countries (mostly developed countries)
Staff: 2,500 (Secretariat Staff)
Budget: €342 million EUR (approx. $486 million USD)

Organizational Structure:

- Council, with one representative from each member, which provides guidance regarding OECD activities and establishes the group's annual budget
- Secretary General, who oversees the Council and the Secretariat, which is responsible for the group's daily operations

System of Voting: Consensus based

Primary Goals:

- Promoting good governance
- Conducting economic surveys and offering economic policy recommendations
- Promoting economic development
- Providing a forum for multilateral discussion of economic, development, social, and governance challenges related to globalization

FIGURE 2 (*continued*)

After World War II, the lessons of the 1930s were on the minds of American leaders, and in 1944 an international conference at *Bretton Woods*, New Hampshire, established institutions to maintain an open, international economy. The *International Monetary Fund (IMF)* lends money, usually to developing countries and new market economies, to help when they have difficulties with their balance of payments or with paying interest on their debts. The IMF generally conditions its loans on the recipient country reforming its economic policies—for example, reducing budget deficits and price subsidies. While its policies are sometimes controversial and not always effective, the IMF played a role in helping the Russian economy in the early 1990s as well as in the Asian financial crisis later in the decade. The *World Bank* lends money to poorer countries and new market economies for development projects. (There are also regional development banks for Asia, Latin America, Africa, and Eastern Europe.)

The *General Agreement on Tariffs and Trade (GATT),* later transformed into the *World Trade Organization (WTO),* established rules for liberal trade and has served as the locus for a series of rounds of multilateral negotiations that have lowered trade barriers. The Organization for Economic Cooperation and Development (OECD) serves as a forum for thirty-four of the most developed countries to coordinate their international economic policies. Since the mid-1970s, the leaders of the seven largest economies, which account for two-thirds of world production, have met at annual G7 summit conferences (expanded to the G8 in the 1990s to include Russia) to discuss conditions of the world economy. In 1999, an even larger and more geographically representative group of countries—the G20—was created, and it started to take on an important role in the 2008–2009 global financial crisis. These institutions have helped reinforce government policies that allow rapid growth of private transnational interactions. The period has seen a rapid increase in economic interdependence. In most of the period after 1945, trade grew between 3 and 9 percent per year, faster even than the growth of world product. International trade, which represented 5.6 percent of the U.S. gross domestic product (GDP) in 1960, more than doubled to 11.2 percent of the U.S. GDP by 1995, and reached 27.97 percent of GDP in 2009. Large multinational corporations with global strategies became more significant as international investments increased by nearly 10 percent per year.

Critics have argued that the major international economic institutions are biased in favor of rich rather than poor countries. The IMF and World Bank, for example, have weighted voting that gives a preponderant influence to the United States, Europe, and Japan. The fund has always been directed by a European and the bank by an American (though this may change in the future). The United States is able to run fiscal and trade deficits with only the mildest of criticism, but when poor countries incur similar debts, IMF bureaucrats insist on a return to market discipline as a condition for help. One reason is that the poor countries often need the IMF's help to borrow money, but the United States can borrow without the IMF. In other words, the institutions reflect the underlying power of the asymmetrical interdependence of financial markets. Abolishing the IMF would not change that underlying power reality in financial markets. If anything, leaving matters to private bankers and fund managers might make it even more difficult for poor countries to borrow.

The World Trade Organization does not have weighted voting. It provides a forum in which 153 countries can negotiate trade agreements on a nondiscriminatory basis, as well as panels and rules to help arbitrate their trade disputes. Critics argue that the agreements countries negotiate within its framework (such as the current Doha "development round" of multilateral trade talks) have allowed rich countries to protect areas such as agriculture and textiles from developing-country competition and thus are unfair to the poor. The critics' descriptions are correct, and the protectionist policies hurt poor countries. But the causes of such protectionism lie in the domestic politics of the rich countries, and might be even greater if the WTO did not play a role. Again, international institutions can alleviate but not remove the underlying power realities. If anything, the fact that the United States and Europe have abided by costly decisions made against them by WTO panels suggests that institutions can make a difference, at least at the margin.

Even among the rich and powerful countries, there are problems in managing a transnational economy in a world of separate states. In the 1980s and again after 2001, the United States became a net debtor when it refused to tax itself to pay its bills at home and instead borrowed money from abroad. Some analysts believed this was setting the scene for a repeat of the 1930s, that the United States would experience decline as Britain had. But the United States did not decline, and other countries continued to be willing to lend it money because they had confidence in its economy, and it suited their interests. China, for example, continues to hold large reserves in dollars as a means to facilitate its exports to the United States. In 2009, although Chinese officials spoke of a desire to reduce China's holding of dollars, its practice changed very little.

Financial volatility, however, remains a potential problem. Global financial markets have grown dramatically in recent years, and their volatility poses risks to stability. Much will depend on the willingness of governments to pursue policies that maintain stability in the international economic system. In any case, the global political and economic system is more complicated and complex than before. More sectors, more states, more issues, and more private actors are involved in interdependent relationships. It is increasingly unrealistic to analyze world politics as occurring solely among a group of large states, solid as billiard balls, bouncing off each other in a balance of power.

Realism and Complex Interdependence

What would the world look like if realism were wrong about some of its fundamental propositions? Realism holds that states are the only significant actors; that military force is their dominant instrument; and that power (or security) is their dominant goal. What if states were not the only significant actors—if *transnational actors* working across state boundaries were also major players? What if force were not the only significant instrument—if economic manipulation and the use of international institutions were dominant? What if welfare, rather than security, were the primary goal? Such an antirealist world could be characterized as a situation of *complex interdependence*. Social scientists call complex interdependence an "ideal type." It is an imaginary concept that does not perfectly describe the real world; but then, as we have seen, neither does realism. Imagining a world in a condition of complex interdependence allows us to imagine a different type of global politics—one in which the liberal paradigm would presumably perform much better.

In fact, both realism and complex interdependence represent ideal types. The real world lies somewhere between the two. We can ask where certain country relationships fit on a spectrum between a Hobbesian state of nature and a condition of complex interdependence. The Middle East is closer to the realist end of the spectrum, but relations between the United States and Canada and relations between France and Germany today come much closer to the complex interdependence end of the spectrum. Different politics and different forms of the power struggle occur depending on where on the spectrum a particular relationship between a set of countries is located. In fact, countries can change their position on the spectrum. During the Cold War, the U.S.-Soviet relationship was clearly near the realist end of the spectrum, but with the end of the Cold War, the Russia-U.S. relationship moved closer to the center between realism and complex interdependence (see Figure 3).

A prime example of the interaction in the real world between complex interdependence and realism is the U.S. relationship with China. As with Japan, U.S. imports from China far outstrip U.S. exports to China. The result is a significant trade deficit. While the bilateral trade relationship between the United States and China is asymmetrical in China's favor, the United States is not particularly vulnerable to potential Chinese trade embargoes because it could compensate for the potential loss of Chinese goods by purchasing them elsewhere, and China has strong domestic incentives to export to the United States. Moreover, as we saw earlier, Chinese threats to sell the large holdings of dollars it earns for its exports would hurt Chinese sales to America. At the same time, the potential size of the Chinese market for American goods and the domestic demand for Chinese goods in the United States mean that the ability of the U.S. government to act against China is somewhat constrained by transnational actors, including U.S. multinational corporations that have pressured the U.S. government not to implement sanctions against China for unfair trade practices and human rights violations. The rapid growth of China's economic and military strength had a strong effect on the perceptions of the balance of power in East Asia, however, and contributed to the reinvigoration of the U.S.-Japan security alliance in 1995.

FIGURE 3

Spectrum from Realism to Complex Interdependence

Before the 2003 Iraq War, columnist Robert Kagan argued that many European countries were less willing to confront dangerous dictators such as Saddam Hussein because they had become accustomed to the peaceful conditions of complex interdependence that prevailed inside Europe and tended to generalize them to the Hobbesian world outside Europe, where they were less appropriate. In his words, "Americans were from Mars, and Europeans were from Venus." Of course this clever phrase was too simple (witness the role of Britain in the Iraq War), but it captured different perceptions across the Atlantic. It also illuminated a larger point. In their relations with each other, all advanced democracies form liberal islands of peace in the sea of Hobbesian realism. In its relations with Canada, Europe, and Japan, even the United States is from Venus. It is equally mistaken to pretend that the whole world is typified by Hobbesian realism or by complex interdependence.

Follow Up

- Robert O. Keohane and Joseph S. Nye, Jr., *Power and Interdependence*, 4th ed. (New York: Longman, 2011).
- Mark J. C. Crescenzi, *Economic Interdependence and Conflict in World Politics* (Lanham, MD: Lexington Books, 2005).

THE POLITICS OF OIL

Oil is the most important raw material in the world, in both economic and political terms, and it is likely to remain the key source of energy well into this century. The United States consumes nearly a fifth of the world's oil (compared to almost 9 percent for China, though Chinese consumption is growing rapidly). Even with high Chinese growth, the world is not about to run out of oil in the short run. More than a trillion barrels of reserves have been proven, and more are likely to be found. But two-thirds of the proven reserves are in the Persian Gulf and are therefore vulnerable to political disruption, which could have devastating effects on the world economy. Oil was not the primary cause of the two Gulf wars in the simple sense of seizing and owning it, but the strong positive relationship between the stability of Middle East oil supplies and global economic stability was a major consideration of policy makers when they debated policy toward Iraq. As one wag put it, if the Persian Gulf produced broccoli instead of oil, the wars might not have occurred. Thus, oil not only is important in itself, but is also an issue that illustrates aspects of both realism and complex interdependence.

Interdependence in a given area often occurs within a framework of rules, norms, and institutions that are called a *regime*. The international oil regime has changed dramatically over the decades. In 1960, the oil regime was a private oligopoly with close ties to the governments of the major consuming countries. Oil at that time sold for about $2 a barrel, and seven large transnational oil companies, sometimes called the "seven sisters," determined the amount of oil that would be produced. The price of oil depended on how much the large companies produced and on the demand in the rich countries where most of the oil was sold. Transnational companies set the rate of production, and prices were determined by conditions in rich countries. The strongest powers in the international system in traditional military terms occasionally intervened to keep the system going. For example, in 1953, when a nationalist movement tried to overthrow the shah of Iran, Britain and the United States covertly intervened to return the shah to his throne. The oil regime was then largely unchanged.

After 1973 there was a major turning point in the international regime governing oil. The producing countries set the rate of production and therefore had a strong effect on price, rather than price being determined solely by the market in the rich countries. There was an enormous shift of power and wealth from rich to relatively poor countries. Confidential documents released in 2004 showed that in response to the Arab oil embargo of 1973, the United States had considered the use of force to seize Persian Gulf oil fields, as realist theory might have predicted. But it did not do so, and the regime changed in favor of the weaker countries. How could such a dramatic change be explained?

A frequently offered explanation is that the oil-producing countries banded together and formed the *Organization of Petroleum Exporting Countries (OPEC)*. The trouble with this explanation is that OPEC was formed in 1960, and the dramatic change did not occur until 1973. Oil prices fell despite OPEC, so there is more to the story. There are three ways to explain these changes in the international oil regime: the overall balance of power, the balance of power in the oil issue, and international institutions.

Realists look at changes in the balance of power resting primarily on military force, particularly with regard to the Persian Gulf, the major oil-exporting region of the world. Two changes affected that balance: the rise of nationalism and decolonization. In 1960, half the OPEC countries were colonies of Europe; by 1973, they were all independent. Accompanying the rise in nationalism was a rise in the costs of military intervention. It is much more expensive to use force against a nationalistically awakened and decolonized people. When the British and Americans intervened in Iran in 1953, it was not very costly, but if the Americans had tried to keep the shah on his throne in 1979, the costs would have been prohibitive.

Relative changes in U.S. and British power also affected the balance of power in the Persian Gulf. When OPEC was formed, and even earlier, Britain was to a large extent the policeman of the Persian Gulf. In 1961, it prevented an earlier Iraqi effort to annex Kuwait. But by 1971, Britain was economically weakened, and the British government was trying to cut back on its international defense commitments. In 1971, Britain ended what used to be called its role "east of Suez." That may sound a bit like 1947, when Britain was unable to maintain its role as a power in the eastern Mediterranean. At that time, the United States stepped in to help Greece and Turkey and formulated the Truman Doctrine. But in 1971, the United States was not well placed to step in to replace Britain as it did in 1947. The United States was deeply embroiled in Vietnam and unwilling to accept an additional major military commitment in the Persian Gulf. As a result, President Nixon and then–National Security Adviser Henry Kissinger designed an American strategy that relied heavily on regional powers. Their chosen instrument was Iran. By using Iran as the regional hegemon, they thought they could replace the departing British policeman cheaply. A realist would point to these changes in the overall structure of power, particularly the balance of military power in the Persian Gulf region, to explain the change in the oil regime.

A second way of explaining the change is a modified form of realism that focuses on the relative symmetry of economic power of various countries in a given issue area. Between 1950 and 1973, serious changes occurred in global oil consumption that altered U.S. dependence on foreign oil. Specifically, the United States, until 1971, was the largest oil producer in the world. But American production peaked in 1971; American imports began to grow thereafter, and the United States no longer had any surplus oil. During the two Middle East wars of 1956 and 1967, the Arab countries tried an oil embargo, but their efforts were easily defeated because the United States was producing enough oil to supply Europe when it was cut off by the Arab countries. Once American production peaked in 1971 and the United States began to import oil, the power to balance the oil market switched to countries such as Saudi Arabia and Iran. No longer was the United States the supplier of last resort that could make up any missing oil.

A third way to explain the difference in the oil regime after 1973 relies less on realism than on changes in the role of international institutions, particularly the multinational corporations and OPEC that are emphasized by liberal and constructivist approaches. The "seven sisters" gradually lost power over this period. One reason was their *obsolescing bargains* with the producer countries. When a multinational corporation goes into a resource-rich country with a new investment, it can strike a bargain in which the multinational gets a large part of the joint gains. From the point of view of the poor country, having a multinational come in to develop its resources will make it better off. Even if it gets only 20 percent of the revenues and the multinational gets 80 percent, the poor country has more than it had before. So at the early stages when multinationals have a monopoly on capital, technology, and access to international markets, they strike a bargain with the poor countries in which the multinationals get the lion's share. But over time, the multinationals inadvertently transfer resources to the poor countries, not out of charity but in the normal course of business. They train locals. Thus Saudis, Kuwaitis, and others learned how to run oil fields, pumping stations, and loading docks. Locals also developed expertise in marketing and associated tasks.

Eventually the poor countries wanted a better division of the profits. The multinational could threaten to pull out, but the poor countries could credibly threaten to run the operation by itself. So over time, the power of the multinational companies, particularly in raw materials, diminished in terms of their bargaining with host countries. This was the "obsolescing bargain."

From the 1960s to 1973, the multinationals inadvertently transferred technology and skills that developed the poor countries' capacity to run oil operations themselves.

There were other developments. The seven sisters were joined by "little cousins" when new transnational corporations entered the oil market. Although they were not as large as the seven sisters, they were still big, and they began to strike their own deals with the oil-producing countries. Thus, when an oil-producing country wanted to get out of the hands of the seven sisters, it could strike a deal with smaller independent multinationals. That again reduced the bargaining power of the largest multinationals.

Institutionally, there was a modest increase in the effectiveness of OPEC as a cartel. Cartels restricting supply had long been typical in the oil industry, but in the past these had been private arrangements of the seven sisters. Cartels generally have a problem because there is a tendency to cheat on production quotas when markets are soft and the price drops. Cartels work best when there is a shortage of oil, but when there is a surplus, people want to sell their oil and tend to cut the price in order to get a bigger share of the market. With time, market forces tend to erode cartels. OPEC represented an effort to shift from a private to a governmental cartel of the oil-producing countries. In its early years, OPEC had trouble exercising power because there was plenty of oil. As long as oil was in surplus, the OPEC countries had incentives to cheat to get a larger share of the market. OPEC was unable to enforce price discipline from the year it was founded, 1960, until the early 1970s. But after oil supplies tightened, OPEC's role in coordinating the bargaining power of the producers increased.

The Middle East War of 1973 gave OPEC a boost, a signal that now it could use its power. The Arab countries cut off access to oil during the 1973 war for political reasons, but that created a situation in which OPEC could become effective. Iran, which is not an Arab country, was allegedly the American instrument for policing the Persian Gulf, but the shah of Iran moved to quadruple oil prices, and the other OPEC countries followed suit. Over the long term, OPEC could not maintain permanently high prices because of market forces, but there was stickiness on the downside that was an effect of the OPEC coalition.

A more important institutional factor was the role the oil companies played in "smoothing the pain" in the crisis itself. At one point in the crisis, Henry Kissinger, by now secretary of state, said that if the United States faced "strangulation," force might have to be used. Fifteen percent of traded oil was cut, and the Arab embargo reduced oil exports to the United States by 25 percent. However, oil companies made sure that no one country suffered much more than any other. They redistributed the world's traded oil. When the United States lost 25 percent of its Arab oil imports, the companies shipped it more Venezuelan or Indonesian oil. They smoothed the pain of the embargo so the rich countries all lost about 7–9 percent of their oil, well below the strangulation point. They helped prevent the economic conflict from becoming a military conflict.

Why did they do this? It was not out of charity. Transnational companies are long-run profit maximizers; that is, they want to maximize their profit in the long term. To do so, they want stability and market access. The multinational companies feared situations in which they would be nationalized in a country if they refused to sell to that country. For example, Prime Minister Edward Heath of Britain demanded that British Petroleum sell only to Britain and not to other countries. The head of British Petroleum replied that if he followed such an order, the company would be nationalized by those other countries, which would destroy British Petroleum. The British prime minister backed down. Essentially, because the oil companies were long-run profit maximizers, they tried to stabilize the market rather than have the pain strike any one country strongly. By reducing the threat of strangulation, they reduced the probability that force would be used.

In short, oil is an illustration of an issue that falls between the ideal types of realism and complex interdependence. Changes in three dimensions—the overall balance of military power, the symmetry of interdependence within the issue structure of economic power, and the institutions within the oil issue area—help explain the dramatic difference between the oil regime of 1960 and the oil regime after 1973.

The Deepwater Horizon offshore oil drilling platform, which exploded and sank in the Gulf of Mexico in August 2010, causing the largest oil spill in U.S. history

Oil as a Power Resource

How powerful was the oil weapon at the turning point of 1973? By cutting production and embargoing sales to countries friendly to Israel, Arab states were able to bring their issues to the forefront of the U.S. agenda. They also created temporary disarray in the alliances between Japan, Europe, and the United States, each of whom responded somewhat differently. The oil weapon encouraged the United States to play a more conciliatory role in arranging the settlement of the Arab-Israeli dispute in the aftermath of the Yom Kippur War, but it did not change the basic policy of the United States in the Middle East: Washington did not suddenly switch from their alliance with Israel to support of the Arab cause. Oil was a power resource that had an effect, but not a strong enough effect to reverse American policy.

Why was the oil weapon not more effective? Part of the answer is reciprocity in interdependence. Saudi Arabia, which became the key country in oil markets, had large investments in the United States. If the Saudis damaged the U.S. economy too much, they would also hurt their own economic interests. In addition, Saudi Arabia depended on the United States in the security area. In the long run, the United States was the only country able to keep a stable balance of power in the Persian Gulf region. The Saudis knew this, and they were careful about how far they pushed the oil weapon. Moreover, in the aftermath of the oil crisis, major oil consumers took measures to reduce somewhat their sensitivity and vulnerability in the future. The United States, for example, established a Strategic Petroleum Reserve—an oil stockpile, in effect—and with other OECD countries established the International Energy Agency to promote transparency in world energy markets and sound energy policy.

What was the role of force as a power resource in the oil crisis of 1973? There was no overt use of force. There was no military intervention, because strangulation never occurred. Moreover, the Saudis were benefiting from the long-run security guarantee provided by the United States. Thus force played a background role. There was an indirect linkage between security interdependence and oil interdependence. Force was too costly to use overtly, but it played a role as a power resource in the background.

This complex set of factors persists. Oil remains an exception among raw materials, and this contributed in part to the two Gulf Wars and to the continuing strong U.S. naval presence in the Persian Gulf. But oil prices are sensitive to global market forces, and multinationals' exploration for new supplies in Central Asia and other regions has increased supply. Prices at the end of the twentieth century had returned to pre-1973 levels.

The nightmare oil scenarios predicted during the 1970s failed to materialize. The U.S. Department of Energy, for instance, forecast that oil would cost more than $100 a barrel by 2000.[12] While oil prices passed that level in 2008, they had dropped as low as $11 a barrel in the late 1990s. A number of factors helped keep these earlier predictions from coming true. On the demand side, policy measures and price increases led to more efficient use of energy. For example, the Corporate Average Fuel Efficiency law in the United States mandated that automakers manufacture cars that achieved minimum standards for gas mileage. This is an example of a domestic policy that had a clear intended effect on foreign policy. (In addition, cost-conscious drivers who had felt the pinch of high gasoline prices also contributed to this effect.)

On the supply side, the emergence of non-OPEC oil sources that were unavailable during the Cold War meant that OPEC faced more competition on the world market. By the late 1990s Russia had become a major oil supplier to the West. The Caspian Sea reserves also offered another promising outlet outside OPEC's control. Advances in technology led geologists to gain access to oil that had previously been impossible to reach, exposing the limitations of the projections that were made in the 1970s about global reserves.

But after 2005, oil prices spiked again, partly in response to disruptions from war, hurricanes, and terrorist threats, but also because of projections of rising demand. The rise in oil and gas prices boosted the political leverage of energy-producing countries such as Russia, Venezuela, and Iran that had suffered from the low oil prices of the 1990s. Two new consumer giants influenced the future of energy markets: China and India. As the two most populous countries on earth, both are experiencing rapid increases in demand for energy as they modernize and industrialize. Both are making mercantilist efforts to buy and control foreign oil supplies, though the lessons of the 1970s crisis should teach them that oil is a fungible commodity, and markets tend to spread supplies and even out the pain no matter who owns the oil. China also has vast coal reserves as well as natural gas and is trying to develop renewable energy, but it will increasingly rely on oil imports to meet its growing needs. Both countries also face serious environmental challenges from their use of fossil fuels that may have global implications in terms of air pollution and climate change. In any event, their rapid economic growth will contribute significantly to the global demand for oil.

The United States will also likely continue to rely on imported oil to meet its energy needs, despite conservation efforts, and this means that the biggest global oil-producing regions, such as the Persian Gulf, will still play a key role in geopolitics. Despite new sources such as Russia, experts anticipate that Saudi Arabia and its neighbors will meet two-thirds of the increased global oil demand between now and 2030.[13] Because Saudi Arabia is the world's number one producer, any major changes in its political stability could have dramatic consequences.

Prices could rise suddenly for rich and poor countries alike if conflicts disrupt supplies from the Persian Gulf. The drama regarding oil is not over. While raw materials are less crucial in information age–economies than in the industrial age, oil still matters. And while growing global networks of economic interdependence produce joint gains, they can also create political problems. Power politics just becomes more complex in an era of economic globalization.

Over the course of the twenty-first century, the politics of oil are likely to become even more complex—although exactly how will depend upon our collective foresight and ingenuity. Oil is a nonrenewable resource, and if we continue to extract it at a high rate, easily available oil will run dry. Most of the easily tapped oilfields have already been exploited. In its 2008 World Energy Outlook, the International Energy Agency predicted that the decline rate for mature oil fields was likely to increase from 6.7 percent today to 8.6 percent in 2030—or, put another way, even if global demand were to remain constant during the next 20 years (which is highly unlikely, given rapidly growing demand in countries such as China and India), we would need to find four new Saudi Arabia's worth of oil production between now and then just to offset the decline of existing oilfields. Inevitably, the world will have to turn increasingly to unconventional sources of oil, such as oil sands, but these are much more difficult and expensive to tap. These three problems—the exhaustion of oilfields that are easy to exploit, the declining productivity of existing fields, and an increasing reliance on unconventional sources—are reflected in a useful statistic called the energy return on investment (EROI), which indicates how much energy can be extracted from an investment of one unit of energy in production. Any petroleum extraction operation requires electricity to run pumps and drills, gasoline to fuel vehicles, and so forth. In the United States in the early 1930s, with an input of one barrel of oil worth of energy, it was possible to extract 100 barrels of oil. Today the EROI has shrunk from 100-to-1 to 17-to-1. Exploiting tar sands, which requires vast quantities of heat to extract usable oil from the sandy soil, has an EROI of less than 6-to-1.[14]

In the long run, the world will have to find a way to end its dependence upon oil. No one knows exactly what will power a postcarbon economy—nuclear, solar, wind, tidal, geothermal, and biomass sources of energy will no doubt all be part of the mix, though in what proportion it is impossible to say.

In the meantime, oil will continue to figure prominently in global politics. The longer Hobbesian parts of the world dominate the oil industry, the more oil politics is likely to resemble realist power politics. The more the world comes to depend upon countries such as Canada, the more oil politics will reflect the dynamics one would expect under conditions of complex interdependence. Either way, however, oil politics and environmental politics will probably intertwine to the point where they will become inseparable, for attempts to solve the world's long-term energy and climate-change problems could easily work at cross-purposes in the absence of significant progress toward a postcarbon world.

Follow Up

- Francisco R. Parra, *Oil Politics: A Modern History of Petroleum* (New York: I. B. Tauris, 2004).
- Daniel Yergin, "Ensuring Energy Security," *Foreign Affairs*, March/April (2006), pp. 28–36.

STUDY QUESTIONS

1. What are the major types of globalization? Is globalization an irreversible process? How is contemporary globalization different from past periods of globalization?
2. What are the implications of globalization in the cultural realm? Does globalization necessarily result in global cultural homogenization? More specifically, will globalization ultimately lead to universal "Westernization"?
3. What kinds of political responses has globalization sparked? What is the relationship between antiglobalization sentiment and economic inequality in the international sphere?
4. What is "complex interdependence"? How does it differ from simple "interdependence"? What paradigm is best at making sense of it? Where do we find complex interdependence most closely approximated today?
5. What makes economic interdependence a source of power? How do sensitivity and vulnerability differ?
6. What were the underlying and immediate causes of the 1973 oil crisis? Why didn't it occur earlier—say, in 1967? Was it a unique event or the beginning of a revolution in international politics? Why was force not used? Could it be used today?
7. Liberal theory was optimistic that increasing international commerce would seriously decrease the attractiveness of military force as a tool in international politics. What does the international oil regime indicate either to support or to falsify this thesis?
8. Under classical realist assumptions, we would not expect to see cooperation among states under conditions of anarchy. How can you explain the degree of cooperation achieved by states in international economic relations? Do institutions play a role?

NOTES

1. Dani Rodrik, *Has Globalization Gone Too Far?* (Washington, DC: Institute for International Economics, 1997), p. 2.
2. James J. McCarthy, "The Scope of the IPCC Third Assessment Report," *Climate Report* (Winter 2001), p. 3.
3. Thomas Friedman, *The Lexus and the Olive Tree: Understanding Globalization* (New York: Farrar, Straus & Giroux, 1999), pp. 7–8.
4. Joseph Stiglitz, "Weightless Concerns," *Financial Times* (London), February 3, 1999, p. 14.
5. John Maynard Keynes, *The Economic Consequences of the Peace* (New York: Penguin, 1988), p. 11.
6. Robert Wade, "Winners and Losers" and "Of Rich and Poor," *The Economist,* April 28, 2001, pp. 72–74, 80. Global inequality is difficult to measure, and there is always a degree of uncertainty; but while it is clear that income inequality has risen dramatically since the Industrial

Revolution, there is reason to believe that it may have declined slightly in recent decades. David Dollar, "Globalization, Poverty and Inequality since 1980," in David Held and Ayse Kaya, eds., *Global Inequality: Patterns and Explanations* (Cambridge: Polity Press, 2007), pp. 73–103.
7. UK Special Representative for Climate Change John Ashton, Speech at the School of Oriental and African Studies (SOAS) in London, September 27, 2006.
8. Edmund Andrews, "Snow Urges Consumerism on China Trip," *The New York Times,* October 14, 2005, p. 1.
9. Lester Brown, *World Without Borders* (New York: Random, 1972), p. 194.
10. Rakesh Mohan, Valedictory Address, Reserve Bank of India, Asia Regional Economic Forum, September 20, 2007.
11. The 1959 Defense Production Sharing Arrangements, the 1965 Auto Pact, and the 1988 Canada-U.S. Free Trade Agreement. Michael Hart, *A Trading Nation: Canadian Trade Policy from Colonialism to Globalization* (Vancouver: UBC Press, 2002), pp. 214–217, 240–247, 367–393.
12. "Still Holding Customers over a Barrel," *The Economist,* October 25, 2003, pp. 61–63.
13. Ibid.
14. Thomas F. Homer-Dixon, *The Upside of Down: Catastrophe, Creativity, and the Renewal of Civilization* (Washington, DC: Island Press, 2006), pp. 90, 93.

PHOTO CREDITS

Credits are listed in order of appearance:

Andrew Wood/E+/Getty Images

EPA/Landov.

BOX CREDIT

"Ecological and Economic Interdependence": Excerpted from "North-South Divide is Marring Environmental Talks," *The New York Times*, March 17, 1992, p. 8.

The Information Revolution and Transnational Actors

An International Committee of the Red Cross/Red Crescent tent supports refugees from the Libyan civil war in the spring of 2011

POWER AND THE INFORMATION REVOLUTION: FROM THE INVENTION OF WRITING TO THE ARAB SPRING

An information revolution is currently transforming world politics. Four centuries ago, the English statesman-philosopher Francis Bacon wrote that knowledge is power. In the twenty-first century, a much larger portion of the population both within and among countries has access to this power. Governments have always worried about the flow and control of information, and the current period is not the first to be strongly affected by changes in information technology. In the fifteenth century, Johann Gutenberg's (1398–1468) invention of movable type, which allowed printing of the Bible and made it accessible to large portions of the European population, is often credited with playing a major role in the onset of the Reformation. Pamphlets and committees of correspondence paved the way for the American Revolution. As constructivists point out, rapid changes in information flows can lead to important changes in identities and interests.

The current information revolution is based on rapid technological advances in computers, communications, and software that in turn have led to dramatic decreases in the cost of processing and transmitting information. Computing power has doubled every two years since the invention of the integrated circuit in 1958, and by the beginning of the twenty-first century it cost one-thousandth of what it did in the early 1970s. If the price of automobiles had fallen as quickly as the price of semiconductors, a car today would cost less than five dollars.

In 1993, there were about 50 websites in the world; by the end of 2010, that number had reached 255 million. Between 2000 and 2011, global Internet usage grew by 480 percent, with Africa and the Middle East experiencing the largest gains. Communications bandwidths are expanding rapidly, and communications costs continue to fall even more rapidly than computing power. As late as 1980, phone calls over copper wire could carry only one page of information per second; today, a thin strand of optical fiber can transmit 90,000 *volumes* in a second. In terms of current dollars, the cost of a brief transatlantic phone call had fallen from $250 in 1930 to considerably less than a dollar at the beginning of the new century. Now with Voice over Internet Protocol (VoIP), it can be virtually free. Webcams allow people to have personal video conferences from the comfort of their home office. In 1980, a gigabyte of storage occupied a room; now an Apple iPod that fits in your pocket comes with up to 160 gigabytes of storage.

The key characteristic of the information revolution is not the *speed* of communications between the wealthy and powerful: For more than 130 years, virtually instantaneous communication has been possible, at least between Europe and North America. The two crucial changes are an enormous reduction in the *cost* and a mind-boggling increase in *capacity*. For all practical purposes, the cost of transmitting and receiving information has become negligible. At the same time, storage and bandwidth have exploded. Cisco, a major manufacturer of communications equipment, estimates that by 2015 more than 15 billion devices will be connected to the Internet—more than twice the world's population—generating a total information flow close to one zettabyte (a trillion gigabytes). These dramatic changes have led to what some call the "third industrial revolution," which is changing the nature of governance, affecting sovereignty, and creating a diffusion of power.

Lessons from the Past

Technology has always had an important impact on how human beings interact and organize their world. The invention of writing 5,000 years ago in Mesopotamia (specifically, in ancient Sumeria) made possible for the very first time a rudimentary bureaucratic state. The invention of movable type in Europe permitted the transformation of medieval fiefdoms into modern states.[1] Revolutions in communications, transportation, and military technology permitted governance over larger and larger areas. It is no accident that in Western Europe, where the modern sovereign state was first invented, countries are physically small.[2] France—the largest—ranks only forty-ninth in the world. You could fit twelve Frances into Australia, and fifteen into the United States or Canada. What will ongoing technological developments mean for world politics in the future?

We can get some idea of where we are heading by looking back at the past. In the first industrial revolution around the turn of the nineteenth century, the application of steam to mills and transportation had a powerful effect on the economy, society, and government. Patterns of production, work, living conditions, social class, and political power were transformed. Public education arose, as literate, trained workers were needed for increasingly complex and potentially dangerous factories. Police forces such as London's "bobbies" were created to deal with urbanization. Subsidies were provided for the necessary infrastructure of canals and railroads.

The "second industrial revolution," around the turn of the twentieth century—electricity, synthetics, and the internal combustion engine—brought similar economic and social changes. The United States went from a predominantly agrarian to a primarily industrial and urban nation. In the 1890s, most Americans still worked on farms or as servants. A few decades later, the majority lived in cities and worked in factories. Social class and political cleavages were altered as urban labor and trade unions became more important. And again, with lags, the role of government changed. The bipartisan progressive movement ushered in antitrust legislation, early consumer protection regulation by the forerunner of the Food and Drug Administration, and economic stabilization by the Federal Reserve Board. The United States rose to the status of a great power in world politics. Some expect the third industrial revolution to produce analogous transformations in the economy, society, government, and world politics.

These historical analogies help us understand some of the forces that will shape world politics in the twenty-first century. Economies and information networks have changed more rapidly than governments have. The political scales of sovereignty and authority have not yet grown at a similar rate. As the sociologist Daniel Bell noted, "If there is a single overriding sociological problem in postindustrial society—particularly in the management of transition—it is the management of scale."[3] Put more simply, the basic building blocks of world politics are being transformed by the new technology. If we focus solely on the hard power of states, we will miss the new reality.

We are still at an early stage of the current information revolution, and its effects on economics and politics are uneven. As with steam in the late eighteenth century and electricity in the late nineteenth century, productivity growth lagged as society had to learn to fully utilize the new technologies. Social institutions change more slowly than technology. For example, the electric motor was invented in 1881, but it was nearly four decades before Henry Ford pioneered the reorganization of factory assembly lines to take full advantage of electric power. Similar lags were true for information technology and computers. The increase in productivity of the American economy began to register only as recently as the mid-1990s.

The advent of truly mass communications and broadcasting a century ago, which was facilitated by newly cheap electricity, provides some lessons about possible social and political effects today. It ushered in the age of mass popular culture. The effects of mass communication and broadcasting, though not the telephone, tended to have a centralizing political effect. While information was more widespread, it was more centrally influenced even in democratic countries than in the age of the local press. President Roosevelt's use of radio in the 1930s worked a dramatic shift in American politics. These effects were particularly pronounced in countries where they were combined with the rise of totalitarian governments that were able to suppress competing sources of information. Indeed, some scholars believe totalitarianism would not have been possible without the mass communications that accompanied the second industrial revolution.

In the middle of the twentieth century, people feared that the computers and communications of the current information revolution would create the central governmental control dramatized in George Orwell's novel *1984*. Mainframe computers seemed set to enhance central planning and increase the surveillance powers of those at the top of a pyramid of control. Government television would dominate the news. Through central databases, computers can make government identification and surveillance easier, and commercialization has already altered the early libertarian culture and code of the Internet. Nonetheless, the technology of encryption is evolving, as well as programs that enable users to

Traders working at the New York Mercantile Exchange

trade digital information anonymously. Governments are increasing their efforts to control cyberspace, but the Internet is more difficult for governments to control than was the technology of the second information revolution.

As computing power has decreased in cost and computers have shrunk in size and become more highly mobile, their decentralizing effects have outweighed their centralizing effects. The Internet creates a system in which power over information is much more widely distributed. Compared to radio, television, and newspapers, controlled by editors and broadcasters, the Internet creates unlimited communication one-to-one (via e-mail), one-to-many (via a personal homepage, blog, or Twitter feed), many-to-one (via electronic broadcast), and, perhaps most important, many-to-many (an online chat room or message board). Comparing these electronic methods of communication to previous advances in communication, political scientist Pippa Norris wrote, "Internet messages have the capacity to flow farther, faster, and with fewer intermediaries."[4] Central surveillance is possible, but governments that aspire to control information flows through control of the Internet face high costs. What this means is that world politics will decreasingly be the sole province of governments. Both individuals and private organizations, ranging from corporations to NGOs to terrorists, will be empowered to play direct roles in world politics. The spread of information means that power will be more widely distributed, and informal networks will undercut the monopoly of traditional bureaucracy. The speed of Internet time means that governments everywhere will have less control of their agendas. Political leaders will enjoy fewer degrees of freedom before they must respond to events, and then they will have to share the stage with more actors. Constructivists warn that we will have to avoid being mesmerized by terms such as *balance of power* and *hegemony*, and measures of strength that compare only the hard power of states run by centralized governments. They say that realist images of sovereign states balancing and bouncing off each other like billiard balls will blind us to the new complex reality.

A New World Politics?

The effects of the information revolution are still in their early stages. Is it really transforming world politics? Realists would say no. States will remain the most important actors, and the information revolution will still benefit the largest states. The information revolution is making world politics more complex by empowering nonstate actors, for better or for worse, and, by reducing control by central governments, it is also affecting power among states. Here the rich states benefit, and many poorer countries lag behind. While some poor countries such as China, India, and Malaysia have made significant progress in entering the information economy, more than a third of all Internet users in 2011 lived in either Europe or North America. Four out of five North Americans use the Internet today; fewer than 6 percent of Africans do. The world remains a mixture of agricultural, industrial, and service-dominated economies. The postindustrial societies and governments most heavily affected by the information age coexist and interact with countries thus far less affected by the information revolution.

Will this digital divide persist? Decreasing costs may allow poor countries to leapfrog or skip over certain stages of development. For example, in many African countries, inexpensive cell phones provide banking and monetary as well as communications roles. Wireless communications are already replacing costly landlines, and voice recognition technologies can give illiterate populations access to computer communications. Technology spreads over time, and many countries are keen to develop their own Silicon Valleys. But it is easier to identify the virtual keys to the high-tech kingdom than to open the actual gates. Well-developed communications infrastructure, secure property rights, sound government policies, an environment that encourages new business formation, deep capital markets, and a skilled workforce, many of whom understand English (still the dominant language of the Internet), will come to some poor countries in time, but not quickly. Even in India, which meets some of the criteria, software companies employ hundreds of thousands, but less than two-thirds of India's nearly 1.2 billion people are literate.

The information revolution has an overall decentralizing and leveling effect, but will it also equalize power among states? In principle, as it reduces costs and barriers of entry into markets, it should reduce the power of large states and enhance the power of small states and nonstate actors. But in practice, international relations are more complex than such technological determinism implies. Some aspects of the information revolution help the small; but some help the already large and powerful. Realists give several reasons why.

First, size still matters. What economists call barriers to entry and economies of scale remain in some of the aspects of power that are related to information. For example, soft power is strongly affected by the cultural content of what is broadcast or what appears in movies and television programs. Large, established entertainment industries often enjoy considerable economies of scale in content production and distribution. The dominant American market share in films and television programs in world markets is a case in point. It is hard for newcomers to compete with Hollywood (though India's "Bollywood" has a wide following). Moreover, in the information economy, there are "network effects" with increasing returns to scale. As we know, one telephone is useless. The second adds value, and so forth as the network grows.

Second, even though it is now cheap to disseminate existing information, the collection and production of new information often requires major investment. In many competitive situations, *new* information matters most. In some dimensions, information is a public good: One person's consumption does not diminish that of another. Thomas Jefferson used the analogy of a candle. If you give someone a light, it does not diminish your light. But in a competitive situation, it may make a big difference if someone else has the light first and see things before you do. Intelligence collection is a good example. America, Russia, Britain, France, and China have capabilities for collection and production that dwarf those of other countries. The United States spends $55 billion a year on non-defense-related intelligence alone. In some commercial situations, a fast follower can do better than a first mover, but in terms of power among states, it is usually better to be a first mover than a fast follower. It is ironic, but no accident, that for all the discussion of the Internet shrinking distance, firms still cluster in Silicon Valley, a congested little area south of San Francisco, because of what is called "the cocktail party effect." What makes for success is informal access to new information before it becomes public. Douglas McGray notes, "In an industry where new technology is perpetually on the verge of obsolescence, firms must recognize demand, secure capital, and bring a product to market quickly or else be beaten by a competitor."[5] Market size and proximity to competitors, suppliers, and customers still matter in an information economy.

First movers are often the creators of the standards and architecture of information systems. As in Robert Frost's famous poem, once two paths diverge in the wood and one is taken, it is difficult to get back to the other. Sometimes, crude low-cost technologies open shortcuts that make it possible to overtake the first mover, but in many instances, the path-dependent development of information systems reflects the advantage of the first mover. The use of the English language and the pattern of top-level domain names on the Internet is a case in point. Partly because of the transformation of the American economy in the 1980s, and partly because of large investments driven by Cold War military competition, the United States was often the first mover and still enjoys a lead in the application of a wide variety of information technologies. But being a first mover also makes America more dependent upon the Internet, and thus more vulnerable to disruption than isolated countries such as North Korea.

Finally, as we have seen, military power remains important in critical domains of international relations. Information technology has some effects on the use of force that benefit the small and some that favor the already powerful. The off-the-shelf commercial availability of formerly costly military technologies benefits small states and nongovernmental actors and increases the vulnerability of large states. For example, today anyone can order satellite images from commercial companies or simply use Google Earth to see what goes on in other countries at little or no cost. Commercial firms and individuals can go to the Internet and get access to satellite photographs that were top secret and cost governments billions of dollars just a few years ago. When a nongovernmental group felt that American policy toward North Korea was too alarmist a few years ago, it published private satellite pictures of North Korean rocket launch pads. Obviously, other countries can purchase similar pictures of American bases.

Global positioning system (GPS) devices that provide precise locations, once the property of the military alone, are readily available at stores such as Walmart and make possible the navigation systems that are available now in many new cars. What is more, information systems create vulnerabilities for rich states by adding lucrative targets for terrorist (including state-sponsored) groups. It is conceivable that a sophisticated adversary (such as a small country with cyberwarfare resources) will decide it can blackmail large states. There is also the prospect of freelance cyberattacks, and deterrence becomes more difficult when a country cannot be sure of the origin of an attack.

Other trends, however, strengthen already powerful countries. Information technology has produced a revolution in military affairs. Space-based sensors, direct broadcasting, high-speed computers, and complex software provide the ability to gather, sort, process, transfer, and disseminate information about complex events that occur over a wide geographic area. This dominant battle-space awareness combined with precision targeting and networking of military systems produces a powerful advantage. As the two Gulf Wars showed, traditional assessments of balances of weapons platforms such as tanks or planes become irrelevant unless they include the ability to integrate information with those weapons. That was the mistake Saddam Hussein made (as well as those in Congress in 1990 who predicted massive American casualties). Many of the relevant technologies are available in commercial markets, and weaker states can be expected to purchase many of them. The key, however, will not be possession of fancy hardware or advanced systems, but the ability to integrate a system of systems, or to dominate crucial nodes of the modern military information infrastructure. While anyone can purchase a GPS receiver, for example, the U.S. military, in time of emergency, has the ability to alter the signals that make them work, because the satellites that broadcast them are American. At a moment's notice, in other words, the United States could throw into disarray any hostile force that uses GPS for navigation. Since even a small edge makes a huge difference in information warfare, the United States' dramatic head start is likely to remain an important source of power, though also a source of vulnerability. At the same time, China and Europe are moving to create their own systems so as not to be vulnerable to American power. Realists see a change in style, but not a basic transformation of world politics.

Liberals agree that states will remain the basic units of world politics, but they argue that the information revolution will increase the role of democratic states, and thus the eventual prospects of a Kantian democratic peace. As far as countries are concerned, most information shapers are democracies. This is not accidental. Their societies are familiar with the free exchange of information, and their institutions of governance are not threatened by it. They can shape information because they can also take it. Authoritarian states, typically among the laggards, have considerably more trouble. Governments such as China's can attempt to control their citizens' access to the Internet by controlling Internet service and content providers, and by monitoring and censoring users. It is possible, but costly, to route around such restrictions, and control does not have to be complete to be effective for political purposes. Singapore, a state that combines political control with economic liberalism, has thus far combined its political controls with an increasing role for the Internet. But as societies such as Singapore reach levels of development in which a broader range of knowledge workers want fewer restrictions on access to the Internet, Singapore runs the risk of losing its creative knowledge workers, its scarcest resource for competing in the information economy. Thus Singapore is wrestling with the dilemma of reshaping its educational system to encourage the individual creativity that the information economy will demand, while at the same time relaxing controls over the flow of information. Closed systems become more costly, as Egypt discovered when it briefly disconnected from the Internet during the demonstrations of February 2011.

Another reason closed systems become more costly is that it is risky for foreigners to invest funds in an authoritarian country where the key decisions are made in an opaque fashion. Liberals point out that transparency is becoming a key asset for countries seeking investments. The ability to keep information from leaving, which once seemed so valuable to authoritarian states, undermines the credibility and transparency necessary to attract investment on globally competitive terms. This point was illustrated by the 1997 Asian financial crisis. Governments that are not transparent are not credible, because the information they offer is seen as biased and selective. Moreover, as economic development progresses and middle-class societies develop, repressive measures become more expensive not only at home, but also in terms of international reputation. Both Taiwan and South Korea discovered in the late 1980s that repressing rising demands for democracy and free expression would be expensive in terms of their reputation and soft power. By beginning to democratize, then, they strengthened their capacity to cope with economic crisis. One of the great questions for China will be how it manages increased demands for political participation as it grows wealthier.

Whatever the future effects of interactivity and virtual communities, one political effect of increased flows of free information through multiple channels is already clear: States have lost much of their control over information about their own societies. States that seek to develop need foreign capital and the technology and organization that go with it. Geographical communities still matter most, but governments that want to see rapid development will have to give up some of the barriers to information flows that protected officials from outside scrutiny. No longer will governments that want high levels of development be able to afford the comfort of keeping their financial and political situations inside a national black box, as North Korea and Myanmar do. As openness and democracy spread, the liberals see a change in the nature of the relations among states.

Constructivists provide a more radical perspective on whether the information revolution is transforming world politics. Some even see the beginnings of the end of the Westphalian state system. Peter Drucker and Heidi and Alvin Toffler argue that the information revolution is bringing an end to the hierarchical bureaucratic organizations that typified the age of the industrial revolution.[6] In civil societies, as decentralized organizations and virtual communities develop on the Internet, they cut across territorial jurisdictions and develop their own patterns of governance.

If these prophets are right, the result would be a new cyberfeudalism, with overlapping communities and jurisdictions laying claim to multiple layers of citizens' identities and loyalties. In short, these transformations suggest the reversal of the modern centralized state that has dominated world politics for more than 350 years. Instead of "international" politics, we may have a broader "world politics." A medieval European might have owed equal loyalty to a local lord, a duke, a king, and the pope. A future European might owe loyalty to Brittany, Paris, Brussels, as well as to several cybercommunities concerned with religion, work, and various interests.

While the international system is still best understood as a system of sovereign states, constructivists argue that we can begin to discern a pattern of cross-cutting communities and governance that resembles the situation before the Peace of Westphalia in 1648. Transnational contacts across political borders were typical in the feudal era, but they were gradually constrained by the rise of centralized states. Now the world is changing. Three decades ago, transnational contacts were already growing, but they involved relatively small numbers of elites involved in multinational corporations, scientific groups, and academic institutions. Now the Internet offers a low-cost means of transnational communication that is open to millions of people.

Sovereignty and Control

The issue of sovereignty is hotly contested in world politics today. Many political leaders resist anything that seems to diminish national autonomy. They worry about the political role of the United Nations in limiting the use of force, the economic decisions handed down by the World Trade Organization, and efforts to develop environmental institutions and treaties. In their eyes, the notion of an international community of opinion is illusory.

But the debate over the fate of the sovereign state has been poorly framed. As the constructivist political scientist John Ruggie put it, "There is an extraordinarily impoverished mind-set at work here, one that is able to visualize long-term challenges to the system of states only in terms of entities that are institutionally substitutable for the state."[7] A better historical analogy is the development of markets and town life in the early feudal period. Medieval trade fairs were not substitutes for the institutions of feudal authority. They did not tear down the castle walls or remove the local lord. But they did bring new wealth, new coalitions, and new attitudes summarized by the maxim, "Town air brings freedom."

Medieval merchants developed the *Lex Mercatoria* ("Merchant Law") that governed their relations largely as a private set of rules for conducting business. Similarly, today, everyone from hackers to large corporations is developing the code and norms of the Internet partly outside the control of formal political institutions. The development of transnational corporate intranets behind firewalls and encryption "represent(s) private appropriations of a public space."[8] These private systems, such as corporate intranets or worldwide newsgroups devoted to specific issues such as the environment, do not frontally challenge the governments of sovereign states; they simply add a layer of relations that sovereign states do not effectively control. People will participate in transnational Internet communities without ceasing to be loyal citizens, but their perspectives will be different from those of typical loyal citizens before the Internet.

Even in the age of the Internet, the roles of political institutions are likely to change gradually. After the rise of the territorial state, other successors to medieval rule such as the Italian city-states and the Hanseatic League in Northern Europe persisted as viable alternatives, able to tax and fight for nearly two centuries. The real issue today is not the continued existence of the sovereign state, but how its centrality and functions are being altered. "The reach of the state has increased in some areas but contracted in others. Rulers have recognized that their effective control can be enhanced by walking away from some issues they cannot resolve."[9] All countries, including the largest, are facing a growing list of problems that are difficult to control within sovereign boundaries—financial flows, drug trade, climate change, HIV/AIDS, refugees, terrorism, and cultural intrusions—to name a few. Complicating the task of national governance is not the same as undermining sovereignty. Governments adapt. However, in the process of adaptation they change the meaning of sovereign jurisdiction, control, and the role of private actors.

Take, for example, the problems of controlling U.S. borders. Airports, seaports, and land border crossings all pose their own particular challenges. In 2010—at land crossings alone—234 million people, 93 million cars, 10 million trucks, 335,000 buses, and 34,000 trains entered the United States. By some estimates, half a million undocumented migrants simply walk or ride across the border from Mexico or Canada. As 9/11 illustrated, terrorists can easily slip across borders, and it is easier to bring in a few pounds of a deadly biological or chemical agent than to smuggle in the tons of illegal heroin and cocaine that arrive annually. The best way for the Department of Homeland Security to cope with such flows is to expand intelligence sharing with and cooperation inside the jurisdiction of other states and to rely on private corporations to develop transparent systems for tracking international commercial flows so enforcement officials can conduct "virtual" audits of inbound shipments before they arrive. Today, customs officers are working throughout Latin America to help businesses implement security programs that reduce the risk of being exploited by drug smugglers, and cooperative international mechanisms are being developed for policing trade flows. The sovereign state adapts, but in doing so it transforms the meaning and exclusivity of governmental jurisdiction. Legal borders do not change, but they blur in practice.

National security—the absence of threat to major values—is another example. Damage done by climate change or imported viruses can be larger in terms of money or lives lost than the effects of some wars. But even if one restricts the definition of national security more narrowly to organized violence, the nature of military security is changing. As the U.S. Commission on National Security in the Twenty-First Century pointed out, the country has not been invaded by foreign armies since 1814, and the military is designed to project force and fight wars far from our shores. But the U.S. military was not well equipped to protect us against an attack on the homeland by terrorists using civilian aircraft as weapons. In absolute numbers, the United States suffered more casualties from the transnational terrorist attacks on 9/11 than from the Japanese government's attack on Pearl Harbor in 1941 (though, in proportion to the total population of the United States, Pearl Harbor was almost twice as deadly). Today, attackers may be governments, groups, individuals, or some combination. The al Qaeda network that attacked the United States on 9/11 involved individuals and groups from many countries and is alleged to have had cells in as many as fifty (including the United States). But some aggressors may be anonymous and may not even come near the targeted country. Cyberattacks can pose a real transnational threat to security. Hence, nuclear deterrence, border patrols, and stationing troops overseas to shape regional power balances will continue to matter in the information age, but they will not be sufficient to ensure national security.

Competing interpretations of sovereignty arise even in the domain of law. Article 2.7 says nothing shall authorize the United Nations to intervene in matters within domestic jurisdiction. There has been a clear, if not monotonic trend toward understanding nonintervention as a privilege states must earn through good behavior, rather than a right to which they are absolutely entitled. Thus, evolving global norms of antiracism and repugnance at the South African practice of apartheid led a large majority at the United Nations to abridge the principle of nonintervention. In 2011, the UN Security Council authorized military intervention in the Libyan civil war on the basis of the doctrine of the Responsibility to Protect, even though it had failed to authorize NATO's intervention in Kosovo in 1999 under what were, in fact, very similar circumstances from the very beginning the Charter of the United Nations enshrined principles of human rights as well as provisions that protect the sovereignty of states, but the former are gaining at the expense of the latter. And new actors are projecting themselves into these debates. In 1998, General Augusto Pinochet was detained in Britain in response to a Spanish magistrate's request for extradition based on human rights violations and crimes committed while he was president of Chile. Britain ultimately denied the request, but on narrow legal grounds, not by invoking British or Chilean sovereignty.

Information technology, particularly the Internet, has eased the tasks of coordination and strengthened the hands of human rights activists. But political leaders, particularly in formerly colonized countries, cling to the protections legal sovereignty provides against outside interventions. Tensions between the principle of state sovereignty and emerging human rights norms are likely to coexist for many years to come.

For many people, the state provides an important source of political identity. As we have seen, people are capable of multiple cross-cutting identities—family, village, ethnic, religious, national, cosmopolitan—and which one predominates often depends on the context. In many preindustrial countries, subnational identities at the tribe or clan level prevail. In some postindustrial countries, including the United States and the countries of Europe, cosmopolitan identities such as "global citizen" or "custodian of planet Earth" are beginning to emerge. It is still too early to understand the full effects of the Internet, but the shaping of identities can move in contradictory directions at the same time—up to Brussels, down to Brittany, or fixed on Paris—as circumstances dictate.

A fascinating use of the Internet to wield soft power can be found in the politics of diaspora communities. In the words of communications expert David Bollier, "The Internet has been a godsend to such populations, because it enables large numbers of geographically isolated people with a shared history to organize into large virtual communities."[10] The Internet enables them to present attractive alternative ideas to those back home. Internet connections between foreign nationals and local citizens helped spark protests in Beijing against anti-Chinese riots taking place in Indonesia in 1998. The frustration of ethnic Chinese living in Indonesia was transferred to Beijing with remarkable speed. Similarly, in Zimbabwe in 2008, and in Iran in 2009, the Internet was crucial in spreading news about government manipulation during disputed elections. At the same, although cell phones and the Internet helped bring repression and violation of human rights to the world's attention, they did not alone lead to a change of government. Nor did the new technologies end the repression in 2007 when the government of Burma (Myanmar) cracked down on Buddhist monks and other protesters.

The Internet has also allowed protests to be quickly mobilized by freewheeling amorphous groups, rather than hierarchical organizations. In the Vietnam era, planning a protest required weeks and months of pamphlets, posters, and phone calls, and it took four years before the size of the first rallies of 25,000 reached half a million in 1969. In contrast, 800,000 people turned out in the United States and 1.5 million in Europe on one weekend in February 2003 to protest the looming war in Iraq.[11] Protests do not represent the "international community," but they do often affect the attitudes of editorial writers, parliamentarians, and other influential people in important countries whose views are summarized by that vague term.[12] The continual contest for legitimacy illustrates the importance of soft power.

The result may be greater volatility rather than consistent movement in any one direction. As Pippa Norris puts it, "The many-to-many and one-to-many characteristics of the Internet . . . seem highly conducive to the irreverent egalitarian, and libertarian character of the cyber-culture."[13] One effect is "flash movements"—sudden surges of protest—triggered by particular issues or events, such as antiglobalization protests, or the sudden rise of the anti–fuel tax coalition that captured European politics in the autumn of 2000, or the protests around the world during the 2003 Iraq War.[14] Politics becomes more theatrical and aimed at global audiences. In the mid-1990s, the Zapatista rebels in Mexico's Chiapas province relied less on bullets than on transnational publicity, much of it coordinated on the Internet, to pressure the Mexican government for reforms. In 2004, activists used cell phones to organize peaceful revolutions in the former Soviet states of Georgia and Ukraine.

Perhaps the most spectacular examples of the power of the Internet to mobilize efforts for political change may be found in the recent *Arab Spring* uprisings. Unplanned and unforeseen by anyone anywhere, a tidal wave of protest and discontent swept North Africa and the Middle East in 2011, triggered by a lone desperate act of a young street vendor in Tunisia named Mohamed Bouazizi on December 17, 2010. Frustrated and humiliated by corrupt officials repeatedly harassing him and ultimately confiscating his wares, Bouazizi set himself on fire in protest. Within weeks, mounting public outrage at his mistreatment and pent-up anger at systemic malfeasance and corruption ended the twenty-three-year rule of President Zine El Abidine Ben Ali and inspired similar mass uprisings in Egypt, Yemen, Syria, Bahrain, and Libya. Egypt's longtime strongman Hosni Mubarak fell shortly thereafter, on February 11, 2011. Other besieged autocrats tried to hold on to power, either by making small concessions or cracking down with violence (and sometimes both). While governments did not topple everywhere, politics nowhere would ever be quite the same.

In what sense was the Arab Spring a demonstration of the transformative political power of the Internet? Along with satellite television stations such as al Jazeera, Internet connectivity made it easy for North African and Middle Eastern youths and young adults to see that life prospects were dramatically better for others in their age brackets with similar levels of education elsewhere—for example, in Europe and North America. By enabling them to interact with and to see how much better were the material lives and opportunities of emigrants in their diaspora communities, or even just their Facebook friends, Internet penetration in the Arab world made it harder and harder for kleptocratic regimes to hide their own sins and underperformance as leaders. In addition, once protests began to break out, social media made it easy to mobilize and coordinate them.

We can use the very same concepts of deep, intermediate, and precipitating causes to explain the Arab Spring that we used to explain the outbreak of

World War I in Chapter From Westphalia to World War I. Among the deep causes were demographic considerations (the enormous proportion of young people in North Africa and the Middle East), economic considerations (massive underemployment, growing inequality, and perceptions of relative deprivation), and political causes (a sense of powerlessness and loss of identification with national leaders, resulting in declining levels of legitimacy). A single Tunisian street vendor provided the precipitating cause; but the information revolution provided a set of crucial intermediate causes. Communications technology and social media enabled an explosion of economic and political disaffection that simply would not have been possible twenty or thirty years earlier.

All of this seems clear enough in retrospect. But it is interesting and important to note that no one saw it coming. Most likely this is simply because our understanding of political dynamics in areas such as North Africa and the Middle East had simply not yet absorbed the implications of the new information revolution. It often takes a shocking failure of foresight to make one notice that one's eyeglass prescription is out of date.

Although the Arab Spring made clear that the information revolution has fundamentally changed regional political dynamics, there is little evidence yet that it has affected political identities. In every country experiencing upheaval, the dominant political cleavages during and after were the same as the dominant political cleavages before: for example, secular/religious in Egypt; tribal in Libya; Sunni/Shi'a in Bahrain. But connectivity can soften the hard edges of these distinctions, as people more easily identify with member of different kinds of groups, both at home and abroad. Political scientist James Rosenau has tried to capture this notion by inventing a new word, *fragmegration,* to express the idea that both integration toward larger identities and fragmentation into smaller communities can occur at the same time. But one need not alter the English language to realize that apparently contradictory movements can occur simultaneously. They do not spell the end of the sovereign state, but they do make its politics more volatile and less self-contained within national shells.

Follow Up

- Ronald J. Deibert, *Parchment, Printing, and Hypermedia: Communication in World Order Transformation* (New York: Columbia University Press, 1997).
- Elizabeth C. Hanson, *The Information Revolution and World Politics* (Lanham, MD: Rowman & Littlefield, 2008).

TRANSNATIONAL ACTORS

As we have seen, a characteristic of the global information age is the increased role of *transnational actors*—nonstate entities acting across international borders. Traditional international politics is discussed in terms of states. We use shorthand expressions such as "Germany wanted Alsace" or "France feared Britain." That shorthand is a useful simplification, especially in the classical period of international politics. In the eighteenth century, the monarch spoke for the state. If Frederick the Great wanted something for Prussia, Frederick was Prussia. In the nineteenth century, a broader elite class controlled foreign policy decisions, but even on the eve of World War I, European diplomacy was a relatively narrowly held, cabinet-level affair. In addition, in the classical period of international politics, the agenda was more limited. Military security issues dominated, and they were handled primarily by the foreign office or its equivalent.

Qualitatively, transnational actors have played a role for centuries, but the quantitative shift in the last half of the twentieth century marks a significant change in the international system. In a world of global interdependence, the agenda of international politics is broader, and everyone seems to want to get into the act. In the United States, for example, almost every domestic agency has some international role. The Department of Agriculture is interested in international food issues; the Environmental Protection Agency is interested in acid rain and global warming; the Coast Guard is interested in ocean dumping; the Department of Commerce is interested in trade; the Treasury Department is interested in exchange rates. The State Department does not control all these issues. Every bureau of the U.S. government has its own little foreign ministry. In fact, if we look at the representation of the United States abroad, only a minority of the Americans in most embassies are from the State Department.

In complex interdependence, societies interact at many points. There is too much traffic for one intersection or for one cop at one intersection. These interactions across state borders outside the central control of the foreign policy organs are called *transnational relations*. They include but are not limited to migration of populations, the rapid transfer of capital from one country to another that occurs daily in the world stock and money markets, illicit trafficking in weapons and drugs, and certain forms of terrorism. Governments can try to control these activities, and in the case of terrorism or smuggling they need to, but control often comes at a very high price. For example, the Soviet Union closely controlled transnational relations, and the Soviet economy suffered gravely for it. In circumstances with high degrees of interdependence and a large number of transnational actors, we can be led astray by the shorthand that was so useful in the classical period. We say things like "Japan agreed to import more" or "America opposed broad claims to the continental shelf under the ocean," but looking more carefully, we notice that Japanese firms acted transnationally to export more or that some U.S. citizens lobbied internationally to promote a broad definition of the continental shelf at the same time that the U.S. Navy sought the opposite.

This complexity of interests has always existed, but it is greater in economic and social issues than in the traditional military security issues. Security issues are often more collectively shared. The survival of a people as a whole is obviously a collective good. Social and economic issues are often less broadly shared; there are more differences of interest. Thus, with the rise of economic interdependence and the rise of economic issues on the agenda of international politics, we find that our traditional shorthand less adequately describes the political process.

Consumer countries wanted low prices and the producer countries wanted high prices in 1973. But the politics was a lot more complex than that. Producing interests inside the consumer countries wanted high oil prices. Small Texas oil producers were not at all unhappy that OPEC raised oil prices, for they had the same economic interests as the Arabs, not the same as the consumers freezing in New England. Producers of nuclear energy were not unhappy to see oil prices rise because that might help nuclear energy become a more competitive energy source. Those affected by the declining coal industry in Europe and unemployed coal miners were not unhappy about the rise of oil prices either. Neither were ecologists who believed higher prices would curtail consumption and pollution. So inside the consumer countries there were enormous differences in the interests over oil prices. In a situation of interdependence, politics looks different if we lift the veil of national interest and national security. One of the reasons why consumer countries did not use more extreme measures such as force during the oil crisis was that the sensitivity interdependence that led to high energy prices was regarded as good by important political actors inside the consumer countries. There was a de facto transnational coalition that was not unhappy with higher oil prices.

Of course, the existence of contradictory interests inside states is not new. In nineteenth-century America, politics was marked by differences over tariffs between Southern farmers and Northern industrialists. When President George W. Bush raised tariffs on steel in 2002, he pleased companies and unions that produce steel, but hurt those companies, such as car manufacturers, who use it. Domestic politics has always been important to foreign policy, but with the expansion of participation in domestic politics it becomes more so. Moreover, as some of those domestic interests develop the capability to communicate and interact directly with other interests in other countries, they develop a different type of world politics.

Two forms of world politics are illustrated by Figure 1. The traditional form of international politics is the outside shell in the left-hand diagram of the figure. Traditional international politics follows the indicated lines. If people in Society 1 want to put pressure on Government 2, they ask Government 1 (through regular domestic politics, the vertical line) to talk to Government 2 (through regular intergovernmental politics, the horizontal line). But

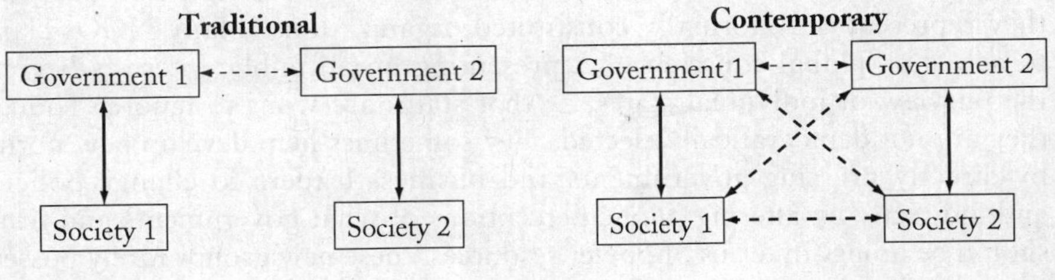

FIGURE 1

Traditional versus Transnational World Politics

in transnational relations, people in Society 1 put pressure on Government 2 directly, or people in Society 1 may put pressure on people in Society 2 directly. The transnational links are the diagonal lines and the lower horizontal line on the right, which represents direct contacts across borders between individuals and/or NGOs. (Not shown in the diagram are the increasingly diverse and important direct connections between subunits of different governments, called *transgovernmental relations*. Sometimes departments or ministries have warmer ties with their foreign counterparts than either of them has with their own political leaders, a phenomenon illustrated, for example, in the Cuban missile crisis, where the U.S. and Canadian militaries cooperated seamlessly despite tensions between the White House and the Pentagon on the one hand, and between the Canadian Armed Forces and 24 Sussex Drive on the other.)[15]

When we talk about the politics of interdependence, we must not assume that everything is captured by the traditional model of government-to-government relations. One of the distinguishing characteristics of complex interdependence is the significance of other actors in addition to the states. The traditional shorthand is not wrong; it remains the best first approximation even for the politics of interdependence. States usually are the major actors. But "global civil society" actors are increasingly important. As constructivists remind us, when you have said that states are the major actors, you have not said everything that is important to know about the politics and conflicts of interdependence.

Nongovernmental Organizations (NGOs)

Private organizations also increasingly cross national boundaries (Figure 2). Transnational religious organizations opposed to slavery date back to 1775, and the nineteenth century saw the founding of the Socialist International, the Red Cross, peace movements, women's suffrage organizations, and the International Law Association, among others. Before World War I, there were 176 international *nongovernmental organizations (NGOs)*. In 1956, they numbered nearly 1,000; in 1970 nearly 2,000. More recently, there has been an explosion in the number of NGOs that operate across borders, increasing from 6,000 to approximately 40,000 during the 1990s alone. (There is now even a meta-NGO—an NGO NGO, in other words!—called WANGO, the World Association of NGOs.) The numbers do not tell the full story, because they represent only formally constituted organizations. Many NGOs claim to act as a "global conscience" representing broad public interests beyond the purview of individual states, or that states are wont to ignore. Though they are not democratically elected, they sometimes help develop new norms by directly pressing governments and business leaders to change policies and indirectly by altering public perceptions of what governments and firms should be doing. In terms of power resources, these new groups rarely possess much hard power, but the information revolution has greatly enhanced their soft power.

Human Rights Watch

Website: http://www.hrw.org
Founded: 1978
Headquarters: New York
Budget: $48 million USD (total support and revenue)

- Largest U.S.-based human rights organization
- Shames human rights offenders by documenting human rights abuses in more than 80 countries, generating media attention regarding abuses and lobbying governments and institutions to pressure offending governments diplomatically
- Was part of a coalition for groups and individuals that won the Nobel Peace Prize in 1997 for work related to the Campaign to Ban Landmines

International Crisis Group

Website: http://www.crisisgroup.org
Founded: 1995
Headquarters: Brussels
Budget: $17 million USD

- Analyzes countries "at risk of outbreak, escalation or recurrence of violent conflict" and offers policy recommendations, targeted to policy makers, regarding ways to reduce tensions and resolve specific conflicts
- Board includes influential figures from politics, diplomacy, business, and media who help shape the group's operations and lobby for implementation of its policy recommendations

Amnesty International

Website: http://www.amnesty.org
Founded: 1961
Headquarters: London
Budget: £45 million GBP (approx. $73 million USD)

- Mobilizes a network of more than 3 million members, supporters, and activists in more than 150 countries to help prevent and end "grave abuses of the rights to physical and mental integrity, freedom of conscience and expression, and freedom from discrimination" and promote human rights

Doctors Without Borders (Médecins Sans Frontières)

Website: http://www.msf.org
Founded: 1971
Headquarters: Geneva
Budget: €200 million EUR (approx. $287 million USD)

- International humanitarian aid organization assisting more than 70 countries
- Assistance provided to "populations in distress, to victims of natural or man-made disasters and to victims of armed conflict, without discrimination and irrespective of race, religion, creed or political affiliation"

Bill and Melinda Gates Foundation

Website: http://www.gatesfoundation.org
Founded: 2000
Headquarters: Seattle
Staff: 957
Assets: $36.3 billion USD (endowment)

(continued)

FIGURE 2

Overview of Select Nongovernmental Organizations (NGOs)

- Founded by Microsoft founder Bill Gates and his wife, Melinda
- Works to "promote greater equity in four areas: global health, education, public libraries, and support for at-risk families"

Oxfam International

Website: http://www.oxfam.org
Founded: 1942
Headquarters: Oxford, UK
Budget: $894.7 million USD (program expenditure)

- A confederation of "13 organizations working together to find lasting solutions to poverty and injustice."

International Committee of the Red Cross (ICRC)

Website: http://www.icrc.org
Founded: 1863
Headquarters: Geneva
Budget: 1.1 billion CHF (approx. $1.4 billion USD)

- Tasked by the Geneva Convention with responsibility for "visiting prisoners, organizing relief operations, re-uniting separated families and similar humanitarian activities *during armed conflicts*"
- An "impartial, neutral and independent organization whose exclusively humanitarian mission is to protect the lives and dignity of victims of war and internal violence and to provide them with assistance"

Greenpeace

Website: http://www.greenpeace.org
Founded: 1971
Headquarters: Amsterdam
Budget: €226 million EUR (approx. $324 million USD)

- Mobilizes 2.8 million supporters in more than 40 countries to support efforts against climate change, degradation of the oceans, whaling, and genetic engineering
- Supports efforts to preserve ancient forests, eliminate toxic chemicals, and encourage sustainable trade

FIGURE 2 (*continued*)

Governments now have to share the stage with actors who can use information to enhance their soft power and press governments directly or indirectly by mobilizing their publics. Given the power of credible editors and cue givers who can cut through the avalanche of available information in the Internet age, a rough way to gauge the increasing importance of transnational organizations is to look at the number of mentions these organizations receive in mainstream media publications. By this measure, the biggest NGOs have become established players in the battle for the attention of influential editors. For example, after Human Rights Watch released its "2003 World Report," which included strong criticism of the U.S. government for its conduct in the war on terrorism, articles appeared in 288 newspapers and magazines over the next ten days mentioning the organization.[16]

News coverage has reflected the growth of this general sector. The term "nongovernmental organization" or "NGO" appeared 70 times in English-language newspapers in July 1991, 576 times in July 2001, and 4,371 times in

July 2011—an increase of 62 times in 20 years. In addition to Human Rights Watch, other NGOs, such as Amnesty International, the International Red Cross, Greenpeace, Doctors Without Borders (*Médecins Sans Frontières*, or MSF), and Transparency International have undergone exponential growth in terms of mainstream media mentions. As the information revolution has lowered the costs of global communication, the barriers to entry into world politics have been lowered.

Not only is there a great increase in the number of transnational and governmental contacts, but there has also been a change in type. Earlier transnational flows were heavily controlled by large bureaucratic organizations such as multinational corporations or the Catholic Church that could profit from economies of scale. Such organizations remain important, but the lower costs of communication in the Internet era have opened the field to loosely structured network organizations with a small headquarters staff, and even to individuals. These nongovernmental organizations and networks are particularly effective in penetrating states without regard to borders. Because they often involve citizens who are well placed in the domestic politics of several countries, they are able to focus the attention of the media and governments on their preferred issues. The treaty banning landmines, as mentioned earlier, was the result of an interesting mixed coalition of Internet-based organizations working with middle-power governments such as Canada and some individual politicians and celebrities such as the late Diana, princess of Wales. On global poverty issues, rock stars, NGOs, and political leaders worked together to press for debt relief for heavily indebted poor countries.

Environmental issues are another example. NGOs have played an important role at every major climate change conference since Kyoto in 1997, either acting as channels of communication between official delegations, as agenda setters, or as mobilizers of public pressure. For example, former U.S. vice president Al Gore's Live Earth coalition organized concerts over a period of 24 hours in eight major cities across the world in 2007. This event brought together a global audience to try to persuade governments to take action against climate change.

Geographical communities and sovereign states will continue to play the main role in world politics for a long time to come, but they will be less self-contained and more porous. They will have to share the stage with actors who can use information to enhance their soft power and press governments directly or indirectly by mobilizing their publics. Governments that want to see rapid development will find that they have to give up some of the barriers to information flow that historically protected officials from outside scrutiny. No longer will governments that want high levels of development be able to afford the comfort of keeping their financial and political situations inside a black box, as Burma (Myanmar) and North Korea have done. That form of sovereignty proves too expensive. Even large countries with hard power, such as the United States, find themselves sharing the stage with new actors and having more trouble controlling their borders. Cyberspace will not replace geographical space and will not abolish state sovereignty, but like the town markets in feudal times, it will coexist and greatly complicate what it means to be a sovereign state or a powerful country.

The Information Revolution and Complex Interdependence

The information revolution has not equalized power among states. Thus far it has had the opposite effect, and realists might feel vindicated. But what about reducing the role of governments and the power of all states? Here the changes are more along the lines predicted by liberals and constructivists. Complex interdependence is certainly much greater in the dimension of multiple channels of contact between societies.

The explosion of information has produced a "paradox of plenty."[17] Plenty of information leads to scarcity of attention. When people are overwhelmed with the volume of information confronting them, they have difficulty discerning what to focus on. Attention rather than information becomes the scarce resource, and those who can distinguish valuable information from background clutter gain power. Editors and cue givers are in increasingly high demand, and this is a source of power for those who can tell us where to focus our attention. Brand names and the ability to bestow an international "Good Housekeeping" seal of approval will become increasingly more important.

In addition, publics have become more wary and sensitized about propaganda. Propaganda as a form of free information is not new. Hitler and Stalin used it effectively in the 1930s. Slobodan Milošević's control of television was crucial to his power in Serbia in the 1990s. Credibility is the crucial resource, and an important source of soft power. Reputation becomes even more important than in the past, and political struggles occur over the creation and destruction of credibility. Governments compete for credibility not only with other governments, but with a broad range of alternatives including news media, corporations, nongovernmental organizations, intergovernmental organizations, and networks of scientific communities.

Politics has become a contest of competitive credibility. Narratives become more important. The world of traditional power politics is typically about whose military or economy wins. But in an information age, it is increasingly important whose story wins. Governments compete with each other and with other organizations to enhance their own credibility and weaken that of their opponents.

Witness the struggle between Serbia and NATO to frame the interpretation of events in Kosovo in 1999 and the events in Serbia a year later. Prior to the demonstrations that led to the overthrow of Milošević in October 2000, 45 percent of Serb adults were tuned to Radio Free Europe and the Voice of America. In contrast, only 31 percent listened to the state-controlled radio station, Radio Belgrade.[18] Moreover, the domestic alternative radio station, B92, provided access to Western news, and when the government tried to shut it down, it continued to provide such news on the Internet. In the 2006 war between Israel and the nonstate actor Hezbollah, Israel had military superiority in the air, but television pictures of children killed by Israeli air strikes gave the propaganda victory to Hezbollah.

Information that appears to be purely propaganda may not only be scorned, but it may also turn out to be counterproductive if it undermines a country's reputation for credibility. In 2003, exaggerated claims about Saddam Hussein's WMD and ties to al Qaeda may have helped mobilize domestic support for the Iraq War, but polls showed that the subsequent disclosure of the exaggeration dealt a costly blow to British and American credibility. Under the new conditions more than ever, a soft sell may prove more effective than a hard sell.

The Iraq example illustrates that power does not necessarily flow to those who can withhold information. Under some circumstances, private information can cripple the credibility of those who have it. As the Nobel Prize winner George Ackerloff has pointed out, sellers of used cars have more knowledge about their defects than potential buyers. Moreover, owners of bad cars are more likely to sell than owners of good ones. These facts lead potential buyers to discount the price they are willing to pay in order to adjust for unknown defects. Hence the result of the superior information of sellers is not to improve the average price they receive, but instead to make them unable to sell good used cars for their real value. Unlike asymmetrical interdependence in trade, in which power goes to those who can afford to hold back or break trade ties, information power flows to those who can edit and credibly validate information to sort out what is both correct and important.

One implication of the abundance of free information sources, and the role of credibility, is that soft power is likely to become less a function simply of material resources than in the past. When the ability to produce and disseminate information is the scarce resource, limiting factors include the control of printing presses, radio stations, and newsprint. Hard power—for instance, using force to take over the radio station—can generate soft power. In the case of worldwide television, wealth can also lead to soft power. For instance, CNN was based in Atlanta rather than Amman or Cairo because of America's leading position in the industry and in technology. When Iraq invaded Kuwait in 1990, the fact that CNN was basically an American

THE NEW GLOBAL ACTORS

It is almost as if the world has arrived at a sort of neomedievalism in which the institutions and sources of authority are multifarious. Just as the leaders of the Knights Templar or the Franciscan order outranked all but the most powerful of princes, so too the secretary general of Amnesty International and the chief executive officer of Royal Dutch Shell cast far longer shadows on the international stage than do leaders of Moldova, Namibia, or Nauru. The state may not be quite ready to wither away, but it's not what it used to be.

—*Peter J. Spiro*[19]

company helped frame the issue worldwide as aggression (analogous to Hitler's actions in the 1930s), rather than as a justified attempt to reverse colonial humiliation (analogous to India's widely accepted "liberation" of the Portuguese colony of Goa in the 1960s). But by 2003, the rise of cable networks in the region, such as al Jazeera and al Arabiya, undercut the American monopoly and provided a local framing of the issues involved in the Iraq War. In an information age, the occupation of Iraq and its coverage were very costly for American soft power.

The close connection between hard and soft power is likely to be somewhat weakened under conditions of complex interdependence in an information age. The power of broadcasting persists, but it will be increasingly supplemented by the Internet with its multiple channels of communication, controlled by multiple actors who cannot use force to control one another. Conflicts will be affected not only by which actors own television networks, radio stations, and websites, but also by who pays attention to which fountains of information and misinformation.

Broadcasting is a type of information dissemination that has long had an impact on public opinion. By focusing on some conflicts and human rights problems, broadcasters have pressed politicians to respond to some foreign conflicts rather than others—for example, Somalia rather than southern Sudan in the 1990s. Not surprisingly, governments have sought to influence, manipulate, or control television and radio stations and have been able to do so with considerable success, since a relatively small number of physically located broadcasting sites were used to reach many people with the same message. However, the shift from broadcasting to "narrowcasting" has major political implications. Cable and the Internet enable senders to segment and target audiences. Even more important for politics is the interactive role of the Internet; it not only focuses attention, but also facilitates coordination of action across borders. YouTube videos can affect how political issues are perceived and framed. Interactivity at low cost allows for the development of new virtual communities: people who imagine themselves as part of a single group regardless of how far apart they are physically from one another. Transnational communications have made borders more porous.

"MAN BITES DOG"

Defense Secretary Robert M. Gates called Monday for the United States government to commit more money and effort to "soft power" tools, including diplomacy, economic assistance, and communications, because the military alone cannot defend America's interests around the world. . . . Mr. Gates joked that having a sitting secretary of defense travel halfway across the country to make a pitch to increase the budget of other agencies might fit into the category of "man bites dog."

—*The New York Times, November 27, 2007*[20]

Transnational Terrorism and the "War on Terror"

Not all transnational actors are benign. Drug cartels, human smuggling rings, and organized criminal syndicates are all cases in point. For groups such as these, the information revolution has opened up new opportunities for action over longer distances than ever before. Yet terrorist groups have captured the public's imagination as particularly dangerous transnational actors. When in the wake of 9/11 President George W. Bush proclaimed a "War on Terror" in his speech to a joint session of Congress (on September 20, 2001), he signaled a fundamental change in U.S. foreign policy that would have far-reaching implications for the world as a whole.[21]

The terrorist attacks of 9/11 took the lives of 2,974 innocent citizens from more than 90 countries, not counting the 19 hijackers. Horrific video of the second plane to hit the World Trade Center circulated the globe almost instantly, generating a massive outpouring of shock, anger, grief, and sympathy for the United States almost everywhere in the world. One thing that made the attacks so horrifying was the fact that they were so low-tech. Armed only with box cutters available at any hardware store, the hijacker terrorists managed to avoid detection and turn civilian airliners into weapons of mass destruction. The ease with which they did so made it seem likely to be repeated.

Kenneth Waltz's first image (the individual level of analysis) helps us understand why 9/11 had such a profound effect on the American psyche, and hence on American policy. As Harvard psychologist Daniel Gilbert explains, human beings are hard-wired to be particularly sensitive to threats that are intended by others, that trigger moral outrage, that seem clear and present, and that catch us by surprise. Terrorism is like theater, and terrorists rely on the dramatic impact of their actions to magnify the effects. As Gilbert notes, global warming will almost certainly kill many times as many people as al Qaeda and will probably also cause much more damage to U.S. property; but it will do so anonymously, unintentionally, and gradually.[22] Thus we have a "War on Terror," but not a "War on Climate Change."

How serious a threat to world order is transnational terrorism? The answer depends upon the angle one takes and the time scale one considers. If one is primarily concerned with transnational terrorism as a cause of premature death, it is not, at present, a serious global problem. Globally, transnational terrorist attacks peaked in 1987. Not counting 9/11 and insurgent attacks against foreign targets in Afghanistan and Iraq—made possible precisely because the War on Terror placed foreigners in vulnerable positions there—over the past fifteen years transnational terrorism has killed fewer than 5,000 people per year globally. Terrorist attacks take place at a rate far less than once per day. As a cause of premature death transnational terrorism is well down the list, behind such things as unsafe drinking water, infectious disease, traffic accidents, tobacco, allergic reactions, and obesity.

Of the total amount of transnational terrorism in the world, al Qaeda is responsible for relatively little. Drug cartels and paramilitaries in Latin

America account for dramatically more. Al Qaeda's operational tempo, not including Afghanistan and Iraq, has historically been roughly two attacks per year. Aside from 9/11, the average al Qaeda attack has killed roughly 50 people. Although reliable information about counterterrorist operations is hard to come by—governments do not like to release information that might compromise future operations—it is clear that many al Qaeda attacks are prevented by timely interdiction. Others fail because of incompetence or unprofessionalism. Al Qaeda's attack on the USS *Cole* was actually its second attempt on a U.S. warship in the Yemeni port of Aden: The first failed when terrorists overloaded their boat with so many explosives that it sank when they attempted to launch it. U.S. authorities captured the "Millennium Bomber," Ahmed Ressam, when he lost his nerve and attempted to flee upon being questioned at his port of entry. Al Qaeda's first attack on the World Trade Center in 1993—a truck bombing of the underground parking garage—was partially successful in the sense that it managed to kill six and wound 1,400, but it failed in its goal of toppling the towers, and the terrorists involved in the attack were caught when they foolishly returned to the rental agency in New Jersey to get their deposit back without the truck.

While transnational terrorists succeed in causing a relatively low level of death and destruction today, they could cause calamitous levels of death and destruction if they managed to acquire, transport, and detonate WMD. It is for this reason that Western governments take counterterrorism so seriously, and rightly so. Yet even if al Qaeda or some other transnational terrorist group managed to get its hands on a nuclear, chemical, or biological weapon, it would not pose an existential threat to a modern developed state. During the latter half of the Cold War, the Soviet Union had the capacity to destroy the United States as a functioning society within half an hour of deciding to do so. The most al Qaeda could do is wreak havoc within an American city in an area of perhaps a few miles' radius. There are many reasons for this. First, the organizational characteristics required for a successful transnational terrorist operation are very different from the organizational characteristics needed to mount an existential threat. Terrorist groups must operate under the radar, and this requires small groups of loosely connected operatives with minimal financial requirements and minimal communications needs. To acquire, transport, and detonate a weapon of mass destruction requires a significant number of well-resourced people, a sophisticated security team, and the ability to design around or thwart the detection and interdiction capabilities of modern sovereign states. Such things are expensive and require a great deal of technical expertise. Al Qaeda's annual operations budget is probably not more than about $30 million, or less than five one-hundredths of 1 percent of the U.S. defense budget. In addition to face-to-face meetings, terrorists operate through a communications infrastructure (cell phone, radio, and Internet) that can relatively easily be monitored by national intelligence communities, making it harder to avoid being thwarted or caught.

What al Qaeda can do, however, is destroy the character of American democracy, tie down its hard power assets, and erode its soft-power attractiveness. Terrorism is like the sport of jiu jitsu, in which the small attacker leverages the strength of the larger defender against himself. Arguably, al Qaeda has already accomplished much of this by provoking the United States to overreact to 9/11. While Operation Enduring Freedom (the use of air power and special forces to topple the Taliban regime and destroy al Qaeda's infrastructure in Afghanistan) enjoyed a UN mandate and broad-based international support, Operation Iraqi Freedom—the 2003 invasion and occupation of Iraq—did not. The 2002 National Security Strategy of the United States, which proclaimed a right and intention to wage preventive war to deal with distant possible future threats (inaccurately termed "preemptive" war in the document itself), struck the international community as dangerously unilateral and provocative. Some provisions of the Patriot Act and the creation of the terrorist detention facility at Guantánamo Bay, Cuba, struck many around the world as a retreat from the principles of democracy, individual freedom, and rule of law that represented America's most attractive soft-power asset. According to some, in other words, 9/11 was an unusually "successful" terrorist attack not so much because of the death and destruction that it caused, but because of the reaction that it provoked.

All countries have an interest in protecting their citizens and their territory from terrorist attack, as well as an obligation to do so. The United States is no exception. But the most effective way of combating transnational terrorism is through steady, painstaking security and intelligence work, conducted in collaboration with friends and allies, combined with policies designed to starve terrorist groups of recruits and cut off their access to the material and financial resources necessary to mount deadly attacks. While military operations in Iraq and Afghanistan have attracted the bulk of the world's attention, the behind-the-scenes conduct of the War on Terror has, in fact, been relatively successful. President Barack Obama's decision in August 2009 to drop the term "War on Terror" was not a declaration of victory, but an acknowledgment that emphasizing the muscular, visible, militarized dimensions of counterterrorism policy has been somewhat counterproductive. As many critics have long noted, one cannot wage war on a noun: One can only ever hunt down and thwart terrorists.

The great danger is that al Qaeda or an affiliate group will get its hands on a "loose nuke" and manage to detonate it somewhere. Accordingly, the United States has spent millions of dollars to help ensure that the former Soviet Union's nuclear weapons are properly accounted for and securely stored. Also of particular concern is Pakistan, the one nuclear power whose military and intelligence communities harbor radical Islamic sympathizers. Small wonder that Pakistan has consistently been one of the largest recipients of American financial and technical assistance. But Pakistan is, at best, a half-hearted ally, and American attempts to thwart Islamic terrorism in the region have on more than one occasion threatened to undermine this important strategic relationship. For example, American attempts to kill known or suspected Taliban or al Qaeda leaders on Pakistani soil by means of remotely controlled unmanned Predator drones that sometimes kill civilians have been a major bone of contention for years. In January 2011, the killing of two Pakistanis in Lahore by Raymond David, a CIA agent with diplomatic accreditation (and hence diplomatic immunity), triggered a national uproar. But by far the most serious strain on the U.S.-Pakistani strategic relationship was Operation Neptune Spear, the U.S. special forces mission on May 2, 2011, that resulted in the killing of Osama bin Laden in his compound in Abbottabad, where he had been living for years just blocks away from the Pakistan Military Academy. Outraged by Washington's lack of prior consultation and its violation of Pakistani airspace and sovereignty, and embarrassed also by the failure of its own military to detect the operation, the government of Pakistan condemned American high-handedness and throttled back its cooperation in U.S. antiterror operations. American officials were equally outraged by, and unusually blunt about, what they inferred must have been Pakistani complicity in bin Laden's hiding. This delicate relationship, which is important yet frustrating to both sides, illustrates very clearly that sometimes the hardest part of fighting unconventional wars is not engaging and defeating your adversaries, but engaging and managing your allies.

Follow Up

- Peter Mandaville and Terence Lyons, eds., *Politics from Afar: Transnational Diasporas and Networks* (New York: Columbia University Press, 2011).
- Christer Jönsson and Jonas Tallberg, eds., *Transnational Actors in Global Governance: Patterns, Explanations, and Implications* (New York: Palgrave Macmillan, 2010).

CONCLUSIONS

We are at such an early stage of the information revolution that any conclusions must be tentative. Nevertheless, current evidence suggests four main arguments. First, realists are correct to challenge predictions that the information and communications revolutions will have an equalizing effect on the distribution of power among states. In part this is because economies of scale and barriers to entry persist with regard to commercial and strategic information, and in part because with respect to free information, larger states are often well placed in the competition for credibility. Second, cheap flows of information have created an enormous change in channels of contact across state borders, and this may have liberalizing effects over time. Nongovernmental actors operating transnationally have much greater opportunities to organize and propagate their views. Sovereign states are more easily penetrated and less like black boxes. Political leaders will find it more difficult to maintain a coherent ordering of foreign policy issues. Third, the information revolution is changing political processes in a way that enables open democratic societies and transnational actors to compete more successfully than authoritarian states for the key power resource of credibility. Finally, soft power is becoming more important in relation to hard power than it was in the past as credibility becomes a key power resource for both governments and NGOs. Although the coherence of government policies may diminish in more pluralistic and penetrated states, those same countries may be better placed in terms of credibility and soft power. In short, geographically based states that realists emphasize will continue to structure politics in an information age, but the constructivists are correct that the processes of world politics within that structure are undergoing profound changes. States remain the most important actors on the stage of world politics, but in an information age, the stage has become more crowded.

STUDY QUESTIONS

1. What is the third industrial revolution? How does it differ from previous industrial revolutions?
2. How are the information revolution and the Internet affecting world politics?
3. Which have been stronger—the centralizing or decentralizing effects of advances in information technology?
4. What kind of impact has the information revolution had on state sovereignty? What kind of changes in the international system of states and in global governance is it producing?
5. Has the information revolution brought about an equalizing effect in terms of power and wealth among states?
6. What is the "digital divide"? What implications does it have for developing countries in particular?
7. What do realists, liberals, and constructivists see as the main effects of the information revolution?
8. What are transnational actors? Are they likely to gain in importance? What are some examples of the power of transnational actors in the information age?
9. What is the role of large states in the governance of the international economy? What is the role of institutions?
10. What has been the relationship between the information revolution and democracy? Have globalization and the information revolution strengthened civil societies in nondemocratic states? What kind of impact have they had on political participation?
11. How does the information revolution enable terrorism? How does it facilitate counterterrorism? Who has the upper hand in the "War on Terror," states or transnational terrorist groups?

NOTES

1. Ronald J. Deibert, *Parchment, Printing, and Hypermedia: Communication in World Order Transformation* (New York: Columbia University Press, 1997).
2. Daniel Deudney, *Bounding Power: Republican Security Theory from the Polis to the Global Village* (Princeton, NJ: Princeton University Press, 2007).

3. Daniel Bell, *The Coming of Post-Industrial Society: A Venture in Social Forecasting* (New York: Basic Books, 1999), pp. 94, 97.
4. Pippa Norris, *The Digital Divide: Civic Engagement, Information Poverty, and the Internet Worldwide* (New York: Cambridge University Press, 2001), p. 232.
5. Douglas McGray, "The Silicon Archipelago," *Daedalus* 128:2 (Spring 1999), p. 167.
6. Alvin Toffler and Heidi Toffler, *The Politics of the Third Wave* (Kansas City, MO: Andrews & McMeel, 1995); and Peter Drucker, "The Next Information Revolution," *Forbes,* August 24, 1998, pp. 46–58.
7. John G. Ruggie, "Territoriality and Beyond: Problematizing Modernity in International Relations," *International Organization* 47:1 (Winter 1993), pp. 143, 155.
8. Saskia Sassen, "On the Internet and Sovereignty," *Indiana Journal of Global Legal Studies* 5 (Spring 1998), p. 551.
9. Stephen Krasner, "Sovereignty," *Foreign Policy* 121 (January/February 2001), p. 24, and Linda Weiss, *The Myth of the Powerless State* (Ithaca, NY: Cornell University Press, 1998).
10. David Bollier, "The Rise of Netpolitik" (PDF document), pp. 21, 23, 24, The Aspen Institute; http://www.aspeninstitute.org (accessed March 15, 2006).
11. Jennifer Lee, "How Protesters Mobilized So Many and So Nimbly," *The New York Times,* February 23, 2003, "Week in Review," p. 4.
12. For various views of what it means, see "What Is the International Community?" in the September 2002 issue of *Foreign Policy.*
13. Norris, *The Digital Divide,* p. 191.
14. Ibid.
15. Peter T. Haydon, *The 1962 Cuban Missile Crisis: Canadian Involvement Reconsidered* (Toronto: Canadian Institute of Strategic Studies, 1993).
16. Search of Factiva/Dow Jones database, January 14–25, 2003.
17. Herbert A. Simon, "Information 101: It's Not What You Know, It's How You Know It," *Journal for Quality and Participation* 21:4 (July/August 1998), pp. 30–33.
18. Edward Kaufman, "A Broadcasting Strategy to Win Media Wars," *The Battle for Hearts and Minds* (Washington, DC: Center for Strategic and International Studies, 2003), p. 303.
19. Peter J. Spiro, "New Global Communities, Nongovernmental Organizations in International Decision-Making Institutions," *Washington Quarterly* 18:1 (Winter 1995), pp. 45–46.
20. "Defense Secretary Urges More Spending for U.S. Diplomacy," *The New York Times,* November 27, 2007.
21. David A. Welch, *Painful Choices: A Theory of Foreign Policy Change* (Princeton, NJ: Princeton University Press, 2005), pp. 1–4.
22. Daniel Gilbert, "If Only Gay Sex Caused Global Warming," *Los Angeles Times*, July 2, 2006; http://www.commondreams.org/views06/0702-26.htm.

PHOTO CREDITS

Credits are listed in order of appearance:

Lefteris Pitarakis/AP Images

Xinhua/Landov.

What Can We Expect in the Future?

Osama bin Laden (1957–2011) as seen in a video captured by U.S. special forces in his hideout in Abbottabad, Pakistan, May 2011

ALTERNATIVE VISIONS

International politics remains a realm of self-help where states face security dilemmas and force plays a considerable role. There are mitigating devices such as the balance of power and international norms, law, and organization, but they have not prevented all wars. The "Prisoner's Dilemma" logic of international conflict that we see reflected even in the writings of Thucydides still applies in some parts of the world today.

With the end of the Cold War, there was a good deal of talk about the prospects for a "new world order." There was far less clarity about what that meant than optimism that it could be so. There was a new world order in the sense that the bipolar system established after World War II had broken down. But that was order within the anarchic state system, and it was not necessarily a just order. Others thought a new world order meant escaping from the problems of the anarchic state system. Is such a world possible? British historian Arnold Toynbee wrote at the beginning of the Cold War that the sovereign state and the atom bomb could not coexist on the same planet. In a world of sovereign states, where the ultimate form of defense is war and the ultimate weapons are nuclear, he believed that something had to go—preferably the state. Globalization and the information revolution present new challenges to state sovereignty, for better and for worse.

The territorial state has not always existed, so it need not necessarily exist in the future. Fragmented units and state systems have existed since the days of Thucydides, but the large territorial state as the basis of international politics developed only after the Renaissance of the fourteenth and fifteenth centuries. The Thirty Years' War (1618–1648) still had some features of a feudal war and was thus both the last of the wars of feudalism and the first of the wars of the territorial state. The large territorial state as we know it today has been the dominant institution of modern world politics for only three and a half centuries. A number of futurists have predicted the decline of the territorial state. Their new world order involves structures that overcome the dilemmas of anarchy. Since World War II, there have been five major efforts to develop alternatives that go beyond the sovereign state as the model for world politics.

World Federalism One of the oldest traditions of European thought, federalism posits a solution for the problem of anarchy by way of an international federation: States would agree to give up their national armaments and accept some degree of central government. Federalists often draw analogies to the way the thirteen American colonies came together in the eighteenth century.

Some believe that history is a record of progress toward larger units. But federalism has not proven to be a very successful design at the global level. Peace is not the only thing people value. People also want justice, welfare, and autonomy, and they do not trust world government to protect them. People of different cultures often cannot agree on what these mean. In addition, few people are convinced that the federal remedy would work, that it would be a cure for the problem of war. Even if the anarchic system of states is part of the cause of war, getting rid of independent states would not necessarily be the end of war. As we have seen, most wars in recent years have been *internal* to states.

Functionalism Because of the inadequacies of federalism, the idea of international functionalism was developed. Popular in the 1940s, functionalism held that if issue-specific international institutions were created that had real decision-making power for handling global problems, states would have less reason to squabble and war would be eliminated. Sovereignty would become less relevant. Even though the formal shell of the state would continue to exist, its hostile content would be drained away. At the end of World War II, functionalist thinking gave rise to some of the specialized UN agencies such as the Food and Agricultural Organization and the World Health Organization (WHO). Functionalism exists to some extent today, and even where genuine international institutions are weak or underdeveloped, transnational actors of various kinds, such as nongovernmental organizations and multinational corporations, often step in to fill the need to promote coordinated management of issue-specific conflicts. So the spirit of functionalism is very much alive and well and responsible for a considerable amount of the international cooperation that we see in the world. But functionalism in the grand sense has not proven a sufficient design for *world* order, because most states are reluctant to allow themselves to become so interdependent that they become highly vulnerable to others.

Regionalism Regional integration became very popular in the 1950s and 1960s. Jean Monnet, head of the French Planning Commission, thought the functional approach at a regional level might lock Germany and France together and thereby prevent a resurgence of the conflicts that had led to World Wars I and II. In 1950, Europe started the process with the Schumann Plan, integrating Western European coal and steel industries. After 1957, the *Treaty of Rome* established the European Common Market, which provided a step-by-step reduction of trade barriers and harmonization of a whole range of agricultural and economic policies that culminated in the creation of the European Union in 1992. As we have seen, other regions have tried to emulate European regionalism, with NAFTA as the most significant example in the Western Hemisphere.

Yet, in 1965 Charles de Gaulle, then president of France (and later, in the 1980s, Margaret Thatcher, then prime minister of Great Britain) set limits on how far regional integration could go. By the mid-1990s there was widespread ambivalence in the countries of the European Union over just how much sovereignty to cede to a regional government. The new common currency, the euro, began to circulate in 2002, but not in all countries. Efforts to create a new constitution for the European Union faltered when voters in France and the Netherlands rejected a proposed draft in referendums held in 2005. But despite these speed bumps in the road toward greater integration and organizational hurdles resulting from the admission of several Eastern European countries, Europe has changed for the better compared with the earlier periods we have studied. The EU represents an ongoing and dynamic experiment in international relations. As its members continue to painstakingly negotiate a thick web of multilateral institutions that deal with issues from agriculture to a common defense force, a distinctly European identity has emerged. While national differences certainly remain at the policy-making level, public opinion polls show that many EU citizens regard themselves as *European* as well as French, German, or Spanish. This fits with constructivist theory, which emphasizes the role ideas and culture play in the construction of political identities and interests. EU members have chosen to increase their complex interdependence in the belief that the cost/benefit ratio favors cooperation over full national independence. In today's Europe, not everybody is in the same boat, but the boats are lashed together in a variety of ways that are very different from those of earlier periods. For example, in many areas EU laws now supersede national laws. The European Union represents a new type of international polity, but it is only a regional one.

Ecologism In the 1970s, ecologism provided a new brand of hope for a different type of world order. Richard Falk's *This Endangered Planet* argued that two things could provide the basis of a new world order: the growing importance of transnational, nonterritorial actors and growing interdependence under conditions of scarcity. Falk argued there would be a gradual evolution of grassroots, populist values that would transcend the state. Anticolonialism, antiracialism, greater equality, and ecological preservation would lead not only to the strengthening of majorities in the United Nations, but to the creation of new regimes for handling the world's dwindling resources. The result would be international norms of peace, justice, and ecological balance, and a new form of world order.

Technological change and economic growth have accentuated ecological problems. Global resource supplies have become further stretched, and as biological diversity decreases, further harm has occurred to the oceans and atmosphere that are part of the global commons. Over the last century, governments have signed more than 170 environmental treaties on subjects of shared concern, including fisheries, acid rain, ozone depletion, endangered species protection, Antarctica, and ocean pollution. Two-thirds have been signed since the first UN Environmental Conference in Stockholm in 1972. Major UN conferences on the environment and climate change were held in Brazil in 1992, in Japan in 1997, in Indonesia in 2007, in Denmark in 2009, in Mexico in 2010, and in South Africa in 2011. Environmental issues have also spawned numerous nongovernmental organizations with transnational lobbying efforts. Citizens and politicians in developed countries are expressing increased awareness and concern regarding matters of environmental degradation and protection. However, Falk overestimated how scarce resources would become and underestimated how much new technologies can compensate for the scarcity there is, and in many countries, ecological concerns take second place to a desire for rapid economic development.

Cyberfeudalism Some theorists of organization in the information age—Peter Drucker, for example, and Alvin and Heidi Toffler—argue that the information revolution is flattening hierarchies and replacing them with network organizations. They predict that the centralized bureaucratic governments of the twentieth century will become decentralized organizations in the twenty-first century, and more governmental functions will be handled by private markets as well as by nonprofit organizations. Moreover, Esther Dyson argues that as decentralized organizations and virtual communities develop on the Internet, they will cut across territorial jurisdictions and develop their own patterns of governance. While states will continue to exist, they will become much less important and less central to people's lives. People will live by multiple voluntary contracts and drop in and out of communities at the click of a mouse. The new pattern of cross-cutting communities and governance will become a modern and more civilized analogue to the feudal world that existed before the Westphalian system of states became dominant.

Although we can discern trends in this direction, this vision of how to get beyond the sovereign state leaves open questions about how the claims of virtual and geographical communities will conflict, and how issues of violence and security will be handled. Moreover, new information technologies can be used for evil as well as for good. Today's terrorists use computers and the Internet to recruit members, obtain instructions for building weapons, transfer funds, and expand their networks. And remote hackers can create damage in other countries without ever crossing borders. In such situations, citizens may want stronger, not weaker, states whose governments can provide protection. As Thomas Hobbes pointed out centuries ago, the anarchy of states has its dangers, but it may be the least of the available evils.

Contrary to the predictions of these five models, the sovereign state has not yet become obsolete. Those who believe it has often use a simple analogy. They say the state today is penetrable by both rockets and electronic messages that can cross its borders in no time. Just as gunpowder and infantry penetrated and destroyed the medieval castle, so have nuclear missiles and the Internet made the sovereign state obsolete. But people want three things from their political institutions: physical security, economic well-being, and communal identity. Changes in international processes are shifting the locus of these values slowly, but thus far the sovereign state has provided more of all three than any other institution. Multinational corporations, NGOs, and international organizations lack the force to provide for security and the legitimacy to provide a focus for communal identity. Moreover, at this stage of human history, democracy has flourished only within the context of sovereign states. Virtual communities are still weaker than geographical ones. So, despite the long tradition of efforts to design alternatives, the territorial state remains central to world politics.

States will persist, but the context of world politics is changing. Revolutionary changes in technology make the world seem smaller and more close-knit. Yet at the same time, many people are reacting to rapid change with divisive ethnic, religious, and nationalistic responses. Globalization can create economic integration and political fragmentation at the same time.

Communications are changing the world. Diplomacy is carried out in real time. In the Gulf War, both Saddam Hussein and George H. W. Bush were watching CNN for the latest news. During the fighting in Afghanistan, both Osama bin Laden and George W. Bush watched CNN and the Arabic station al Jazeera. During the Iraq War, television reporters were embedded with frontline troops and broadcast battles in real time to a global audience. Human rights problems and mass suffering in distant parts of the globe are brought into our living rooms by television. People living on a dollar a day in poor countries are becoming more aware of the lifestyles of people earning millions of dollars a year.

But economic integration does not mean political integration. Most people who watched the wars in Afghanistan and Iraq on al Jazeera had different views of events than those who watched them on CNN. Similarly, the Internet makes more information available to more people, but people do not always seek the same types and sources of information. The Internet, cable, and satellite television all encourage "narrowcasting" of information to specific groups rather than the common denominator that typified television network broadcasting in the past. The Canadian communications theorist Marshall McLuhan once argued that modern communications was producing what he called a "global village." But the metaphor of a global village can be misleading because global political identity remains weak. In much of the world, national, religious, and ethnic identities seem to be getting stronger, not weaker. Instead of a global village, we have villages around the globe that are more aware of each other. And villages connote parochialism as well as community. This simultaneous process of integration and disintegration gave rise to two popular oversimplified visions of the future of world politics after the Cold War.

The End of History or the Clash of Civilizations?

In 1989, Francis Fukuyama published an article titled "The End of History." He did not mean that literally, but rather argued that with the demise of communism we had reached the end point of ideological evolution and "the emergence of Western liberal democracy as the final form of human government." Deep ideological cleavages drove international conflict over the twentieth century, and movements such as fascism and communism were responses to the disruption of traditional life by modernization. Industrialization tore people from their villages or small communities and made them available for mobilization by large ideological movements. Over time, however, liberal capitalism proved more successful in producing a higher level of welfare and citizen participation. The end of the Cold War suggested that liberal capitalism had prevailed. In one sense, Fukuyama was right. There is no longer one single competitor to liberal capitalism as an overarching ideology. And the relations among rich democracies have been profoundly transformed. Neither Germany and France nor the United States and Japan expect or plan for war with each other. Their complex interdependence forms large islands of democratic peace in the world today, along the lines of Kant's liberal predictions.

But in another sense, rather than the "end of history," the post–Cold War world could be described as the *return* of history. The return of history means more normal circumstances in which a single ideological cleavage does not drive the larger conflicts in international politics. Liberal capitalism has many competitors, albeit fragmented ones. China and Russia use capitalism and global markets, yet neither is liberal nor fully capitalist. In other areas, religious fundamentalism challenges the norms and practices of liberal capitalism. We sometimes lump all religious fundamentalisms together, but there are many fundamentalisms. What many have in common is a reaction against and a resistance to secular liberal capitalism. The major response and competitor to liberal capitalism after the Cold War is ethnic, religious, and national communalism.

In 1993, Samuel P. Huntington published an article (later a book) titled "The Clash of Civilizations" that became a well-known counter to Fukuyama's vision. Huntington argued that rather than the fundamental sources of conflict in the new world being primarily ideological or economic, the great divisions that would dominate conflict would be cultural. Building on the work of the British historian Arnold Toynbee, Huntington divided the world into eight great "civilizations" (Western and Latin American, African, Islamic, Sinic, Hindu, Orthodox, Buddhist, and Japanese). He predicted conflict along the fault lines of those civilizations. In contrast to realists who used balance-of-power theory to predict that interstate conflicts would reemerge between Germany and its neighbors, or some liberals who expected the democratic peace to spread around the globe, Huntington saw culture as a source of conflict.

Huntington oversimplified his vision by adopting Toynbee's rather arbitrary categorization of civilizations. As constructivists point out, cultures are neither homogeneous nor static; they are overlapping and fluid. More conflicts have occurred within the large "civilizations" in Huntington's map of the world (e.g., within Africa or Islam) than between them. Some observers argue that Osama bin Laden's terrorist attacks and his call for an Islamic jihad against the West proved that Huntington was correct, but one can more plausibly see the events following 9/11 as a civil war within Islam between extreme fundamentalists and mainstream Muslims. Many faithful Muslims have more in common with moderate Christians and Jews than with Osama bin Laden.

Both Fukuyama's and Huntington's visions suffer from trying to fit the post–Cold War world into a single, simple pattern. But one size does not fit all. Not only are there multiple cultures, but there are very different types of states in terms of levels of economic modernization. Fukuyama's triumph of liberal capitalism and democratic peace fits well with much of the postindustrial world. Huntington's focus on cultural conflict fits better with the preindustrial world and its relations with the rest of the world. Neither fits anywhere perfectly.

Ethnic and cultural conflict tends to rise when identities are challenged by major social changes that accompany modernization and globalization. Ethnic characteristics are a powerful bond, but so are state identities. As we saw in the Middle East, Egyptian and Syrian leaders have more readily acted on the basis of traditional state interests than on pan-Arabism or their common identity as Muslims. Indeed, Egyptian and Syrian leaders are currently engaged in major struggles against transnational Islamic fundamentalism.

Even when states prevail, nationalism varies in intensity. It is instructive to look at the difference between Eastern and Western Europe. Under communist rule, nationalistic and ethnic conflicts in the East were frozen for a half century. The end of the Cold War and the removal of Soviet hegemony thawed many of these tensions. For example, with the end of the Cold War and the demise of its communist government, competition between Serbs, Croats, Muslims, and Kosovar Albanians came to the fore with terrible consequences in the former Yugoslavia. Throughout the former Soviet Union, many ethnic groups spill across borders, stirring up more potential for further ethnic conflict and revivals of nationalism. Contrast this with post–Cold War Western Europe, where intrastate conflict is negligible and countries that previously held strong national rivalries have formed a larger European Union. What can explain it?

Much of the explanation fits well with liberal theories. When people are better off, the animosities may be less tense. Part of the answer may be democracy, for when people have a chance to resolve disputes openly, passions can be better managed. Some Western animosities were exorcised through democratic processes—witness the debate that went on in West Germany at the end of World War II that led to changes in the textbooks and a new understanding of German history. And part of the answer lies in the regional institutions that pulled Western Europeans together in a larger framework in which the more extreme nationalist views were discouraged. Fortunately, the desire of many Eastern European countries to join the European Union had an important moderating effect on their leaders and peoples. Indeed, the soft power of the European Union has helped spur significant economic and political reforms in Eastern Europe, at a pace once considered unachievable.

But even in Western Europe, nationalism is far from dead. Many Europeans do not want their national identity submerged completely in a European identity. There are still residual concerns between the French and Germans. One reason why the French support European integration is to tie the Germans down. In addition, many Western Europeans are concerned about the impact of immigration on their national cultures. They fear migration from the north of Africa as well as from Eastern Europe. Experts point to 9/11 and subsequent attacks in Madrid and London as evidence that European citizens and leaders have failed to adequately address the political and economic grievances of Europe's sizable Muslim immigrant community. And riots in France have demonstrated that many North African immigrants have not been successfully assimilated into the French economy and society. Simultaneously, right-wing parties in Western Europe increasingly appeal to xenophobia and provide a warning signal that the problems of nationalism and ethnic tensions are not totally banished from Western Europe. And as the tragic events in Norway demonstrated in July 2011, xenophobes are just as capable of acts of terrorism as the most extreme members of the groups they hate.

With declining birthrates and porous borders, Europe cannot cut off all immigration from its poorer neighbors across the Mediterranean Sea. Resolving the tensions between a desire to preserve a European identity and the need to better integrate immigrants into society is an ongoing challenge for Europe—as it will increasingly be for wealthy countries with low birthrates everywhere.

Technology and the Diffusion of Power

A third vision of the future is less determinate than that of Fukuyama or Huntington, but comes closer to reality: the view that technology, particularly information technology, is leading to a diffusion of power away from central governments. Just as the twentieth century was the era of centralizing power in national capitals, which reached its peak with the totalitarian governments in the Soviet Union and Nazi Germany, economic and information networks are moving some functions of governance to higher and lower levels of government, and some from formal government to the private and nonprofit sectors, as Table 1 illustrates.

Information affects power, and governments of all kinds will find their control eroding during the twenty-first century as information technology gradually spreads and costs continue to decrease. In the middle of the twentieth century, people worried that computers might produce the centralized, authoritarian world of George Orwell's novel *1984,* but the decentralizing effects have proven to be more powerful.

TABLE 1

The Diffusion of Governance in the Twenty-first Century

	PRIVATE	PUBLIC	THIRD SECTOR
Supranational	Transnational Corporations (e.g., IBM, Shell)	Intergovernmental Organizations (e.g., UN, WTO)	Nongovernmental Organizations (e.g., ICRC, Greenpeace)
National	National Corporations (e.g., Southwest Airlines)	21st-Century Central Government	National Nonprofits (e.g., American Red Cross)
Subnational	Local Businesses	State/Local Government	Local Groups

How far and how fast the information revolution causes decentralization will vary across countries, and countervailing forces may arise. But the general proposition that governments are losing their monopoly over foreign policy and that they will have to share the stage in world politics with the nonstate actors seems highly likely.

This diffusion of power can have both positive and negative consequences. A benign vision paints a picture in which technology will encourage economic development and make authoritarian regimes less tenable. The result will be to speed the spread of islands of democratic peace. A malign vision sees a new feudalism in which destructive individuals, terrorist groups, and otherwise weak states gain access to weapons of mass destruction (WMD), creating true anarchy, rather than the anarchy of the interstate system. In such an insecure world, a negative reaction may slow down or reverse economic globalization; citizens may sacrifice democratic liberties in favor of Hobbesian autocratic governments that provide basic personal security.

The benign vision points out that because of transnational communications, there is much more awareness of what is going on in other parts of the globe, and groups are better able to organize on a global basis. As we have seen, NGOs are able to mount transnational campaigns for environmental and human rights causes. The Internet provides information to citizens that undercuts the controls of authoritarian regimes.

The most impressive transnational actor, of course, is the multinational corporation. By spreading investments around the world and making profits in different parts of the global market, the transnational corporation is producing a different type of world economy. Governments compete to attract international investments. A large part of international trade is trade within multinational corporations. Honda now produces more automobiles in the United States than it does in Japan, and it transports American-made automobiles back to Japan. The U.S. government even pressed the European Union to accept Honda vehicles made in the United States. In other words, the United States defined the export of Japanese cars made in the United States to Europe as an American national interest. Similarly, IBM was the largest producer of mainframe computers in Japan; IBM/Japan does its research in Japan and hires Japanese employees. In 2004, IBM sold its personal computer division to the Chinese computer manufacturer Lenovo, furthering the globalized nature of the computer industry. When an American calls a toll-free service number in the United States, the call is likely to be answered by an Indian in Bangalore who has learned to reply with an American accent.

This has led former secretary of labor Robert Reich to ask, "Who is us?" Should analysts focus on the identity of the headquarters of a company, or on where it does its research and production? He argues that in terms of what is good for the people living within the borders of the United States, a foreign company working inside the United States may be more important than an American company working in Japan. Critics have responded to Reich by saying that he is looking further into the future than is currently justified. Most multinational corporations have a predominant national identity, and three-quarters of American production is done by companies with headquarters in the United States. Nonetheless, it is an interesting way of thinking about the future. Transnational investment is helping to confuse identities, to confuse the question of "Who is us?," and along with ecological interdependence, might affect long-run views of global problems.

If the United States responded by excluding foreign firms from American markets, it would simply create inefficient firms that could no longer compete on a global basis. The trouble with protectionist responses is that they may hurt the protector as much as they hurt the other side. So in the 1990s, the Americans and the Japanese negotiated over domestic impediments to trade. The United States pressed Japan over something strictly within Japanese domestic jurisdiction. Japan had laws restricting supermarket size and other practices restricting access of foreign firms to the distribution system. A number of Japanese politicians and consumers were delighted to have this American pressure because it benefited the Japanese consumer. In a sense, there was a transnational coalition between U.S. producers and Japanese consumers. The Japanese government in turn pressed the United States to reduce its budget deficit, arguing correctly that the U.S. trade deficit was related to the government budget deficit. In other words, Americans and the Japanese officials were dealing with each other not at water's edge, but on matters that were deep within the sovereign jurisdiction of each country.

Proliferation of Weapons of Mass Destruction

The malign vision of the effects of technology on the diffusion of power focuses on a different dimension of the transnational spread of technology. As we saw in the oil case, companies spread technologies and skills. Technology can also be spread through trade, migration, education, and the flow of ideas. What will this dispersal do to security? Already forty countries have the potential to make nuclear, chemical, or biological WMD. The technology of chemical weaponry is nearly a century old; nuclear weaponry and ballistic missiles are half-century-old technologies. To some extent, policies of nonproliferation have slowed the rate of spread of nuclear weapons. But the problem of proliferation was exacerbated when the Soviet Union collapsed, and its successor states have been less able to control the outflow of technology.

Before the Soviet collapse, eight countries had nuclear weapons. Five were formally declared nuclear weapons states in the 1968 Treaty on the Non-Proliferation of Nuclear Weapons (NPT): the United States, the Soviet Union, Britain, France, and China. Three states remained outside the treaty and were widely reputed to have developed nuclear weapons covertly: Israel, India, and Pakistan. In 1998, both India and Pakistan openly tested their nuclear weapons. Three other countries—Iraq, Iran, and North Korea—signed the NPT but were widely viewed as trying to develop weapons anyway. North Korea eventually withdrew from the treaty and exploded two small nuclear devices. Five other countries—South Africa, South Korea, Argentina, Brazil, and Libya—started down that path but changed their minds. Interestingly, more than

30 countries could have produced nuclear weapons but did not; that is, three or four times more states were able to have nuclear weapons than actually had them. That is quite a contrast to President Kennedy's fear, which he articulated when he signed the Limited Test Ban Treaty in 1963, that twenty-five countries would have nuclear weapons by the 1970s.

Why wasn't there more nuclear proliferation? After all, in an anarchic world of sovereign states, nuclear weapons are the ultimate form of self-help. There are several major answers. Realists point to the alliances that arose during the Cold War in which each superpower gave security guarantees to its allies. For example, Germany and Japan did not develop nuclear weapons because they had American security guarantees. American promises to prevent any country from using nuclear blackmail against these allies reassured the Japanese and the Germans that they did not have to develop nuclear weapons. Alliances also made a difference to some of the smaller states. For example, South Korea and Taiwan each began to develop nuclear weapons when it looked as if the United States might withdraw from Asia in the 1970s in the aftermath of Vietnam, but they stopped when the United States protested and promised continued protection. Similarly, the Soviet Union constrained its Eastern European allies and Third World client states from developing nuclear weapons.

Another explanation, favored by liberals, was superpower cooperation and the development of a nonproliferation regime of norms and institutions. In the early stages of the nuclear era, the superpower attitude toward nuclear weaponry was highly competitive. The superpowers tried to use nuclear technology to earn points in the ideological competition. In 1953, President Eisenhower announced with great fanfare the Atoms for Peace program to help other countries develop nuclear technology for peaceful purposes, emphasizing the benign face of the atom to win more points for the United States. Similarly, the Soviet Union extended nuclear assistance to China. But by 1968, the United States and the Soviet Union learned to cooperate to the point that they could agree on a nonproliferation treaty. In 1977, the United States, the Soviet Union, and thirteen other countries that supplied nuclear technology set up the Nuclear Suppliers Group to set guidelines on what sorts of nuclear technology could be exported.

Liberals point out that nuclear proliferation was curbed by the existence of treaties and institutions. One hundred eighty-nine states have ratified or acceded to the NPT, obliging them to develop or to transfer nuclear weapons. Non-nuclear states have agreed to have inspectors from the UN's International Atomic Energy Agency in Vienna (which was awarded the 2005 Nobel Peace Prize) visit their peaceful nuclear facilities to ensure that they are not being misused. As we have seen, only a few countries such as Israel, India, and Pakistan did not sign the treaty, and a few signatories cheated. After Iraq lost the Gulf War in 1991, coalition forces and UN inspectors dismantled its nuclear programs. Constructivists would add that the development of a norm against the use of nuclear weapons since 1945 has helped to reinforce the effects of the treaties and institutions. Finally, the history of many authoritarian states' attempts to acquire nuclear weapons shows quite simply that it is more difficult for most states than President Kennedy imagined. In particular, as University of Southern California political scientist Jacques Hymans has argued, badly run states tend to have badly run nuclear weapons programs. Still, these programs are among the most dangerous. Nuclear weapons in the United States and the Soviet Union were equipped with elaborate technological devices—"permissive action links"—that required a code from a higher authority in order to activate the weapon. But many of the countries with active nuclear weapons programs do not, and may well not, have these elaborate technological devices. The end of the Cold War and the transnational spread of technology may produce a larger prospect of nuclear weapons being used in some of the new countries trying to enter the nuclear race than was true in the last half century.

Two open questions about proliferation concern the future of alliances, institutions, and security guarantees, and whether nuclear technology would leak from countries such as Russia and Pakistan to would-be proliferators and terrorist groups. Neorealists, such as Kenneth Waltz, have argued that the spread of nuclear weapons to more states may be stabilizing because deterrence will work. If nuclear weapons helped prevent the Cold War from becoming hot, why wouldn't their crystal ball effect produce prudence and order in other parts of the world such as the Middle East and South Asia? The trouble with this view is that it rests almost entirely on a rational model of deterrence among coherent unitary actors. But if the real danger of nuclear weapons in the post–Cold War period is likely to be loss of control, then these rational models that provide the basis for confident predictions may be largely irrelevant. Many of the countries that may develop nuclear weapons will have a history of coups and political instability.

Transnational Challenges to Security

One fact about the future seems quite clear: Many of the security challenges states will face will be transnational in character. For most of the Westphalian era, sovereign states had only to worry about other sovereign states. Today there are a range of actors and issues that pose security challenges. Globalization and the information revolution may make possible many wonderful new opportunities, but they have also made possible many new threats—not just to states, but to other possible referent objects of security, including individuals ("human security").

Transnational Terrorism

We discussed transnational terrorism in the context of the information revolution and concluded that while transnational terrorism is exaggerated as a security threat today, it is worth taking seriously because of the danger—small though it may seem—of terrorists acquiring and using WMD. It is worth elaborating on the subject here.

What is terrorism? Under American law it is premeditated, politically motivated violence against noncombatant targets by subnational groups. The UN has passed conventions to suppress terrorist bombings, assassinations, hostage taking, and the financing of terrorism. A Security Council resolution in September 2001 that obligated all member states to deny terrorists safe harbor helped legitimize American actions in Afghanistan. Nonetheless, the General Assembly has found it difficult to agree on a resolution defining terrorism. Arab governments led by Egypt and Syria blocked any text that did not exempt groups such as the Palestinians, whose political goals they endorsed, from being defined as terrorists. As skeptics sometimes put it, "One man's terrorist is another man's freedom fighter."

When President George W. Bush addressed the UN General Assembly in 2001, he said the world must unite in "opposing all terrorists, not just some of them. No national aspiration, no remembered wrong can ever justify the deliberate murder of the innocent." His statement was consistent with the just war doctrine and with international law. Some acts of nonstate political resistance perhaps should not be considered terrorism—for example, much of the antiapartheid struggle in South Africa did not kill civilians. But even if a political group can argue that the absence of democratic procedures for change make violence necessary in a "war of national liberation," the taking of innocent life is not morally or legally acceptable under just war doctrine. Similarly, if states deliberately kill noncombatants to terrorize a population, it is a war crime. If terrorism is defined as the substate use of violence for political purposes, states are excluded (by definition), but they are not thereby exculpated if they engage in similar immoral and illegal behavior. For all the difficulties at the margins of defining terrorism, the core evil of deliberately killing innocent people for political purposes is broadly condemned by the moral codes of all major religions as well as by international law. In 2004, a high-level panel appointed by the UN Secretary-General agreed unanimously that terrorism is any action intended to cause death or serious bodily harm to civilians or noncombatants for the purpose of intimidation.

Transnational terrorism is to the twenty-first century somewhat as piracy was to an earlier era. Some governments gave pirates and privateers safe harbor to earn revenues or to harass their enemies. Today some states harbor terrorists in order to attack their enemies or because they are too weak to control such groups. At the same time, the technology of miniaturization of explosives, the vulnerability of modern systems such as air travel, and the increasing ease of communication via the Internet provide opportunities for nonstate actors to do great harm across borders even without state support. Ironically, the common threat felt by many people may enhance their appreciation of the role of states and the importance of their cooperation in providing security. The anarchy of the interstate system is usually more bearable than the chaotic anarchy of a nonstate actor's war of all against all.

Since transnational terrorists cannot do a great deal of physical damage without WMD, it is vital to be on guard against this danger. We know that Osama bin Laden and the al Qaeda network were making efforts to obtain such weapons and made contact with scientists working in Pakistan's nuclear program. We also know that al Qaeda operatives made contact with arms dealers claiming to have access to material stolen from former Soviet states and smuggled abroad. Fissile material is difficult and costly to produce, and transnational terrorist groups lack the organizational characteristics and resources required to do it. There are reasons to doubt whether they would even be capable of acquiring nuclear weapons from someone else, transporting, and detonating them. But they have certainly tried. Moreover, nuclear weapons are not the only threat. Biological agents have been developed by states. Even though they are unreliable on the battlefield (think of the effect of wind on an aerosol cloud of anthrax spores), biological weapons are easier to make than nuclear weapons—recipes are available on the Internet—and can be used to create terror among defenseless civilian populations. In 1993, if the terrorists who detonated a truck bomb in the basement garage of New York's World Trade Center had used anthrax or the chemical agent sarin in addition to high explosives, they could have claimed thousands of victims. In 2001, terrorists turned hijacked civilian airliners into gigantic cruise missiles to accomplish that purpose. In contrast, however, if the 9/11 terrorists had had access to a nuclear weapon, they could have killed hundreds of thousands of people. More alarmingly, the problem of transnational actors seeking to acquire WMD is not likely to vanish if the al Qaeda network is destroyed. In 1995, a religious cult in Japan, Aum Shinrikyo, killed a dozen people with sarin in the Tokyo subway system, sending shock waves of fear through Japanese society. Interestingly, eight years later a deranged mental patient killed more than ten times as many people without triggering a similar wave of fear or panic simply by setting fire to a milk carton full of flammable liquid in a subway car in Daegu, South Korea. The contrast between the two attacks demonstrates that it is not the consequences so much as the nature of the attack and the identity of the attacker that provoke terror.

Terrorist groups could also wreak havoc by attacking the information systems that control electricity for hospitals, air traffic radar, or banking transactions. Such attacks could be perpetrated with high explosives at the sites of key server computers, but they could also be carried out transnationally by computer hackers tens of thousands of miles away.

Deterrence does not provide adequate protection against terrorist threats because there is sometimes no return address against which to retaliate, unless a foreign state can be proven to have assisted the terrorists, as Afghanistan's Taliban regime did. And the worst case of terrorism in the United States before 2001, the bombing of the federal building in Oklahoma City in 1995, was purely homegrown. In other cases, criminal groups may take control of the government of a state but ostensibly behave according to international law and claim the rights of sovereign protection against interference in their internal affairs. In such circumstances, other states may feel justified in intervening. Some situations in Latin America and the Caribbean have come close to this: witness the 1989 American invasion of Panama; the capture of its president, Manuel Noriega; and his trial in the United States on drug-smuggling charges. In 2002, President George W. Bush issued a new national security strategy that argued in favor of preventive war against state sponsors of terrorism, but intelligence agencies estimate that the subsequent invasion of Iraq increased rather than decreased the number of transnational terrorists.

Terrorism is not new in world politics. It is a method of violence with roots stretching far back in history. Terror means "great fear," and governments as varied as the French First Republic (1792–1804) and Stalin's Soviet Union have used it to control their populations. Terrorism was also used by anarchists and other transnational revolutionaries in the nineteenth century. They killed half a dozen heads of state, and World War I was triggered in part by a terrorist turned assassin. What is new today is that technology could potentially put into the hands of deviant individuals and groups destructive powers that were once reserved primarily to governments. In the twentieth century, heads of government such as Stalin and Hitler could kill large numbers of people. If terrorists are able to obtain WMD, they will develop similar capabilities. That is why some observers refer to terrorism as the privatization of war. Moreover, technology has made the complex systems of modern societies more vulnerable to large-scale attack. As Walter Laqueur argues, "This trend toward increased vulnerability was occurring even before the Internet sped it along."[1]

One of the hardest things for terrorists to do is to organize trustworthy cells across borders that cannot be taken down by intelligence and police agencies. By moving from the physical sanctuaries of the 1990s to virtual sanctuaries on the Internet, the terrorists reduce their risk. No longer does recruiting occur only in physical locations such as mosques and jails. Instead, alienated individuals in isolated national niches can make contact with a new virtual community of fellow believers around the world. The number of jihadist websites is reported to have grown from a dozen in the late 1990s to more than 4,500 today. Such websites not only recruit; they also train. They include detailed instructions on how to make bombs, how to cross borders, how to plant and explode devices to kill soldiers and civilians. And experts use chat rooms and message boards to answer trainees' questions. Plans and instructions are then sent through coded messages. Of course, such websites can be monitored by governments. Some sites are shut down, others left open to monitor. But the cat and mouse game between police agencies and terrorists is a close one.

Cyberwarfare Another threat related to the information revolution combines both governments and transnational actors. Cyberthreats and potential cyberwarfare illustrate the increased vulnerabilities and loss of control of modern societies. For example, "The critical infrastructure of the United States, including electrical power, finance, telecommunications, health care, transportation, water, defense and the Internet, is highly vulnerable to cyber attack. Fast and resolute mitigating action is needed to avoid national disaster."[2] And in the murky world of the Internet, attackers are difficult to identify.

In today's interconnected world, an unidentified cyberattack on nongovernmental infrastructure might be severely damaging. For example, some experts believe that electric power grids may be a particularly susceptible target. The control systems that electric power companies use are thought to be vulnerable to attacks, which could shut down entire cities and regions for days or weeks. Moreover, cyberattacks may interfere with financial markets and cause immense economic loss by closing down commercial websites.

Some scenarios, including an "electronic Pearl Harbor," sound alarmist, but they illustrate the diffusion of power from central governments to individuals. In 1941, the powerful Japanese navy used many resources to inflict damage thousands of miles away. Today, an individual computer hacker using malicious programs has the potential to inflict considerable damage and chaos in faraway places at very little cost to himself. The so-called "love bug virus" launched by a hacker in the Philippines in 2000 is estimated to have cost billions of dollars in damage to information systems. Sabotage is not a new phenomenon, but the information revolution enables individuals to perpetrate sabotage at unprecedented speed and scope. As we have seen, terrorists can engage in asymmetrical warfare with governments and exploit new vulnerabilities in cyberspace.

In 2007, the government of China was accused of sponsoring thousands of hacking incidents against German federal government computers, as well as Pentagon and private-sector computer systems in the United States. But it was difficult to prove the source of the attack, and the Pentagon had to shut down some of its computer systems. More recently, Google accused the government of China of stealing its intellectual property, but China denied it. In 2007, when the government of Estonia moved a World War II statue commemorating Russian war dead, hackers retaliated with a costly denial of service attack that closed down Estonia's access to the Internet. There was no way of proving whether this transnational attack was aided by the Russian government, a spontaneous nationalist response, or both, and in the 2008 war between Russia and Georgia, similar claims were made about cyberattacks on Georgia. In 2009, when Canadian scholars cracked GhostNet—an elaborate back-door cyberespionage network—they were unable to prove that the government of China was behind it, even though the network clearly targeted groups and movements of particular concern to Beijing. In 2010, Iranian nuclear centrifuges were destroyed by a mysterious computer worm called Stuxnet, which some attributed to Israel or the United States.

A new theater of conflict has emerged in the increasingly interconnected and interdependent world. Governments will find it hard to tell where cyberattacks come from, whether from a hostile state or a group of criminals masquerading as a foreign government.

Pandemics World War I was devastating for Europe and is estimated to have killed more than 15 million people worldwide. What is less often remembered is that in 1918, a transnational avian flu pandemic killed far more people than died in World War I. Episodes of flu recur on an annual basis, but occasionally a new strand is transmitted across borders by trade, travelers, or migratory birds and has a devastating effect. Since transnational pandemics can kill more citizens than a world war, governments have to develop a broader conception of national security and new sets of policies to cope with this threat.

Microbes are constantly racing science. Not only do well-known bugs develop resistance to drugs, but over the past three decades, about one new disease has entered the human population each year. The AIDS virus, HIV, was identified in Africa in the 1980s, spread around the world in a matter of decades, and is estimated to have killed more than 25 million people. In dealing with these transnational challenges, governments need to think of foreign policies in new ways. Aid to other countries' public health systems may be the most cost-effective form of defense. Work must be done to improve their databases and surveillance. Stockpiles of vaccines and antibiotics must be developed, along with distribution systems. Just as natural and manmade threats overlap, so too are the national and global public health systems closely connected by direct and indirect linkages.

Microbes do not respect borders. West Nile virus spread to nearly all states east of the Mississippi within a few years after it was first detected in New York in the 1990s. It could have entered the country by a mosquito carried in a plane or in the blood of passenger who was subsequently bitten by a local mosquito. The H1N1 virus that by the summer of 2009 had infected people on every continent probably first evolved in Mexico less than a year earlier. Roughly 140 million people enter the United States by plane each year. At least half of American cases of tuberculosis come from abroad, some with resistance to antibiotics because of faulty foreign health care systems. And of course, terrorists can obtain microbes and viruses from inadequately protected foreign laboratories, or by bribing underpaid scientists in the remnants of the Russian biological warfare system, or from natural sources. The WHO reports that in recent years there have been about a dozen naturally occurring cases of anthrax.

Effective response to these infectious diseases lies in the global public health system of surveillance, detection, communication, and response. The WHO has developed international public health regulations and a reporting system for its 193 members. Its global alert network is supplemented by reports from nongovernmental organizations such as Doctors Without Borders. The WHO has created a network of national laboratories that do early detection work, and it manages all this on a modest annual budget of roughly $3 billion. There are also indirect connections between the national and global public health systems. Many poor states need assistance in developing the laboratories and institutions necessary for surveillance, detection, communication, and response to infectious diseases. In addition to a humanitarian concern, developing their capacity is in the wealthy countries' interest, not only for early warning but also to ensure that improper care does not lead to creation of resistant strains. Even states with better-developed public health systems are more likely to cooperate if assistance meets their broader health needs as well as narrow pandemic concerns. Since there is increasing evidence that improved public health contributes to economic development and greater stability in poor countries, farsighted policies by donor governments can serve their own interests and the interests of others at the same time. With transnational threats, policies to enhance security do not start or stop at the national border.

Only a few years ago, lack of funding was the main constraint to improving global health. Thanks to private and public giving (from organizations such as the Gates Foundation) more money is being donated and spent today. But these funds often go to high-profile cases of diseases and pandemics, not to general improvements in public health and infrastructure, and higher spending is unlikely to lead to improvements if it continues in an unsystematic and disorganized way.[3]

Climate Change In Chapter Globalization and Interdependence we examined climate change as an environmental dimension of globalization, and in the public debate, the issue has been viewed mainly as an environmental problem with economic implications. However, as scientific models that predict future changes in the climate become more reliable and precise, climate change is increasingly being framed as a transnational threat and potential international security issue. When the Nobel Committee awarded the 2007 Peace Prize jointly to former vice president Al Gore and to the UN's Intergovernmental Panel on Climate Change, it cited climate change as a source of "increased dangers of violent conflicts and wars, within and between states."[4]

According to leading scientists, global warming today is to a large extent caused by human activities. Carbon dioxide, a greenhouse gas that accumulates in the atmosphere and is a major cause of rising temperatures, is emitted by a wide range of normal economic activities. Carbon emissions are what economists call a negative externality. This means that emitters do not bear the full cost of the damage they cause and hence produce too much carbon dioxide. A domestic analogy is smoking. Smokers do not face the full costs of their action because society has to bear part of the increased health care costs that are incurred. As a result, governments try to discourage smoking through taxes and regulations. But in the case of global warming this is far more difficult, as there is no global government that can immediately regulate excessive carbon emission, and countries are tempted to take a free ride and leave expensive remedies to others. Moreover, some countries such as Russia—which believes that it stands to benefit economically from a warmer Siberia—have different incentives than Bangladesh—a poor country that is likely to be flooded by rising sea levels that will accompany global warming. In 2001, the United States decided not to ratify the Kyoto Protocol, an agreement to cap greenhouse gas emissions, because it would be too damaging to the U.S. economy and would not involve limits on less-developed emitters such as China.

What are the expected consequences of climate change? Some scientists predict severe disruptions such as weather-related natural disasters, droughts, and famines that may lead to enormous loss of life. Global warming between 1.6 and 2.8 degrees Celsius over the next three decades would raise sea levels by half a meter. That is a conservative estimate, and if warming proceeds more rapidly because of the loss of the reflectivity of Arctic ice and the release of CO_2 and methane from thawing permafrost, rising sea levels could lead to the submersion of low-lying islands and hence threaten the survival of entire countries such as the Maldives and Tuvalu. At the same time, in other places such as Africa and Central Asia, water will become scarcer and drought will reduce food supplies. External shocks brought about by climate change will directly affect advanced economies, but they may also have indirect effects by aggravating the disparities between developed and developing countries and creating additional incentives for mass migration to rich, less affected, and more adaptable regions. In addition, climate change will put stress on weak governments in poor countries and may lead to an increase in the number of failed states.

All of this makes climate change a transnational issue with potentially high economic, environmental, and human costs. But is it also a transnational threat from an international security perspective? If we think of security as protecting vital interests, climate change has both direct and indirect effects on security. If the Maldive Islands ceases to exist as a country, the effects of climate change would be as devastating to them as a nuclear bomb. Even for the United States, the damage to Florida, the Chesapeake, and the San Francisco Bay areas could be as costly as the effects of bombing. Such direct effects of human activities, while not malevolent in intention like terrorism or cyberwarfare, argue for a broadening of our concept of security and the adoption of new policies. But climate changes may also be an indirect source of international conflict. UN secretary-general Ban Ki Moon argued in 2007 that the Darfur conflict "began as an ecological crisis, arising in part from climate change." Some scholars argue that climate change will cause international and civil wars, terrorism, and crime, and that increasingly scarce food and water will lead to violent conflict and mass migration from poor to rich countries. Other scholars play down these effects and see climate as just one of many factors that lead to conflicts. Some realists argue that climate change is a scientific and technological challenge, but that it should not be confused with intentional and organized violent conflict. Other scholars and practitioners concerned with traditional security issues, such as a panel of retired generals from the U.S. military, pay more heed to the indirect effects and call climate change a "threat multiplier for instability in some of the most volatile regions of the world."[5] The Bush administration's 2002 National Security Strategy argued that in an age of transnational terrorism, the United States may face a greater threat from failed states than from great powers, and to the extent that climate change accelerates state failure, the indirect effects as well as the direct effects of climate change must be taken into account in security policies.

There are four basic ways of reducing carbon emissions and mitigating global warming: (1) technological innovation; (2) substitution; (3) economic instruments; and (4) conservation. An example of technological innovation is carbon sequestration, which allows the capture and storage of carbon in underground geological formations so that less carbon dioxide is released

Melting icebergs, Greenland, 2006

into the atmosphere. An example of substitution is switching from coal, oil, or natural gas-fired electricity generation to hydroelectricity, nuclear power, wind power, geothermal, tidal, solar, and other sources of energy that do not involve combustion. Each of these has advantages and disadvantages from both an economic and environmental point of view. Nuclear power generation is undoubtedly the most reliable and arguably the least environmentally costly—but the partial meltdowns at the Fukushima nuclear power plant in the wake of the March 2011 earthquake and tsunami in Japan have made nuclear power generation suddenly far less popular worldwide. Economic instruments include economic incentives and disincentives. The so-called emissions trading system allocates tradable permits and aims to control carbon emissions. This approach has also been used successfully in other cases of environmental pollution. A different method is a carbon tax, which would be a tax on the use of energy resources and, if set accurately, would reflect the cost of the negative externality. This would induce individuals to lower the use of fossil fuels in particular, whose consumption leads to high carbon emissions. Finally, there is conservation. Greenhouse gas emissions can be lowered if people simply learn to use less energy. As the Japanese public response to the immediate shutdown of the country's nuclear power plants in the wake of "3/11" dramatically illustrated, people are capable of getting by with far less energy than we might imagine.

Seeing transnational climate change as a security issue requires a reframing of security policy. For example, in 2007 China surpassed the United States as the world's leading emitter of carbon dioxide. China points out, however, that on a per capita basis, each of its citizens is responsible for only one-fifth the emissions of the average American. China uses coal, a particularly

CO_2-intensive fuel, for 70 percent of its commercial energy supply, while coal accounts for a third of America's total energy. China builds more than one new coal-fired power plant each week. Coal is cheap and widely available in China, which is important as the country scrambles for energy resources to keep its many energy-intensive industries running. What can the United States do about this security threat? The bombs, bullets, and embargoes of traditional security policy are irrelevant. A 2007 report from the International Energy Agency (which was created after the 1973 oil crisis to provide policy advice to industrial countries) urged a cooperative approach to helping China and India become more energy efficient. In other words, to promote its own security, the United States may have to forge a partnership with China to develop creative ideas, technologies, and policies for preventing dangerous climate change.

As realists would argue, the anarchical nature of the international system makes it difficult to address the issue of climate change comprehensively. If a number of states decide to impose costs on their economies in order to slow global warming, other nonparticipating states will benefit from a better climate while paying none of the costs. That is a typical example of the free-rider problem, which we can also observe in a variety of other situations in international politics. Free-riding is often rational behavior from the point of view of the individual country. Moreover, state leaders are first and foremost responsible for their own people and not for others who may be more severely affected by climate change. Hence, a leader may choose to free-ride by not participating in mitigation policies while reaping the benefits of other states' efforts.

Overall, however, the issue of climate change is increasingly being recognized as one of the transnational challenges with greatest environmental, economic, and perhaps security implications. As many governments take action, a powerful global environmental movement constantly highlights the importance of addressing global climate change. Such environmental issues and other transnational challenges will become much more important in the future and inspire new ways of thinking about international conflicts beyond the limited military dimension. In any case, transnational challenges will intensify the already enormously complicated nature of contemporary international politics.

As transnational challenges and threats grow, states will not only begin to question the Westphalian norms that make clear distinctions between what is domestic and international, but they will also find themselves broadening their concepts of security and defense. Many new threats will not be susceptible to solution by armies wielding high-explosive weaponry. Close cooperation of intelligence, customs, and police agencies will play a major role, as will private-sector measures of protection of facilities critical to the global economy. If democracies fail in these tasks, and terrorists using weapons of mass destruction create an anarchy of individuals rather than states, Fukuyama's vision of the future becomes less relevant. But even if governments rise to the challenge and contain transnational threats, more traditional problems of interstate order still remain.

Follow Up

- Francis Fukuyama, "The End of History," *National Interest* no. 16 (Summer 1989), pp. 3–18; Francis Fukuyama, "Second Thoughts: The Last Man in a Bottle," *National Interest* no. 56 (Summer 1999), pp. 16–33; and "Responses to Fukuyama," *National Interest* no. 56 (Summer 1999), pp. 34.–44
- John Mearsheimer, "Back to the Future," *International Security* 15:1 (Summer 1990), pp. 5–56; and Stanley Hoffmann, Robert Keohane, and John Mearsheimer, "Back to the Future: Part II," *International Security* 15:2 (Fall 1990), pp. 191–199.
- Samuel Huntington, "The Clash of Civilizations?" *Foreign Affairs* 72:3 (Summer 1993), pp. 22–49.
- Charles W. Kegley and Gregory A. Raymond, *The Global Future: A Brief Introduction to World Politics* (Boston: Wadsworth, 2011), pp. 377–392.

A NEW WORLD ORDER?

Given the contradictory forces at work, how will world order change over the course of the twenty-first century? The end of the Cold War certainly altered the international system, but claims of the dawning of a "new world order" were undermined by the profoundly different ways in which people interpret the word *order*. Realists argue that wars arise from the effort of states to acquire power and security in an anarchic world (one in which there is no ultimate arbiter of order other than self-help and the force of arms). In this view, *order* refers primarily to the structure or distribution of power among states. Liberals and constructivists argue that conflicts and their prevention are determined not only by the balance of power, but by the domestic structure of states; their values, identities, and cultures; transnational challenges; and international institutions for conflict resolution. In contrast to realists, liberals argue that institutions such as the United Nations can help prevent conflict and establish order by stabilizing expectations, thereby creating a sense of continuity and a feeling that current cooperation will be reciprocated in the future. Order for liberals, then, is tied to values such as democracy and human rights, as well as to institutions. Constructivists focus attention on the norms, interests, and identities of actors, and remind us that "orders" evolve over time through interaction between agents and social structures. Order thus understood is always contested, never a value-neutral term, and not entirely predictable.

For some, order has sinister connotations. In the view of nativist or nationalist groups such as those led by Pat Robertson in the United States or by Jean-Marie Le Pen in France, "new world order" suggests a conspiracy among financial and political elites to dominate the world. In this view, multinational corporations, in league with the financial markets of Wall Street, London, and Tokyo, enrich themselves at the expense of the rest. In the view of certain Islamic fundamentalists, order is a purely Western concept designed to dominate the non-Western world.

These differing conceptions of order mean that a "new world order" is tricky to define. None of these schools of thought is adequate by itself in understanding the causes of conflict in the current world. The realist emphasis on the balance of power is necessary but not sufficient when long-term societal changes are eroding the norms of state sovereignty, as constructivists might expect. The view that peace has broken out among the major liberal democracies is accurate, but it is not a panacea because most states, including some rising great powers, are not liberal democracies. The old, bipolar Cold War order provided a stability of sorts. The Cold War exacerbated a number of Third World conflicts, but economic conflicts among the United States, Europe, and Japan were dampened by common concerns about the Soviet military threat, and bitter ethnic divisions were kept under the tight lid of the Soviet presence in Eastern Europe. With the passing of that bipolar order, conflict did not end. It did, however, have different sources.

Future Configurations of Power

As historians and political observers since Thucydides have noted, rapid power transitions are one of the leading causes of great power conflict and hegemonic wars. Such power transitions were a deep structural cause of recent great power conflicts, including Germany's rise before each of the two world wars and the relative rise and resulting rivalry of the United States and the Soviet Union after World War II. There is a strong consensus that the period after the Cold War was one of rapid power transitions with the rise of the United States and China and the decline of Russia. Considerable debate remains over the description and magnitude of the transitions, however, and these debates indicate the unpredictability that makes such transitions a potential source of conflict.

One alternative is *multipolarity*. Former French President Jacques Chirac, for example, called for a return to a multipolar world. If the term *multipolarity* implies a historical analogy with the nineteenth century, it is highly misleading. That order rested on a balance of power between roughly five equal powers, whereas the great powers after the Cold War are far from equal. Russia declined faster and further after 1991 than almost anyone expected, though it retains an immense nuclear arsenal and has received a recent boost from rising oil prices. China has risen faster than most anticipated, with a long period of double-digit economic growth, but remains a developing country. Japan and Germany have not become the full-fledged superpowers that some incorrectly predicted in 1990. And India, despite its great economic progress, must overcome several hurdles before achieving its full potential as a major world power. The United States is the only military superpower, though the European Union is a peer in economic terms.

Some realists warn that the rapid rise of China will present a hegemonic challenge to the United States in the twenty-first century analogous to what the kaiser's Germany posed to Britain on the eve of World War I. But the historical analogy is flawed. Germany had already surpassed Britain in industrial strength by 1900, while China's economy is only about 40 percent the size of that of the United States (measured at official exchange rates). If the

Chinese economy continued to grow at a spectacular rate of 10 percent and the United States at 3 percent, China would catch up by 2025; but China is already bumping up against limits to growth—including environmental and demographic changes—and it is likely that its growth rate will begin to slow down. In any case, the two countries' economies are so interdependent that they have every incentive to avoid conflict. While conflict is possible if the two governments mismanage their relations, hegemonic war is far from inevitable.

Some analysts predict the world will be organized around *three economic blocs*—Europe, Asia, and North America. Yet even here, global technological changes and the increase of nonbloc, nonstate actors such as multinational corporations and ethnic groups will resist the capacity of these three blocs to constrain their activities. And we have already discussed the problem with describing world order in terms of civilizations.

In the aftermath of the 2003 invasion of Iraq, other analysts described the international order as an American world empire. In many ways the metaphor of empire is seductive. The American military has a global reach with bases around the world, and its regional commanders sometimes act like proconsuls. English is a *lingua franca* just as Latin was during the heyday of Rome. The American economy is the largest in the world, and American culture serves as a magnet. But it is a mistake to confuse the politics of primacy with the politics

Iraq War, 2003

of empire. The United States is certainly not an empire in the way we think of the European overseas empires of the nineteenth and twentieth centuries, because the core feature of such imperialism was political control. Though unequal relationships certainly exist between the United States and weaker powers and can be conducive to exploitation, in the absence of formal political control the term *empire* is inaccurate and misleading.

The United States has more power resources than Britain had at its imperial peak, but the United States has less power in the sense of direct control over the behavior that occurs inside other countries than Britain did when it ruled a quarter of the globe. For example, Kenya's schools, taxes, laws, and elections—not to mention its external relations—were controlled by British officials. The United States has little such control today. In 2003, the United States could not even get Mexico and Chile to vote for a second UN Security Council resolution authorizing the invasion of Iraq. The imperial analysts reply that the term *empire* is merely a metaphor. But the problem with the metaphor is that it implies a control from Washington that fits poorly with the complex ways in which power is distributed today. The United States found it far easier to win the initial battle in Iraq than to manage the occupation.

In the global information age, power is distributed among countries in a pattern that resembles a complex three-dimensional chess game in which you play vertically as well as horizontally. On the top chessboard of political-military issues, military power is largely unipolar with the United States as the sole superpower, but on the middle board of economic issues, the United States is not a hegemon or an empire, and it must bargain as an equal when Europe acts in a unified way. For example, on antitrust or trade issues, it must meet Europe halfway to reach agreements. And on the bottom chessboard of transnational relations that cross borders outside the control of governments and include actors as diverse as bankers and terrorists, power is chaotically dispersed. To take a few examples in addition to terrorism, private actors in global capital markets constrain the way interest rates can be used to manage the American economy, and the drug trade, pandemics, migration, and climate change have deep societal roots in more than one country and are outside American governmental control. It makes no sense to use traditional terms such as *unipolarity, hegemony*, or *American empire* to describe such transnational issues.

Those who portray an empire based on traditional military power are relying on a one-dimensional analysis. But in a three-dimensional game, you lose if you focus only on one board and fail to notice the other boards and the vertical connections among them—witness the connections in the war on terrorism between military actions on the top board where the United States removed a tyrant in Iraq, but simultaneously increased the ability of the al Qaeda network to gain new recruits on the bottom transnational board. Representing the dark side of globalization, these issues are inherently multilateral and require cooperation for their solution. To describe such a world as an American empire fails to capture the real nature of the world the United States faces.

Another issue, often ignored by proponents of the empire model, is whether the American public will tolerate a classical imperial role. America was briefly tempted into real imperialism when it emerged as a world power in 1898, but the interlude of formal empire did not last. Unlike in Britain, imperialism was not a comfortable experience for Americans. Polls have consistently shown little taste for empire. Instead, the public continues to say it favors multilateralism and using the UN. Perhaps that is why Michael Ignatieff, a Canadian advocate of the empire metaphor, qualifies it by referring to the American role in the world as "Empire Lite."

The current distribution of power is one of *multilevel interdependence*. No single hierarchy adequately describes a world politics that is like a three-dimensional chess game. None of this complexity would matter if military power were as fungible as money and could determine the outcomes in all areas. But military prowess is a poor predictor of the outcomes on the economic and transnational playing boards of current world politics. The United States has a more diversified portfolio of power resources than other countries, but the current world order is not an era of American empire in any traditional sense of the word. The world's only superpower cannot afford to go it alone. Globalization is elevating issues on the international agenda that not even the most powerful country can address on its own—witness international financial stability, global climate change, the spread of infectious diseases, and transnational drug, crime, and terrorist networks. The paradox of American power in the twenty-first century is that the strongest military power the world has seen since the days of Rome is unable to provide security to its citizens by acting alone.

The Prison of Old Concepts

The world after the Cold War is *sui generis*. Constructivist theorists are right that we should not overly constrain our understanding by trying to force it into the procrustean bed of traditional metaphors with their mechanical polarities. Power is becoming more multidimensional, structures more complex, and states themselves more permeable. This added complexity means world order must rest on more than the traditional military balance of power alone.

The realist view of world order is necessary but not sufficient to explain today's geopolitical order, because it does not take into account the long-term societal changes that have been slowly moving the world away from the Westphalian system. In 1648, after thirty years of tearing each other apart over religion, the European states agreed in the Peace of Westphalia that the ruler, in effect, would determine the religion of a state regardless of popular preferences. Order was based on the sovereignty of rulers, not the sovereignty of peoples. The mechanical balancing of states treated as billiard balls was slowly eroded over the ensuing centuries by the growth of nationalism and democratic participation, but the norms of state sovereignty persisted. Now the rapid growth in transnational communications, migration, and economic interdependence is accelerating the erosion of the classical conception of order and state control, and increasing the gap between old norms and reality.

This evolution makes more relevant the liberal conception of a world politics of peoples as well as of states, and of order resting on values and institutions as well as on military power. Liberal views that were once regarded as hopelessly utopian, such as Immanuel Kant's plea for a peaceful league of democracies, seem less far-fetched now that political scientists report virtually no cases of liberal democracies going to war with each other. In the debates over the effects of German reunification, for example, the predictions of realists who saw Europe going "back to the future" have fared less well than those of liberals who stressed that the new Germany would be democratic and deeply enmeshed with its Western neighbors through the institutions of the European Union. However, as political scientists Edward Mansfield and Jack Snyder point out, young democracies can be more prone to war, and so increased democratization in tumultuous regions, such as the Middle East, should not be expected to yield instant security dividends.

Indeed, liberal conceptions of order are not entirely new, and they do not apply to all countries. The Cold War order had norms and institutions, but they played a limited role. During World War II, Roosevelt, Stalin, and Churchill had agreed to a United Nations that assumed a multipolar distribution of power. The UN Security Council would enforce the doctrine of collective security and nonaggression against smaller states, while the five great powers were protected by their vetoes.

Even this abbreviated version of Woodrow Wilson's institutional approach to order was hobbled, however, by the unforeseen rise of bipolarity. The superpowers vetoed each other's initiatives, and the organization was reduced to the more modest role of stationing peacekeepers to observe cease-fires rather than repelling aggressors. When the decline of Soviet power led to a new Kremlin policy of cooperation with the United States in applying the UN doctrine of collective security against Iraq in 1990–1991, it was less the arrival of a new world order than the reappearance of an aspect of the liberal institutional order that was supposed to have come into effect in 1945.

But just as the 1991 Gulf War resurrected one aspect of the liberal approach to world order, it also exposed an important weakness in the liberal conception. The doctrine of collective security enshrined in the UN Charter is state-centric, applicable when borders are crossed, but not when force is used among peoples within a state. Liberals try to escape this problem by appealing to the principles of democracy and self-determination: Let peoples within states vote on whether they want to be protected behind borders of their own. But, as we have seen, self-determination is not as simple as it sounds. Who decides what self will determine? Less than 10 percent of the states in today's world are ethnically homogeneous. Only half have one ethnic group that accounts for as much as 75 percent of their population. Most of the states of the former Soviet Union have significant minorities, and many have disputed borders. Africa might be considered a continent of roughly a thousand peoples squeezed within and across fifty-some states. In Canada, the French-speaking majority of Quebec demands special status, and some agitate for independence from the rest of Canada. Once such multiethnic, multilingual states are called into question, it is difficult to see where the process ends. In such a world, local autonomy and international surveillance of minority rights hold some promise, but a policy of unqualified support for national self-determination could turn into a principle of enormous world disorder.

The Evolution of a Hybrid World Order

How, then, is it possible to preserve some order in traditional terms of the distribution of power among sovereign states while also moving toward institutions based on "justice among peoples"? International institutions are gradually evolving in such a post–Westphalian direction. Human rights and the broader concept of human security are becoming more important. International humanitarian law, and within it the notions both that states have an obligation to protect their citizen's human rights and that the international community has a "Responsibility to Protect" (R2P) those whose who are victimized by their own governments, are gaining increased influence. Already in 1945, Articles 55 and 56 of the UN Charter pledged states to collective responsibility for observance of human rights and fundamental freedoms. Even before the 1991 Security Council resolutions authorizing postwar interventions in Iraq, UN recommendations of sanctions against apartheid in South Africa set a precedent of not being strictly limited by the Charter's statements about sovereignty. In Europe, the 1975 Helsinki Accords codified minority rights, and violations could be referred to the European Conference on Security and Cooperation and the Council of Europe. International law is, therefore, gradually evolving. In 1965, the American Law Institute defined international law as "rules and principles . . . dealing with conduct of states and international organizations." Two decades later, the institute's lawyers added, "as well as some of their relations with persons." Human rights are increasingly treated as more than just national concerns. In 2005, the UN General Assembly agreed that while states have the primary responsibility to protect the human rights of their citizens, the international community should take up this responsibility if states are unable or unwilling to do so. In 2011, for the first time, the international community acted on the basis of R2P to protect civilians in the Libyan civil war.

In many, perhaps most, parts of the world, human rights are still flouted and violations go unpunished. To mount an armed multilateral intervention to right all such wrongs would be another enormous principle of disorder. But, as we have seen, intervention is a matter of degree, with actions ranging from statements and limited economic measures at the low end of the spectrum to full-fledged invasions at the high end. Limited interventions and multilateral infringements of sovereignty may gradually increase without suddenly disrupting the distribution of power among states.

On a larger scale, the Security Council may act under Chapter VII of the UN Charter if it determines that internal violence or development of weapons of mass destruction are likely to spill over into a more general threat to the peace in a region. Such definitions are somewhat elastic and may gradually expand over time. In other instances, groups of states may act on a regional basis, as Nigeria and others did in the 1990s by sending troops to Liberia and Sierra Leone under the framework of the Economic Community of West African States, or as NATO did in Kosovo in 1999.

Such imperfect principles and institutions will leave much room for domestic violence and injustice among peoples. But the moral horrors will be less than would be the case if policy makers were to try either to right all wrongs by force or, alternatively, to return to the unmodified Westphalian system. Liberals must realize that the evolution of a new world order beyond the Westphalian system is a project of decades and centuries; realists must recognize that the traditional definitions of power and structure in purely military terms ignore the changes that are occurring in a world of global communications and growing transnational relations.

One thing is clear: World government is not just around the corner. There is too much social and political diversity in the world and not a sufficient sense of community to support world government. Reform of the United Nations or the development of new institutions offer new ways for states to work with each other as well as for nonstate actors to facilitate cooperation. In some instances, transnational networks of government officials will foster such cooperation; in other instances, mixed coalitions of governments and private actors will do the job. But what does this mean for democracy?

Democracy is government by officials who are accountable and removable by the majority of people in a jurisdiction, albeit with provisions for protections of individuals and minorities. Who are "we the people" in a world where political identity at the global level is so weak? "One state, one vote" is not democratic. Using that formula, a citizen of the Maldive Islands would have more than 3,000 times the voting power of a citizen of China. On the other hand, treating the world as one global constituency implies the existence of a political community in which citizens of most states would be willing to be continually outvoted by more than a billion Chinese and more than a billion Indians. Minorities acquiesce to a majority when they feel they participate in a larger community. In the absence of such community, the extension of domestic voting procedures to the global level makes little practical or normative sense. A stronger European Parliament may reduce a sense of "democratic deficit" as a European community evolves, but it is doubtful that the analogy makes sense under the conditions that prevail on the global scale. Thus far in world history, democracy has flourished only in the context of sovereign states.

Accountability, however, is not assured only through voting—even in well-functioning democracies. In the United States, for example, the Supreme Court and the Federal Reserve System are responsive to elections only indirectly through a long chain of delegation. Professional norms and standards can help keep the judges and central bankers accountable, but transparency is essential if they are to play this role. In addition to voting, publics communicate and agitate over issues through a variety of means ranging from letters and polls to protests. Interest groups and a free press can play an important role in increasing transparency at the local, national, and transnational levels.

The private sector can also contribute to accountability. Private associations and codes, such as those established by the international chemical industry in the aftermath of the 1984 explosion of a plant in Bhopal, India, can create common standards. The NGO practice of naming and shaming companies that exploit child labor has helped consumers hold accountable transnational firms in the toy and apparel industries. And while people have unequal votes in markets, in the aftermath of the 1997 Asian financial crisis, accountability to markets may have led to more increases in transparency by corrupt governments than any formal agreements did. Open markets can help diminish the undemocratic power of local monopolies and can reduce the power of entrenched and unresponsive government bureaucracies, particularly in countries where parliaments are weak. Moreover, efforts by investors to increase transparency and legal predictability can have beneficial spillover effects on political institutions. Hybrid networks that combine governmental, intergovernmental, and nongovernmental representatives are likely to play a larger role in the future.

There is no single answer to these questions of global governance. We need to think harder about norms and procedures for the governance of globalization. Denial of the problem, misleading domestic analogies, and platitudes about democratic deficits will not do. We need changes in processes that take advantage of the multiple forms of accountability that exist in modern democracies. International institutions are not international government, but they are crucial for international governance in a global information age.

Follow Up

- Daniel Deudney, *Bounding Power: Republican Security Theory from the Polis to the Global Village* (Princeton, NJ: Princeton University Press, 2007), pp. 1–26, 193–277.
- T. V. Paul and John A. Hall, eds., *International Order and the Future of World Politics* (Cambridge: Cambridge University Press, 1999).
- Heikki Patomäki, *The Political Economy of Global Security: War, Future Crises and Changes in Global Governance* (London: Routledge, 2008).

THINKING ABOUT THE FUTURE

What kind of world would you like to live in? You will almost certainly live in a world that will be anarchic in the sense: a world without a single overarching political authority. With luck, that world will not be a Hobbesian anarchy—a war of all against all. Order will be provided by the realists' balance of power among states, by the liberals' evolving international institutions, and by the constructivists' evolution of new norms and ideas. That order will not always be just. Justice and order are often at odds with each other, even in issues of self-determination. Is it more important to keep borders intact or to pursue humanitarian causes and protection of human rights that violate territorial integrity? What do these choices do to principles of order? Will the role of legitimacy and soft power become more important? These debates are not easily resolved.

But change is occurring. Robert Gilpin argued that international politics has not changed over two millennia, and that Thucydides would have little trouble understanding our world today. If Thucydides were plopped down in the Middle East or East Asia, he would probably recognize some aspects of the situation quite quickly. But if he were set down in Western Europe, he would probably have a more difficult time understanding the relations between France and Germany. Globally, there has been a technological revolution in the development of nuclear weaponry, an information revolution that reduces the role of geography and territory, an enormous growth in economic interdependence, and an emerging global society in which there is increased consciousness of certain values and human rights that cross national frontiers. Interestingly, similar changes were anticipated by Immanuel Kant in his eighteenth-century liberal view of international politics. Kant predicted that over the long run, humans would evolve beyond war for three reasons: the greater destructiveness of war; the growth of economic interdependence; and the development of what he called republican governments and what we call today liberal democracies.

To understand the current world, we must understand both the realist and liberal views of world politics and be alert to social and cultural changes that constructivists emphasize. We need to be able to think about different ideal types at the same time. Neither realism nor complex interdependence exist in pure form; both are abstract models of the world. The realist sees a world of states using force to pursue security. Reversing that produces complex interdependence, in which nonstate actors, economic instruments, and welfare goals are more important than security. Those two views are at the opposite ends of a conceptual continuum on which we can locate different real-world relationships. All three approaches—realism, liberalism, and constructivism—are helpful and necessary to understand international politics in a changing world.

STUDY QUESTIONS

1. What does Francis Fukuyama mean by the "end of history"? What are the strengths and weaknesses of his concept?
2. Are conflicts more likely to occur between large civilizations or within them? What are the strengths and weaknesses of Huntington's argument?
3. Is there a new world order distinct from that which came to be after World War II? Can we characterize it as multipolar? Bipolar? Unipolar? Does it matter?
4. Is nationalism fading in importance in world politics, or is it stronger than ever? Cite examples. Is empire possible in an era of nationalism?
5. Is the threat of nuclear war a thing of the past? What would happen if terrorists obtained weapons of mass destruction?
6. What are the arguments for and against a diffusion of power away from central governments? Why does it matter? What are the implications for democracy?

7. What kinds of power are important and will be important in coming decades? How will this affect America's role in the world? How would your answers to these questions differ if you looked only at the 1991 Gulf War, the 1999 Kosovo crisis, the 2003 Iraq War, or the ongoing war in Afghanistan?
8. What does realist theory predict about the future of Europe? Of Asia? What other factors might affect events? What do liberal and constructivist approaches add?
9. What is the difference between global government and global governance? What role do institutions play? What are the implications for democracy?
10. What are arguments for and against portraying the current world order as an American empire?
11. If the Internet strengthens transnational groups, how will that affect world politics?
12. How does security in the twenty-first century differ from security in the previous century? Will transnational challenges such as climate change and pandemics transform the nature of world politics?
13. Are human rights becoming more important in world politics? How can humanitarian law be reconciled with the norm of sovereignty at the heart of the Westphalian system?

NOTES

1. Walter Laqueur, "Left, Right, and Beyond: The Changing Face of Terror," in James F. Hogue and Gideon Rose, eds., *How Did This Happen? Terrorism and the New War* (New York: PublicAffairs, 2001), p. 73.
2. Professionals for Cyber Defense, "Letter to President Bush," http://www.uspcd.org/history.html (accessed on September 2, 2007).
3. Laurie Garrett, "The Challenge of Global Health," *Foreign Affairs* 86:1 (Jan./Feb. 2007), p. 14.
4. Michael T. Klare, "Global Warming Battlefields: How Climate Change Threatens Security," *Current History* 106:703 (November 2007), p. 355.
5. Center for Naval Analyses, "National Security and the Threat of Climate Change," p. 6; http://www.cna.org/reports/climate.

PHOTO CREDITS

Credits are listed in order of appearance:

AFP/Getty Images/Newscom

Kyodo News/Newscom.

David Leeson/Dallas Morning News.

Index